I0753980

HISTORIC PHOTOS OF DALLAS

TEXT AND CAPTIONS BY MICHAEL V. HAZEL

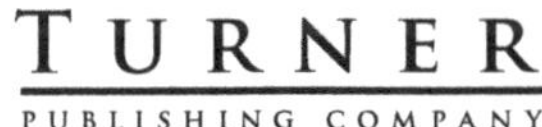
TURNER
PUBLISHING COMPANY

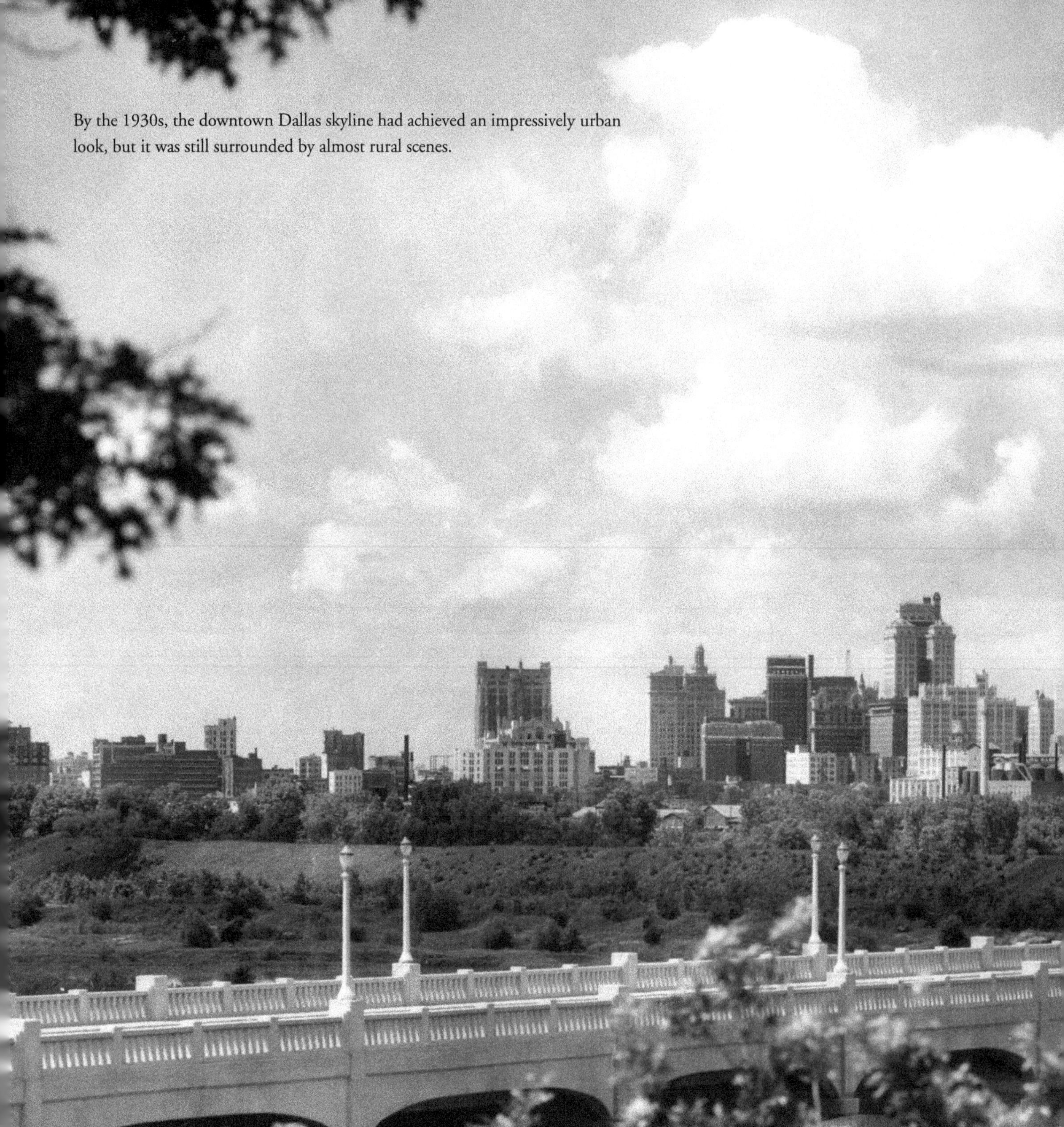

By the 1930s, the downtown Dallas skyline had achieved an impressively urban look, but it was still surrounded by almost rural scenes.

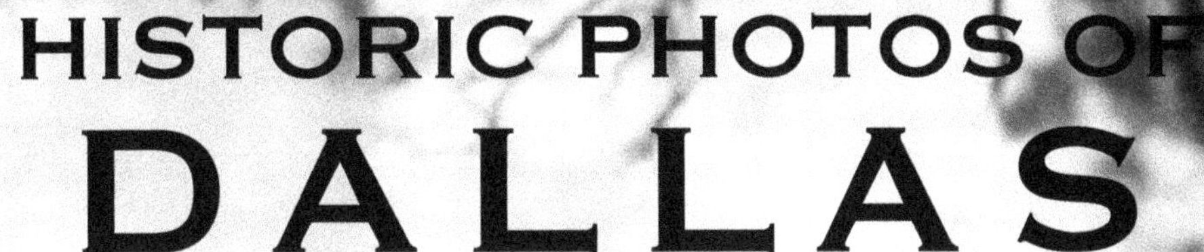

HISTORIC PHOTOS OF DALLAS

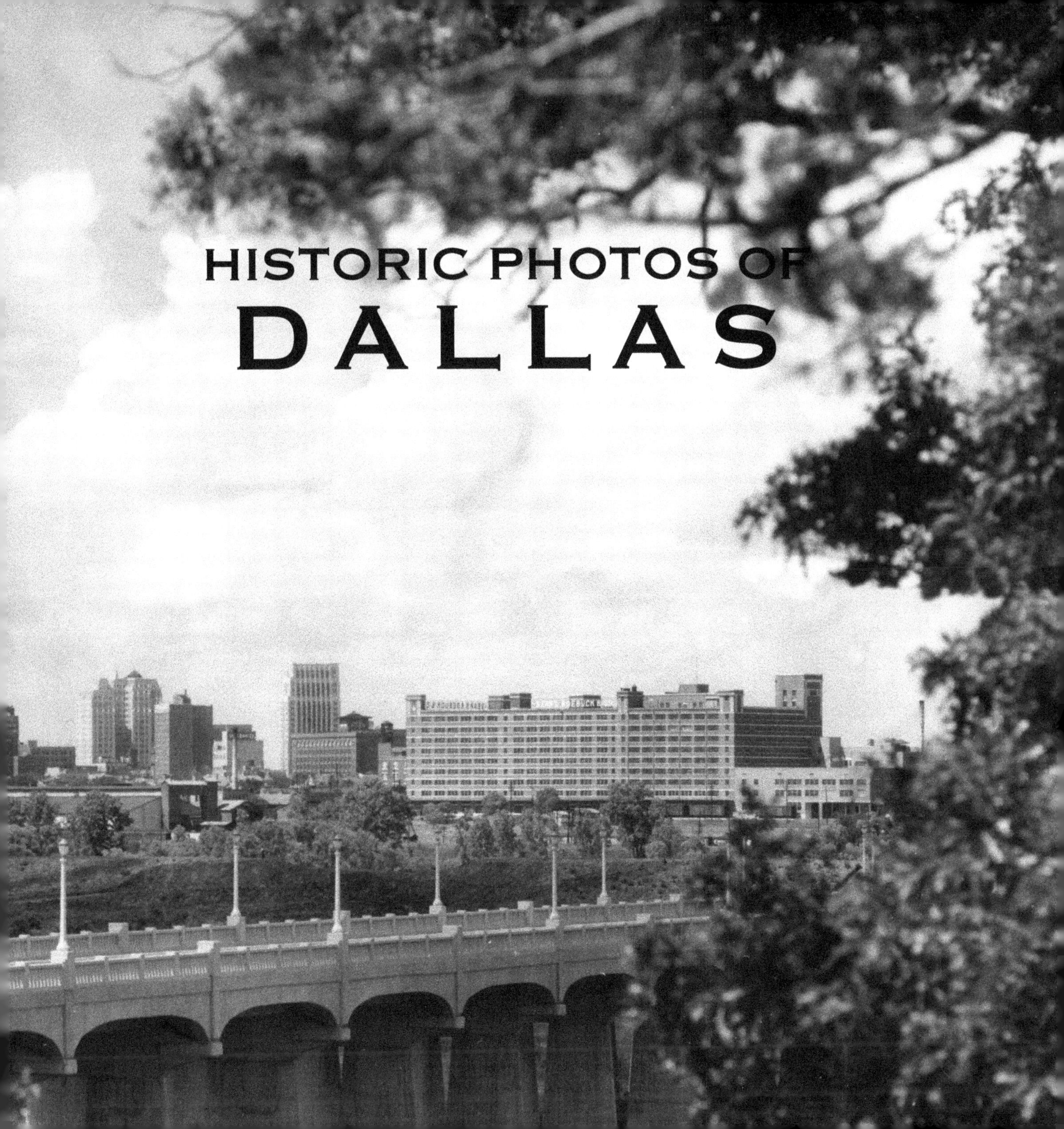

Turner Publishing Company
www.turnerpublishing.com

Historic Photos of Dallas

Library of Congress Control Number: 2006934336

ISBN-10: 1-59652-290-9
ISBN-13: 978-1-59652-290-9

Printed in the United States of America

ISBN 978-1-68336-919-6 (hc)

Contents

Acknowledgments vii

Preface viii

From Outpost to Turn-of-the-century Boomtown (1850s–1899) 1

Stirrings of a New Century (1900–1929) 43

From the Great Depression to Postwar Metropolis (1930–1949) 139

The Modern Age (1950–1969) 179

Notes on the Photographs 201

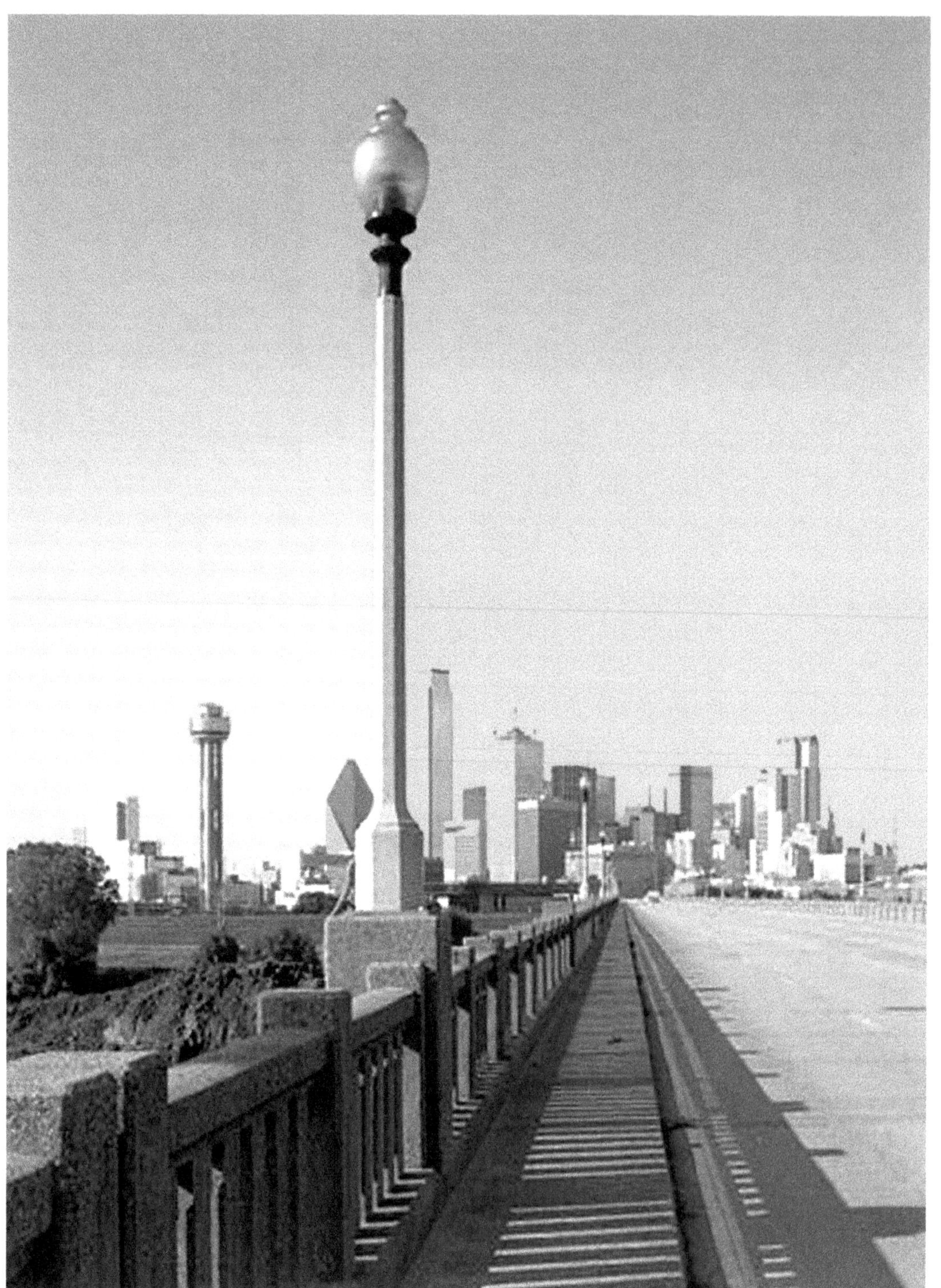

New skyscrapers and the iconic Reunion Tower (left) created a vibrant image for Dallas in the late twentieth century, while the Houston Street Viaduct, which opened in 1911, remained a visible link with the past.

ACKNOWLEDGMENTS

This volume, *Historic Photos of Dallas,* is the result of the cooperation and efforts of many individuals, organizations, institutions, and corporations. It is with great thanks that we acknowledge the valuable contribution of the following for their generous support:

Dallas Historical Society
Dallas Public Library
Library of Congress

We would also like to thank the following individuals for their valuable contributions and assistance in making this work possible:

Beth Andresen, History & Archives Division, Dallas Public Library
Michael Duty, Dallas Historical Society
Michael V. Hazel, Dallas Historical Society, Writer and Editor
Jane Soutner, History & Archives Division, Dallas Public Library

Preface

Dallas has thousands of historic photographs that reside in archives, both locally and nationally. This book began with the observation that, while those photographs are of great interest to many, they are not easily accessible. During a time when Dallas is looking ahead and evaluating its future course, many people are asking, How do we treat the past? These decisions affect every aspect of the city—architecture, public spaces, commerce, infrastructure—and these, in turn, affect the way that people live their lives. This book seeks to provide easy access to a valuable, objective look into the history of Dallas.

The power of photographs is that they are less subjective than words in their treatment of history. Although the photographer can make decisions regarding subject matter and how to capture and present it, photographs do not provide the breadth of interpretation that text does. For this reason, they offer an original, untainted perspective that allows the viewer to interpret and observe.

This project represents countless hours of review and research. The researchers and author have reviewed thousands of photographs in numerous archives. We greatly appreciate the generous assistance of the archivists listed in the acknowledgments of this work, without whom this project could not have been completed.

The goal in publishing this work is to provide broader access to this set of extraordinary photographs that seek to inspire, provide perspective, and evoke insight that might assist people who are responsible for determining Dallas's future. In addition, the book seeks to preserve the past with adequate respect and reverence.

With the exception of touching up imperfections that have accrued with the passage of time and cropping where necessary, no other changes have been made. The focus and clarity of many images is limited to the technology and the ability of the photographer at the time they were taken.

The work is divided into eras. Beginning with some of the earliest known photographs of Dallas, the first section records images through the end of the nineteenth century. The second section spans the beginning of the twentieth century to the close of the 1920s. Section Three moves from the Great Depression to World War II and the early postwar years. The last section covers the postwar era through the 1960s.

In each of these sections we have made an effort to capture various aspects of life through our selection of photographs. People, commerce, transportation, infrastructure, religious institutions, and educational institutions have been included to provide a broad perspective.

We encourage readers to reflect as they go walking in Dallas, strolling through the city, its parks, and neighborhoods. It is the publisher's hope that in utilizing this work, longtime residents will learn something new and that new residents will gain a perspective on where Dallas has been, so that each can contribute to its future.

—Todd Bottorff, Publisher

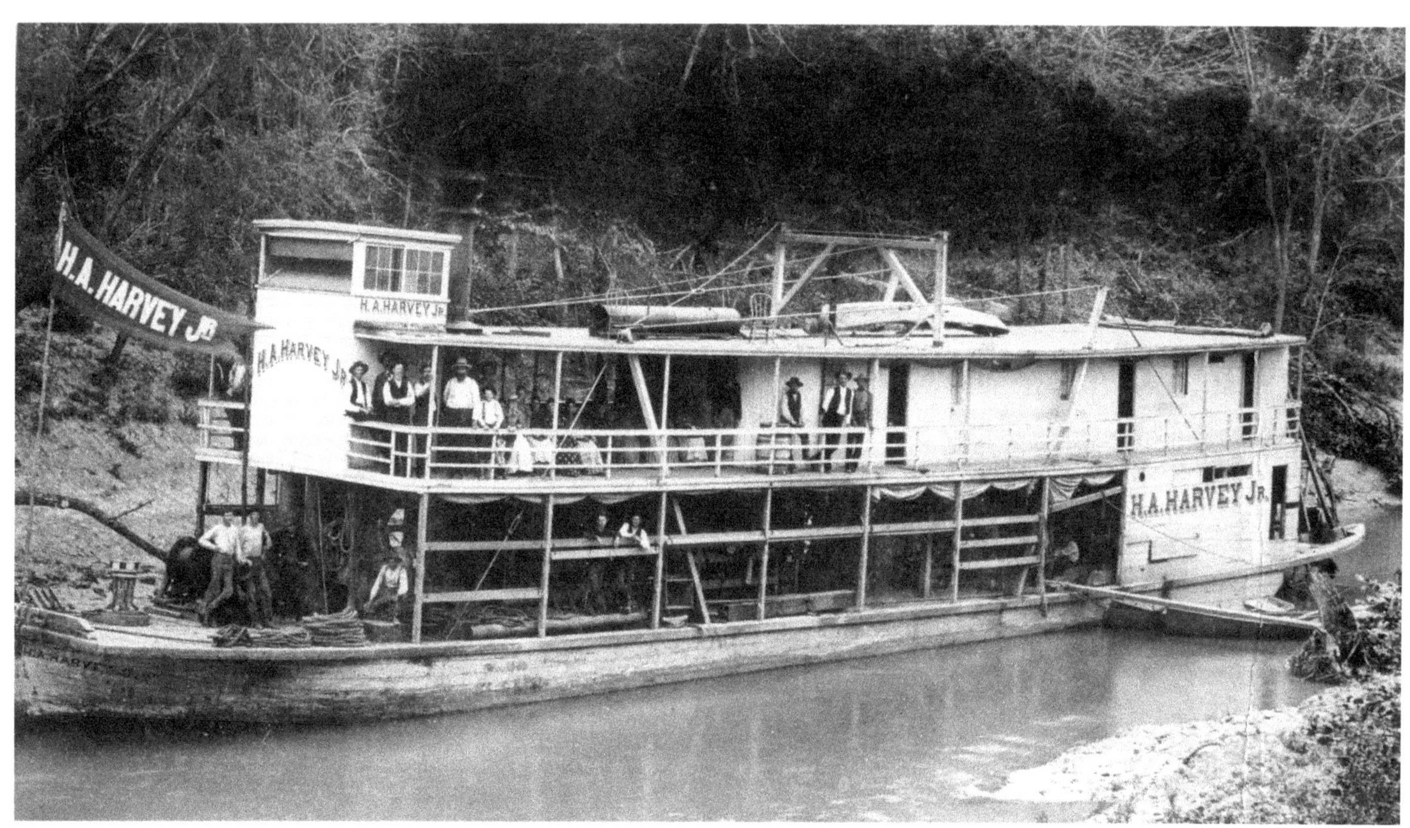

The arrival of the *H. A. Harvey, Jr.*, in 1893 was cause for much rejoicing, but the long-held dream of navigating the Trinity River proved elusive. The river was too obstructed with debris, and its water level was too variable, to make boat traffic practical.

From Outpost to Turn-of-the-Century Boomtown

(1850s–1899)

Dallas began in the 1840s as an outpost at a crossing of the Trinity River. Its founder was John Neely Bryan, a real estate speculator who laid out lots but had trouble finding buyers and eventually sold out to Alex and Sarah Cockrell. More enterprising than Bryan, they built a bridge across the Trinity, set up a sawmill to provide milled lumber for construction, and built a hotel. By the 1850s, several hundred people lived in town.

Dallas got a boost over neighboring villages in 1850 when it was selected as the county seat. Since anybody with legal business had to come to the courthouse, the surrounding livery stables, hotels, stores, and saloons all benefited. But growth was hampered by the lack of good transportation, the roads being primitive and the river unnavigable. Civic leaders pinned their hopes on the railroads and resorted to chicanery and bribery to get them to run lines through Dallas, which they finally did in 1872 and 1873.

With rail outlets, Dallas became a boomtown, attracting immigrants, merchants, and manufactured goods. Area farmers turned to cotton, which could now be economically shipped out by rail, and by the end of the century Dallas was the largest inland cotton market in the world. Gradually, the town acquired the amenities of late-nineteenth-century urban life—gas and electric lights, telephones, streetcars, and protection of police and fire departments. Churches and schools proliferated.

In 1890, for the first and only time in its history, Dallas was the largest city in Texas, with a population of 38,000. It hosted the annual state fair, as well as traveling theatrical troupes and religious evangelists. By the end of the century, it was the largest publishing center south of St. Louis and headquarters for fire and life insurance in the Southwest. It even had suburbs, several of which would eventually be absorbed into the city.

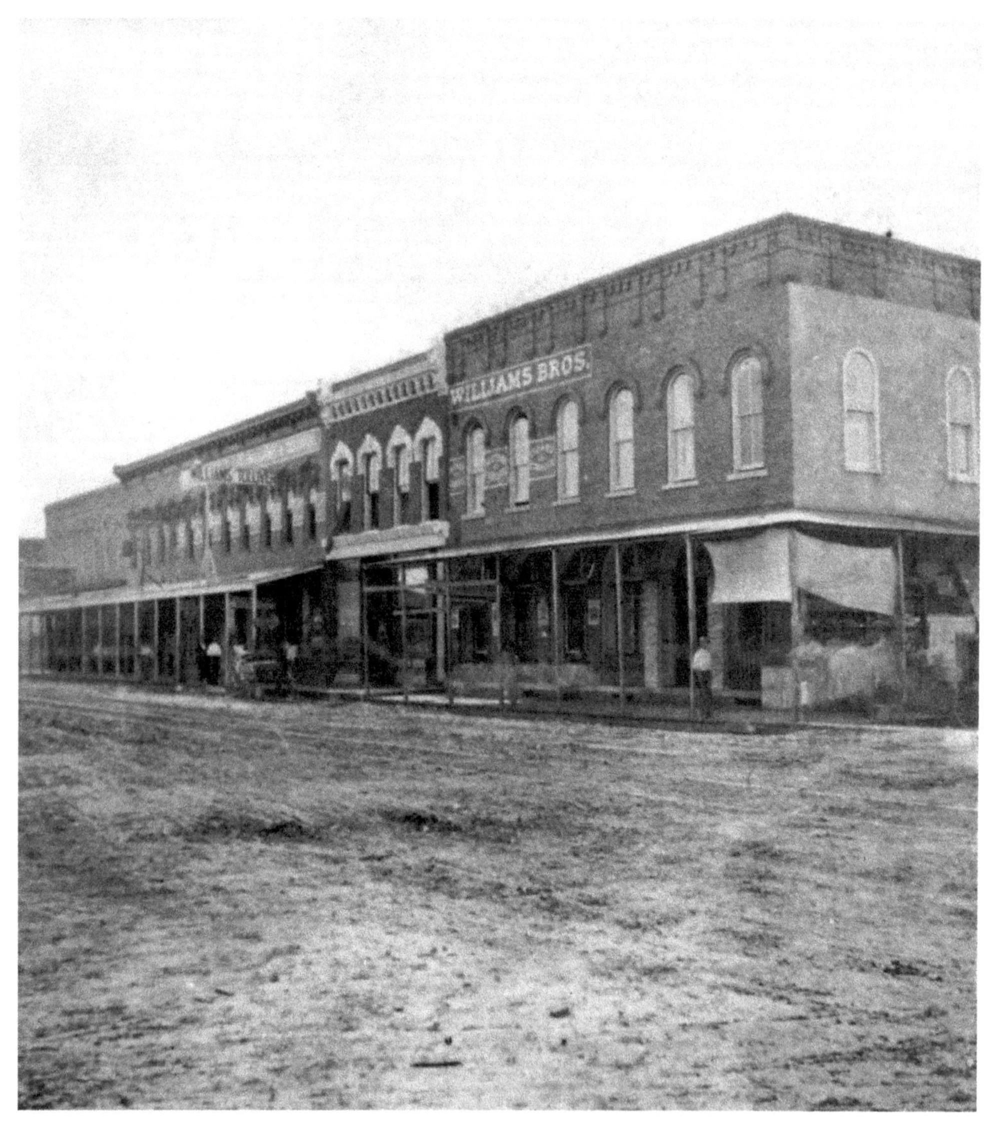

One of the earliest photographs of Dallas is this stereoscope image of a two-story block facing a dirt street.

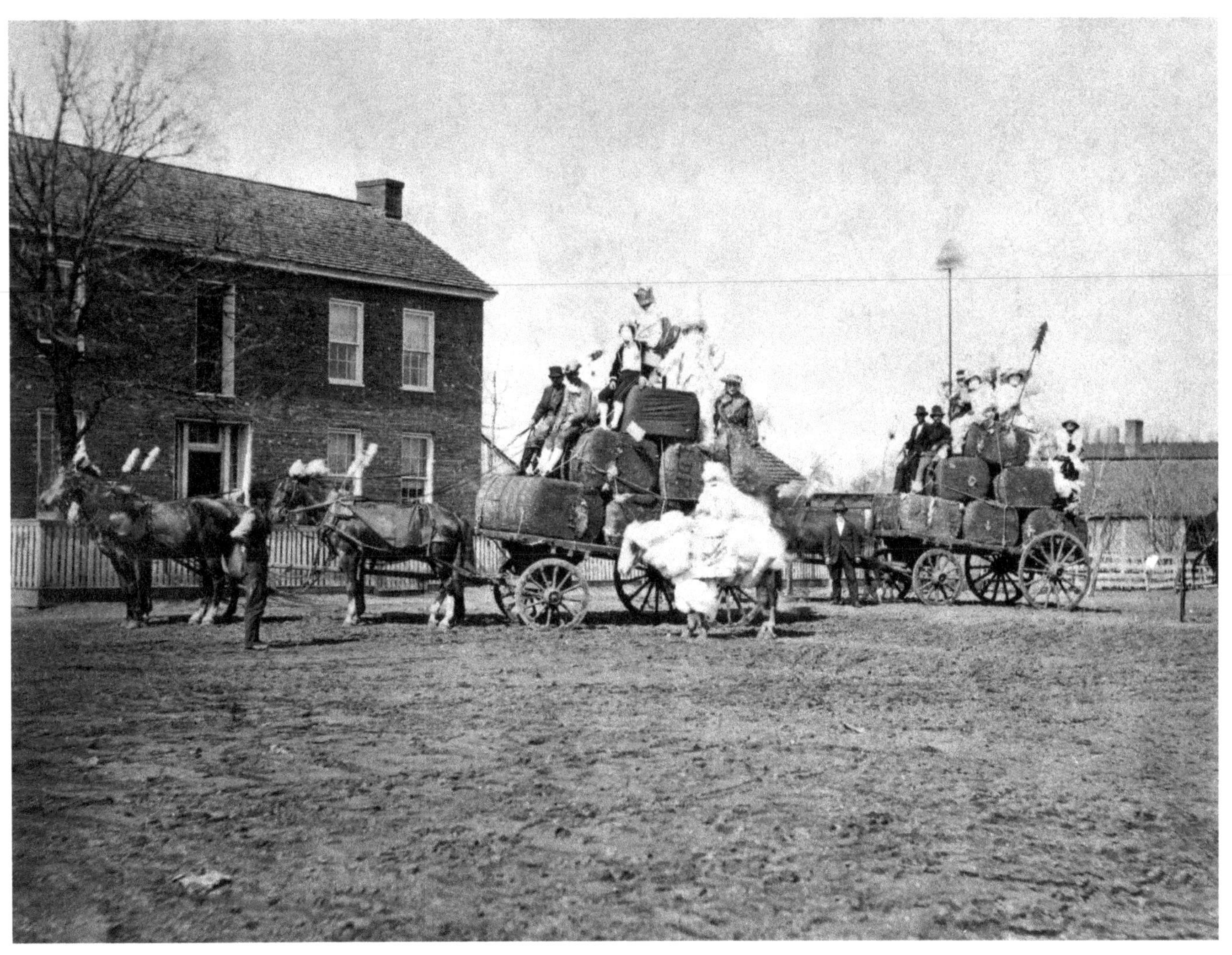

Parades were a popular form of entertainment in the nineteenth century, but they also helped promote local businesses. This Mardi Gras parade was staged in 1876.

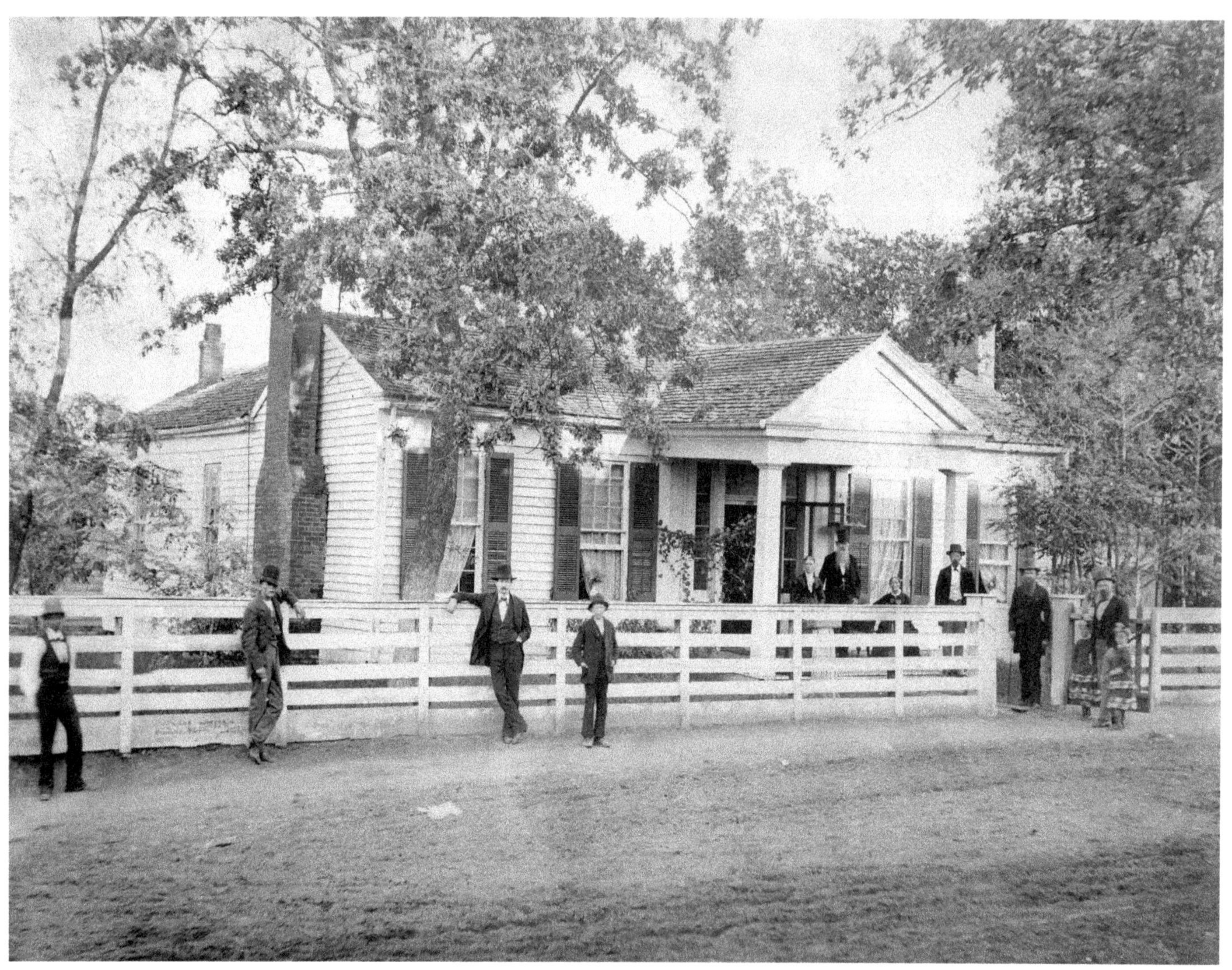

Dallas's first practicing attorney, John C. McCoy, built this cottage in 1852 at the corner of Commerce and Lamar. In this 1879 family photo, McCoy is the bearded man standing on the porch.

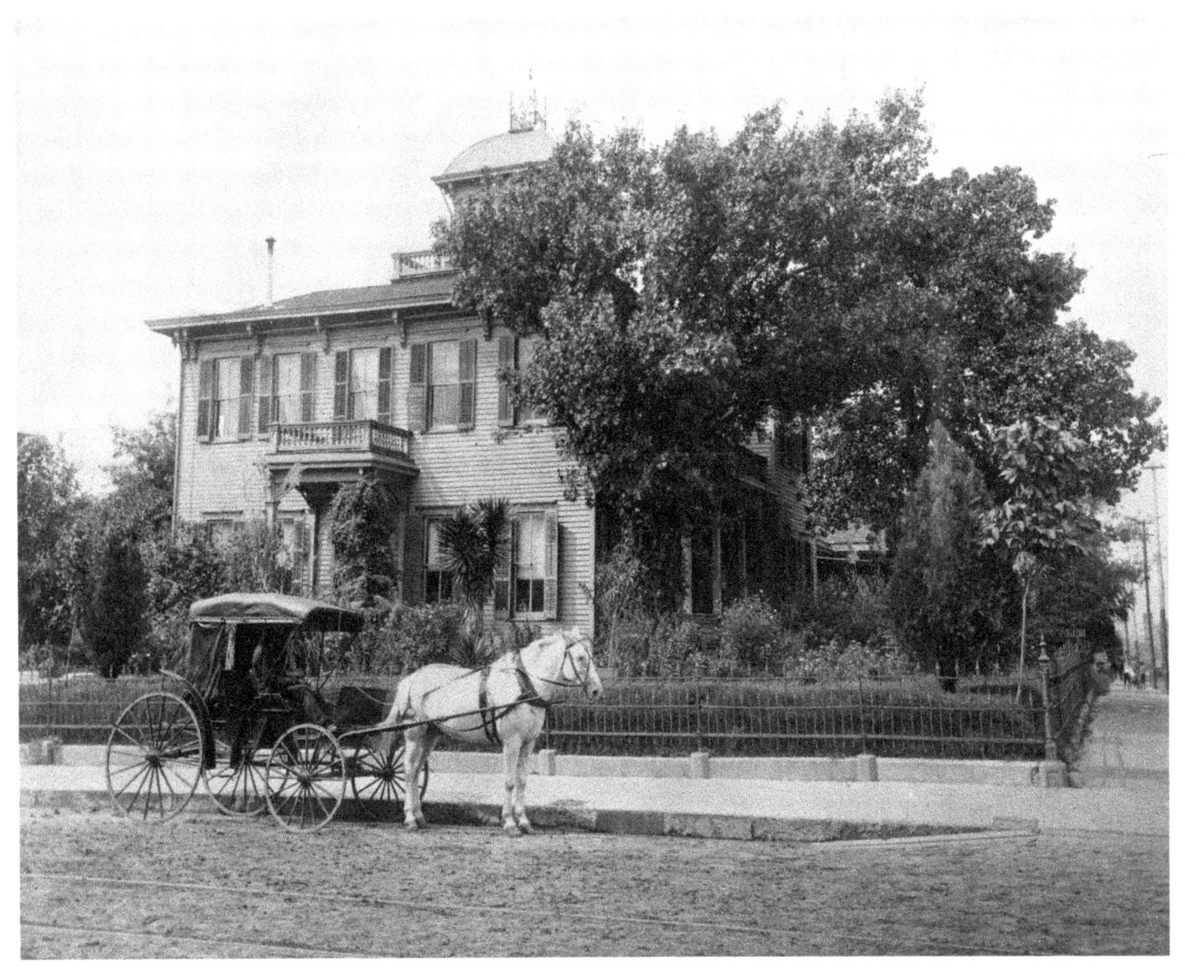

Colonel James B. Simpson, an early Dallas attorney, built this house on the southwest corner of Main and S. Harwood streets in 1878. Colonel John C. McCoy, another early attorney, purchased the residence in 1885. It remained in his family until it was torn down in 1906.

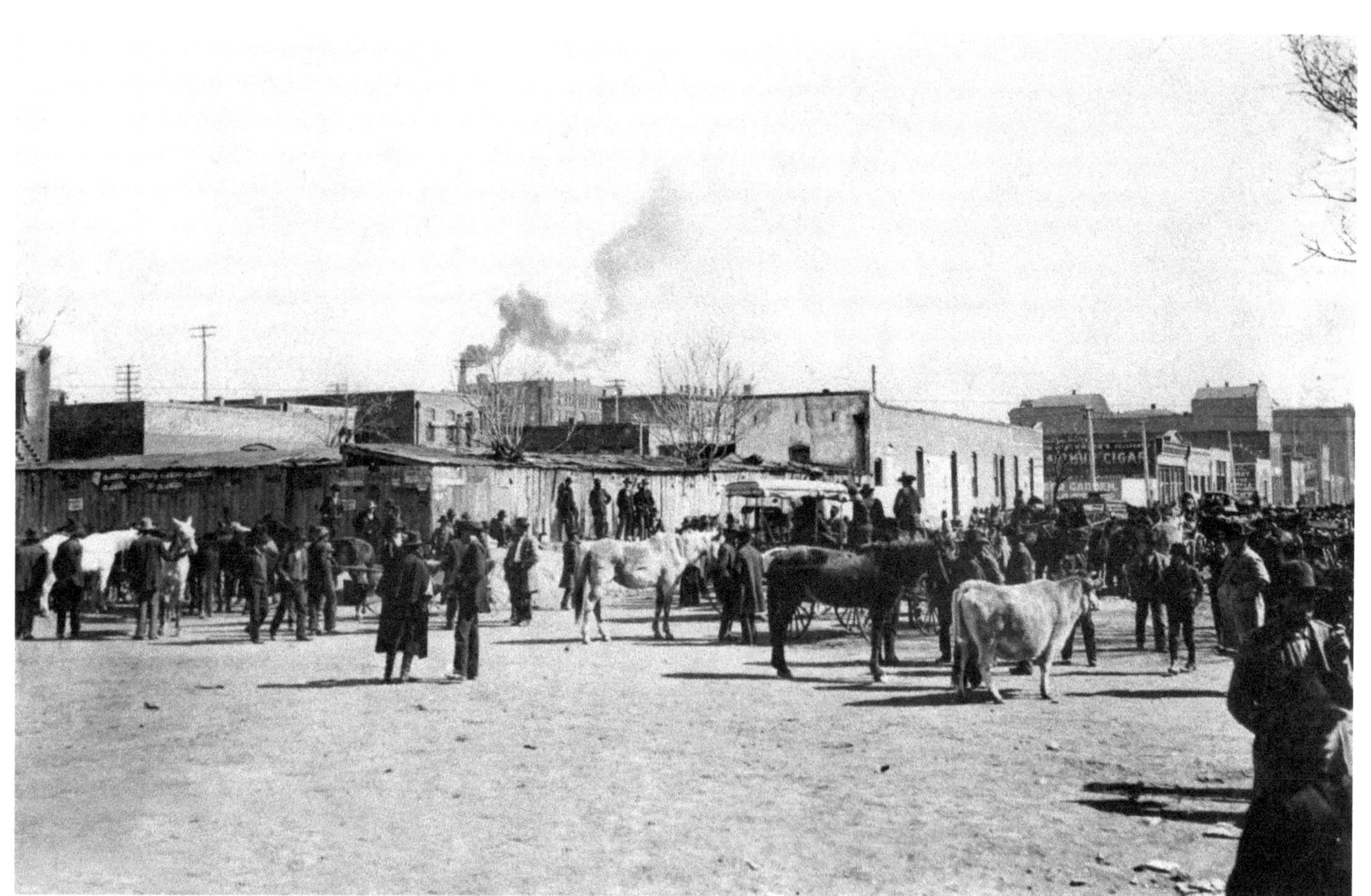

The wagon yard a block south of the courthouse was the scene of monthly trade days. From the 1880s into the twentieth century farmers brought livestock here.

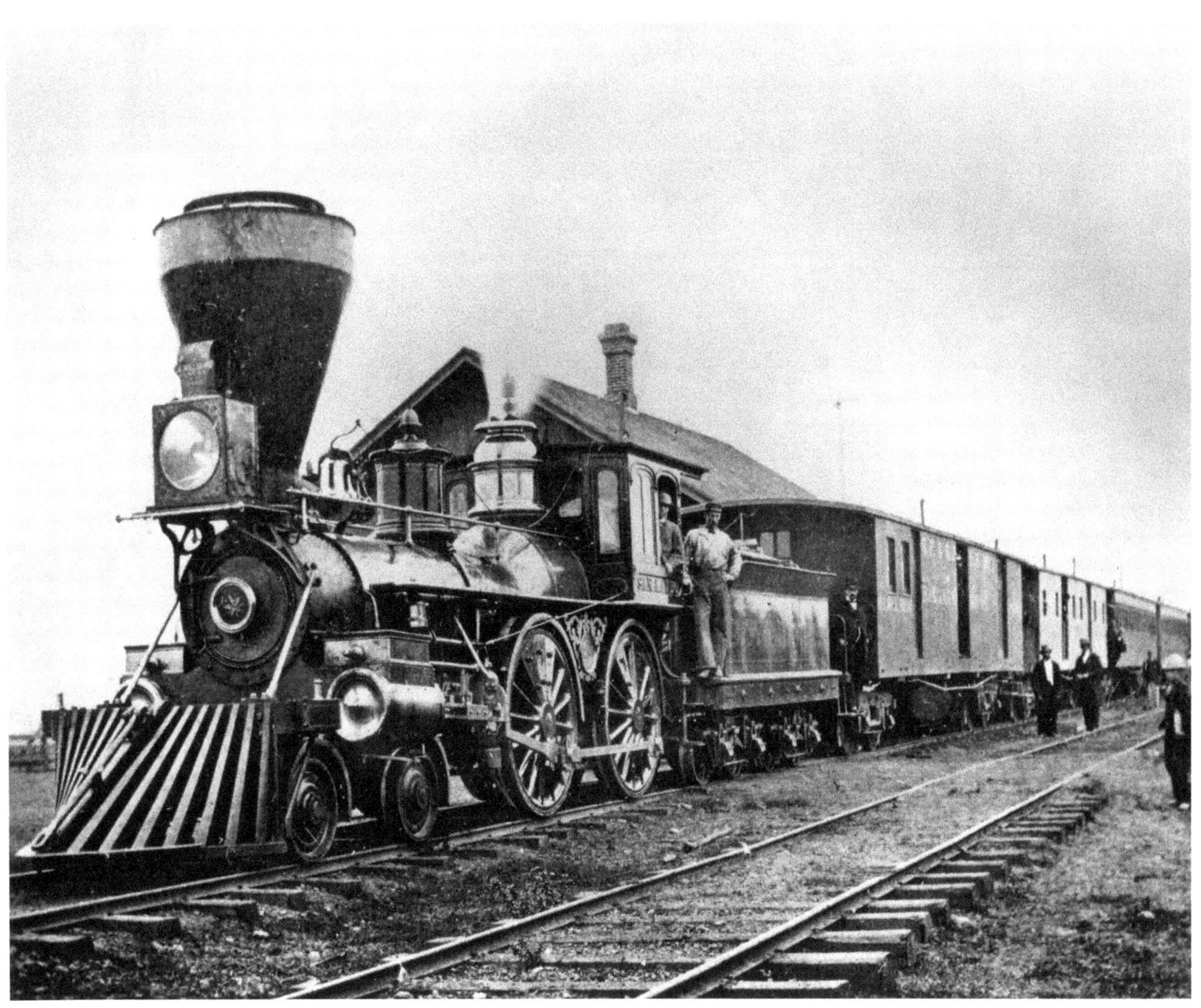

The arrival of the railroads to Dallas in 1872 and 1873 was the key event in the development of the city, turning it almost overnight into a boomtown. Rail transportation gave farmers an outlet for their products, enabled merchants to import manufactured goods, and allowed the population to soar.

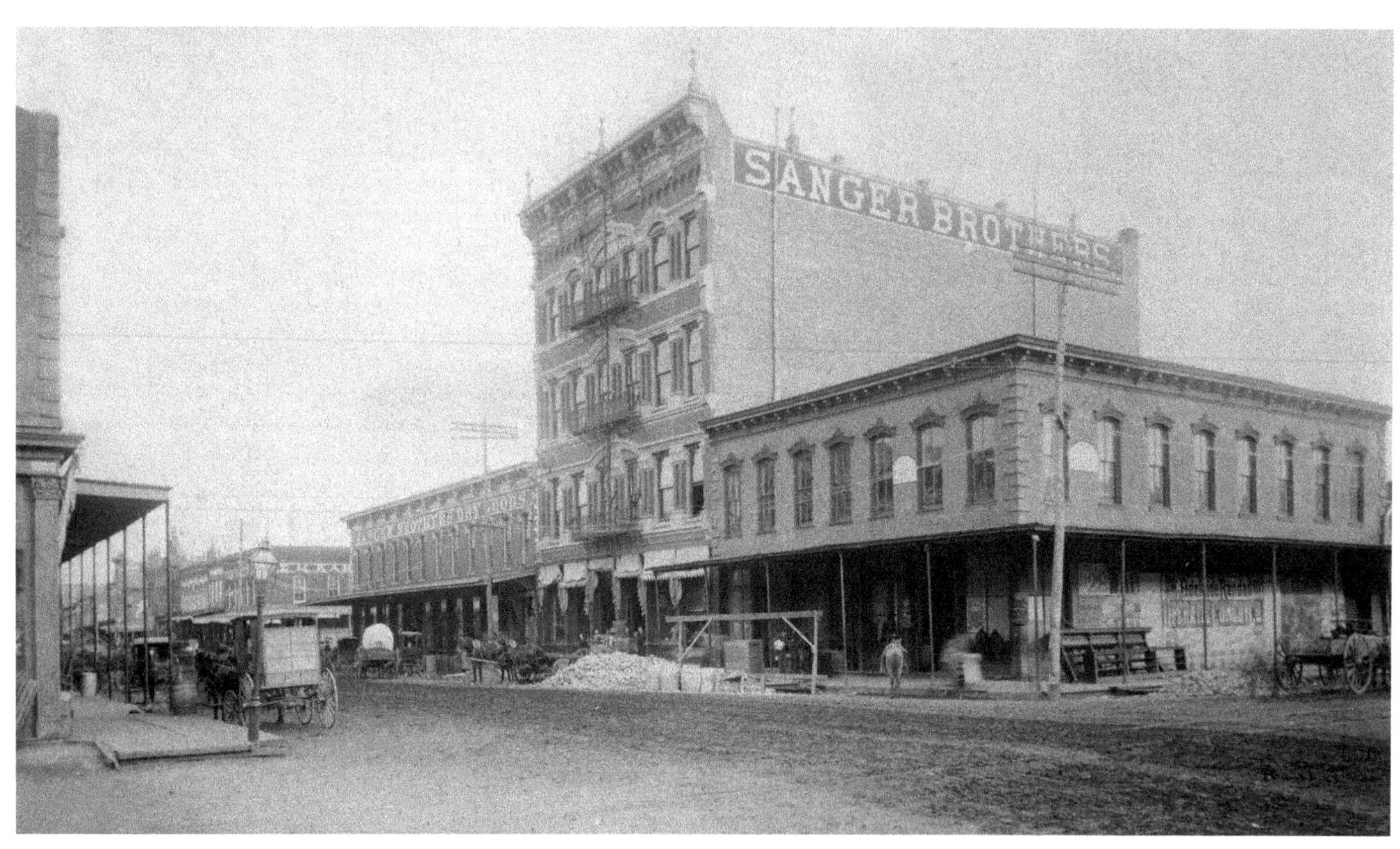

Alex and Philip Sanger brought their family's mercantile business to Dallas with the railroad in 1872, opening what soon became the city's leading department store. Sanger Brothers introduced escalators, fixed prices, and women sales clerks to Dallas.

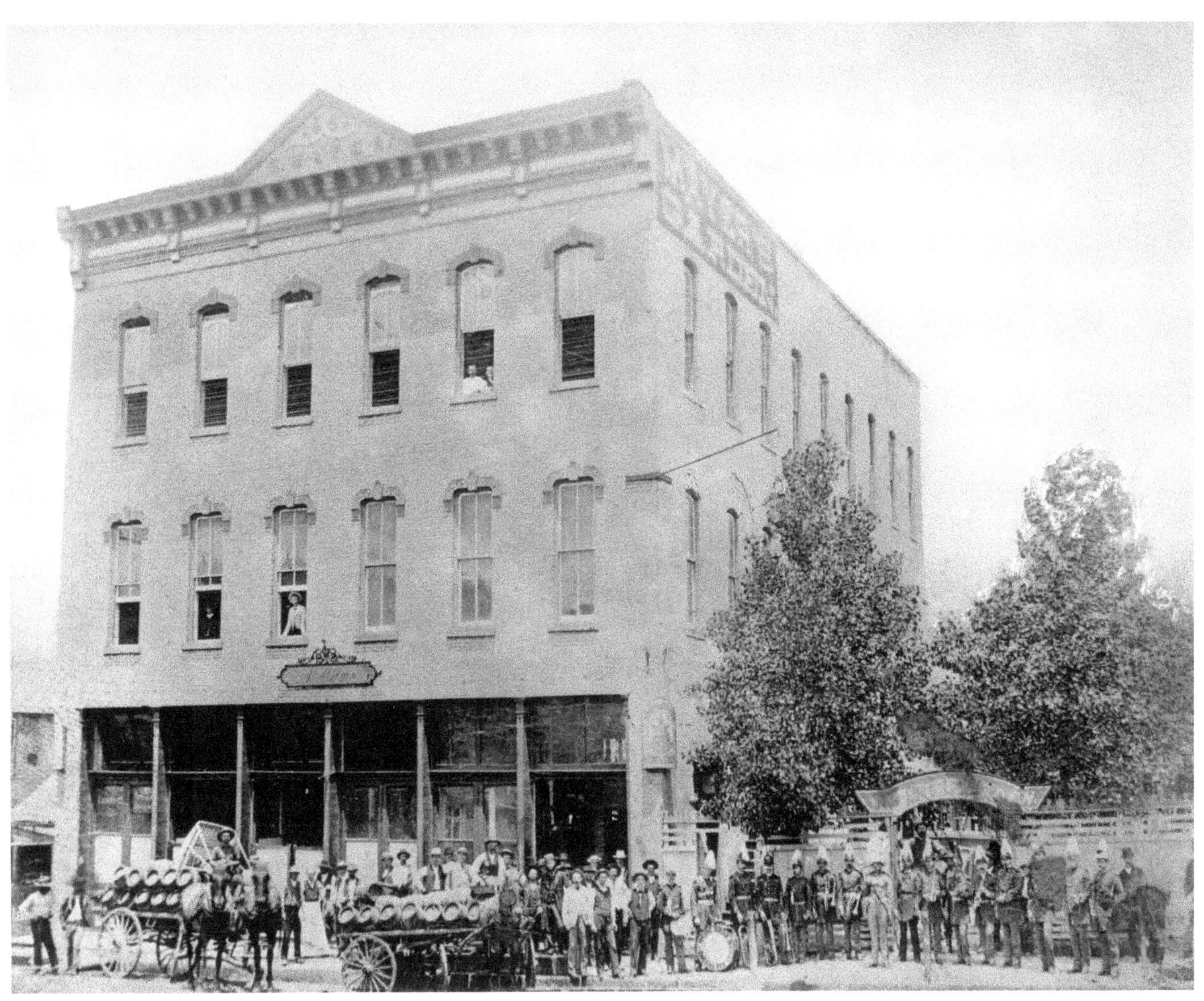

Operated by one of the many German immigrants who flocked to Dallas in the 1870s and 1880s, Mayer's Garden was a popular watering hole, featuring a garden with a small zoo and the city's first outdoor electric lights.

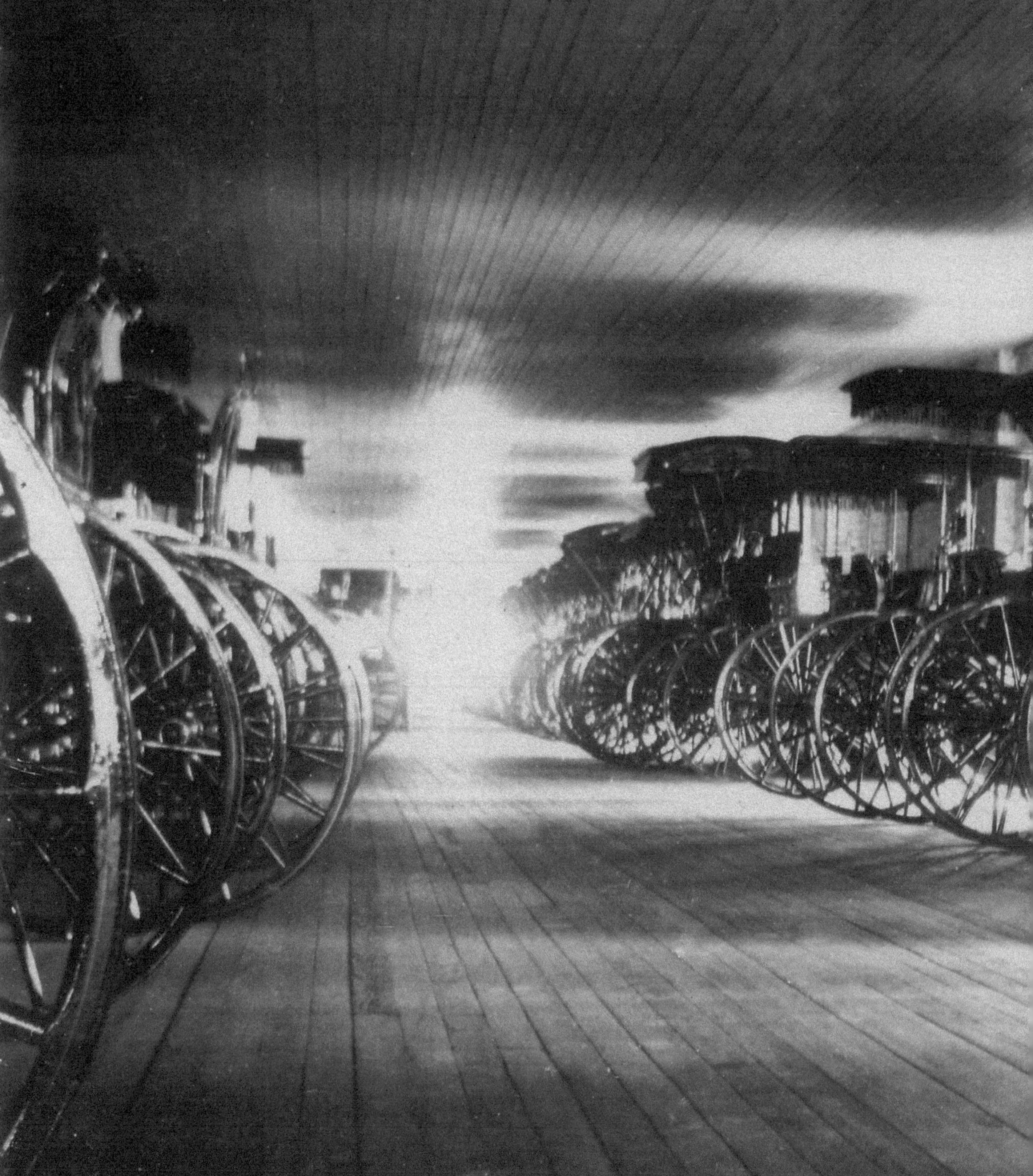

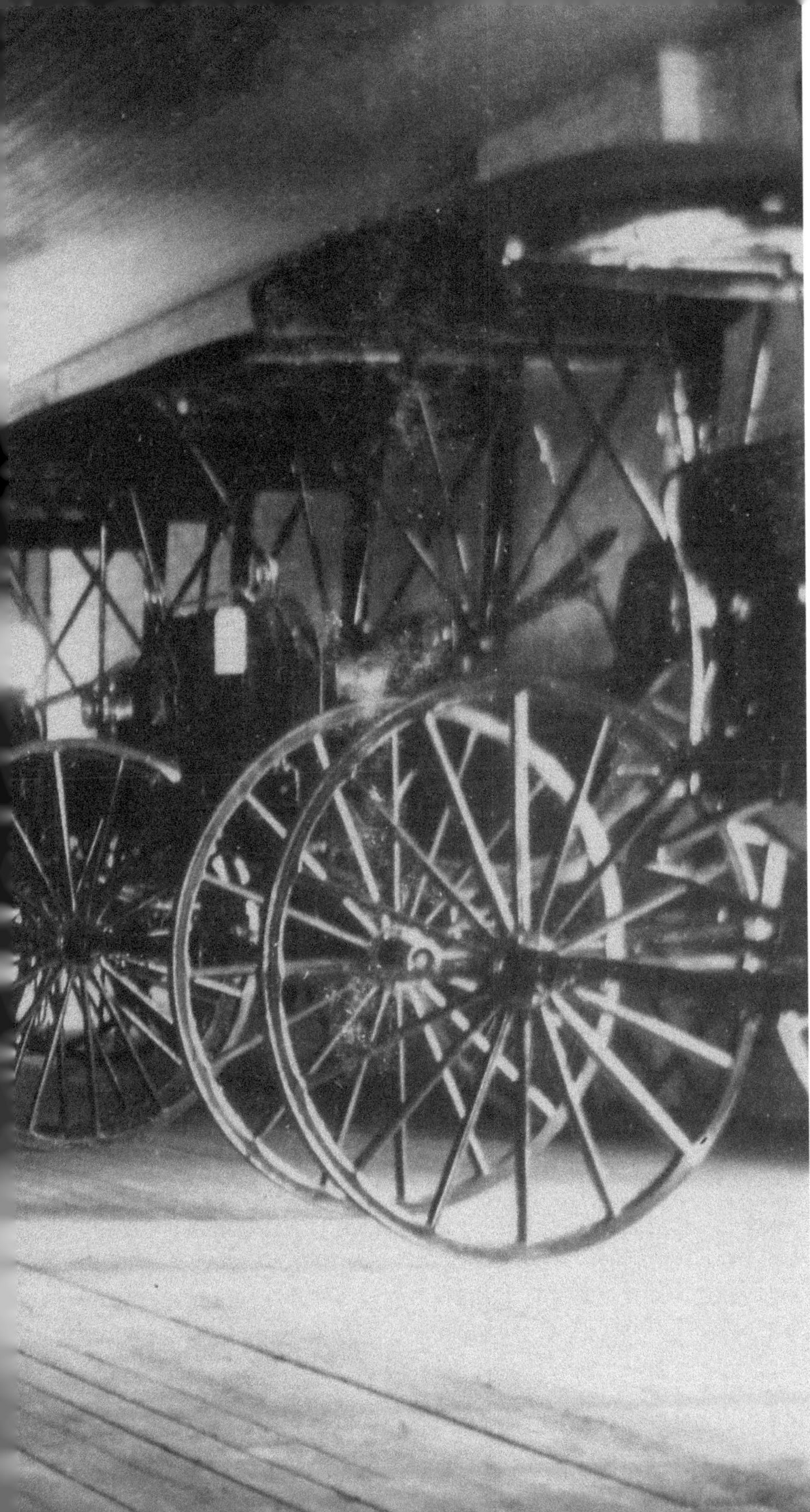

Beginning with saddlery and leather goods in the 1870s, Padgitt Brothers soon branched out into the manufacture and sale of carriages. Dallas had been a center for carriage building since the 1850s.

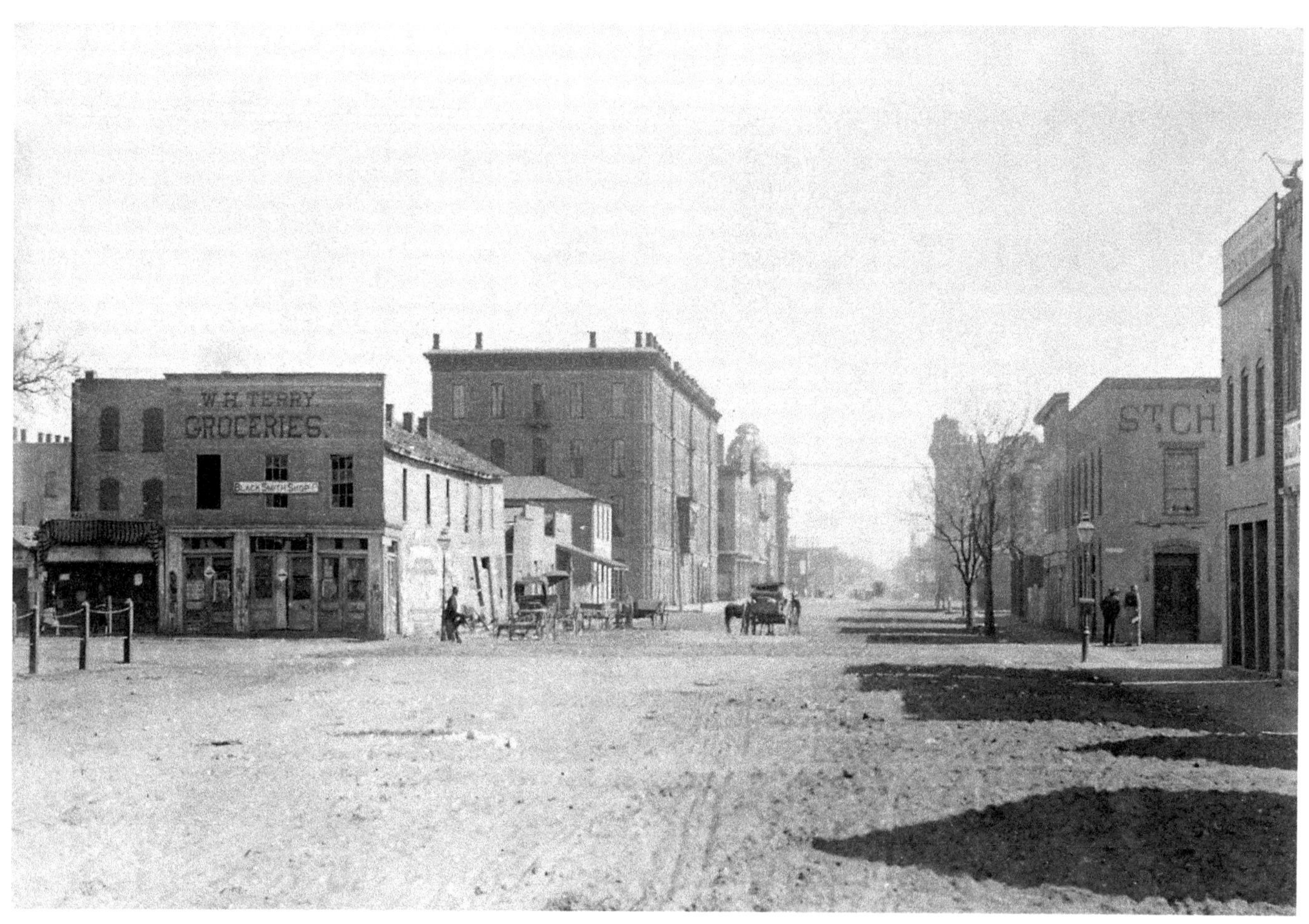

Dallas streets were still unpaved in the 1880s, as this view taken from the courthouse square looking east on Commerce indicates.

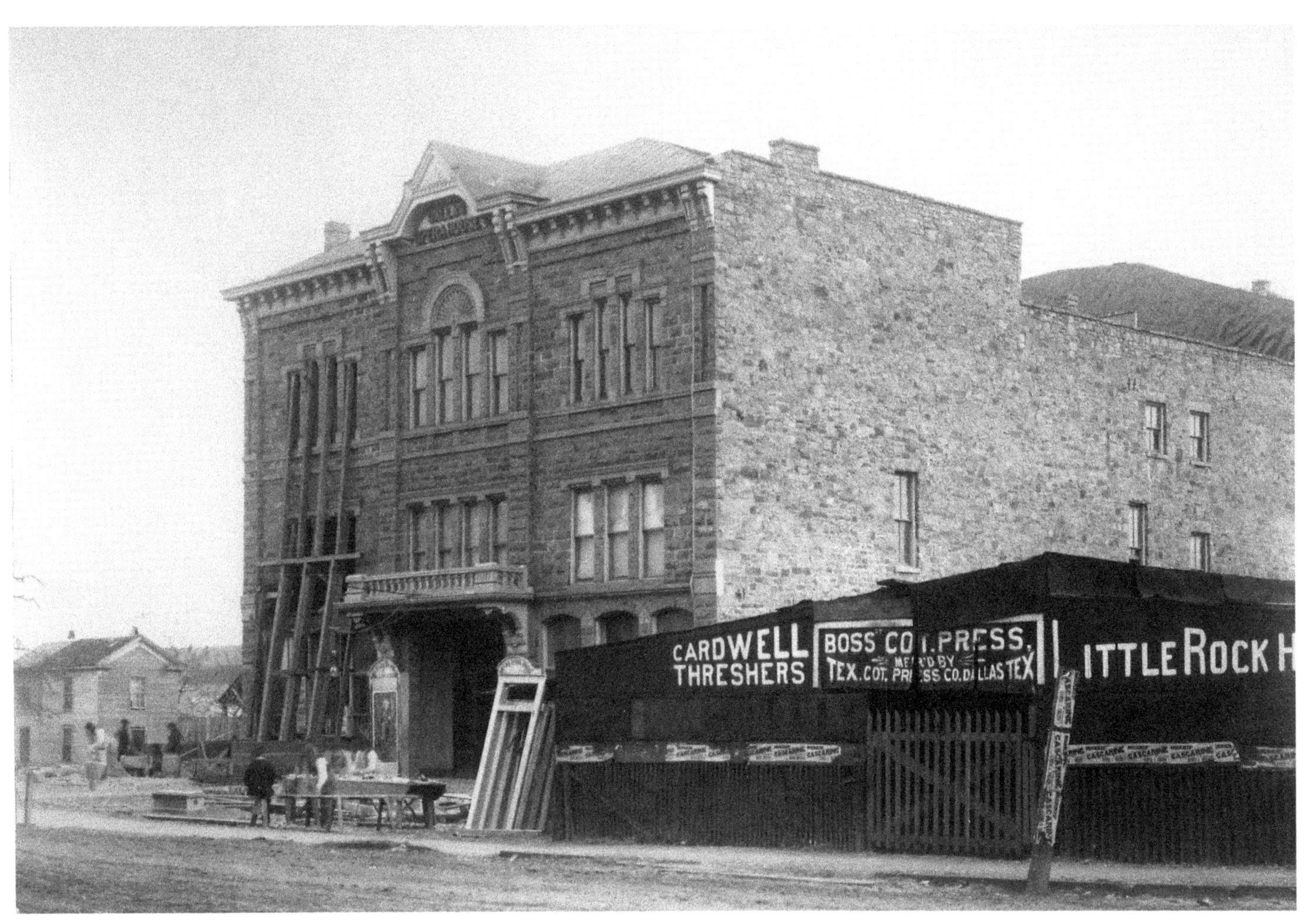

The Dallas Opera House opened in 1883 and hosted such diverse entertainers as actors James O'Neill and Eddie Foy, and bandleader John Philip Sousa before it burned to the ground in 1901.

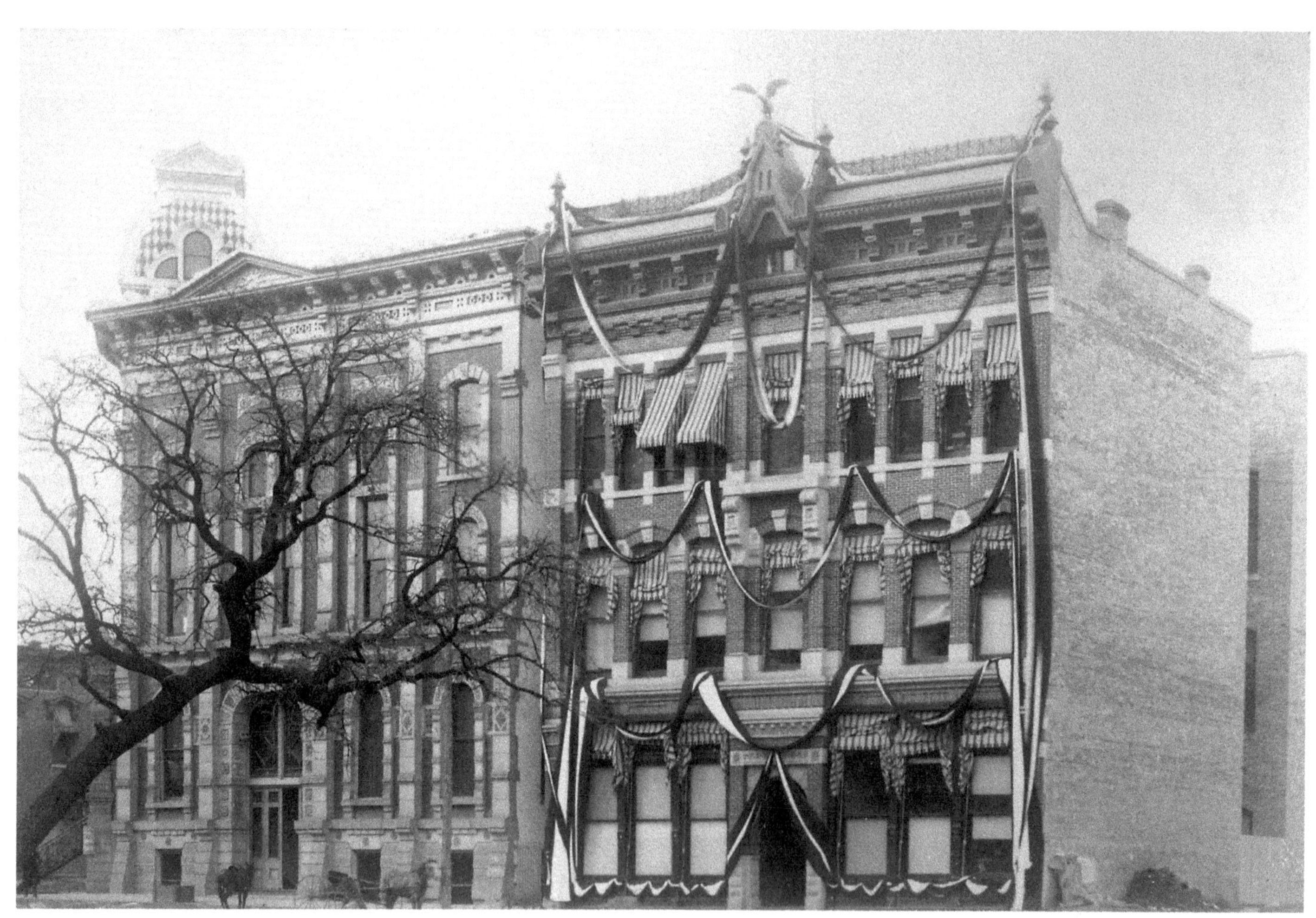

Dallas's most important nineteenth-century architect, James Flanders, designed both the Gaston Building (left) and the Gould Building (decorated for its opening in 1885).

Dallas County's fifth courthouse was designed by the city's leading architect, James Flanders, and was widely touted as being fireproof—until it burned in 1890.

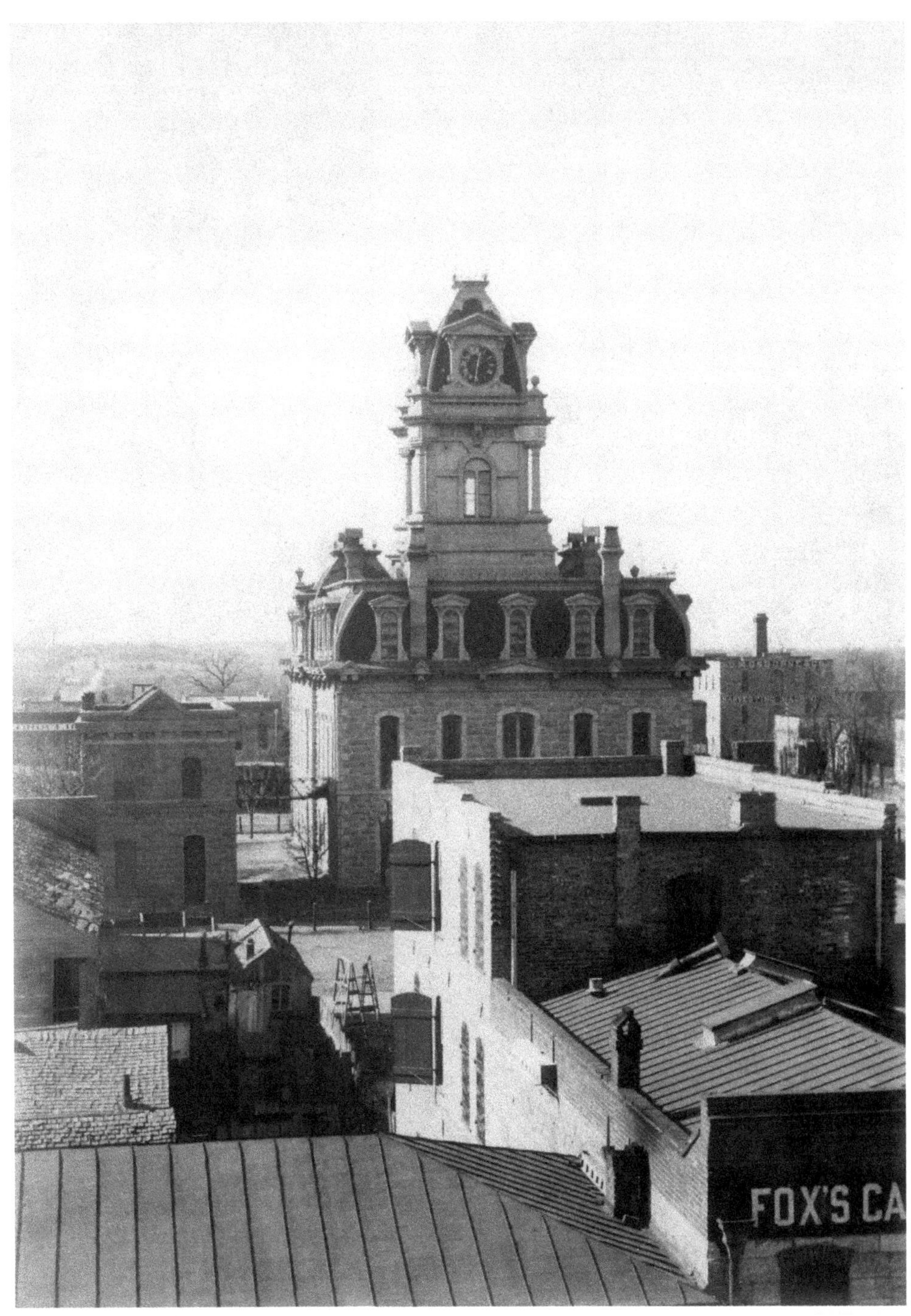

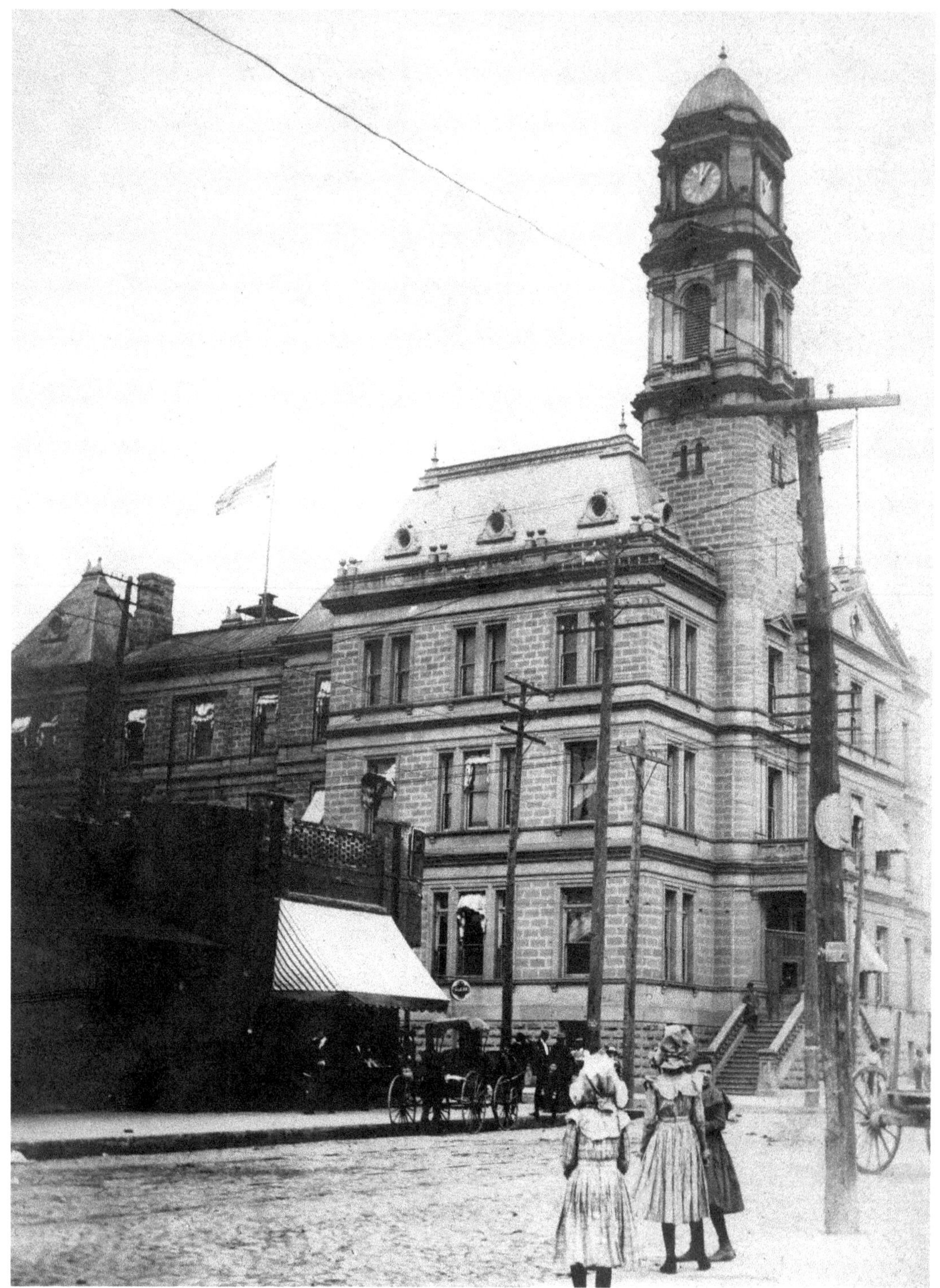

This U.S. Post Office building was constructed in stages between 1884 and 1904 on Ervay Street between Commerce and Main. The government sold the structure for $125 in 1939, and the site was cleared for the new Mercantile Bank Building, which boasted its own clock tower.

A new Dallas City Hall was constructed in 1888-89 at the corner of Commerce and Akard at a cost of $80,000. It was demolished 20 years later so that Adolphus Busch could construct his Adolphus Hotel on the prominent site.

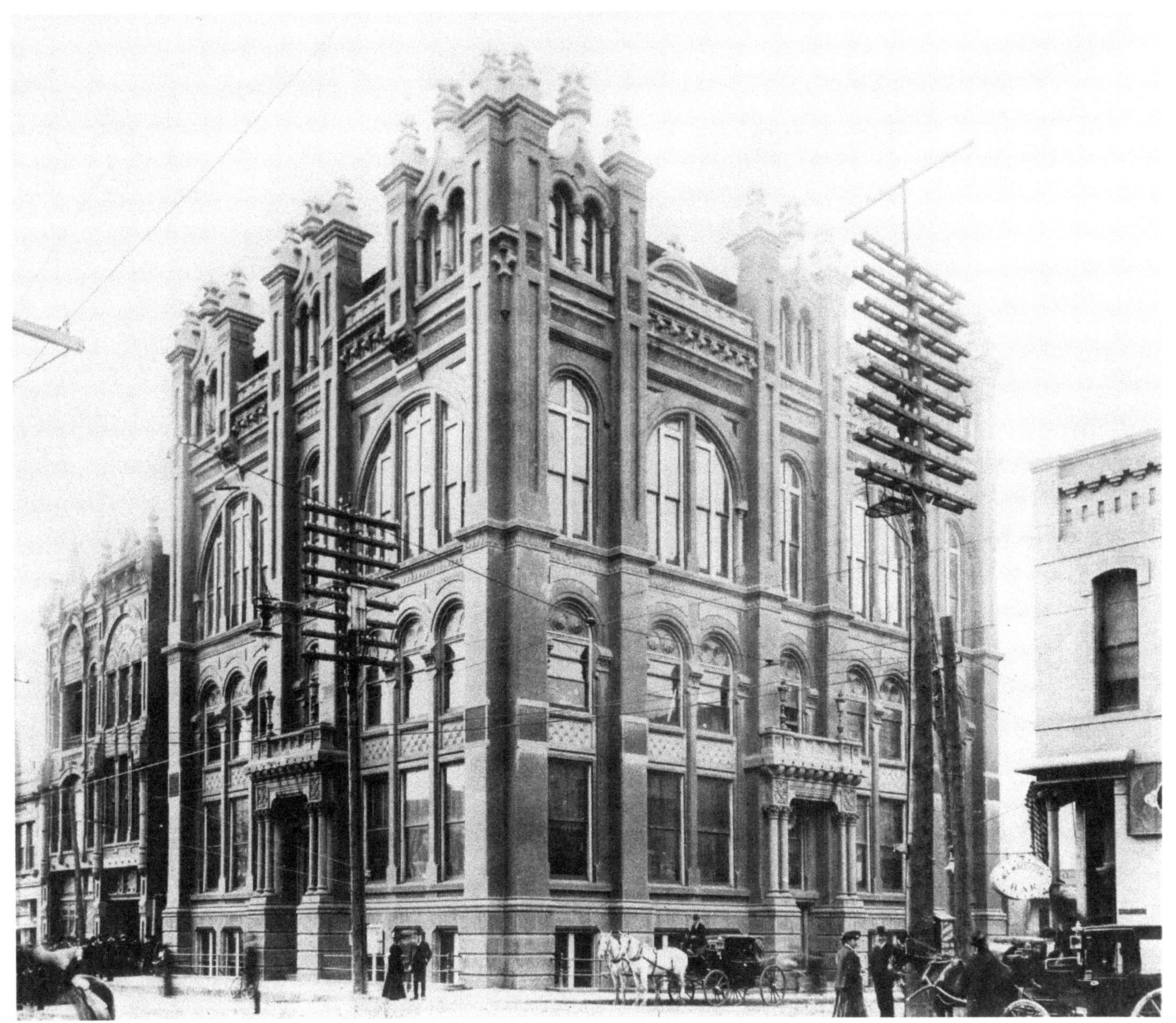

This view of the intersection of Commerce and S. Lamar streets about 1890 shows the Windsor Hotel (1879) at the far left, flanked by the first *Dallas Morning News* plant (1885) and the two-story Dallas City Hall (ca. 1880). Eventually the newspaper expanded to fill the entire block.

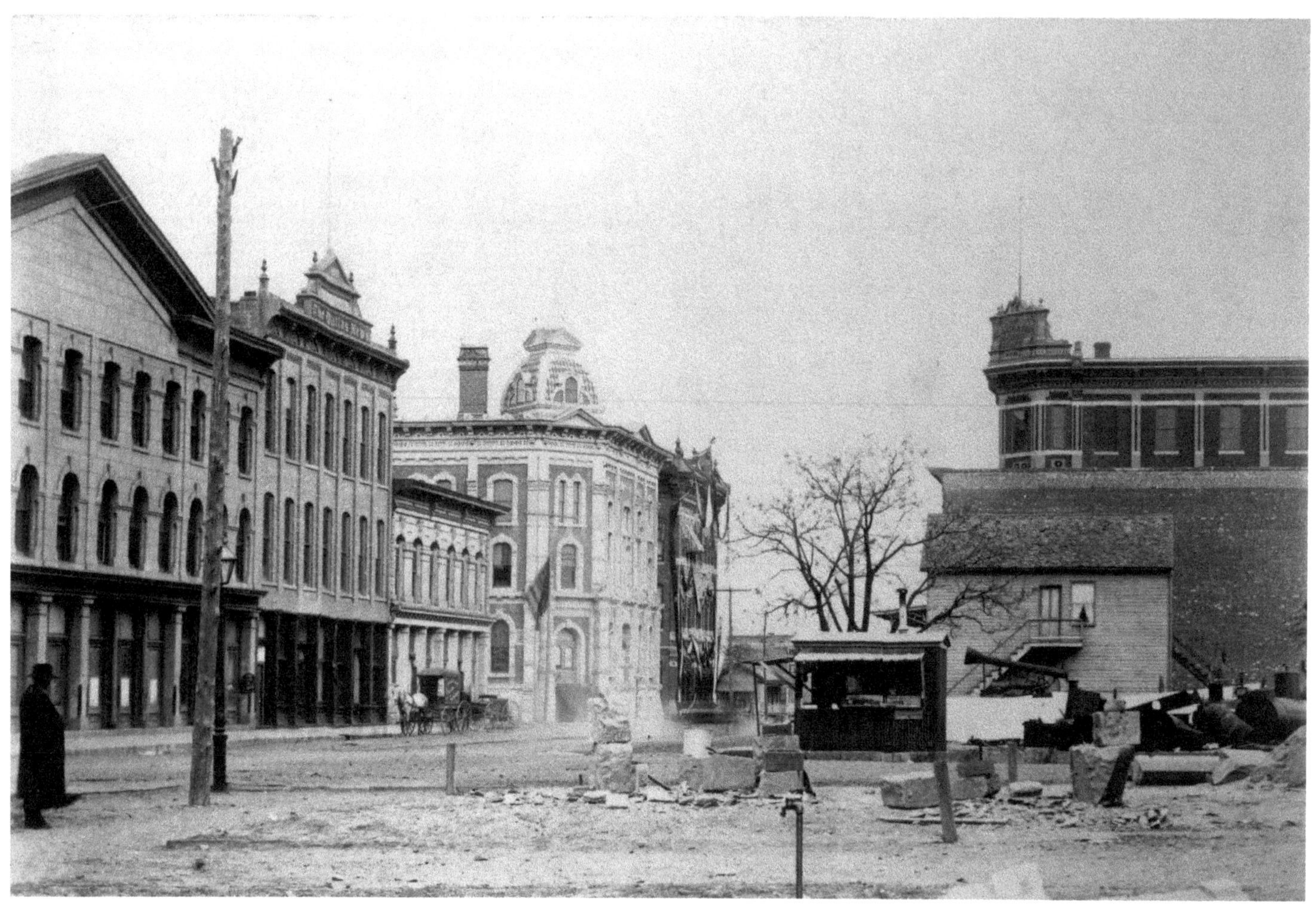

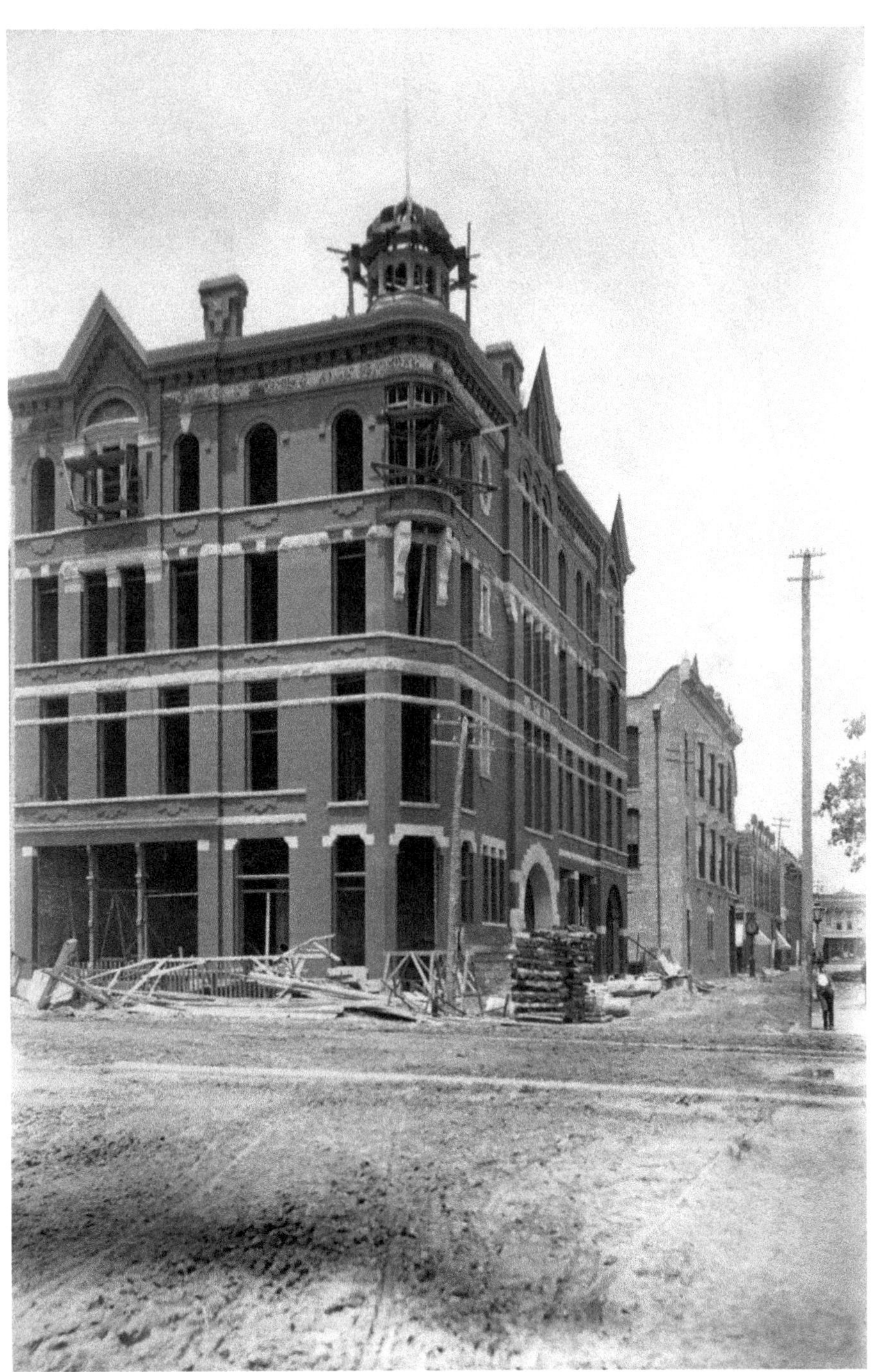

The Dallas Club was founded in 1887 and within a few years had nearly 300 members. About 1890 it built its own structure at the corner of Commerce and Poydras.

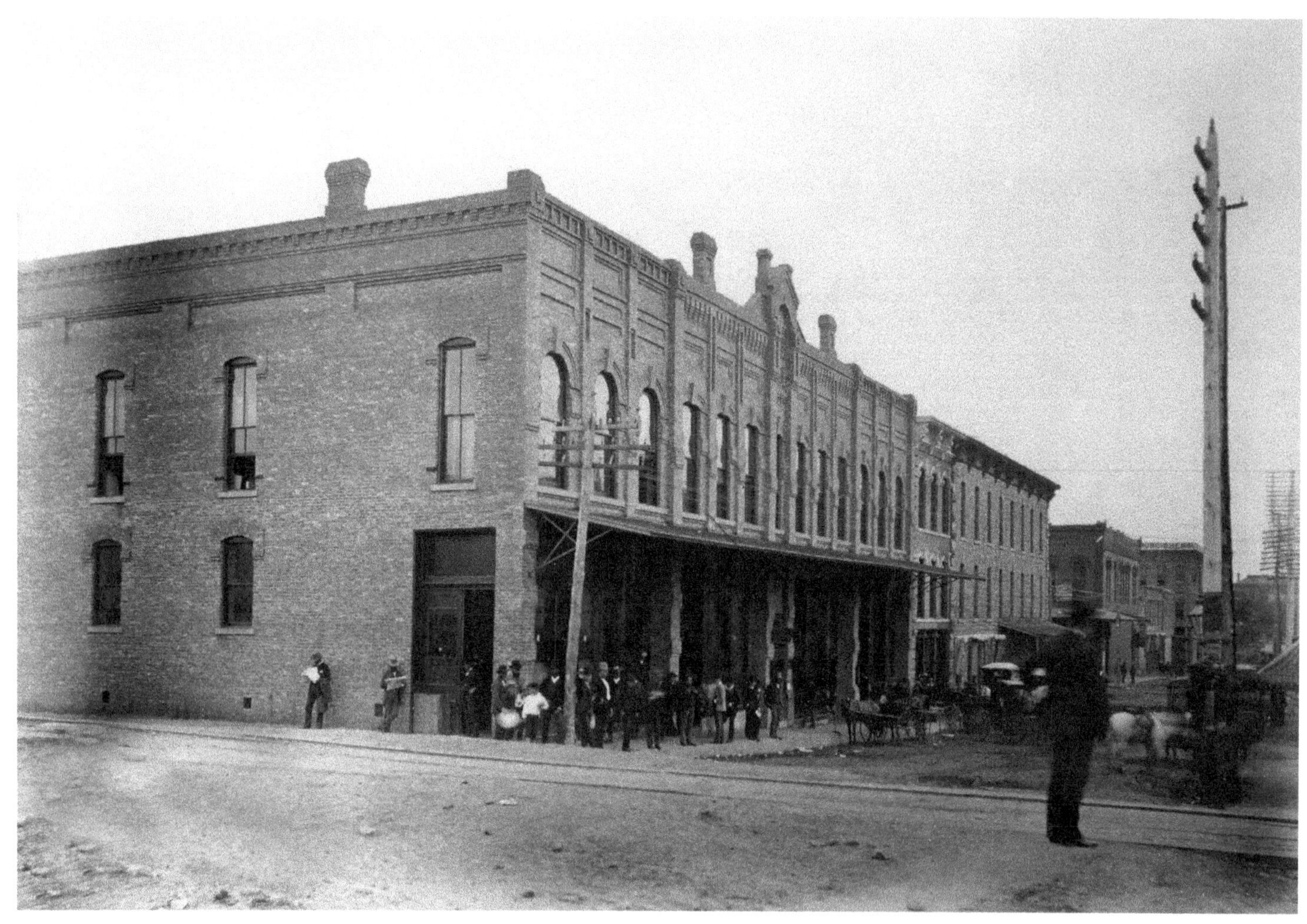

Courtenay E. Wellesley and Richard Potter—Dallas agents for the Texas Land & Mortgage Company of London, England—joined with local attorney Alex Coke to construct this commercial building on Akard Street in the early 1890s.

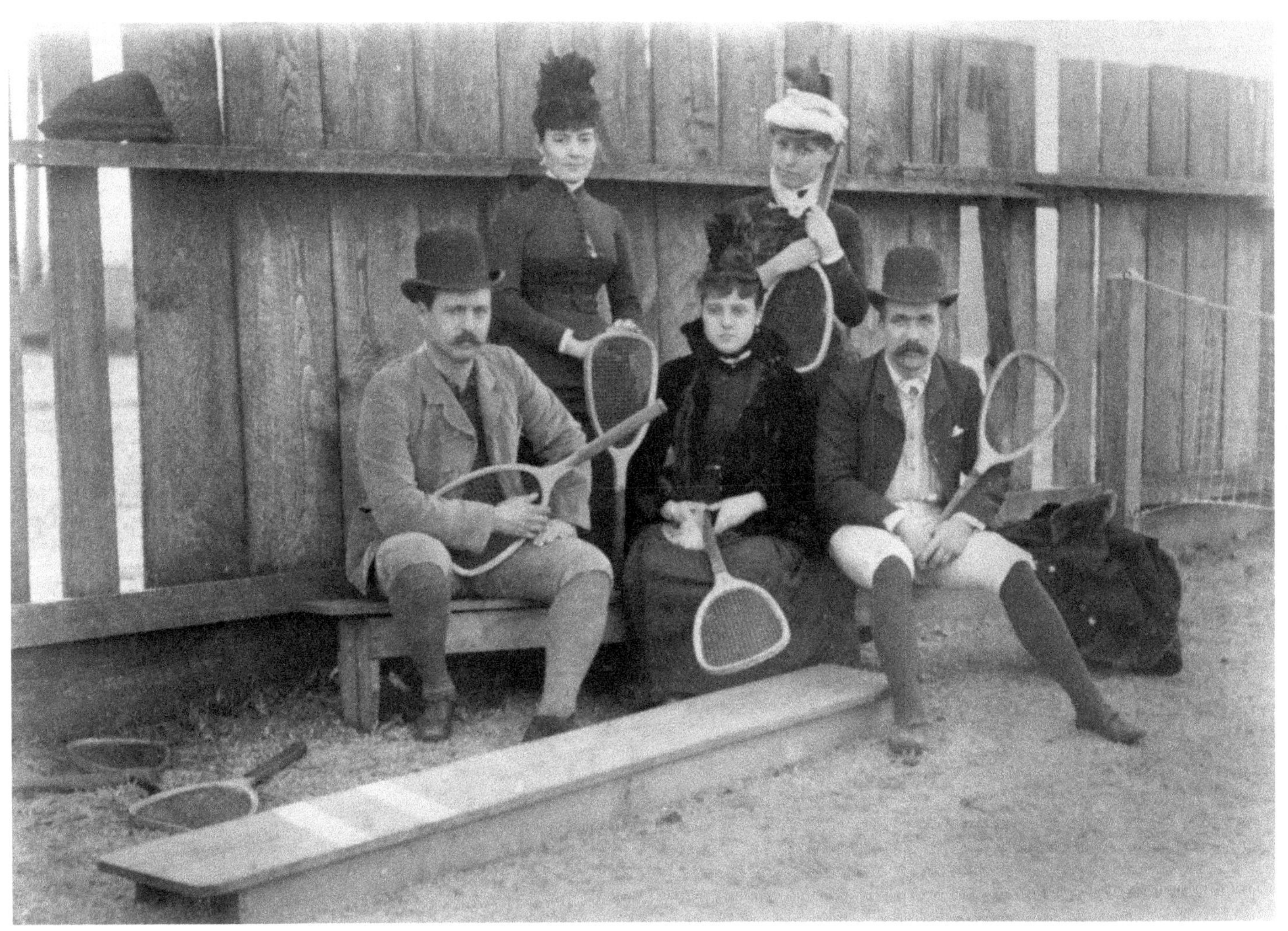

A lawn tennis club was organized in Dallas as early as 1882, with both men and women members. During the early twentieth century, Dallas produced several state champions and nationally known players, including J. B. Adoue, Jr., who later became mayor of Dallas.

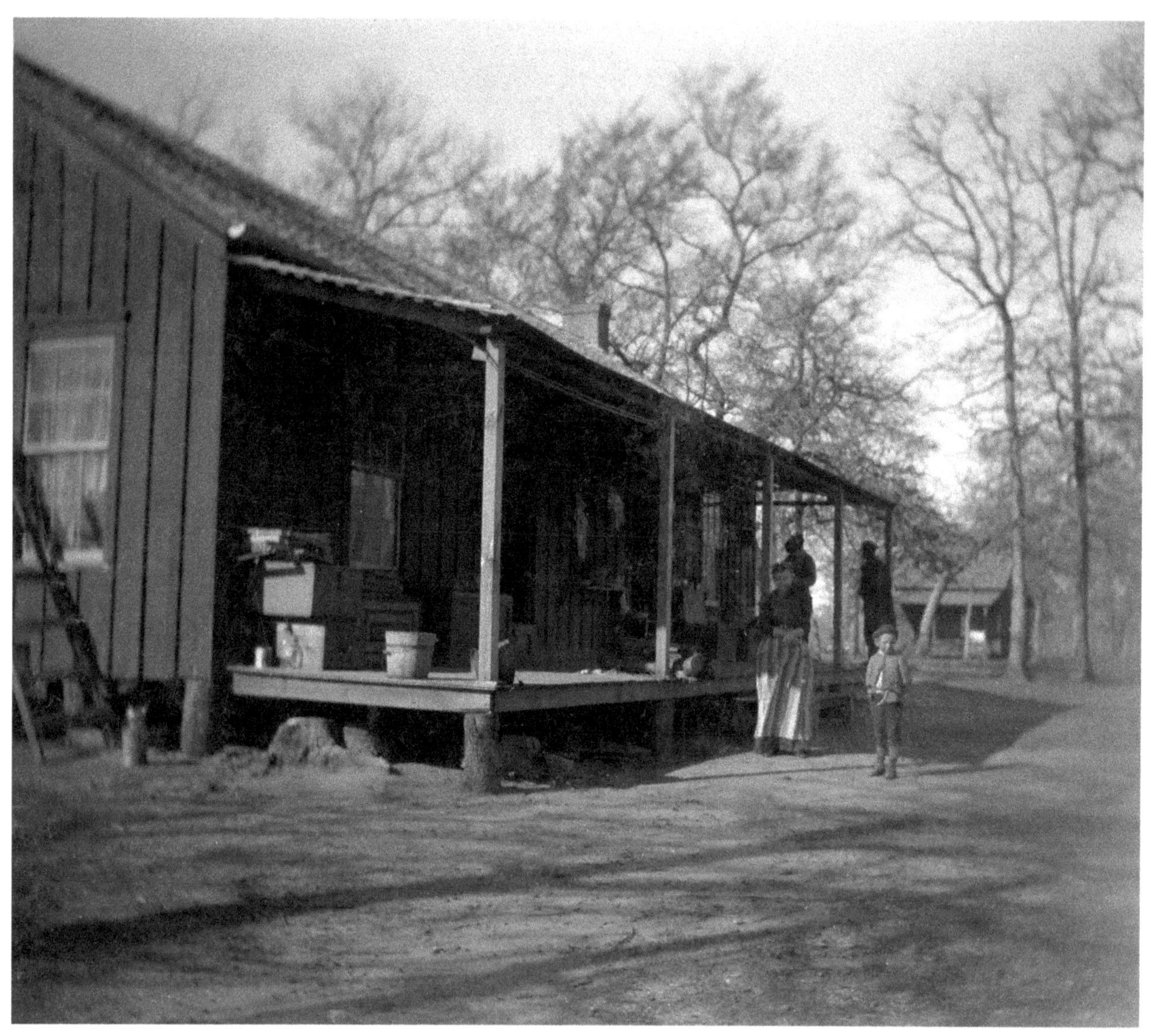

The numerous creeks in Dallas County provided good opportunities for anglers, which could explain why this photo is labeled "Fishing Club."

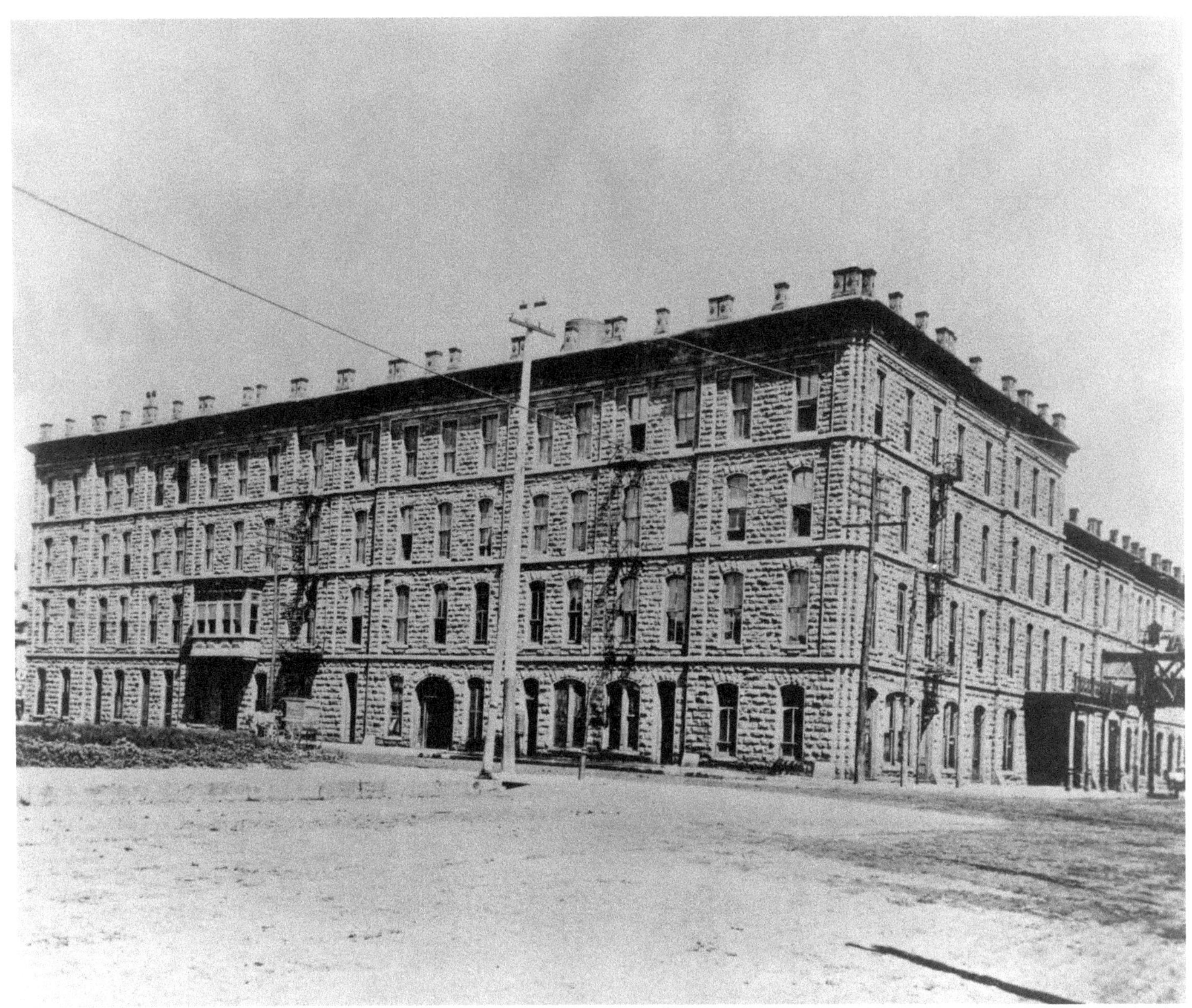

The Windsor Hotel, constructed in 1879, merged with Le Grande across Austin Street, to form the Grand-Windsor. Note the bridge at the far right connecting the two buildings.

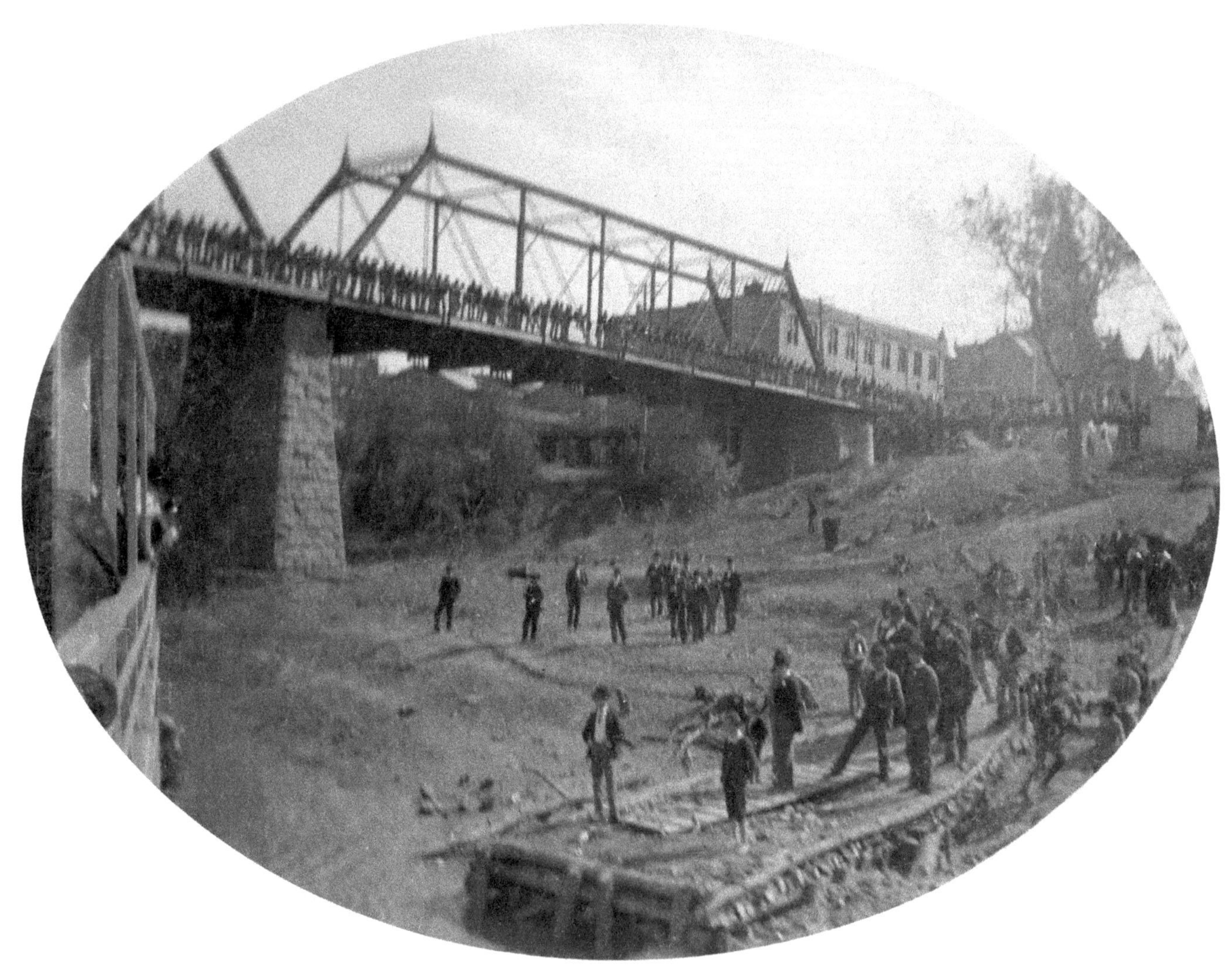

Crowds lined the Commerce Street bridge in May 1893, as they awaited the arrival of the steamer *H. A. Harvey, Jr.*, after its three-month trip up the Trinity River from Galveston.

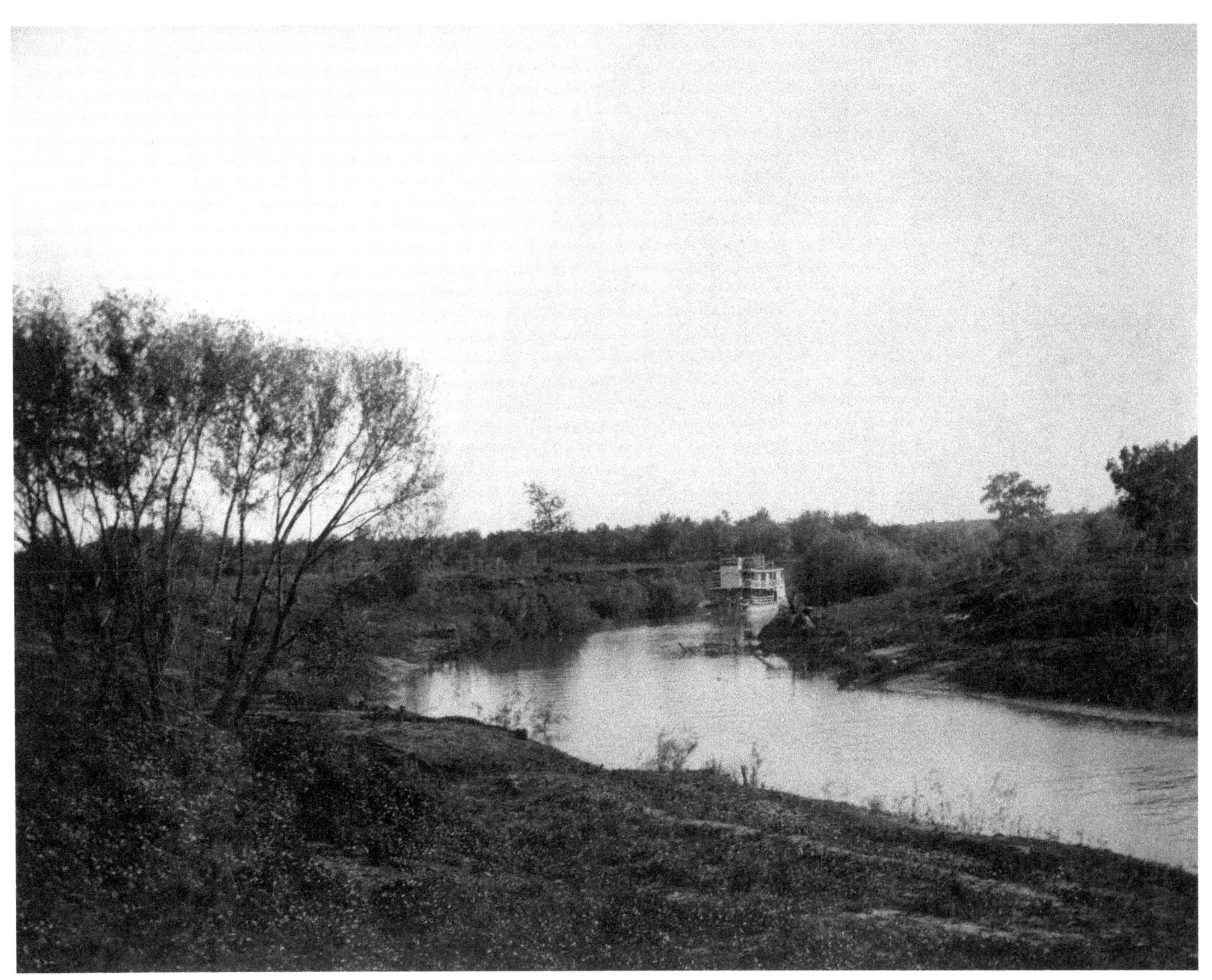

This view of the *Harvey* steaming up a relatively wide, open river is atypical. Most of the Trinity was heavily timbered and filled with debris.

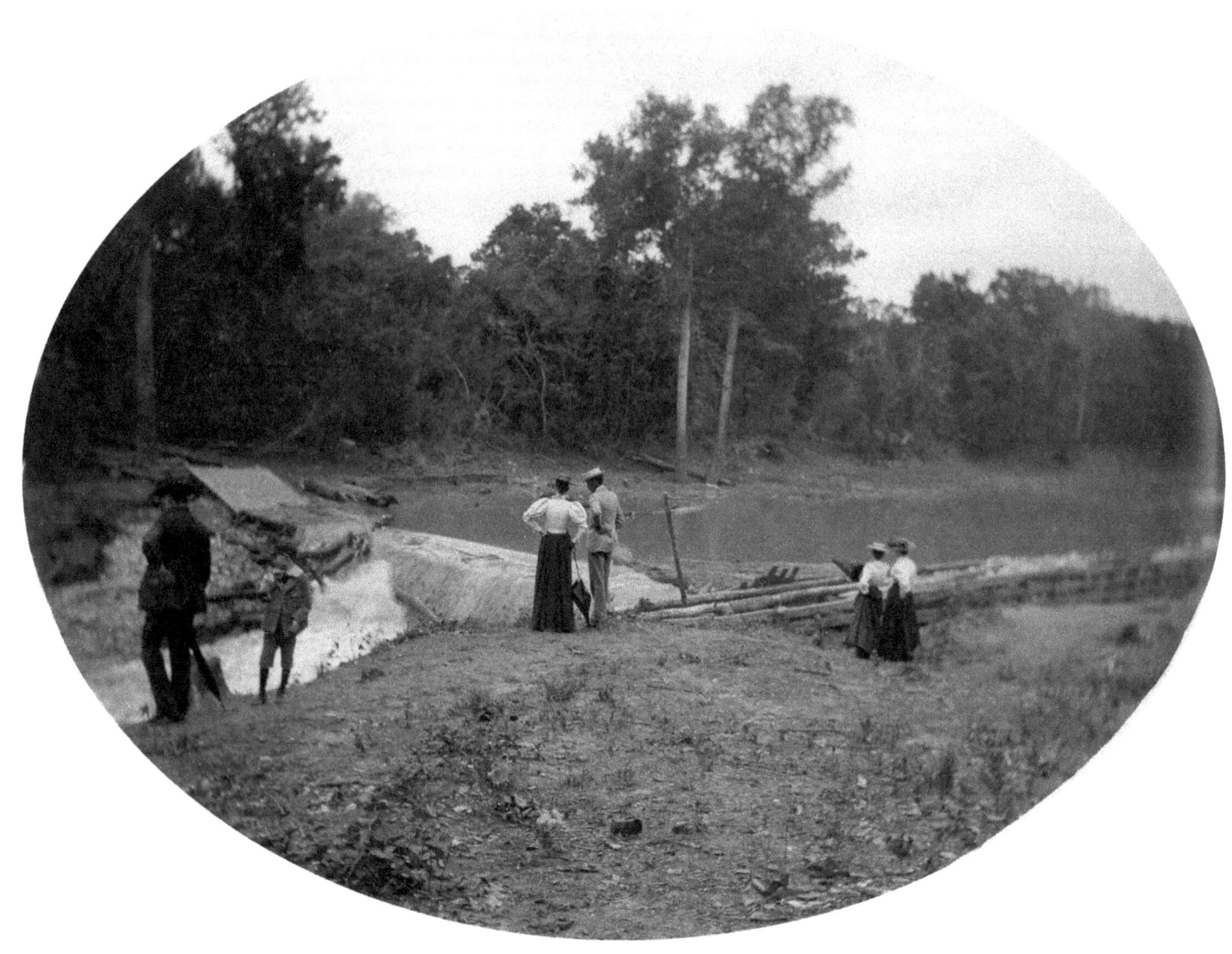

Navigating the Trinity River from Dallas to the Gulf of Mexico had been a dream since the first settlers arrived in the 1840s. A lock and dam to control the water level was constructed at McCommas Bluff, 13 miles south of town, in 1893.

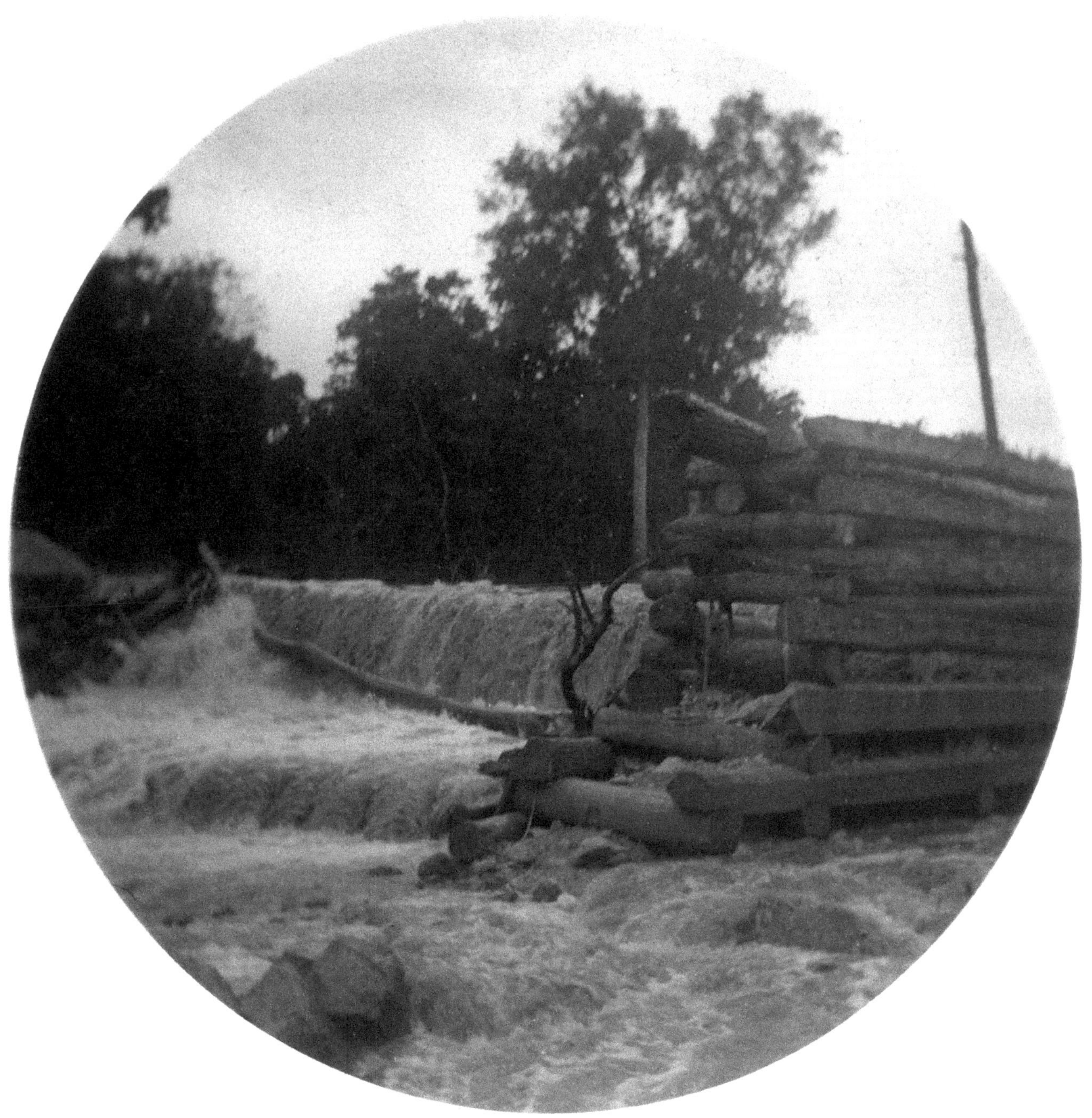

Unfortunately, the McCommas dam was the only one built, leaving navigation south of Dallas impractical.

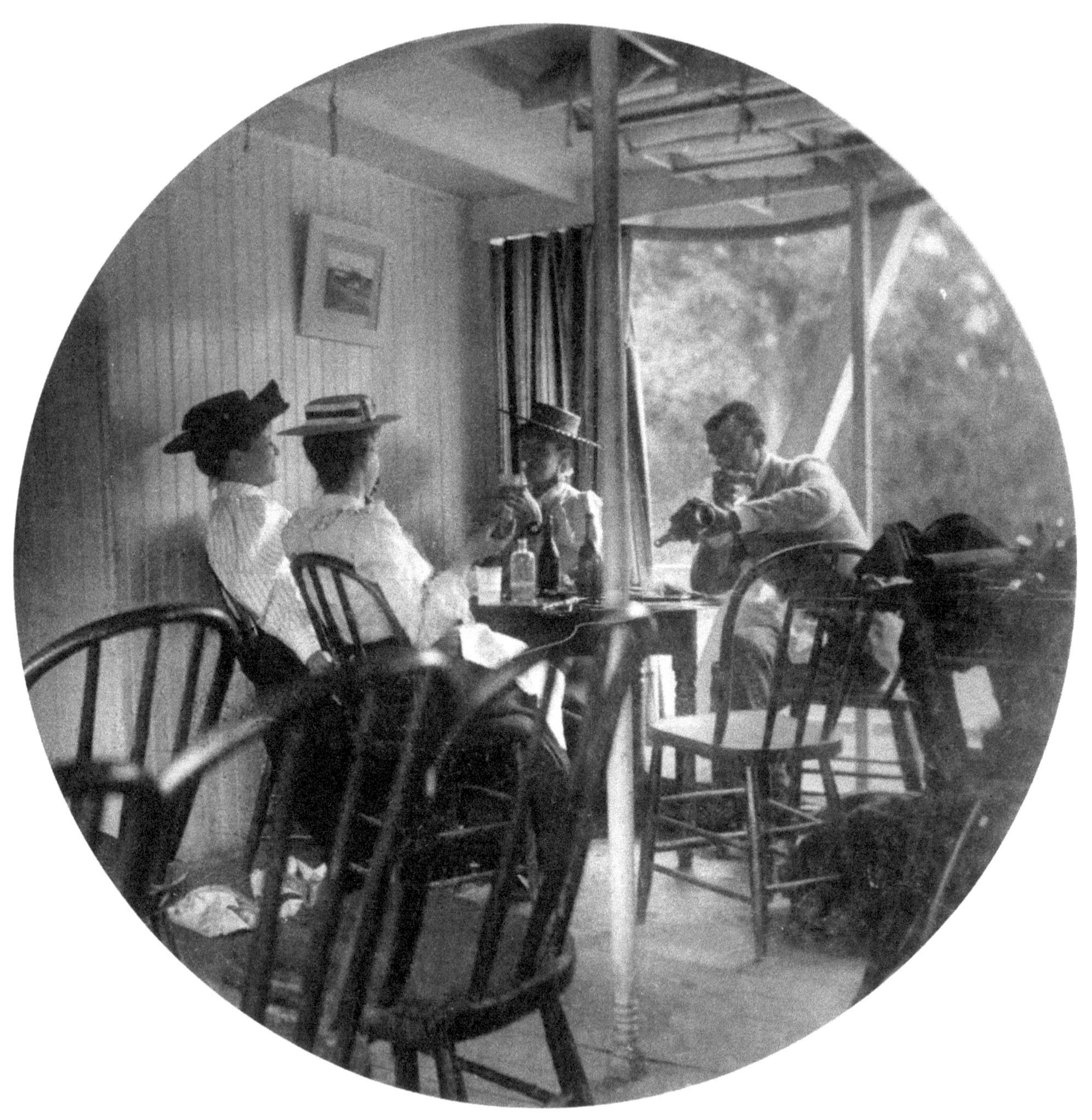

For several years after its arrival in Dallas in 1893, the steamer *H. A. Harvey, Jr.,* offered excursions to McCommas Bluff, 13 miles downstream.

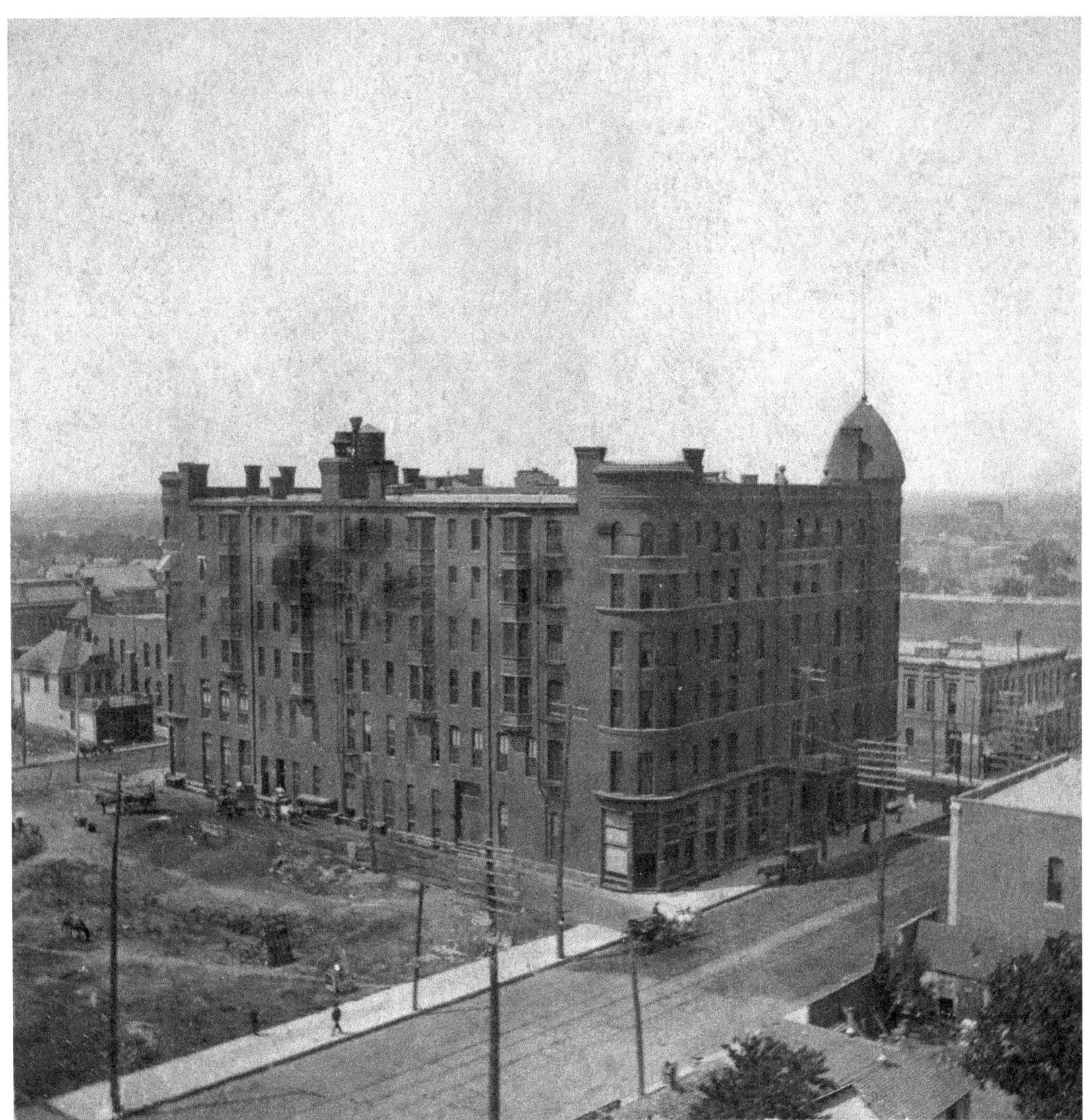

Costing $500,000 to build in 1893, the Oriental Hotel was Dallas's first "luxury" hotel, boasting 200 rooms, electricity, and elevators. Located on Commerce at Akard, it was demolished in 1924 to make way for the Baker Hotel.

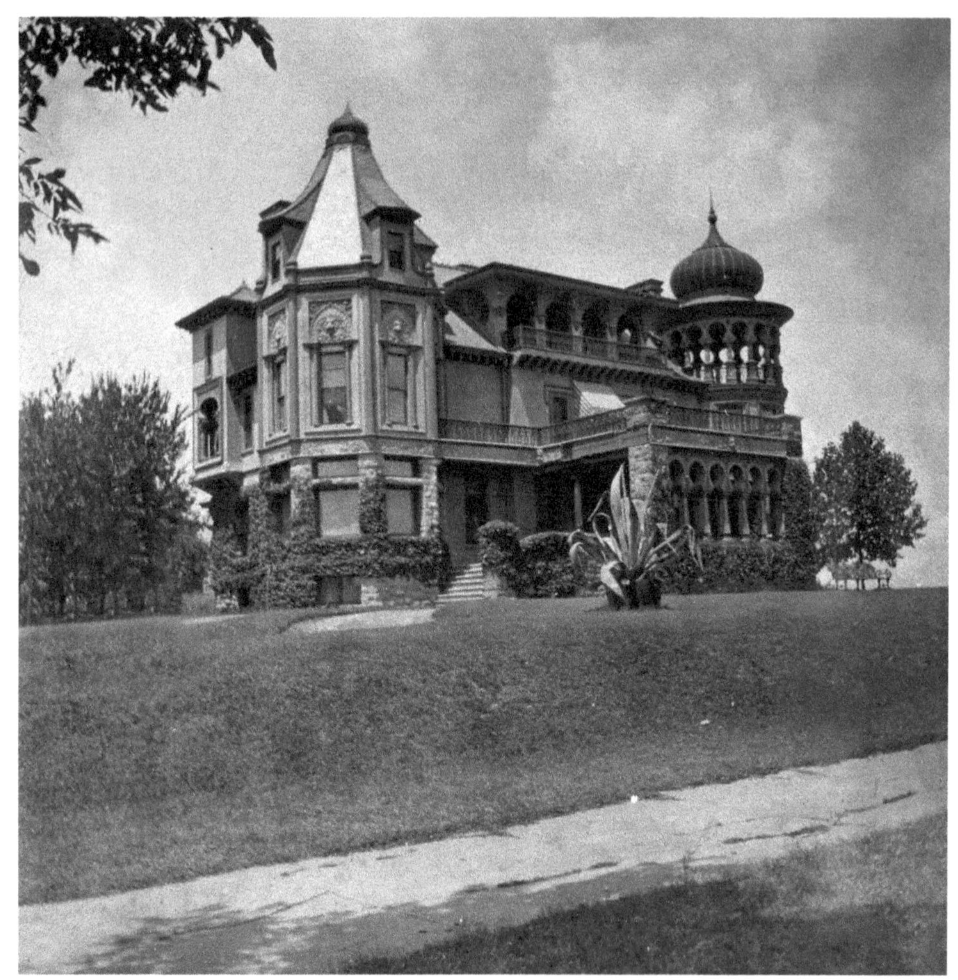

One of the grandest private homes built in Dallas was Ivy Hall, built by George M. Dilley in 1890, using Pecos County gray marble on the exterior and oak and Honduras mahogany for the interior. Later owned by banker Royal Ferris, the house was demolished in 1924 to build the present Maple Terrace Apartments.

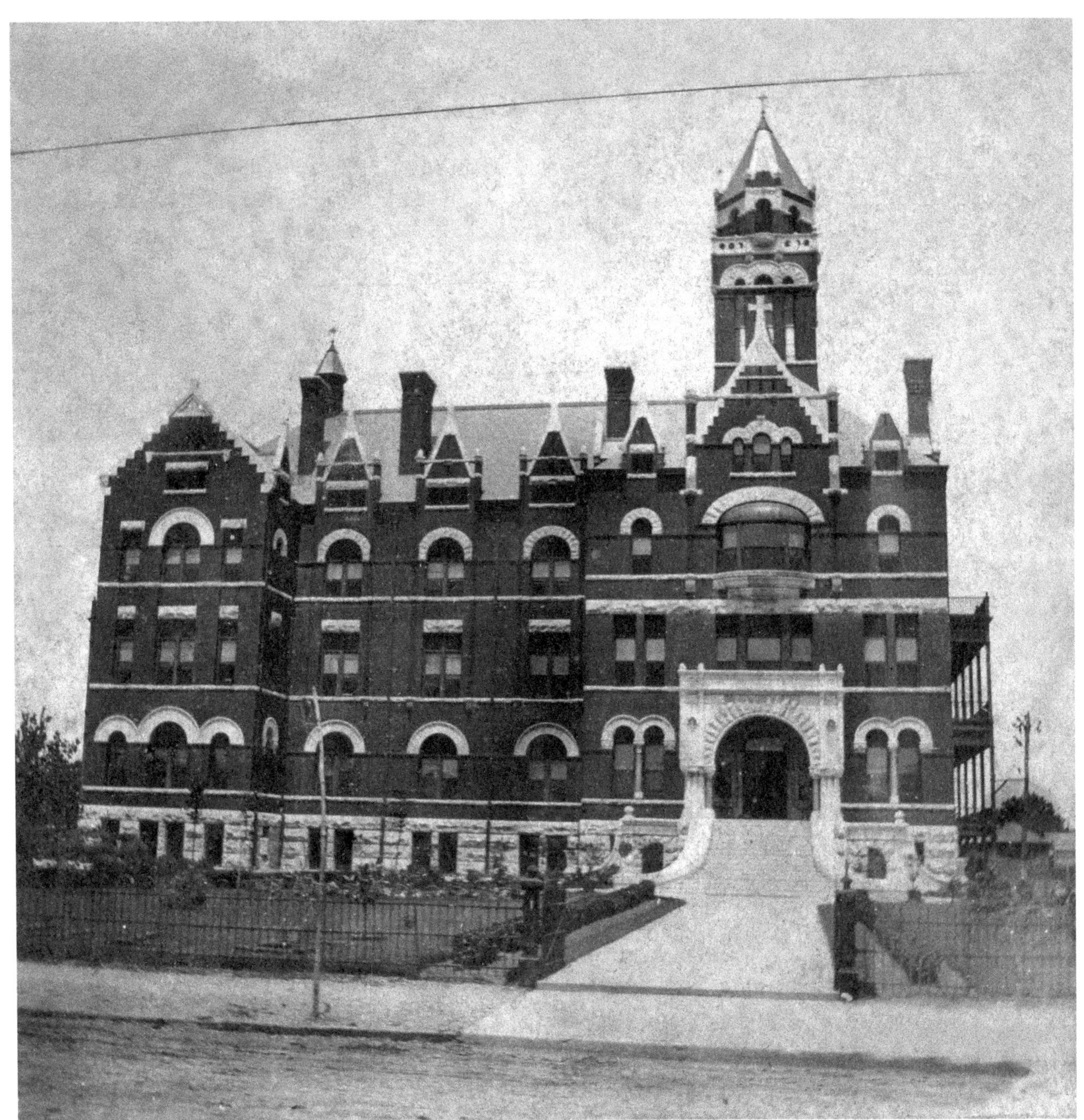

St. Paul's Sanitarium opened in 1898 as Dallas's first "modern" hospital, with electricity, elevators, and hot and cold running water. It cost over $350,000. The 350-bed facility closed in 1963 when a new St. Paul's opened, and the building was demolished in 1968.

This Moorish-influenced synagogue was built by Temple Emanu-El in 1898 at the corner of S. Ervay and St. Louis, in the heart of the heavily Jewish residential neighborhood called the Cedars. In 1913, the Temple built a new structure farther south, and this building became a Unitarian church.

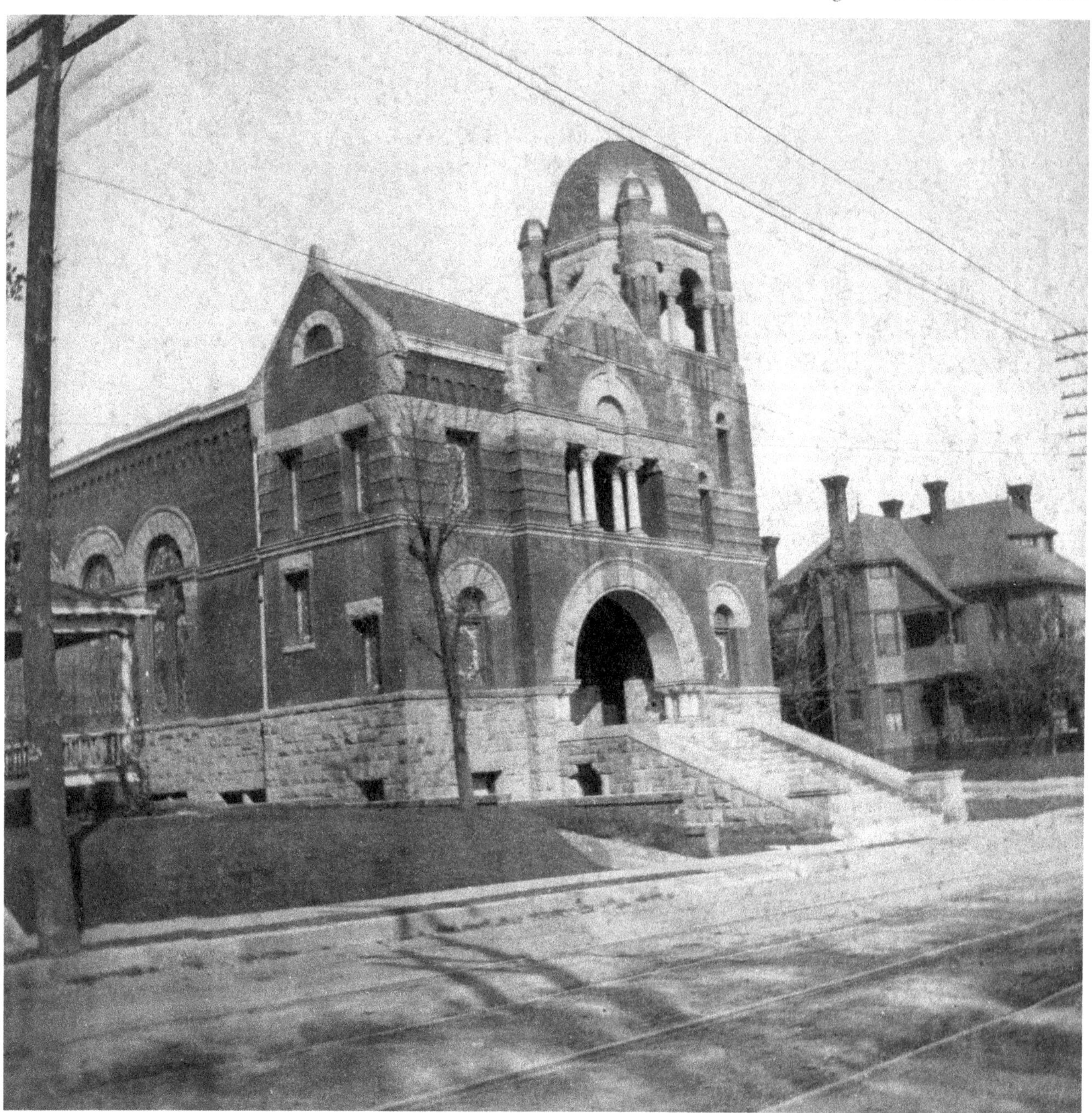

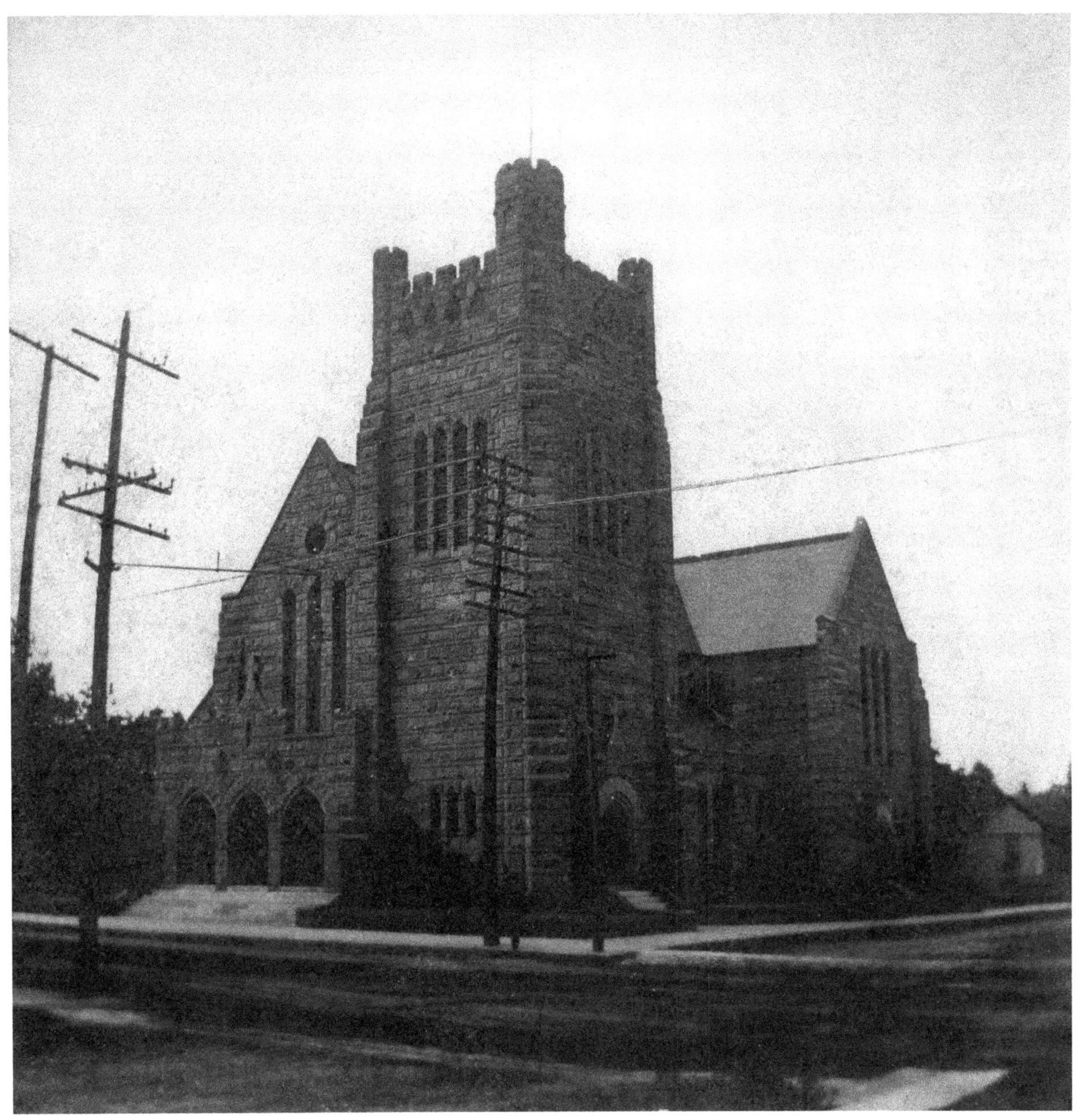

The third St. Matthew's Cathedral, see of the Episcopal Diocese of North Texas, was built on the northeast corner of S. Ervay and Canton streets in 1894-95, at a cost of more than $100,000.

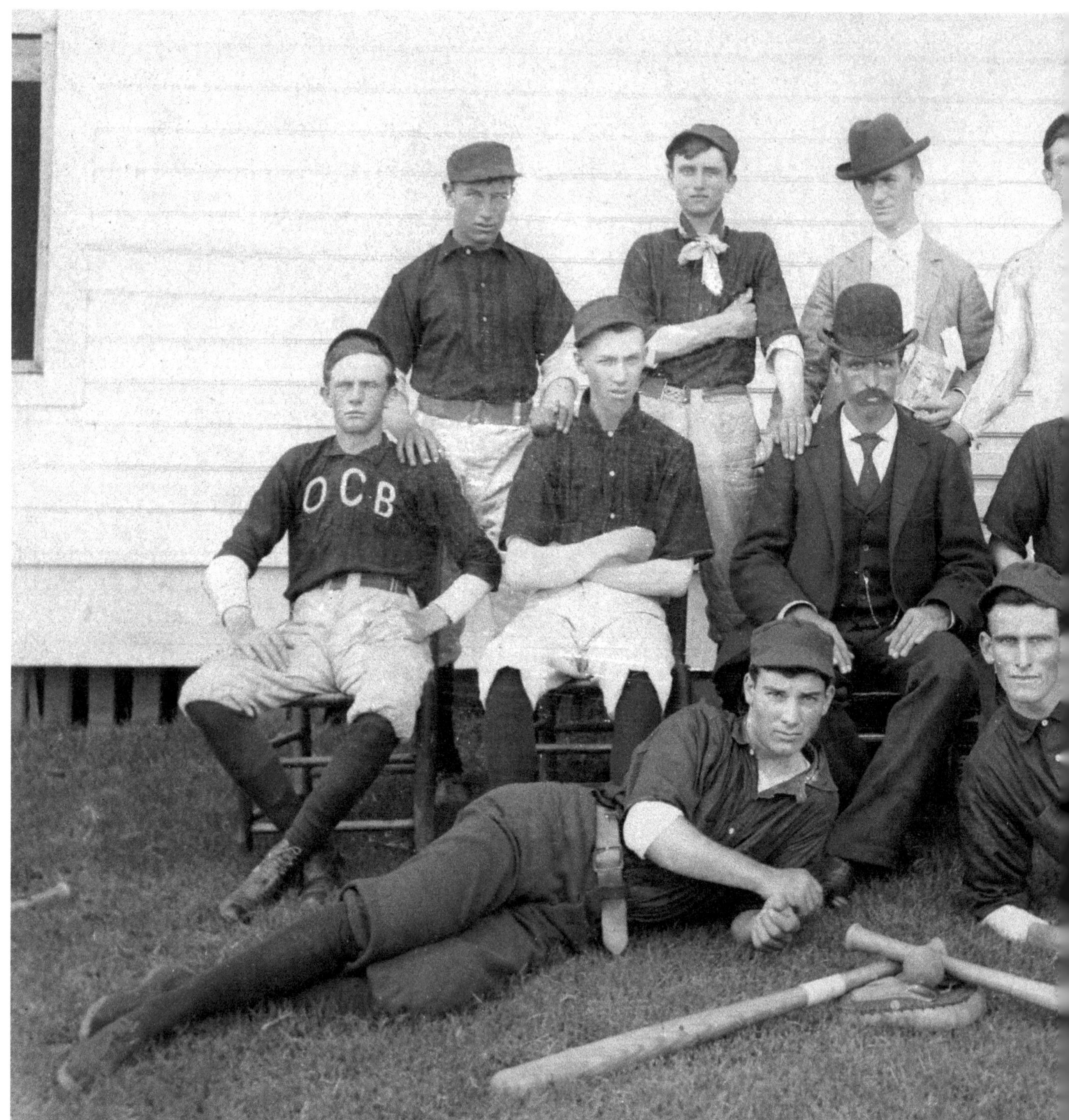
OCB

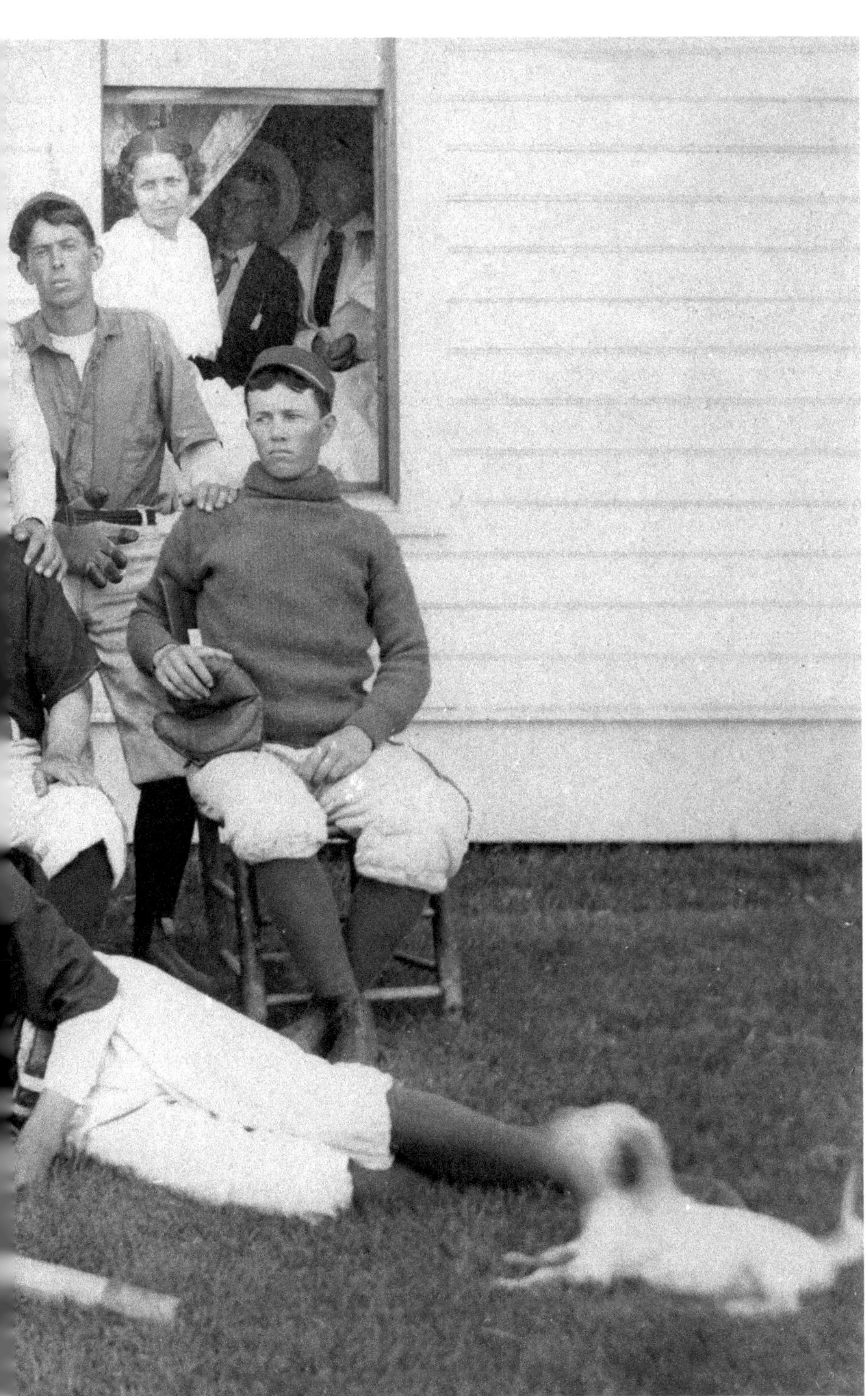

By the 1890s, nearly every community boasted an amateur baseball team. The letters on the jersey in this 1895 photo would suggest that this team hailed from Oak Cliff, south of the Trinity River.

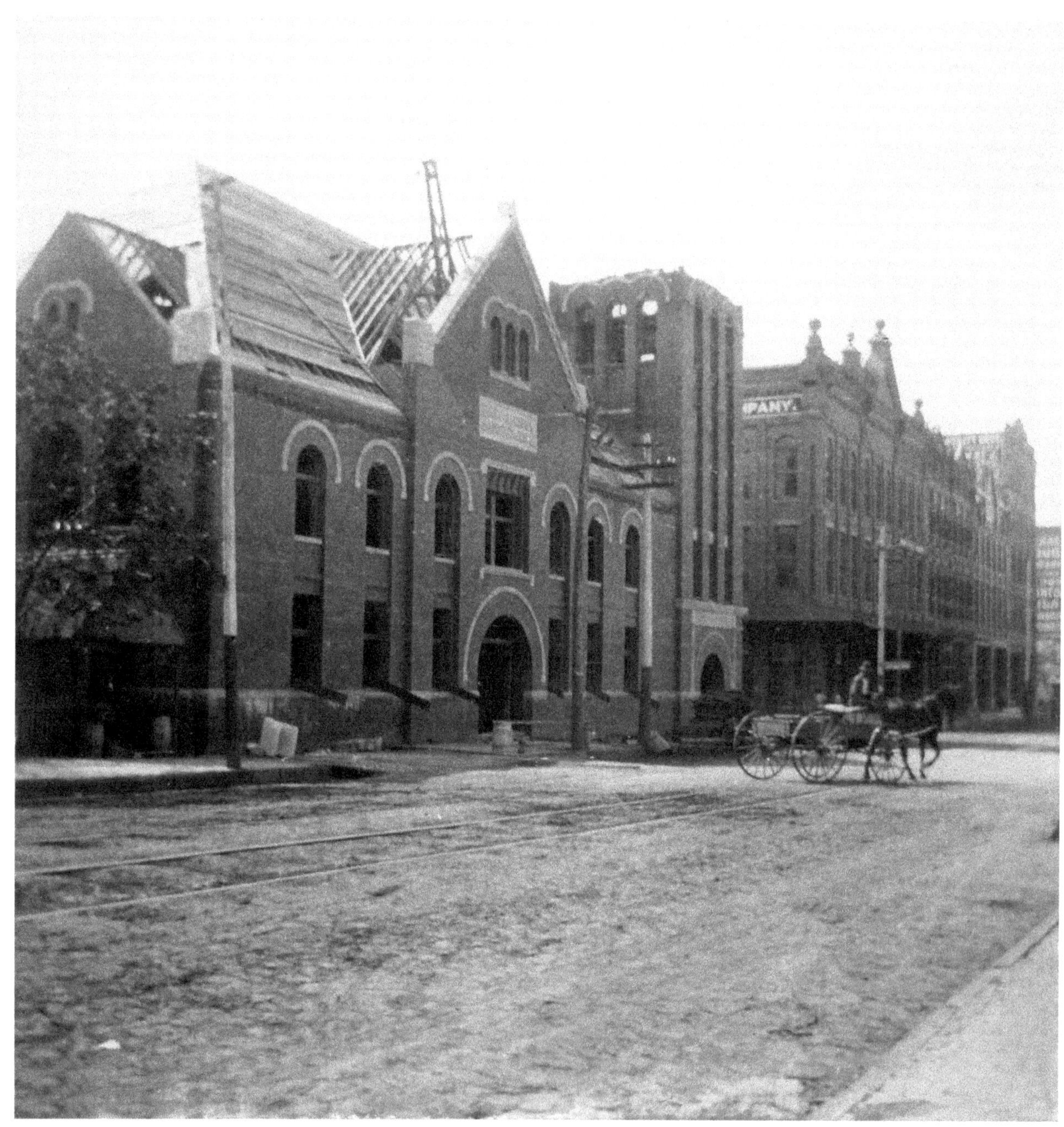

The Gulf, Colorado, and Santa Fe Railroad and the St. Louis and Southwestern Railway (commonly called the Cotton Belt), constructed this Richardsonian Romanesque terminal at the corner of Commerce and Murphy streets in 1896. It was demolished 30 years later to erect the Santa Fe Building, still standing.

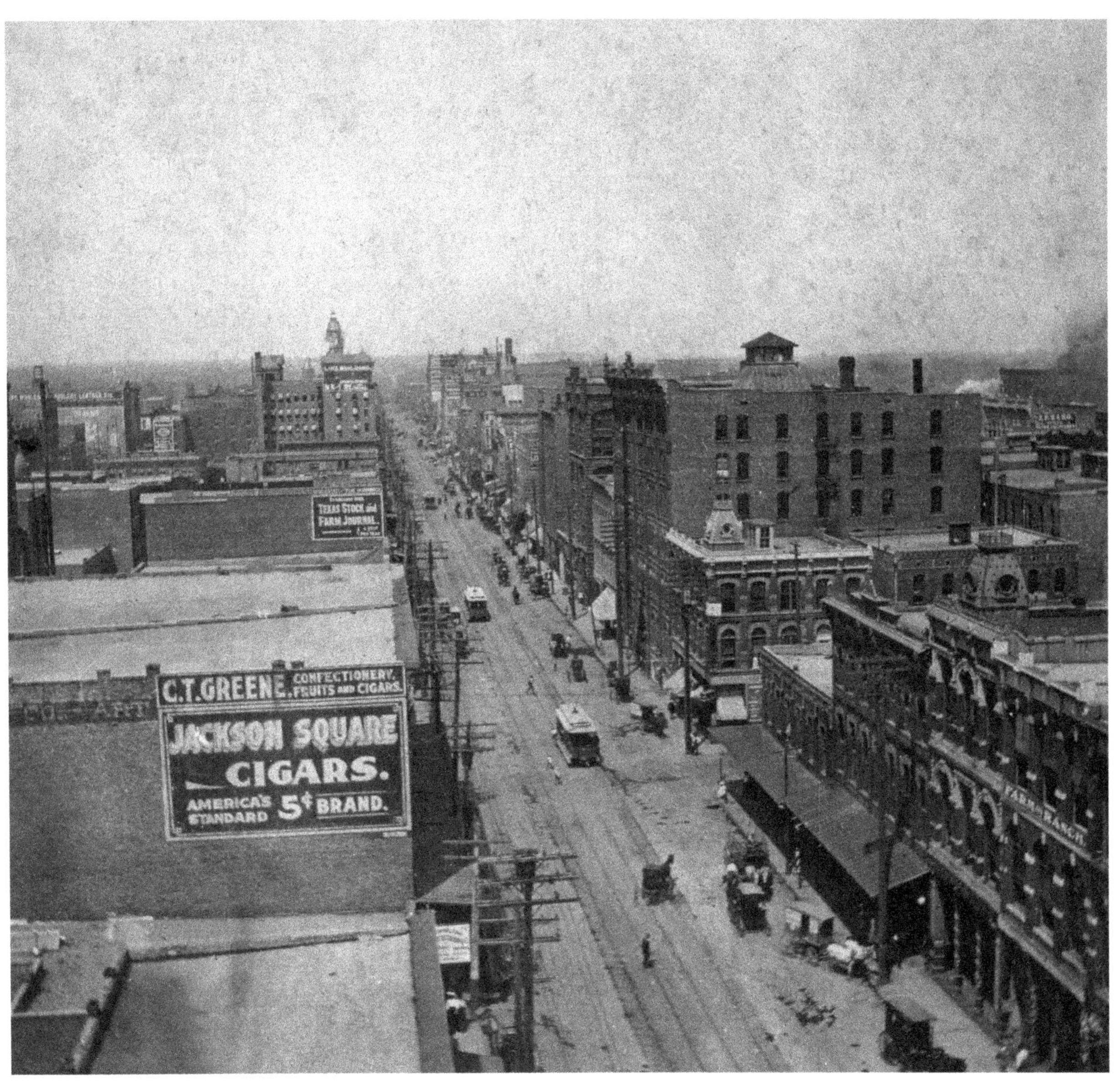

By the early 1900s the trolley lines, first laid in the 1870s, had been electrified and the major downtown streets had been paved.

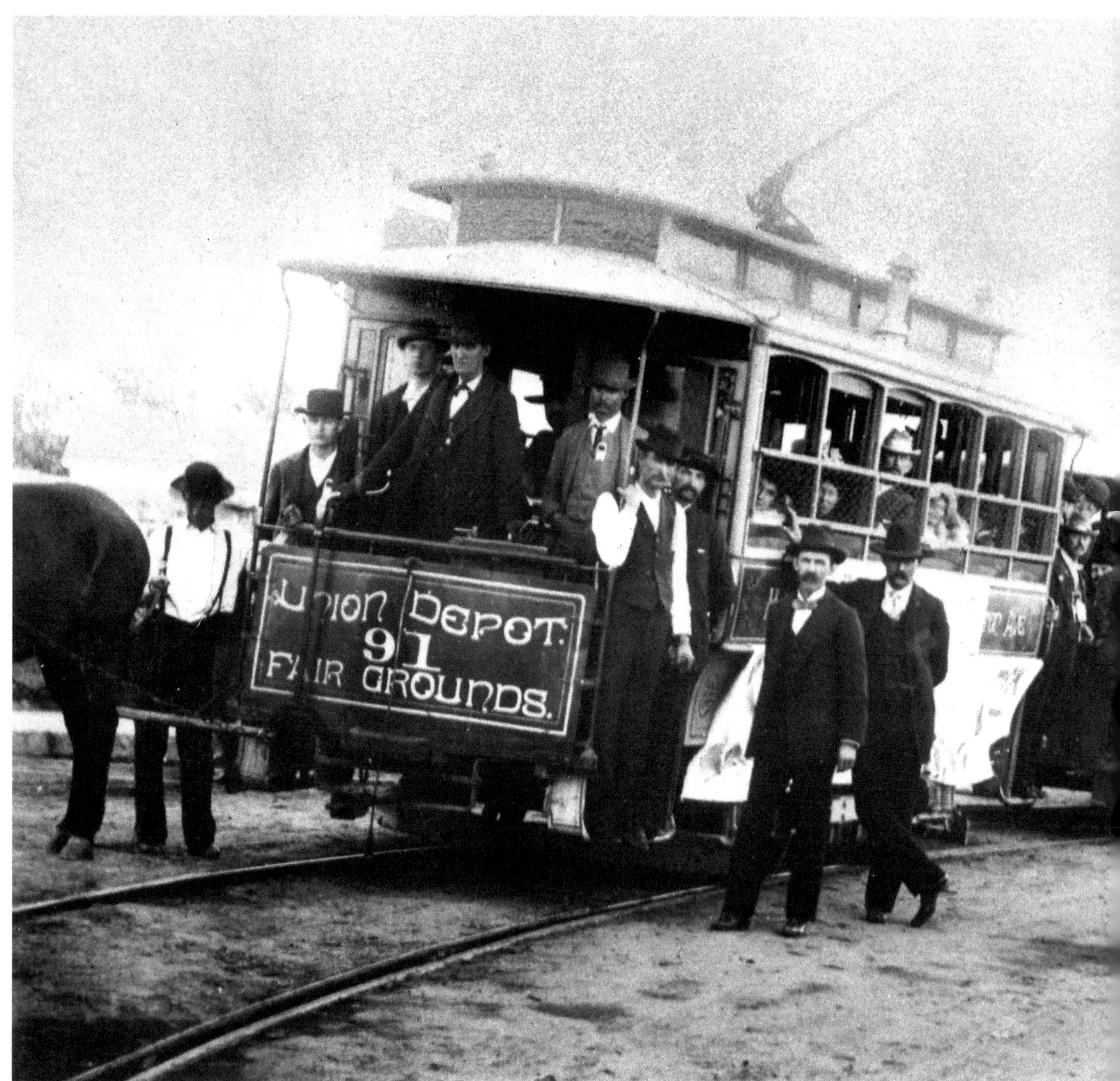
UNION DEPOT.
91
FAIR GROUNDS.

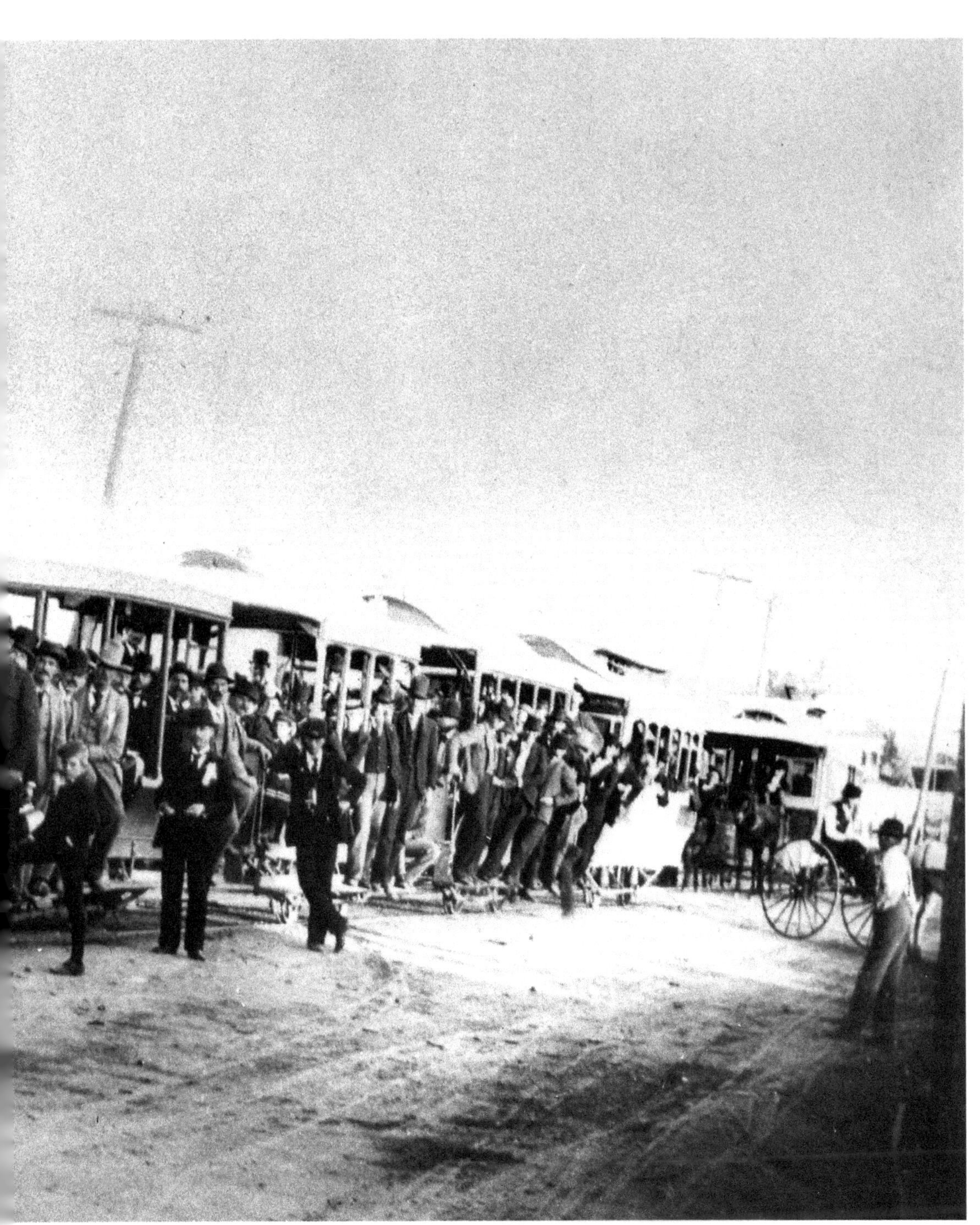

By the 1890s, streetcar lines fanned out from downtown Dallas, providing convenient and inexpensive transportation for workers and shoppers. This streetcar was loaded with passengers headed to the annual state fair in East Dallas.

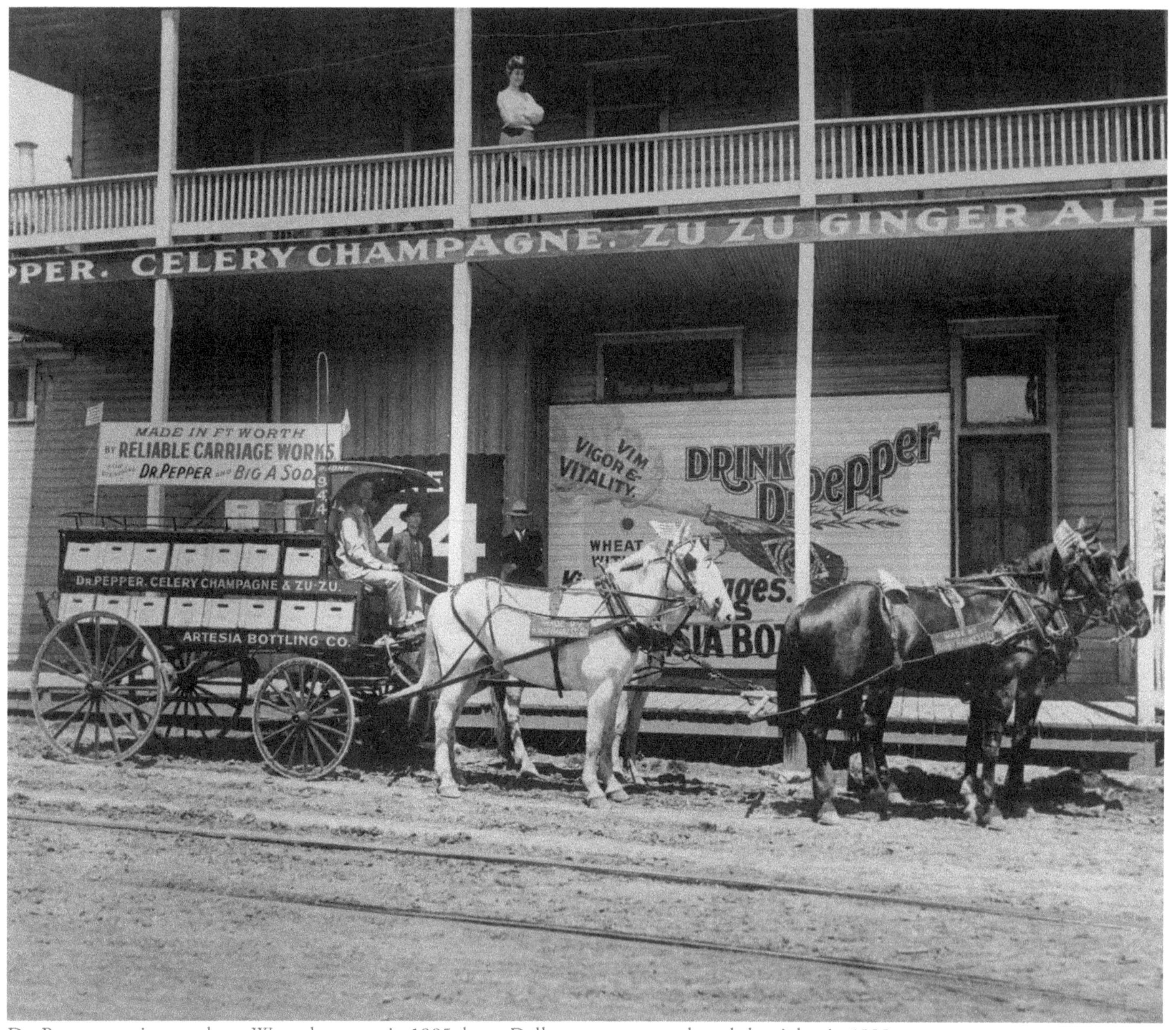

Dr. Pepper was invented at a Waco drugstore in 1885, but a Dallas company purchased the rights in 1898. It was one of a number of popular soft drinks, or elixirs, sold at the turn of the century.

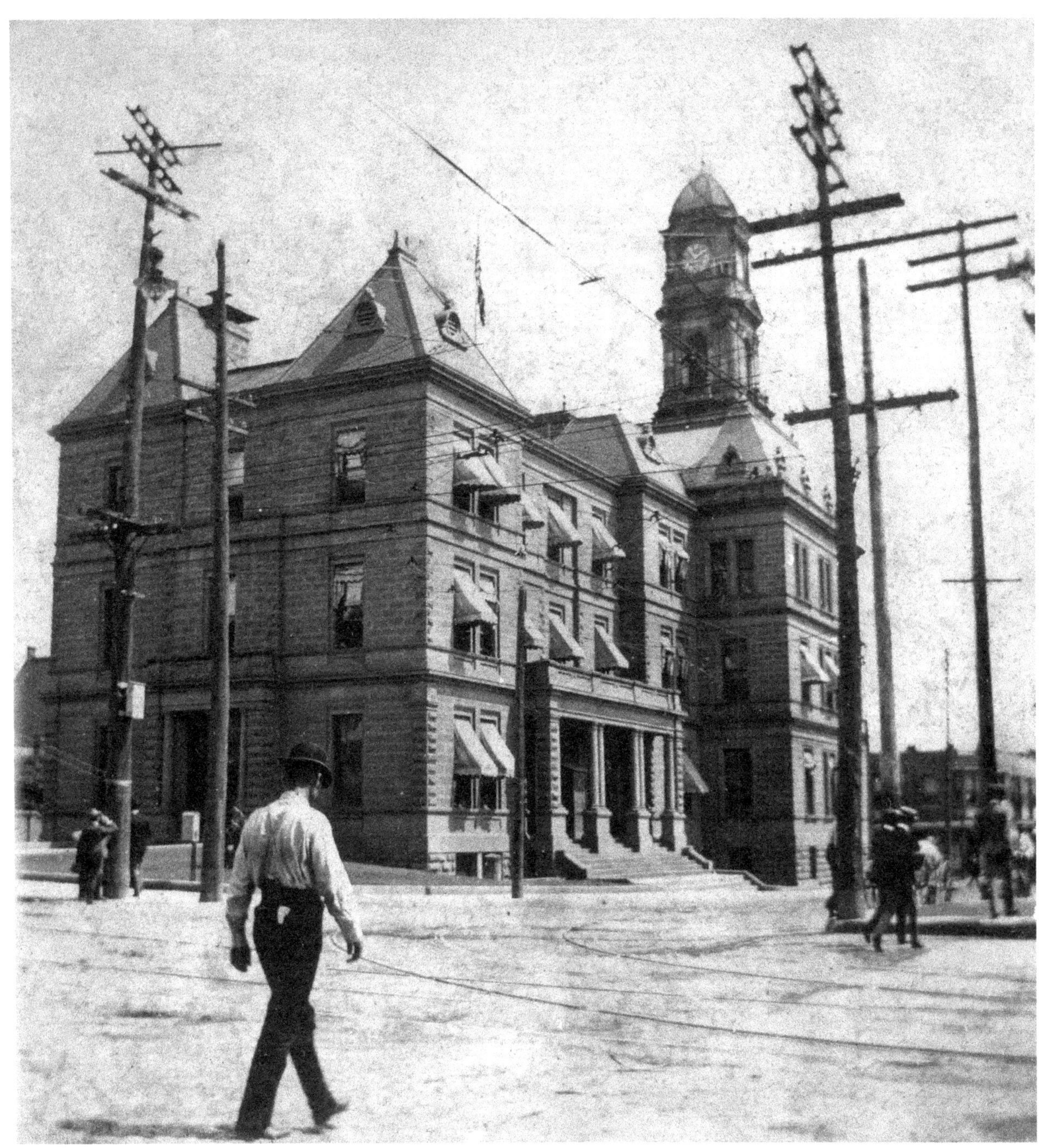

The Federal Building at Ervay and Commerce housed not only the Post Office but also the U.S. Circuit Court for the North Texas District.

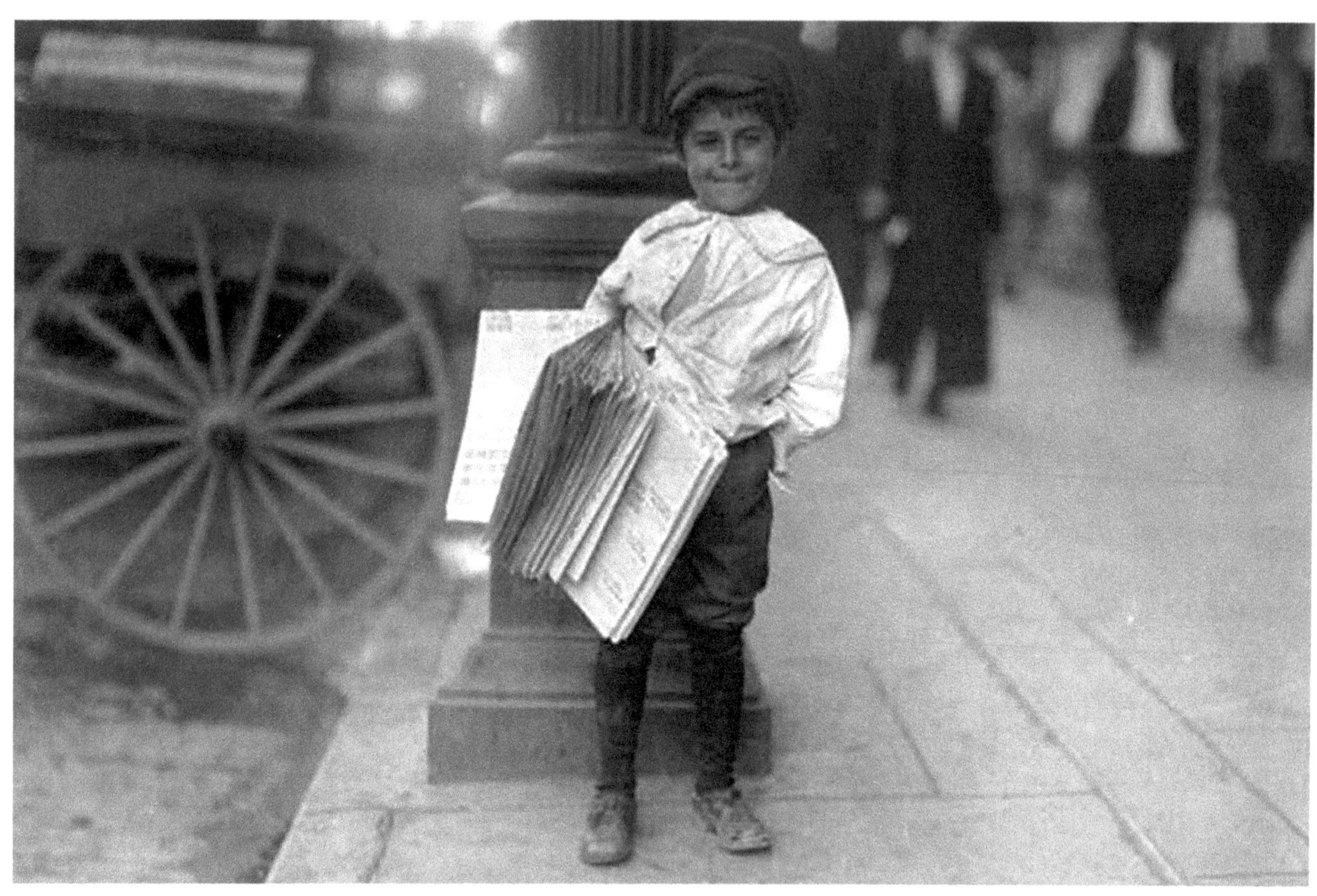

Newsboys were almost a class to themselves, fiercely competitive entrepreneurs who hawked papers on street corners as well as delivered them to homes.

Stirrings of a New Century

(1900–1929)

Rapid growth brought Dallas problems similar to those of many other urban centers at the turn of the century—overcrowding, poor sanitation, disease, and crime. Local women's clubs took the lead in tackling many of these issues, lobbying for pure food and drug legislation, a clean water supply, better sanitation in the schools, and juvenile justice facilities. They funded free kindergartens for the children of working mothers and set up "neighborhood houses" offering classes and services for the poor. Women also led successful movements to build a public library and establish an art museum.

That Dallas had "arrived" as a major city was symbolized in 1905 when President Theodore Roosevelt visited the city—the first U.S. president to do so. President William Howard Taft came four years later. Automobiles began to outnumber horses on the streets, and airplanes flew over the city (in exhibitions) in 1911.

A disastrous flood in 1908 washed away all the bridges across the Trinity River and flooded downtown buildings. But civic leaders were inspired to develop the city's first comprehensive city plan, designed to ensure more orderly growth. As a result, Union Station replaced five different passenger depots downtown, landscaped boulevards were designed, parkland was increased, and eventually the section of the river near downtown was moved and confined between levees, opening up thousands of acres for new development.

Dallas's position as the financial center of the region was confirmed in 1914 when it was selected as the headquarters for the 11th District of the Federal Reserve Bank. The next year, its first major university, Southern Methodist, opened with the largest beginning enrollment of any college to that date except the University of Chicago.

About 8,000 Dallas County residents served in the armed forces during World War I. The Army established an air training facility near Bachman Lake named Love Field, while Fair Park was converted into Camp Dick, where pilots learned strategy and army discipline. In 1919 Dallas County voters approved both prohibition and women's suffrage amendments to the state constitution. And by 1920, Dallas had risen to 42nd among largest cities in the nation, with a population of nearly 159,000.

The 1920s were as colorful in Dallas as in most of the nation's other large cities. Police and sheriff's deputies were kept busy raiding speakeasies and confiscating stills. "Theater Row" along Elm Street filled up with vaudeville houses and movie picture palaces. Downtown bristled with new skyscrapers, dominated by the 29-story Magnolia Building—the tallest structure west of the Mississippi.

But the twenties were also a dark decade for Dallas, when the Ku Klux Klan gained a strong foothold, terrorizing African Americans, Catholics, and Jews, while controlling many municipal offices and enjoying support from many businessmen and clergy. Some courageous individuals challenged the Klan, but only slowly did its influence wane.

Despite KKK threats and Jim Crow laws, Dallas's African American community managed to develop strong institutions and businesses within segregated neighborhoods. And the blues music it fostered in vibrant "Deep Ellum" gained national attention. Mexican Americans, who had first migrated to Dallas in substantial numbers during the 1910s, established barrios in Little Mexico (north of downtown), Cement City, and Juarez Heights (West Dallas).

Transportation remained a key to the city's economic health. Train service (both commercial and passenger) remained basic, but automobile and truck traffic was increasing as Dallas found itself centrally located on the growing national highway system. And when a visiting Charles Lindbergh urged Dallas to turn Love Field into a municipal airfield, citizens listened.

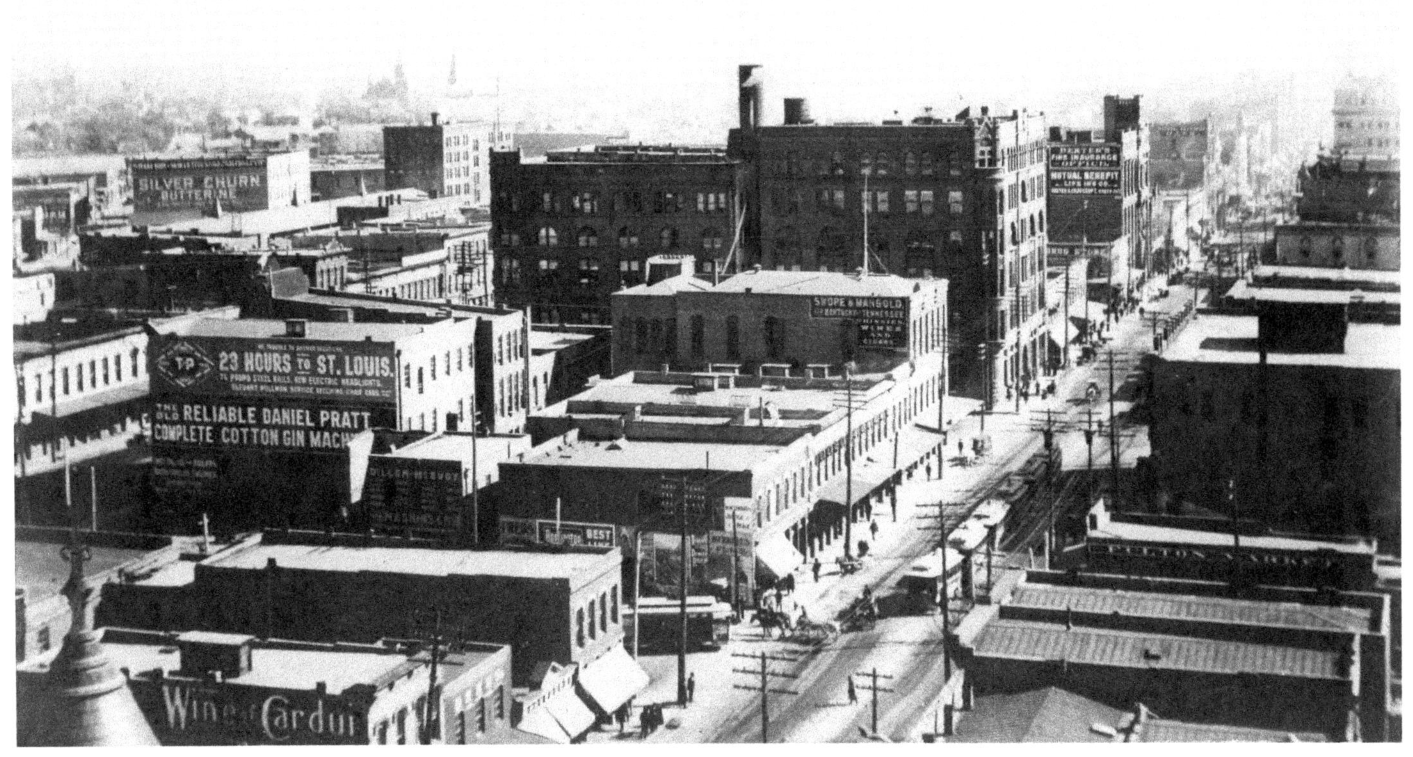

As the tallest building in the west end of town, the courthouse became a favorite vantage point for photographers. Swiss immigrant Charles Arnold took this picture in 1900, looking east.

The Scollard Building on Main Street was designed by M. A. Orlopp, who also designed the Old Red Courthouse. It was demolished in 1923 and replaced with a bank building, now known as the Davis Building.

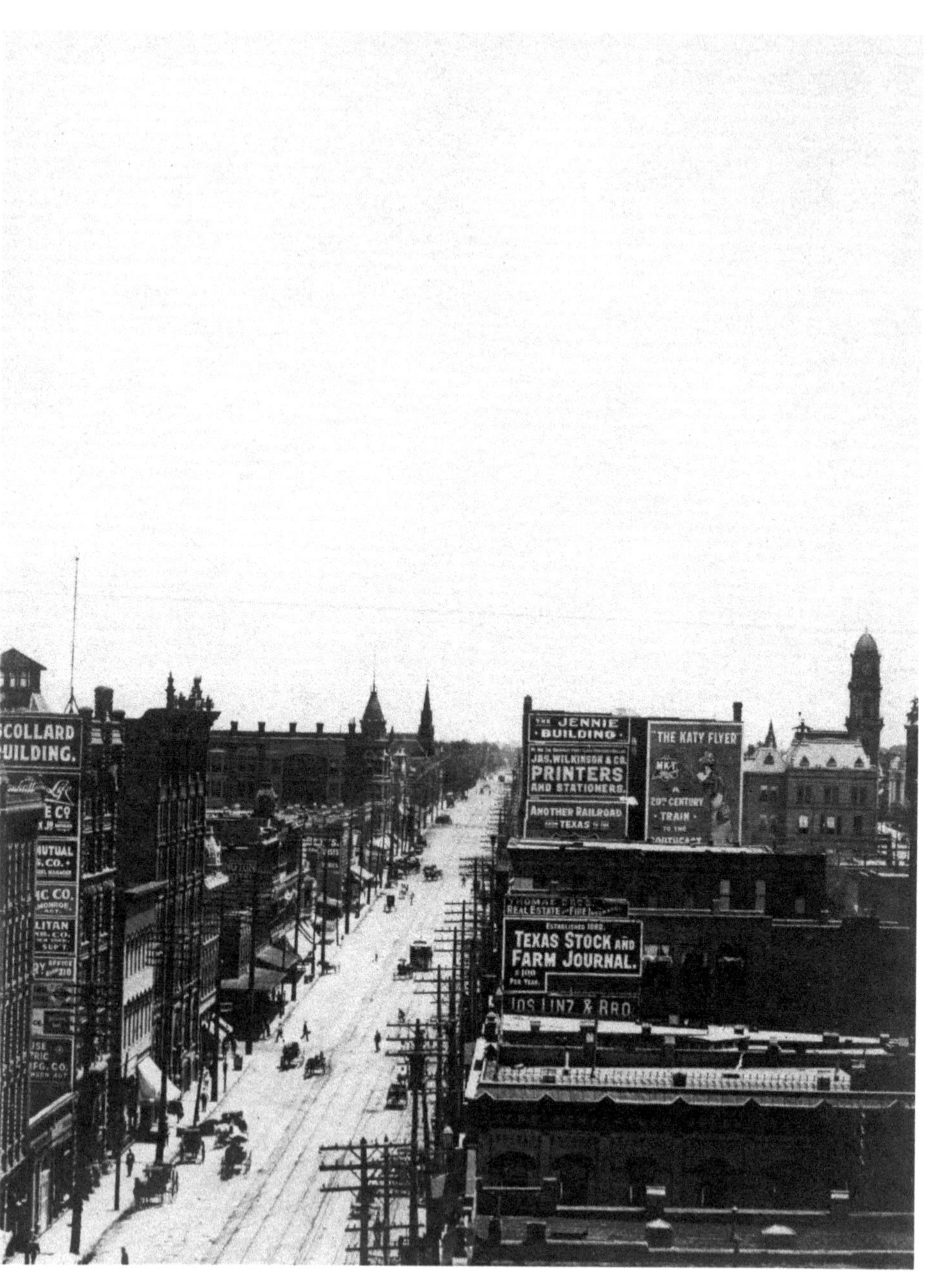

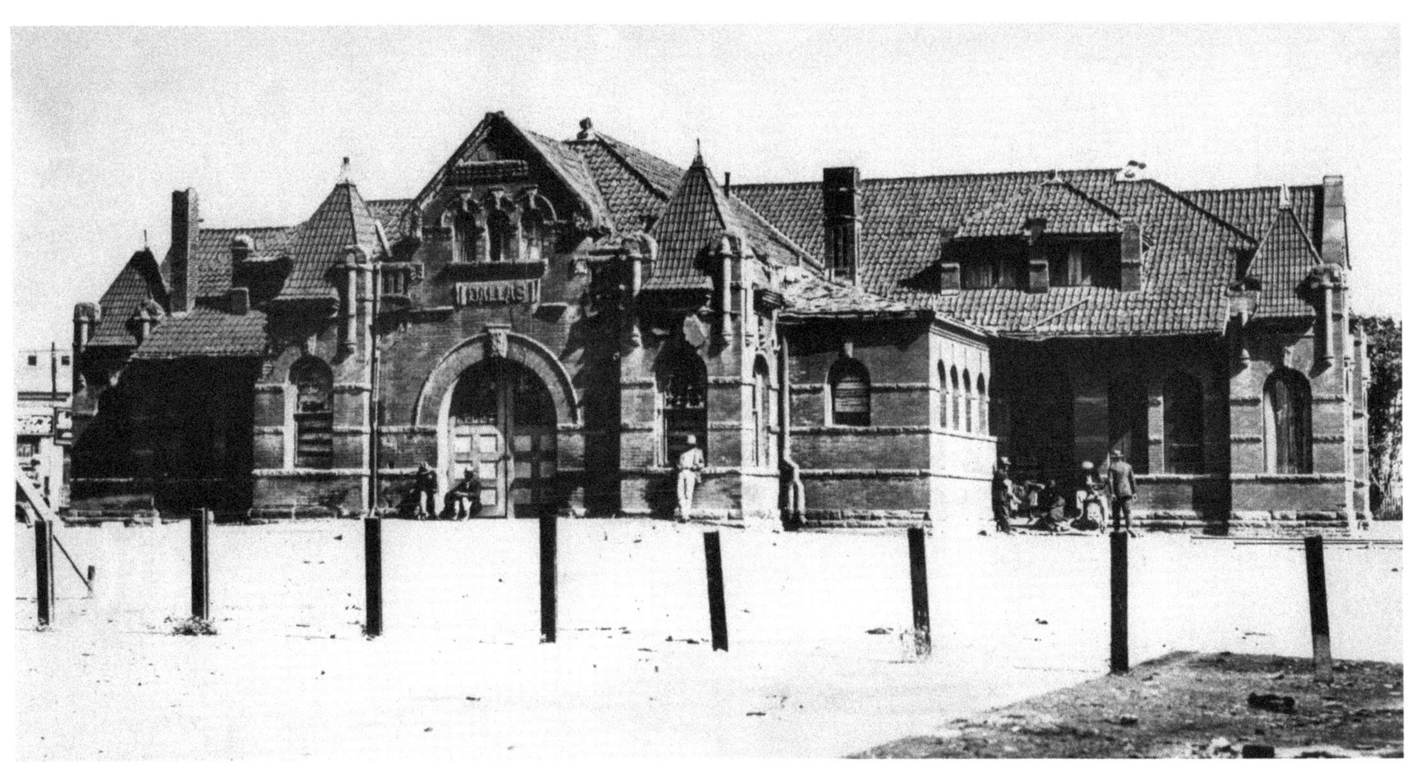

The Houston and Texas Central Railroad brought the first train to Dallas in July 1872, following a route that later became Central Expressway. This massive depot was constructed near the intersection of Central and Pacific avenues in 1885 and demolished in 1935.

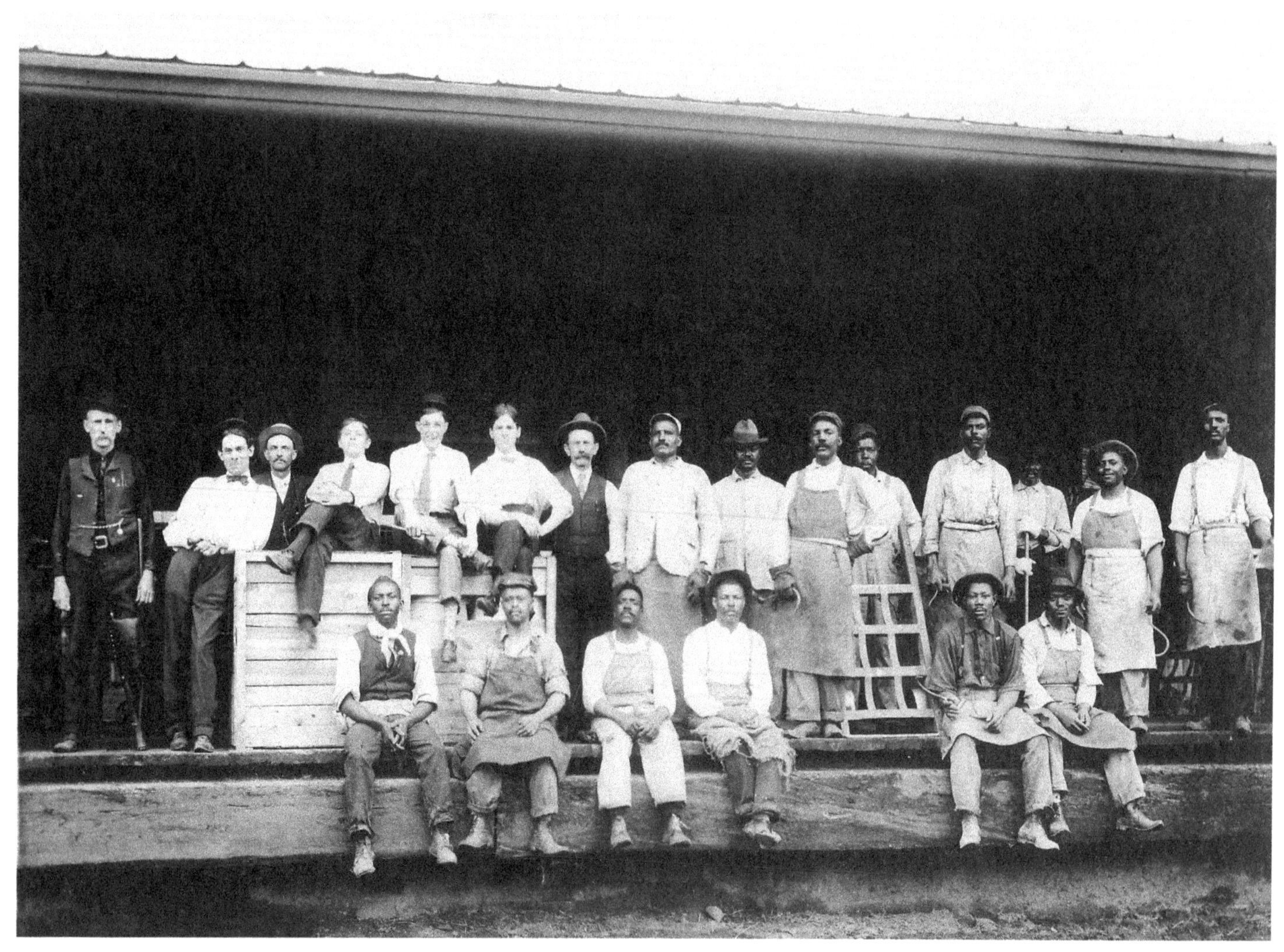

African Americans provided an important source of labor in Dallas at the turn of the century, representing 21 percent of the population.

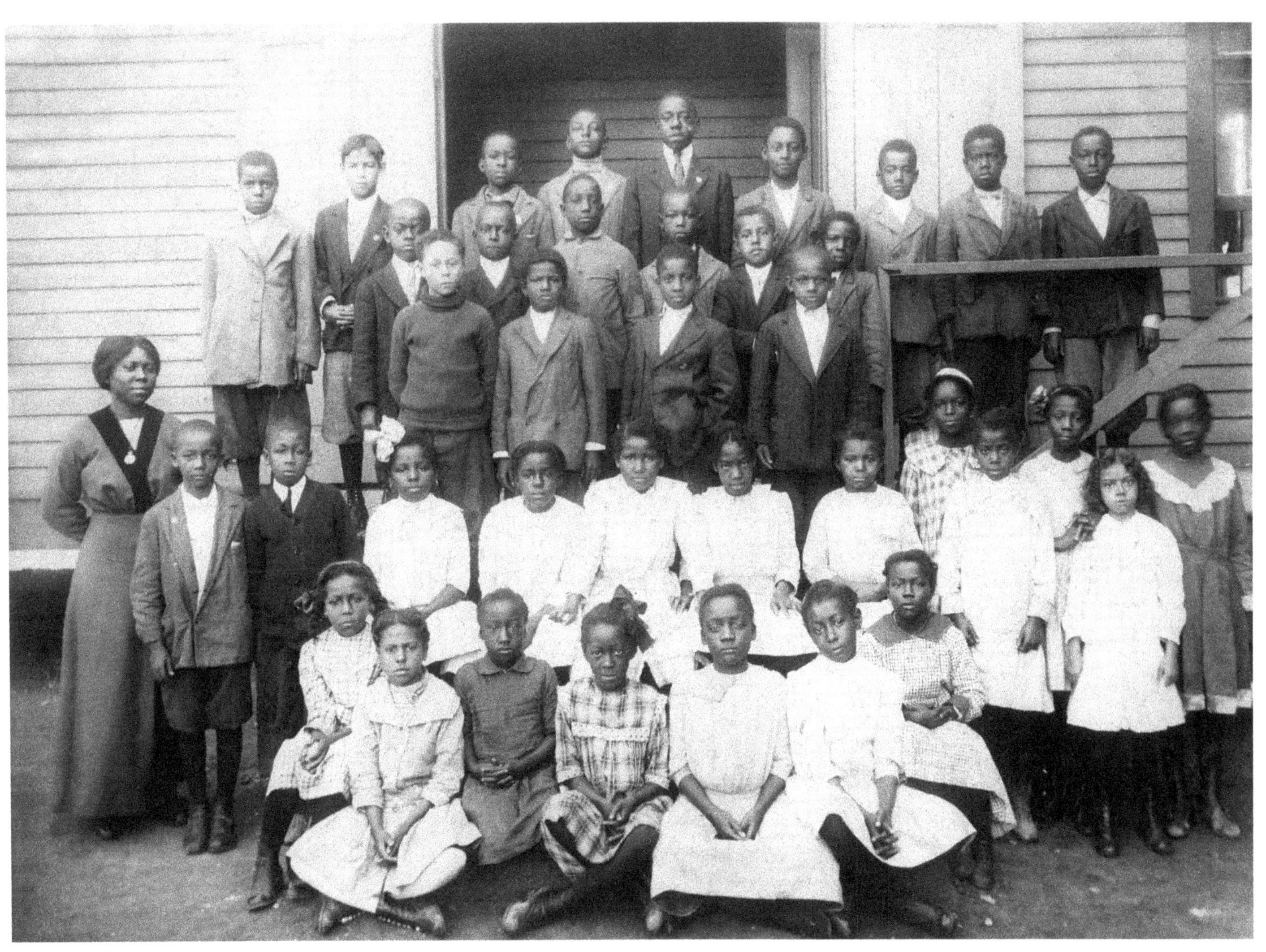

Racial segregation relegated black students to inferior facilities, but dedicated teachers often provided sound educations. John Leslie Patton, one of the students in this photo, became a distinguished principal of Booker T. Washington High School.

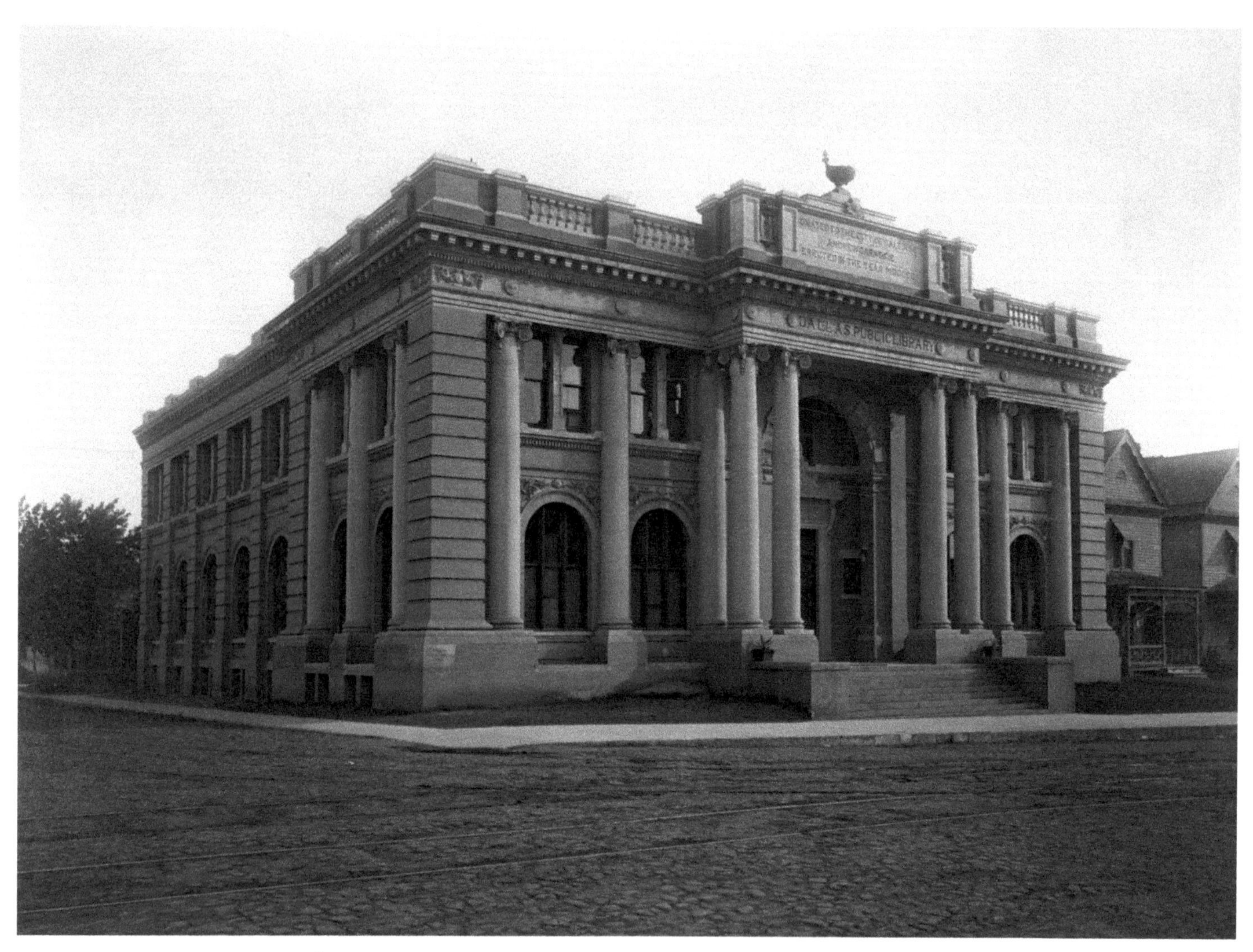

Dallas women's clubs spearheaded the movement to build a public library in Dallas. With help from Andrew Carnegie, they opened this library at the corner of Commerce and Harwood streets in 1901.

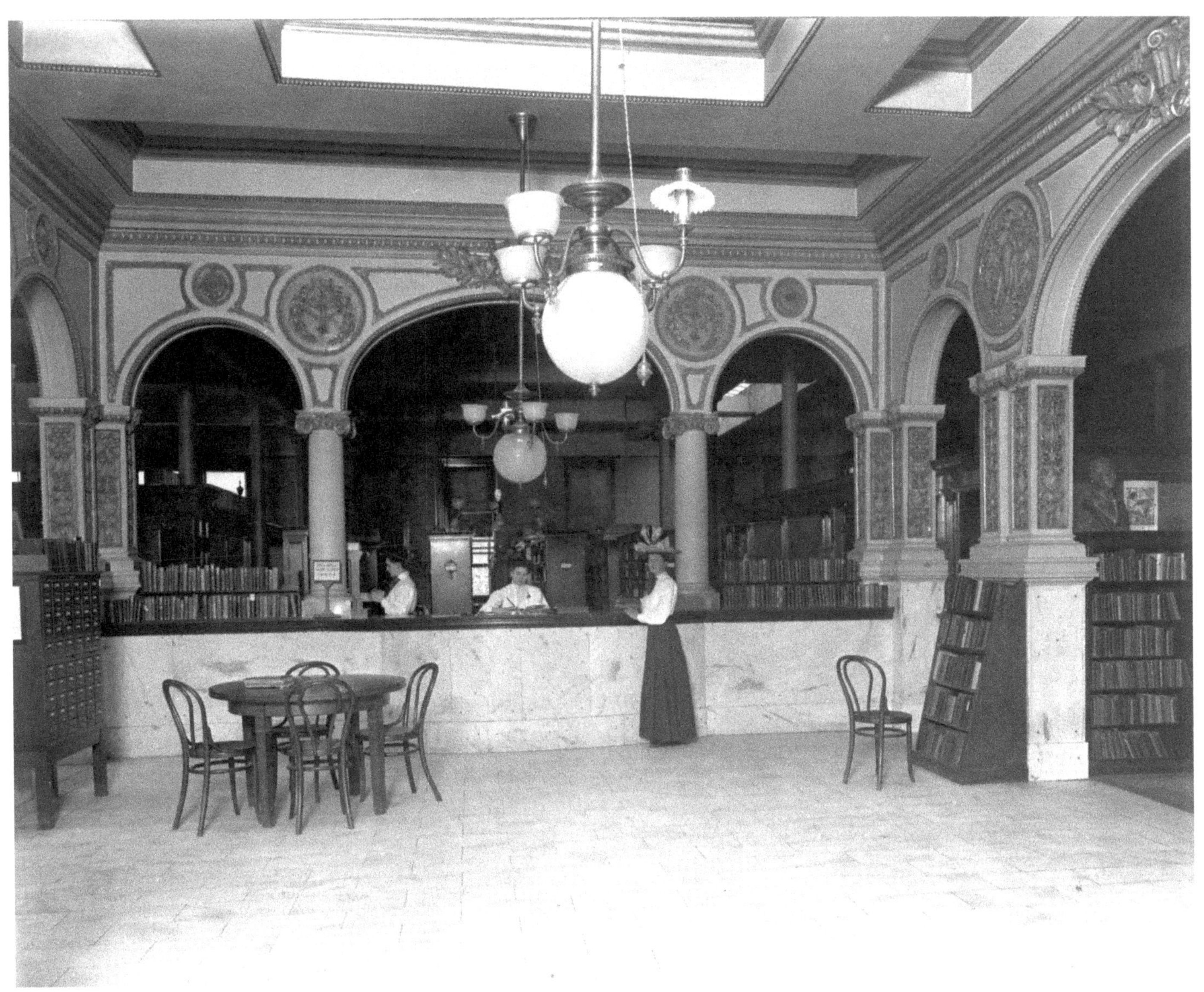

Although it had a beautiful interior, the Carnegie Library soon became overcrowded. It was torn down in 1954 and replaced with a modern structure.

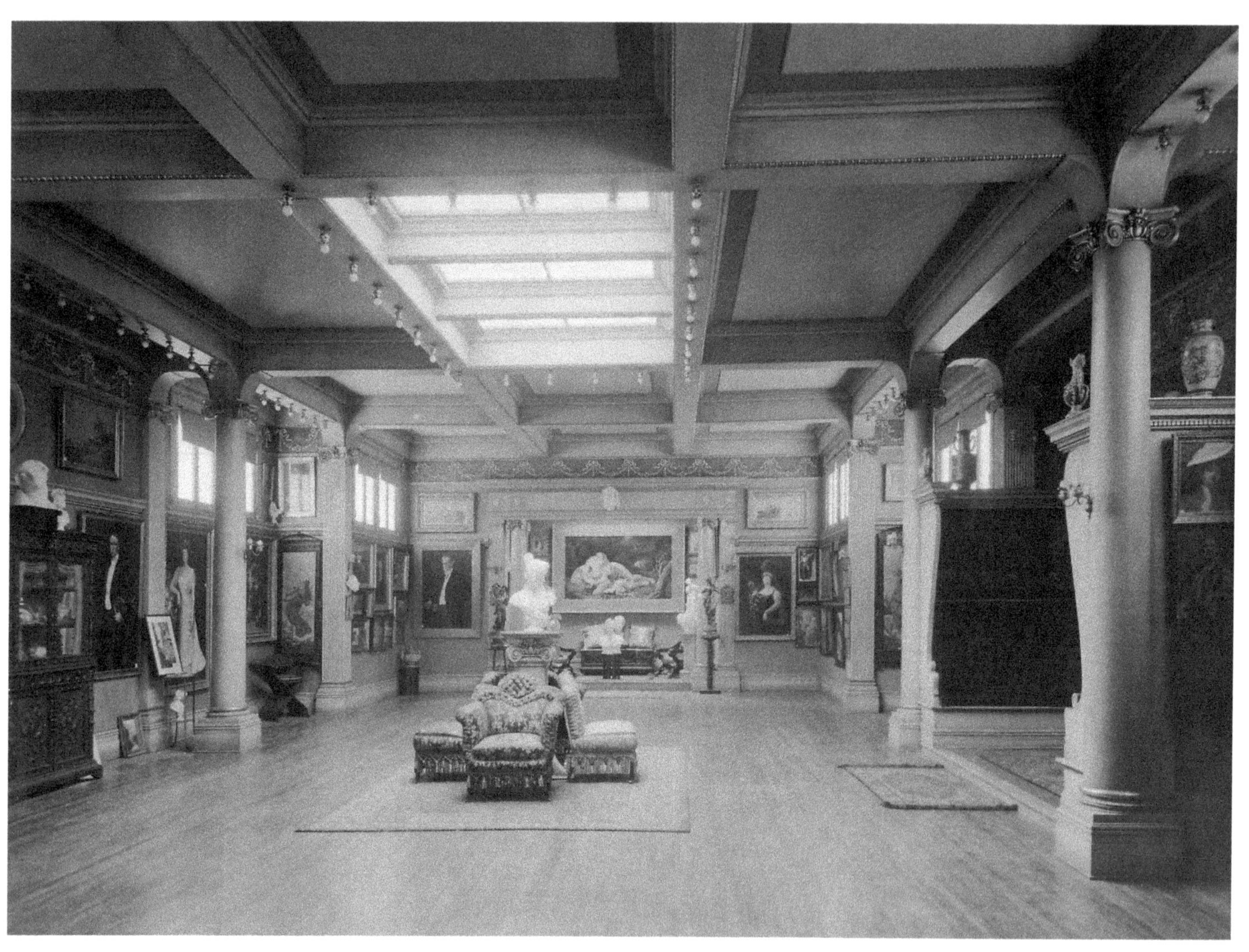

Katherine Crawford, wife of a prominent Dallas attorney, opened the first private art gallery in the Southwest in her Ross Avenue mansion, featuring the work of both European and Texas artists.

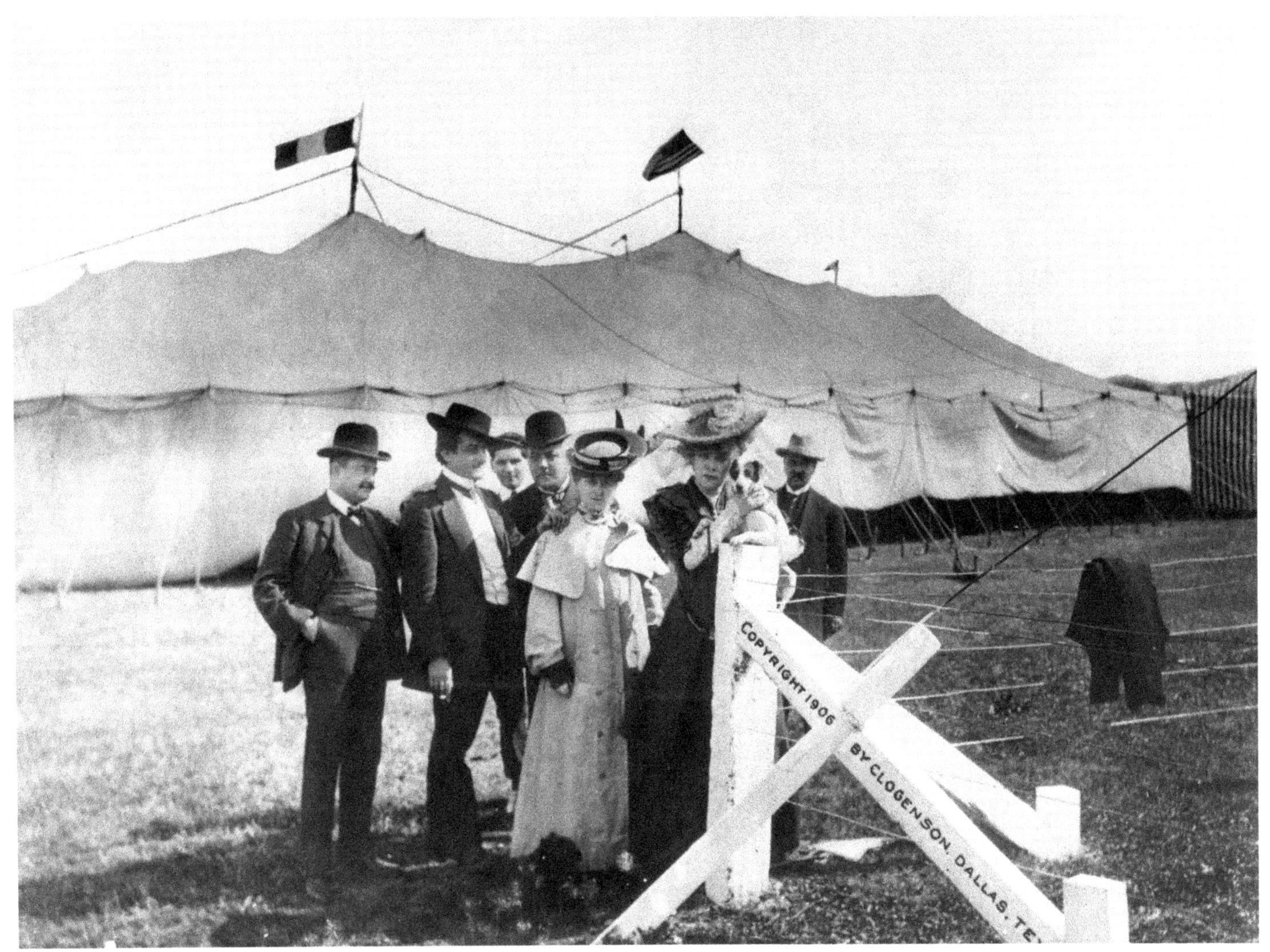

Because of a quarrel with theater owners, legendary actress Sarah Bernhardt performed in a tent when she visited Dallas on one of her "farewell tours" in 1906. The tent was set up in a cornfield adjacent Cycle Park near the fairgrounds.

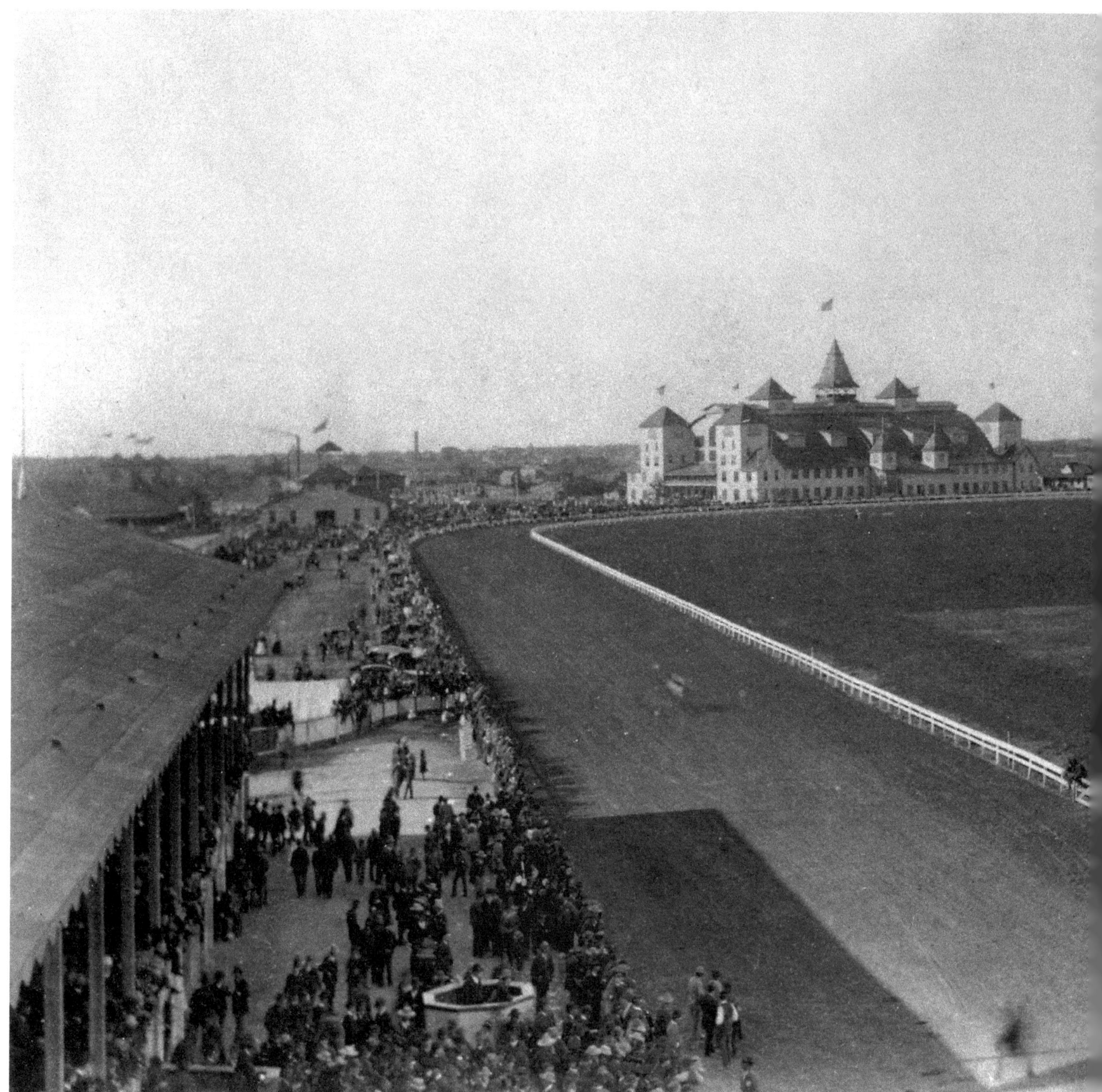

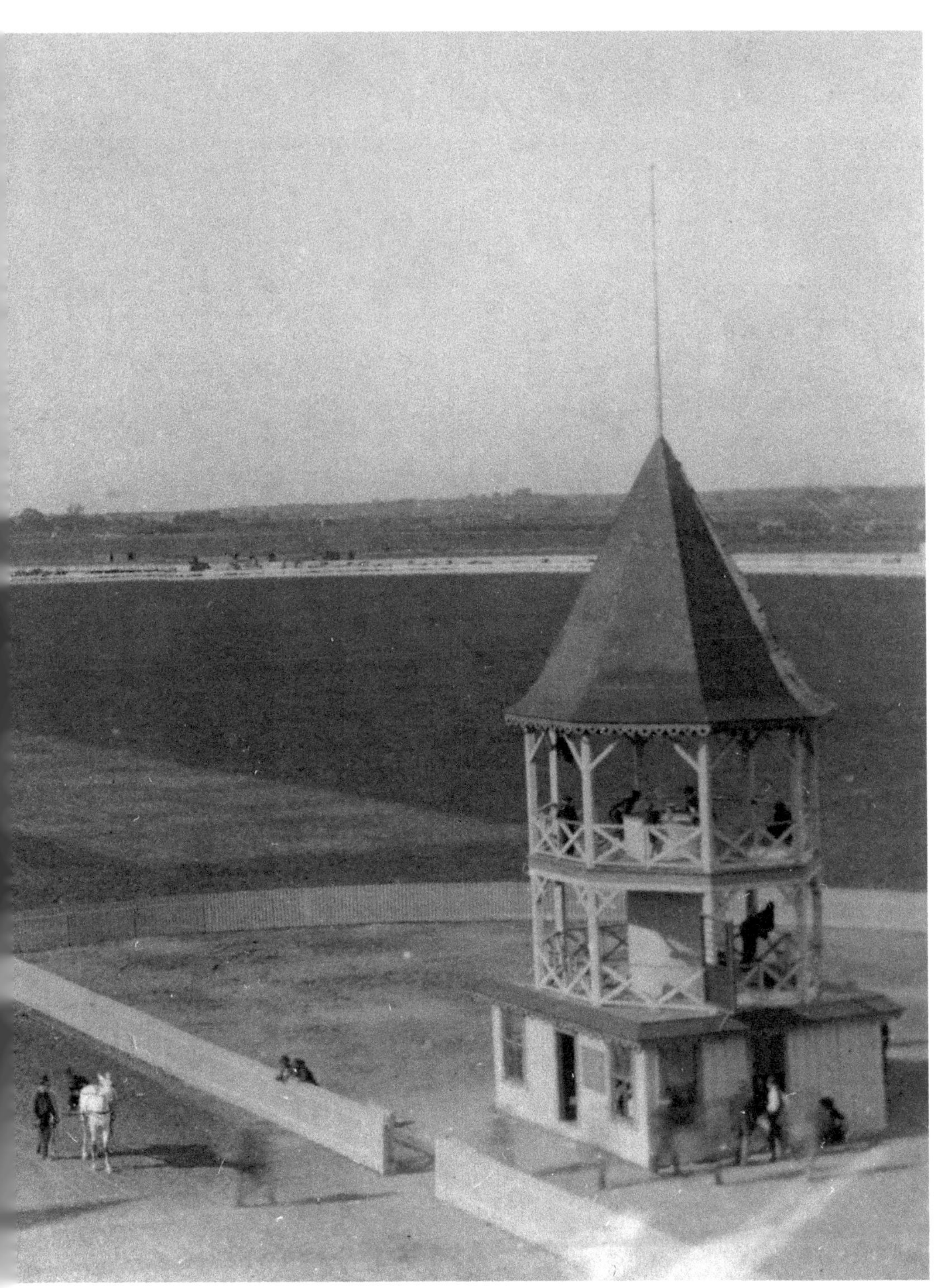

Horse racing was the big draw for the State Fair of Texas until 1903, when the state legislature outlawed betting.

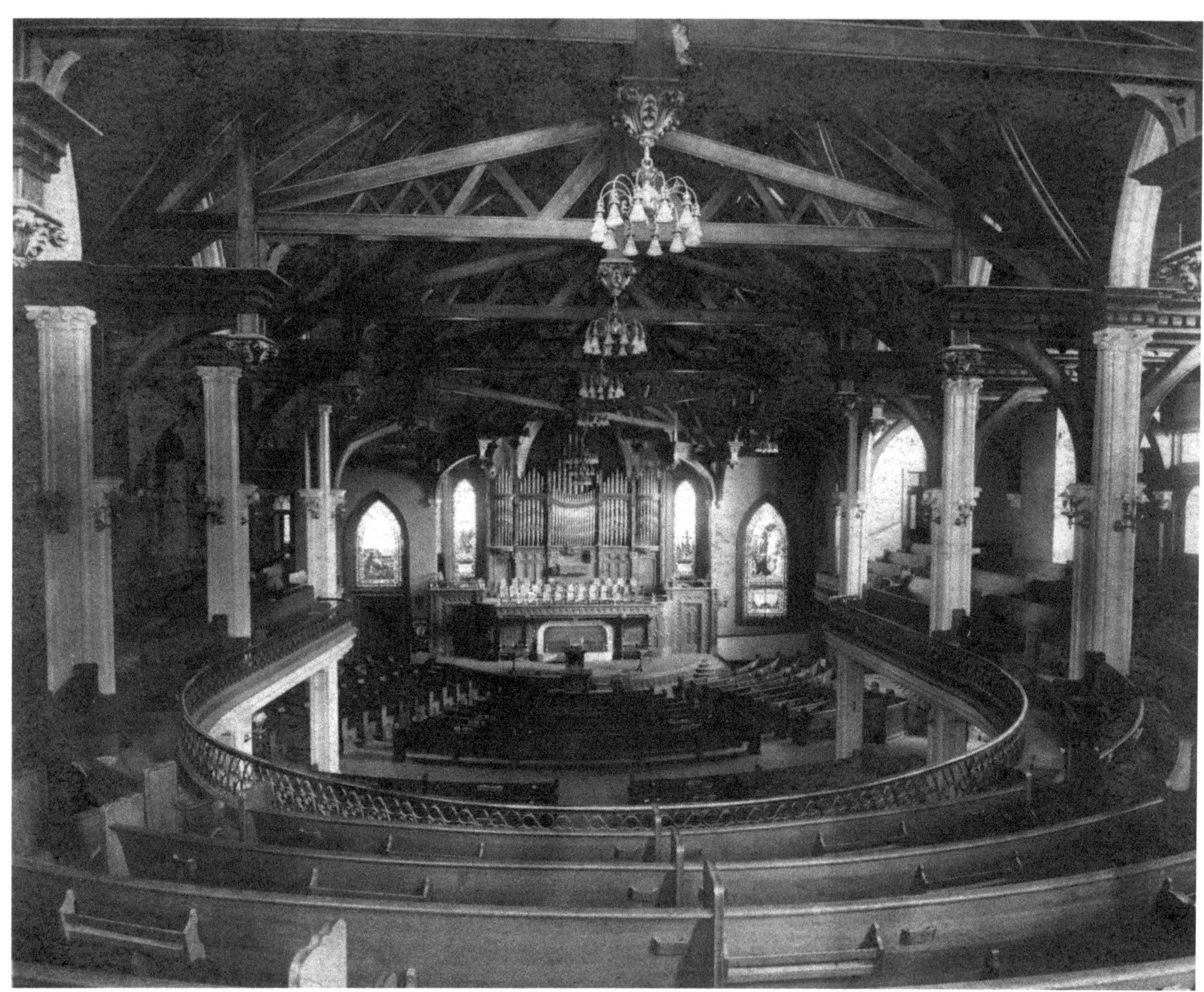

The sanctuary of the First Baptist Church of Dallas was constructed in 1890 and is still in use. This 1908 photograph commemorated the installation of a new organ.

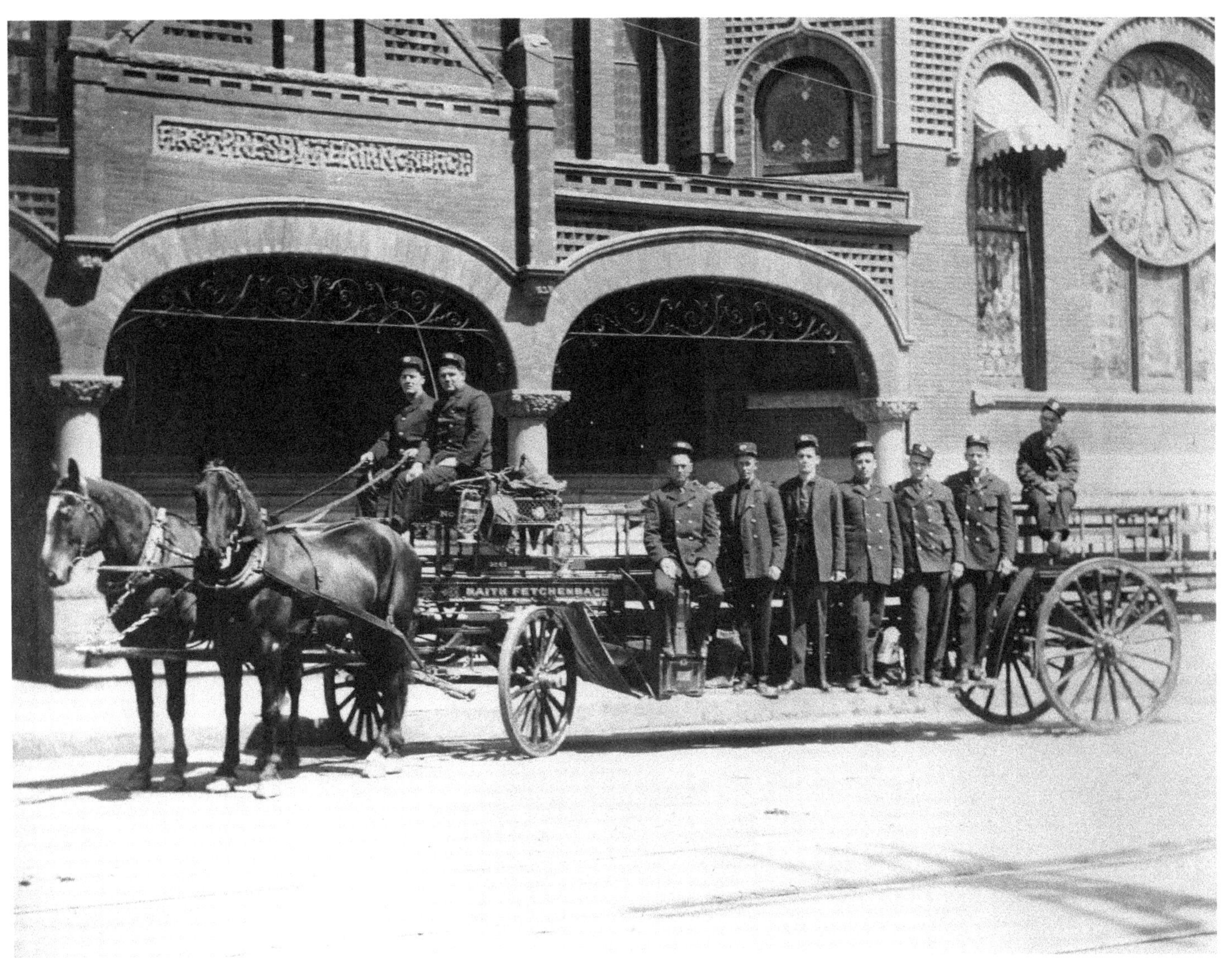

Fire protection at the turn of the century relied on the speed of horse-drawn equipment. These fire fighters are posed in front of the First Presbyterian Church at the corner of Main and Harwood streets.

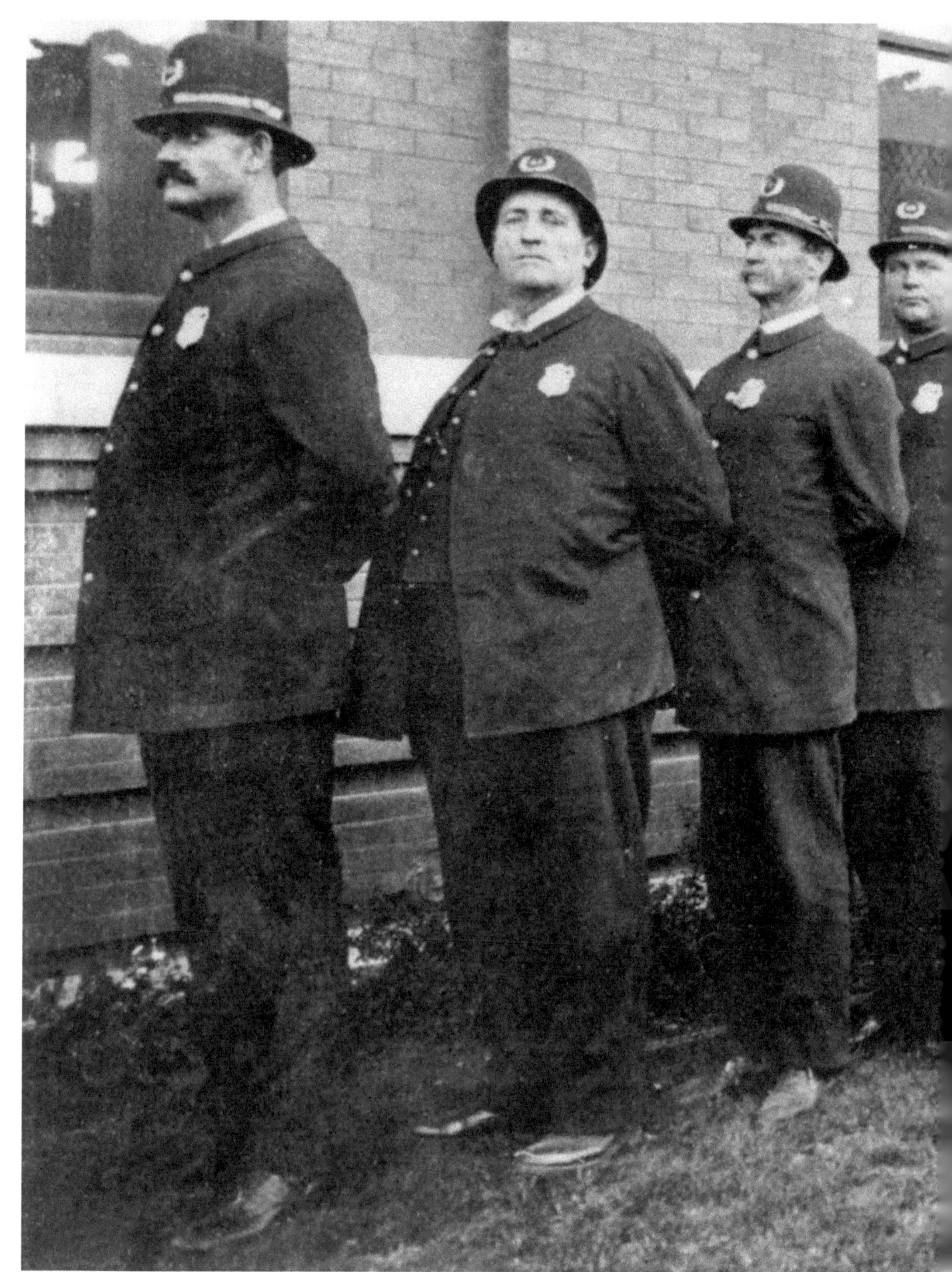

Dallas police lined up around 1908 beside the city jail, a facility that still stands on Ross Avenue near Market.

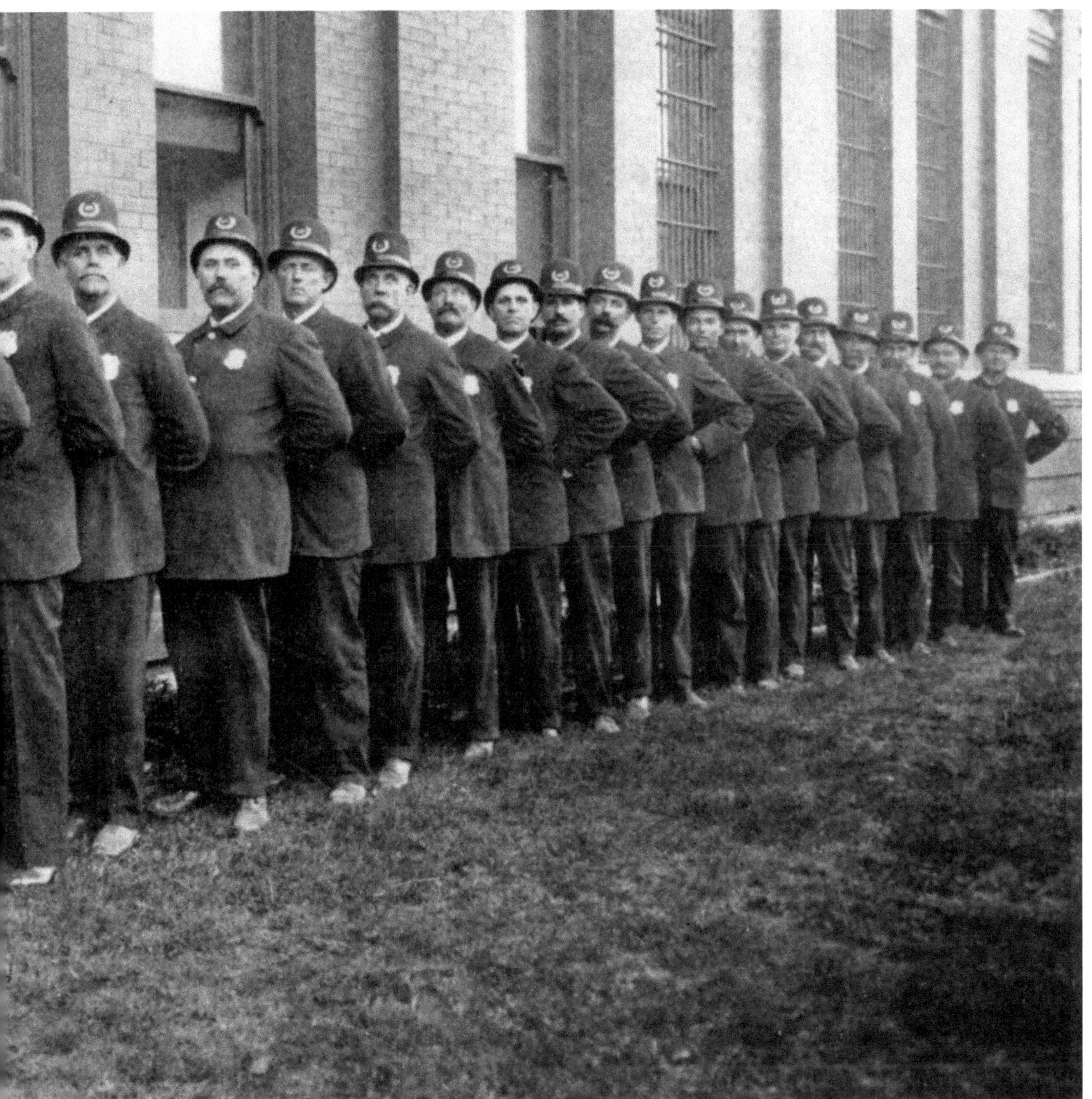

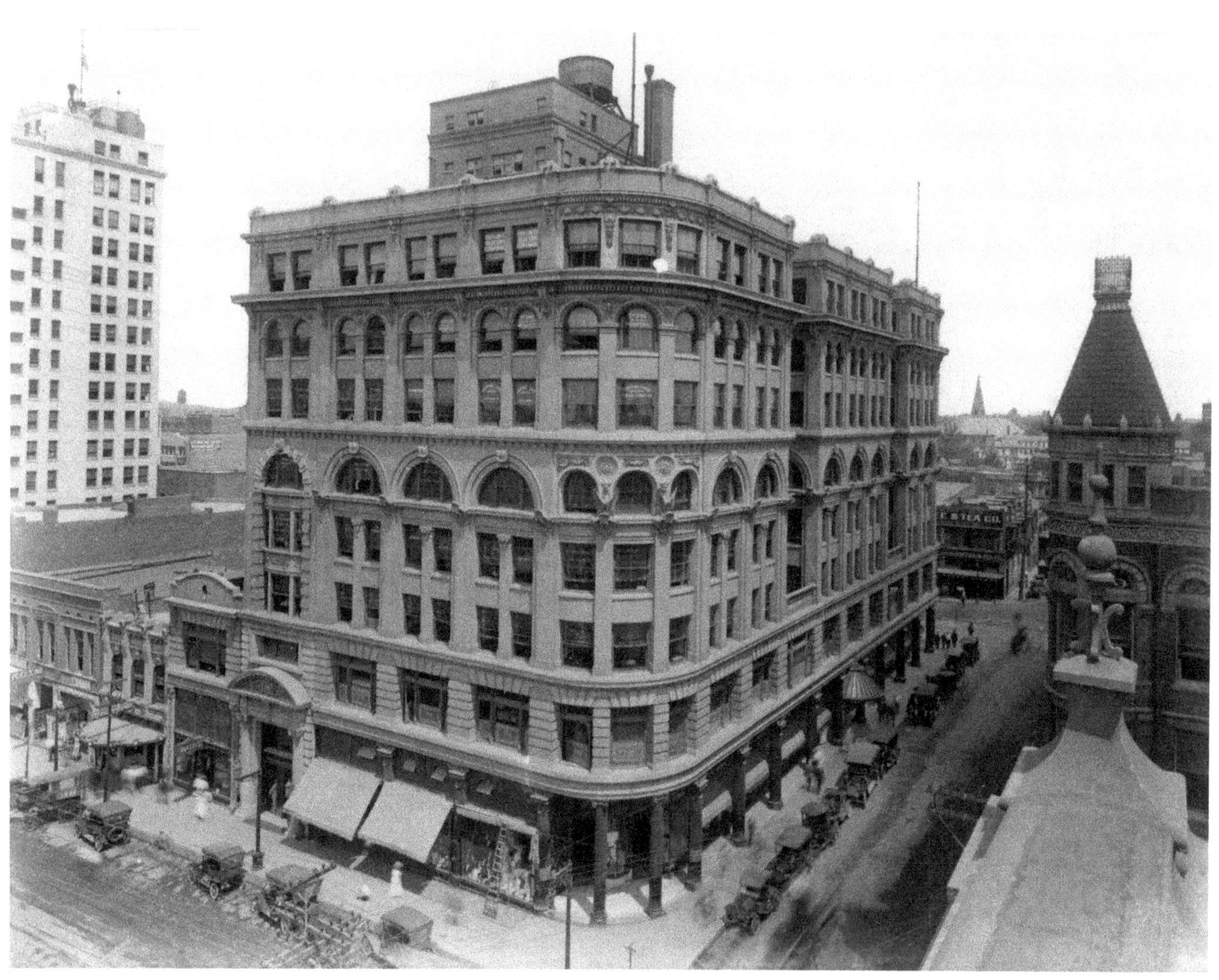

J. B. Wilson, a wealthy cattleman, banker, and investor, constructed this office and retail building in 1903. Designed by the prestigious Fort Worth firm of Sanguinet and Staats, and modeled after the Grand Opera House in Paris, the Wilson Building was the first eight-story building in Texas. Post Properties has restored the exterior of the Wilson Building to its original splendor while redeveloping the interior space into 135 luxury loft apartments and 9,952 square feet of street-level retail space.

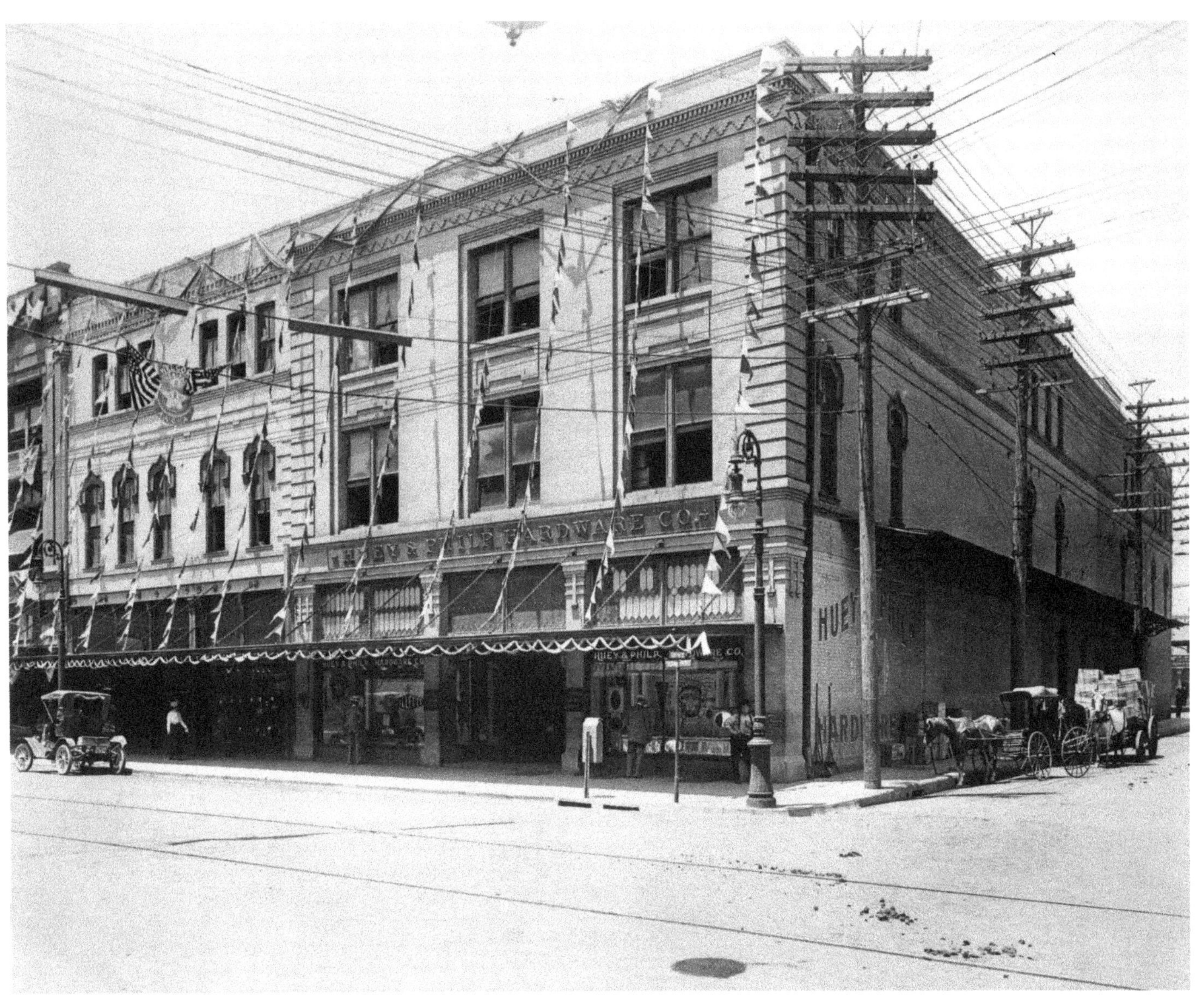

Hardware dealers Huey & Philp were among many "terminus merchants" who followed the railroad from Corsicana to Dallas in 1872. They were sole purveyors of certain brands of barbed wire and cookstoves.

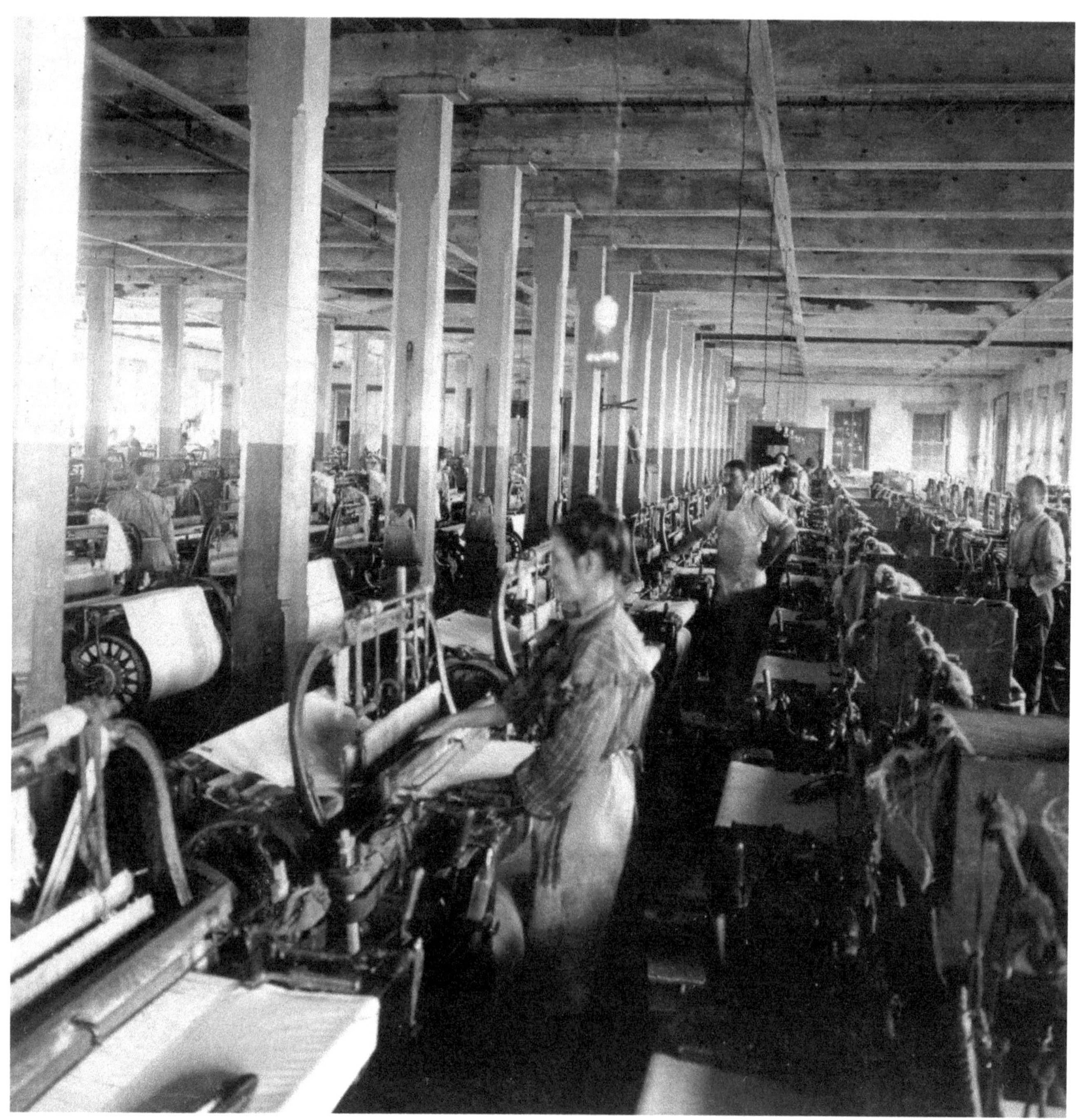

As the leading inland cotton market in the U.S., Dallas was also home to several cotton mills and related industries. This stereoscope card depicts the weaving room in one factory.

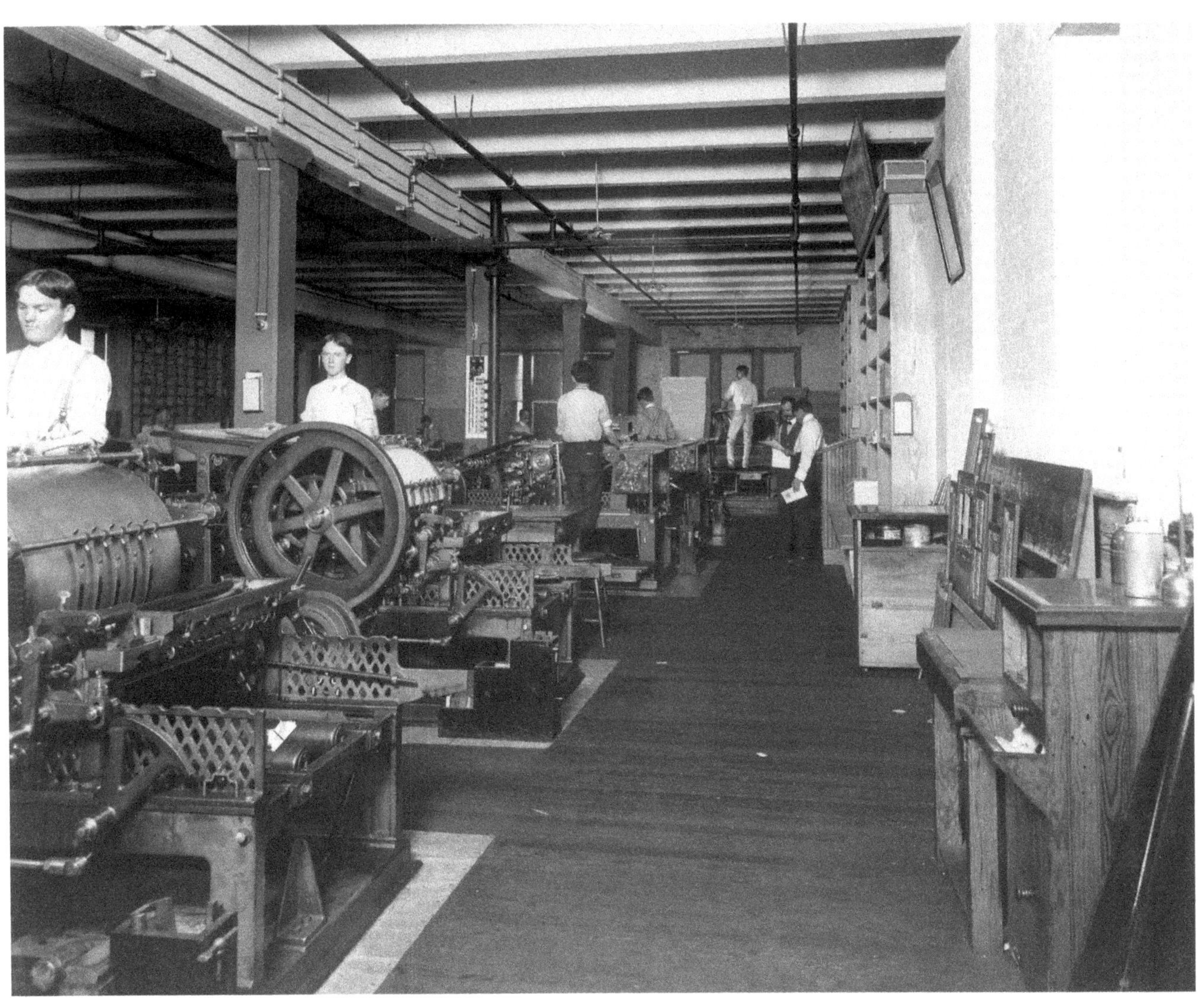

This is the press department at Dorsey Company, established in 1884. Dallas was a major printing center in the early twentieth century, publishing magazines and newspapers distributed throughout the South, as well as books, pamphlets, stationery, and other items.

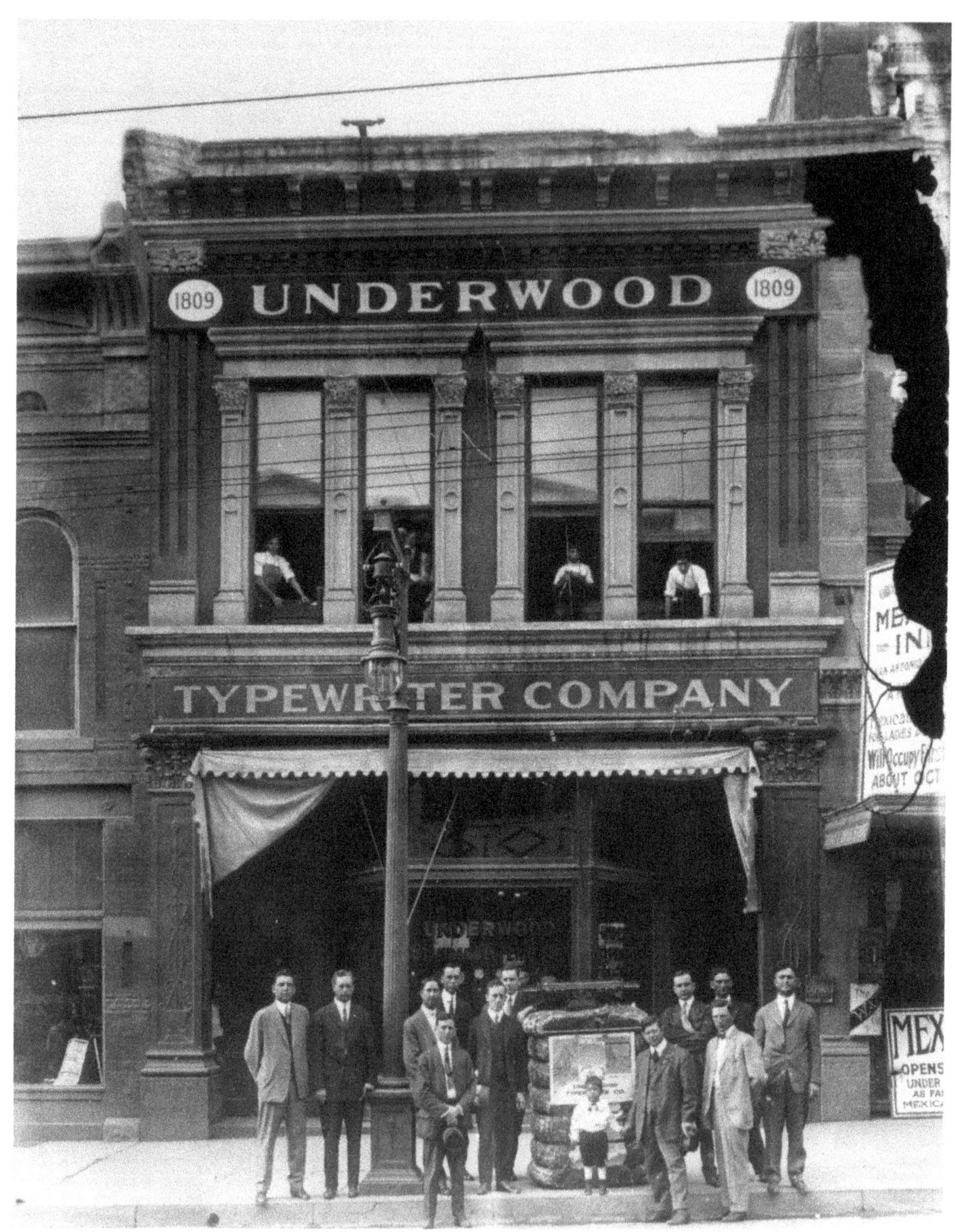

The invention of the typewriter opened up new jobs for women as office clerks and secretaries, but men still controlled management and sales.

Men also took advantage of new office jobs that entailed typing and using an adding machine.

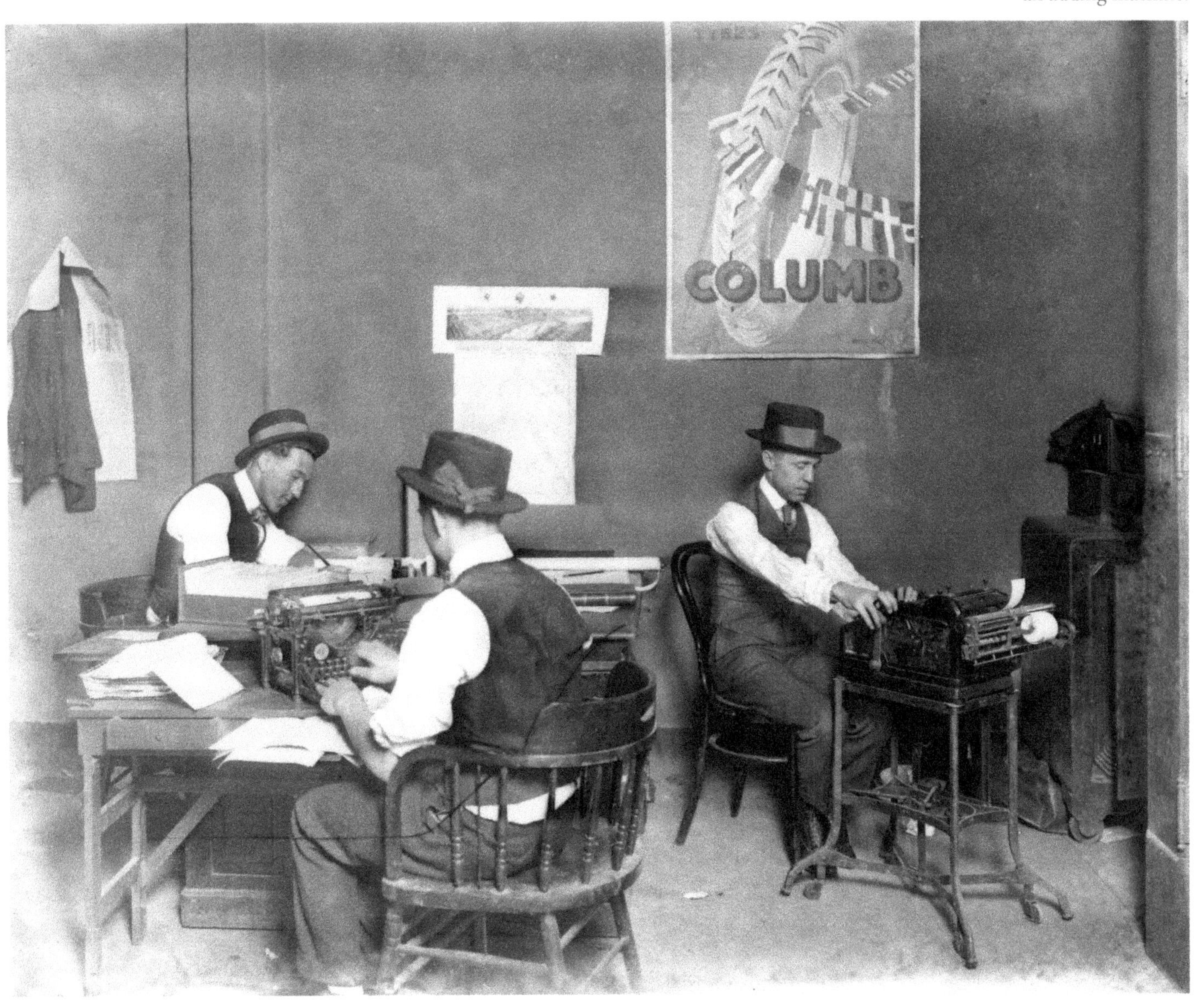

Following Spread: Torrential rains in May 1908 caused the Trinity River to rise 13 feet, washing away bridges and flooding hundreds of buildings. The city lost electricity and water pressure, and numerous animals drowned.

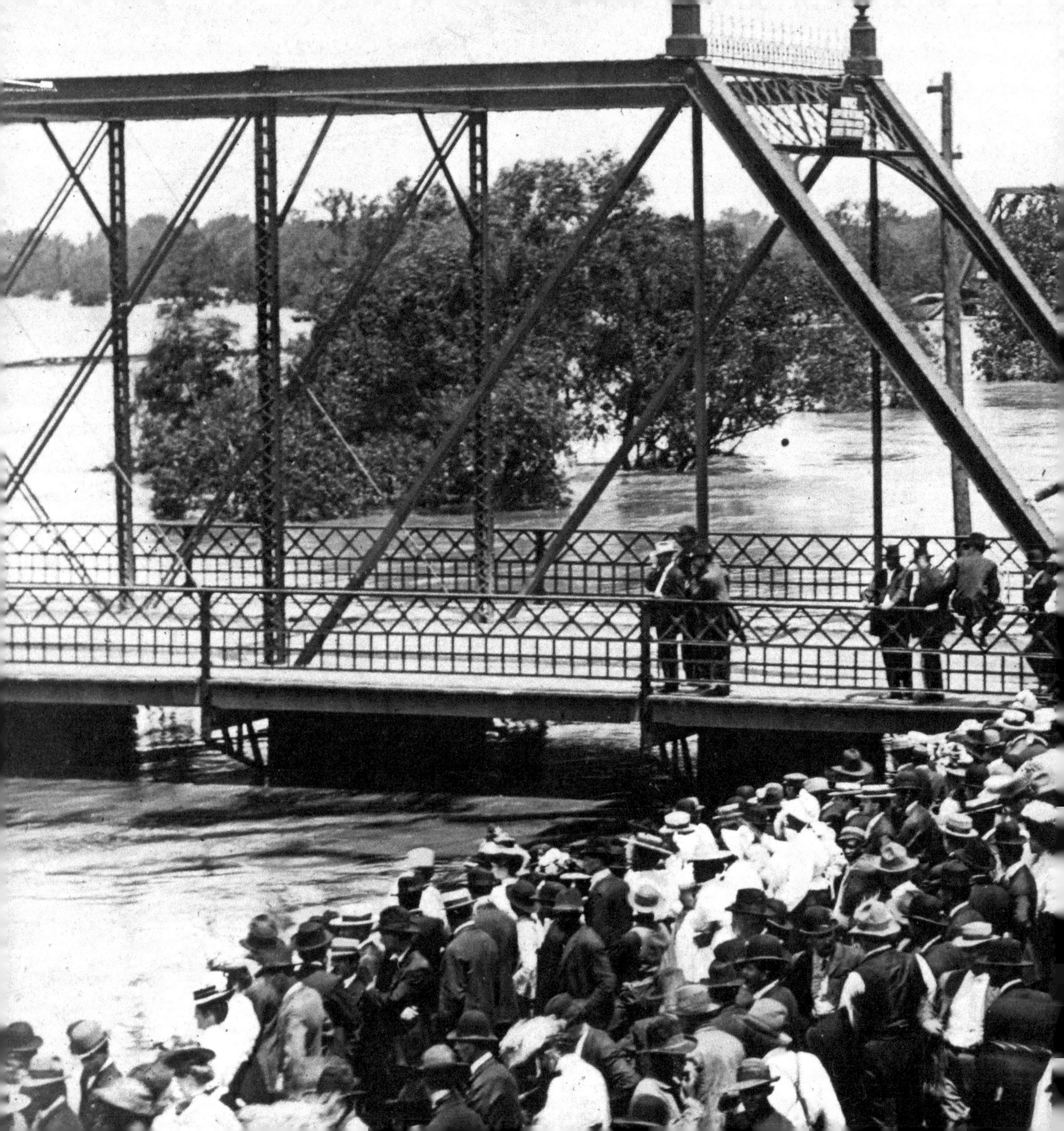

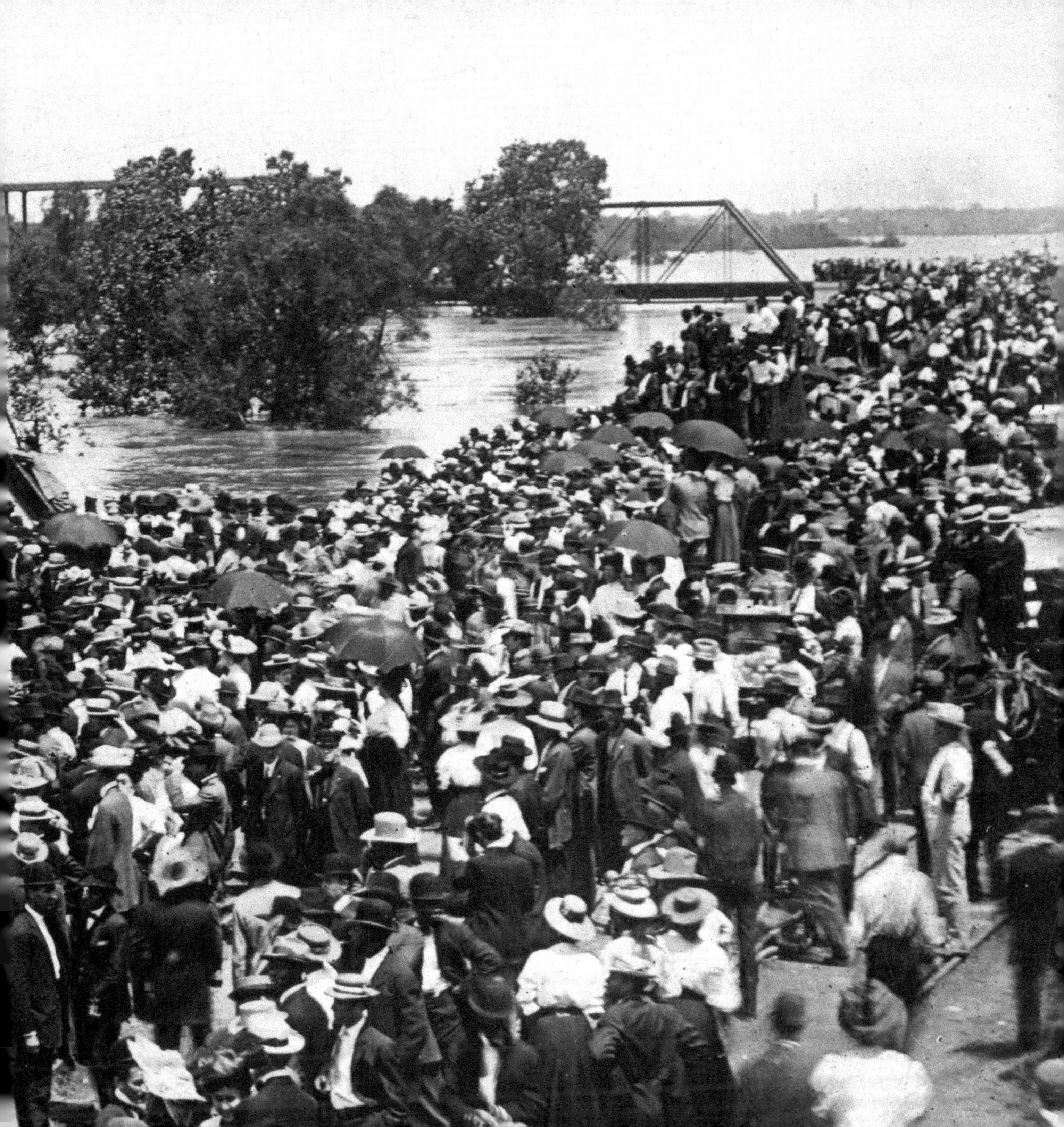

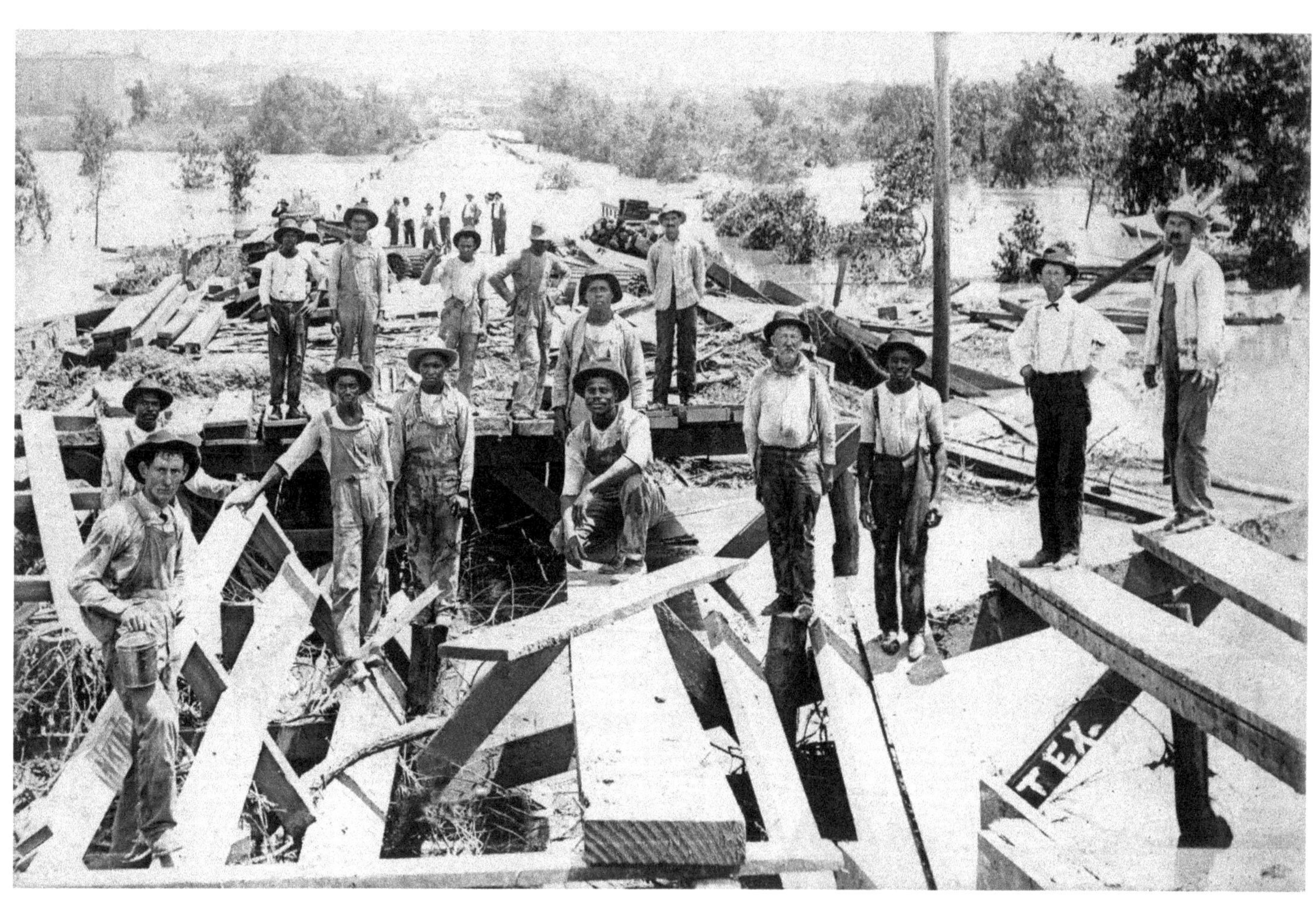

Repairing the flood damage took years, but the catastrophe did inspire civic leaders to undertake a massive project to redirect the Trinity River between levees. In the 75 years since the levees were completed, the river has never again flooded adjacent areas, including downtown Dallas.

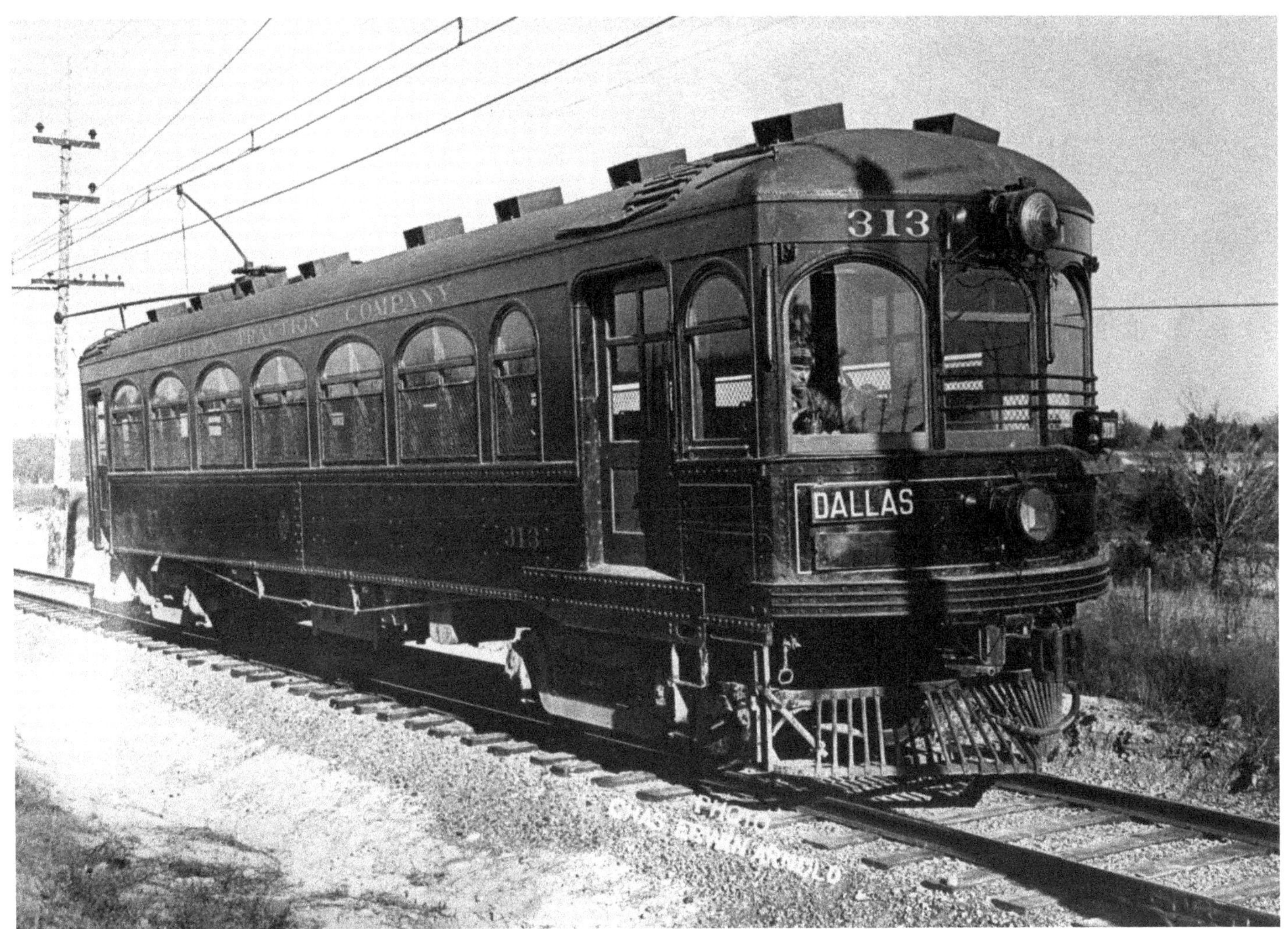

Beginning in 1902, Dallas residents enjoyed fast and easy access from downtown Dallas to neighboring communities such as Sherman, Denison, McKinney, Fort Worth, Corsicana, and Waco on what was known as the "Interurban." Interurban rail lines carried passengers on electrically powered trains, providing fast and inexpensive commuter service.

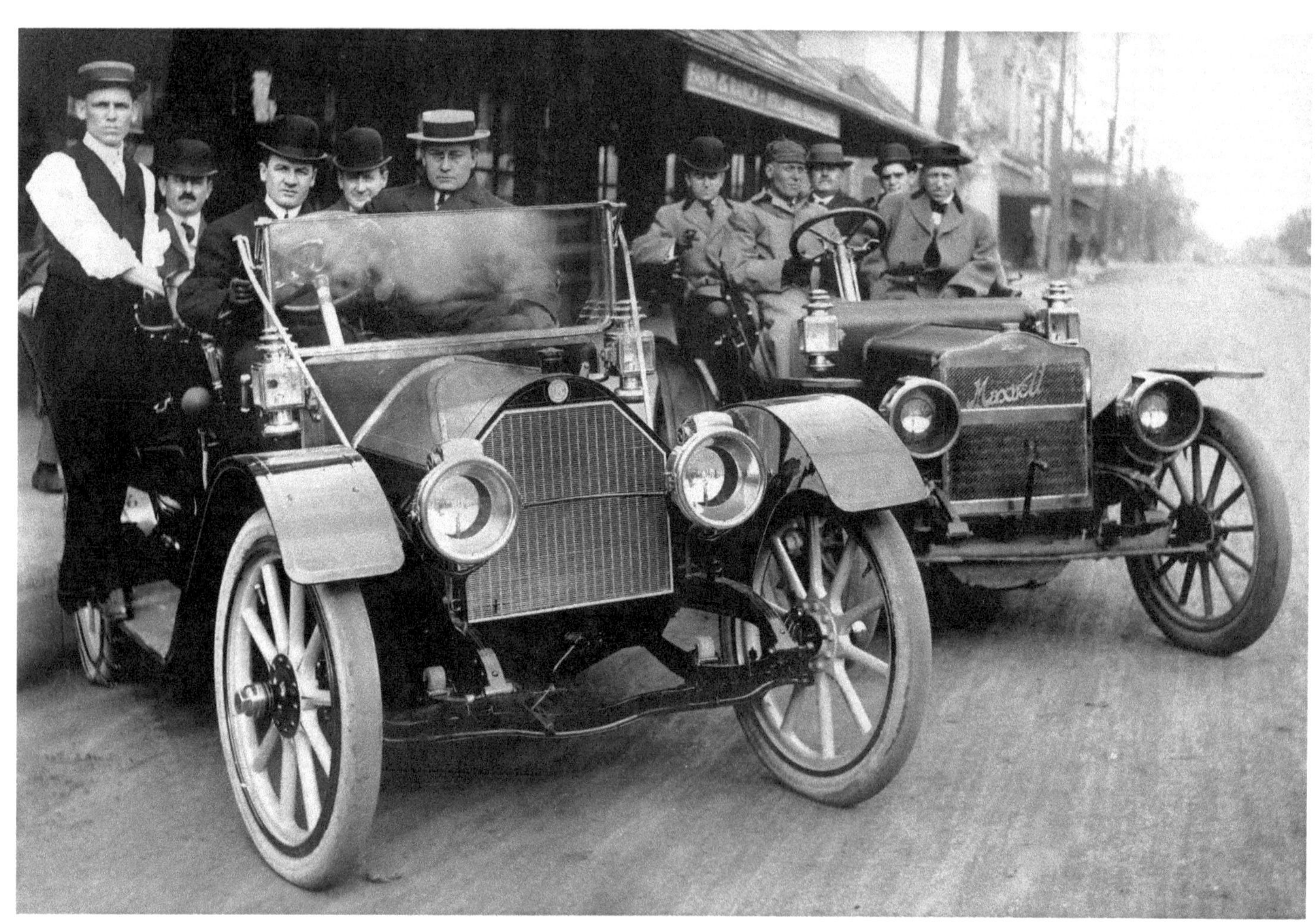

From the day the first privately owned automobile drove into Dallas in 1899, the city's love affair with the horseless carriage began. Hugh Chalmers (at the wheel), president of Chalmers Automobile Company, drove one of his cars from Detroit to Dallas to visit his Dallas dealer, Padgitt Brothers. Charley Padgitt, seated next to Chalmers, was part of the family that founded a carriage and buggy shop in 1869.

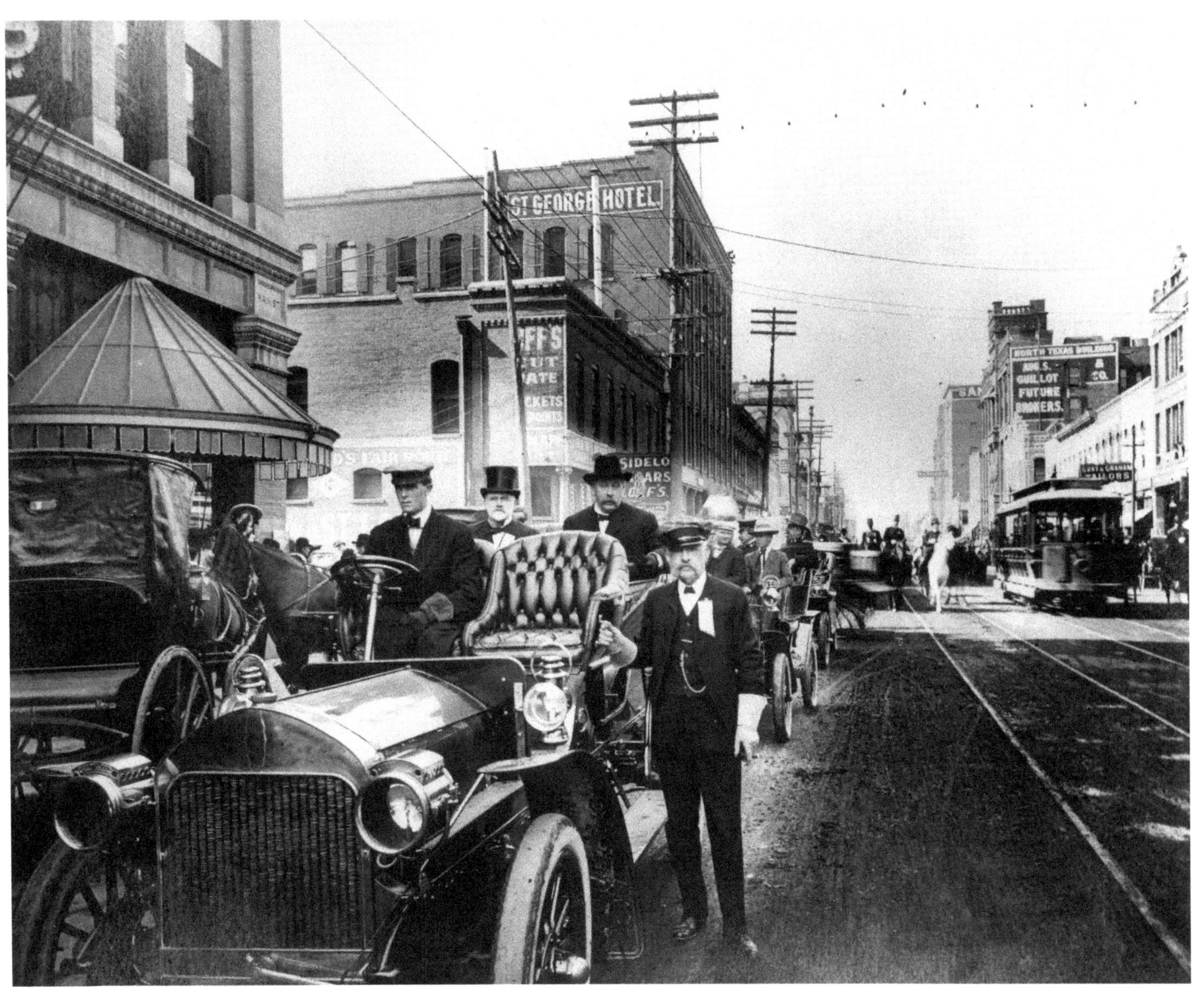

By 1907, automobiles were taking precedence over horses. Leading the annual state fair parade in Eli Sanger's Haynes auto were Texas Governor S. W. T. Lanham (wearing the top hat) and State Fair President C. A. Keating. Standing beside the car is Colonel John G. Hunter, first secretary of the Dallas Chamber of Commerce.

This publicity photo, staged by the Dallas Auto Device Company, shows one of A. J. Shrader's rent cars carrying 14 passengers up a steep hill on Beckley Avenue. The Ford car was equipped with "Double Mileage Manifold," allowing it to make the climb in high gear rather than low.

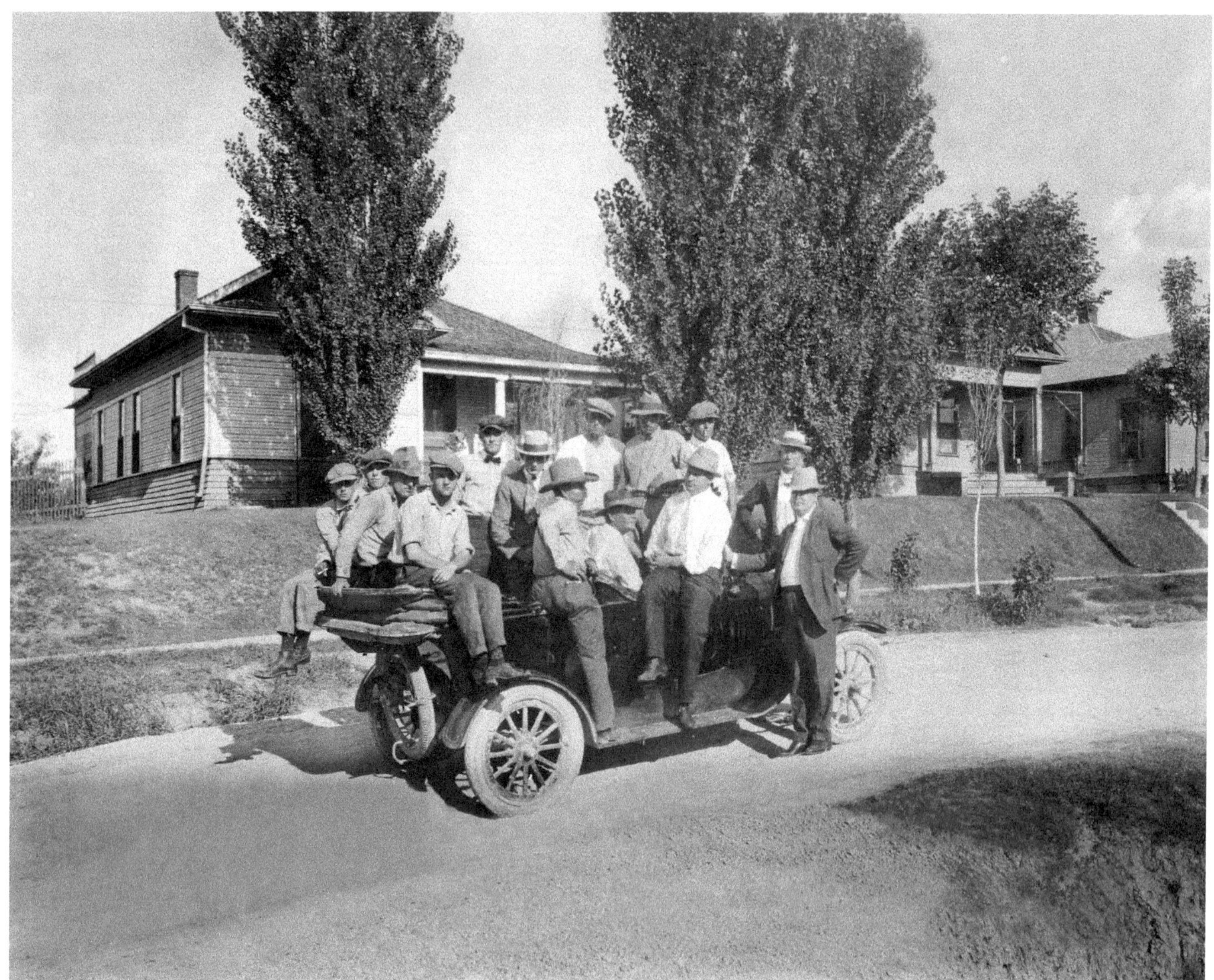

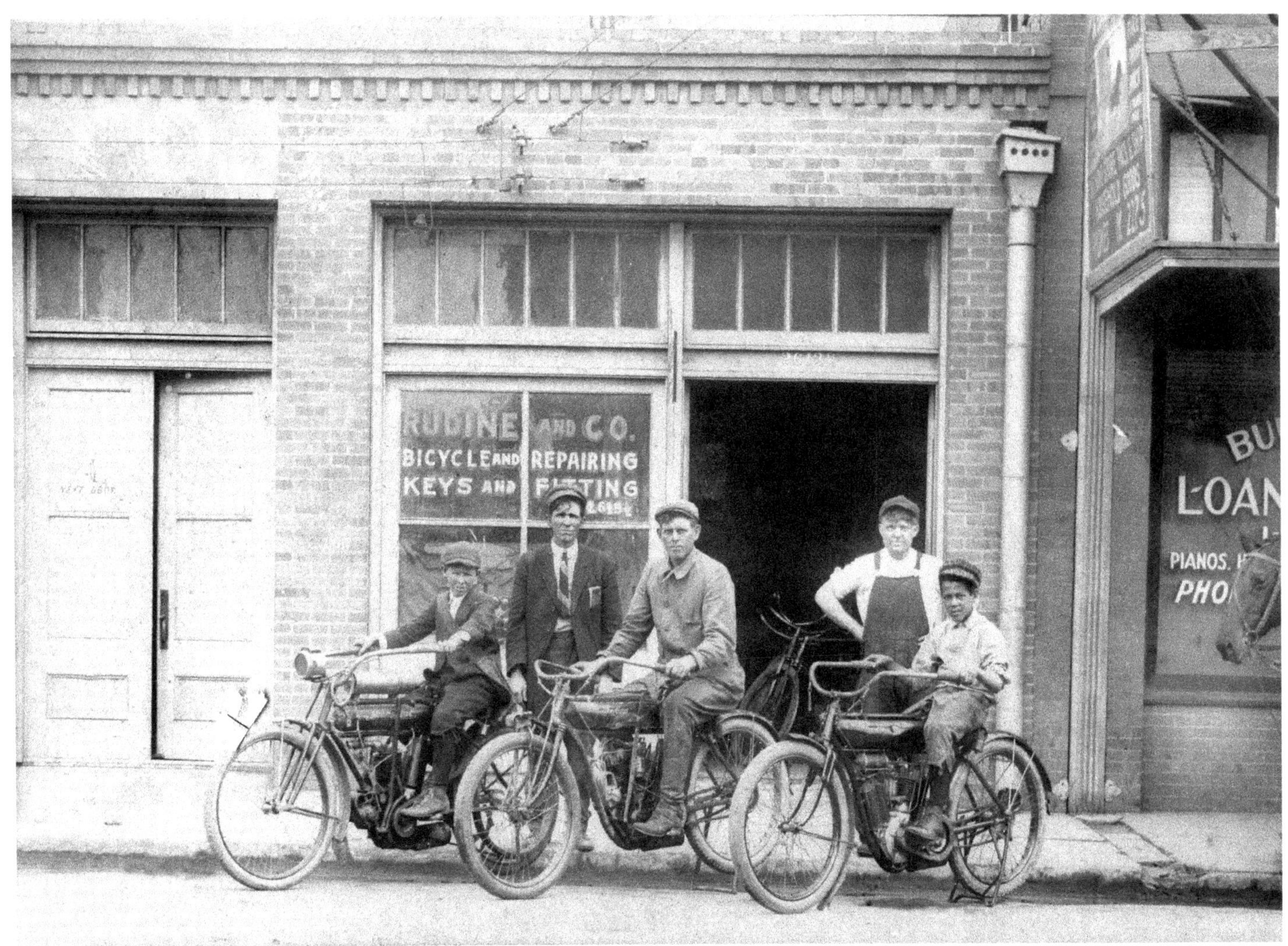

After working as a machinist for the Dallas Rubber & Cycle Company, Ludwig Rudine opened his own bicycle repair shop about 1913 at 2613 Elm. The national bicycle craze hit Dallas in the 1890s and continued until World War I.

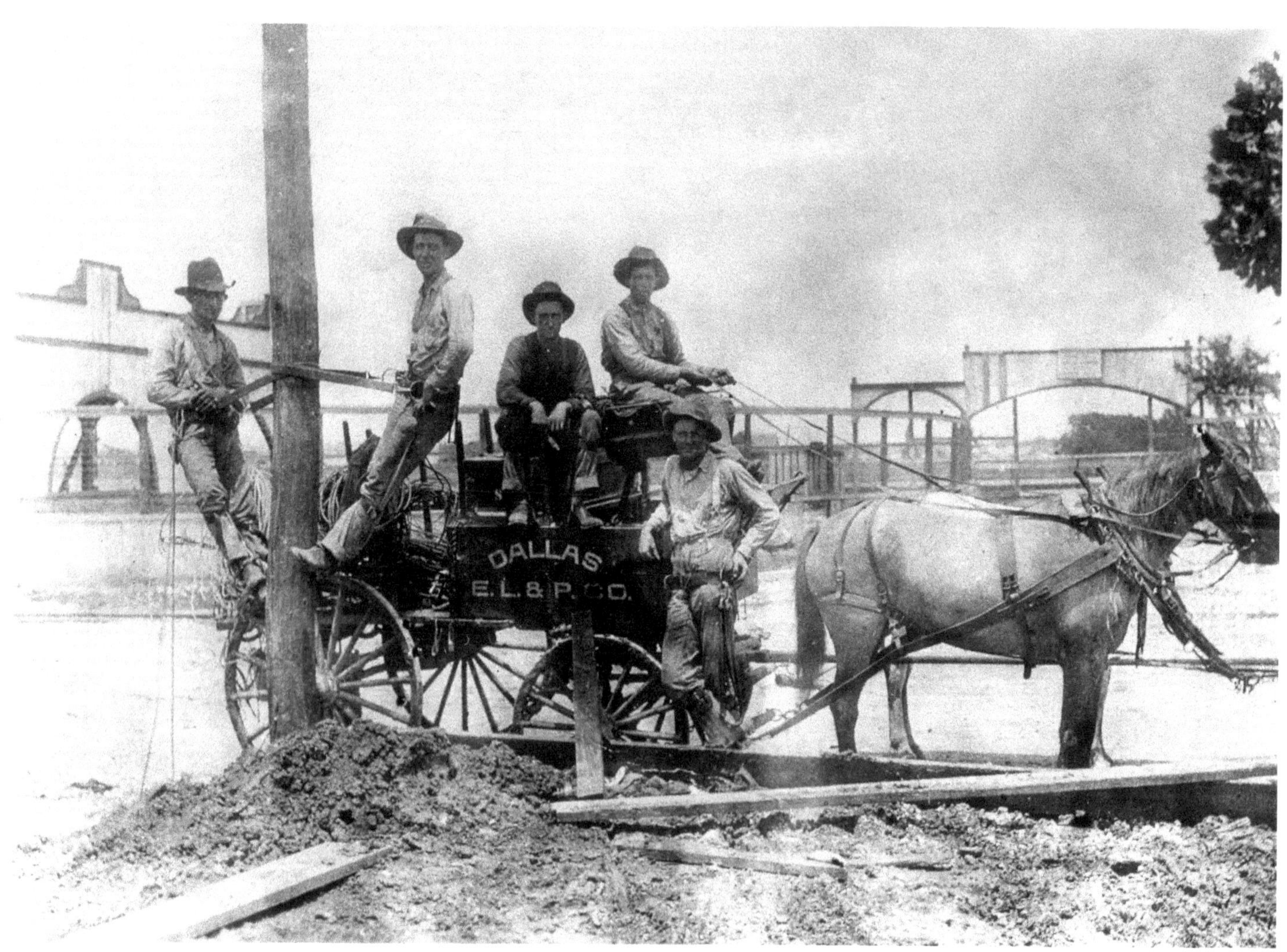

Dallas gained its first electric plant in 1882, not long after Thomas Edison produced his first light bulb. Until they finally merged in 1917, several competing companies offered electric service, stringing lines throughout the city.

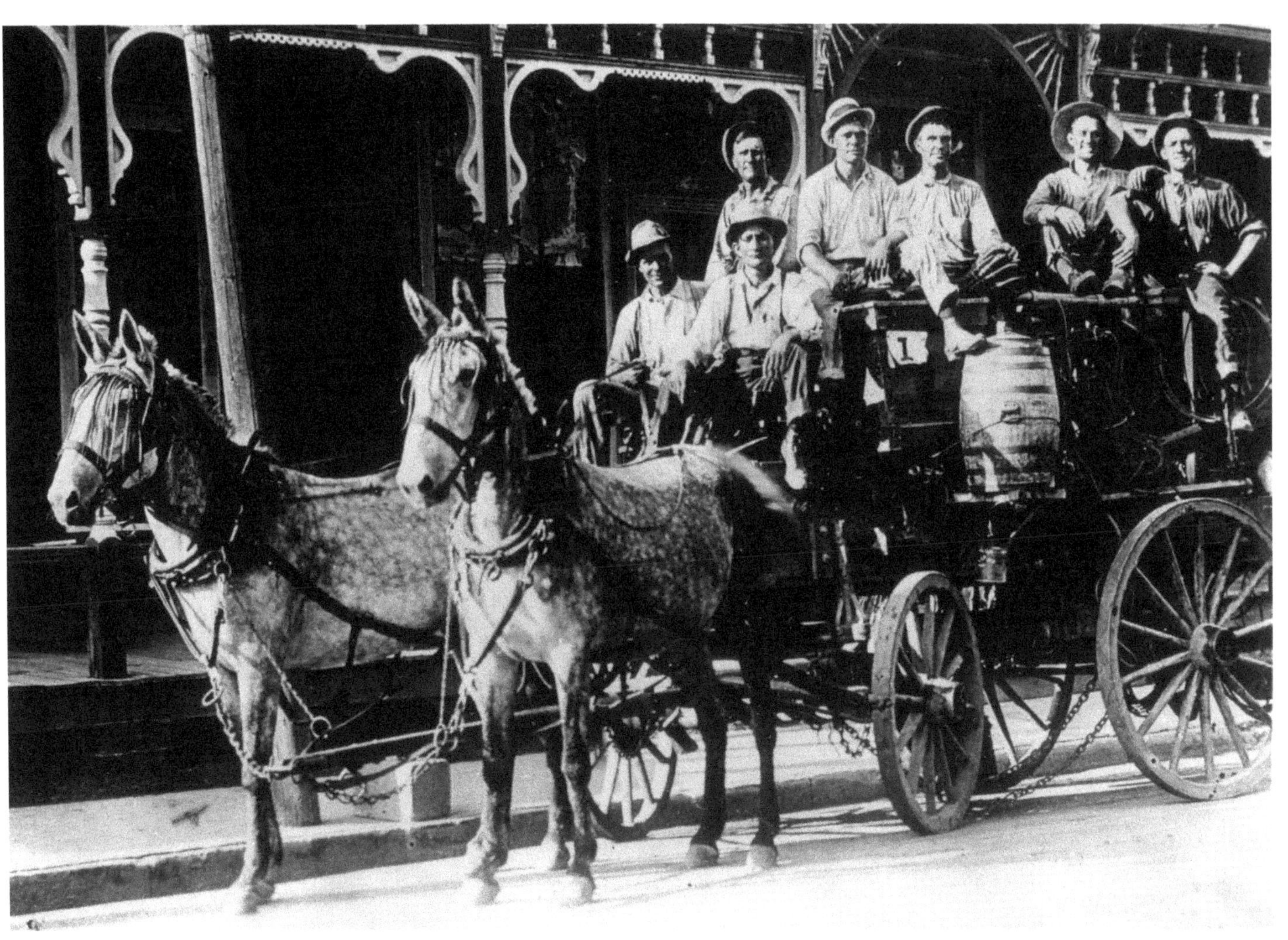

Electric company line crews were still using horse-drawn wagons in 1912, when this photo was taken, but automobiles were close to outnumbering horses on Dallas streets by then.

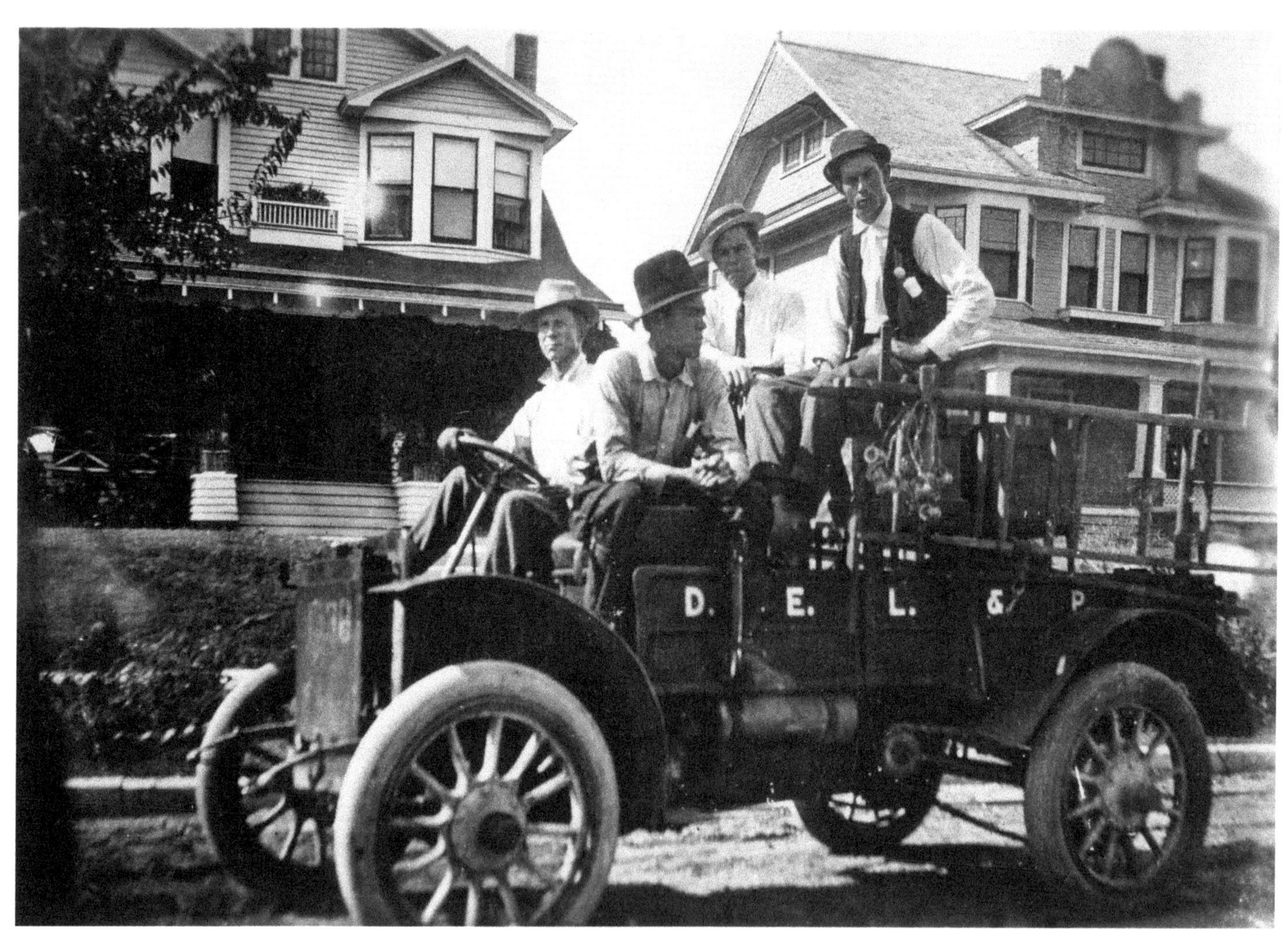

The Dallas Electric Light & Power Company purchased its first motor-driven line construction truck—a two-cylinder Buick—in 1910.

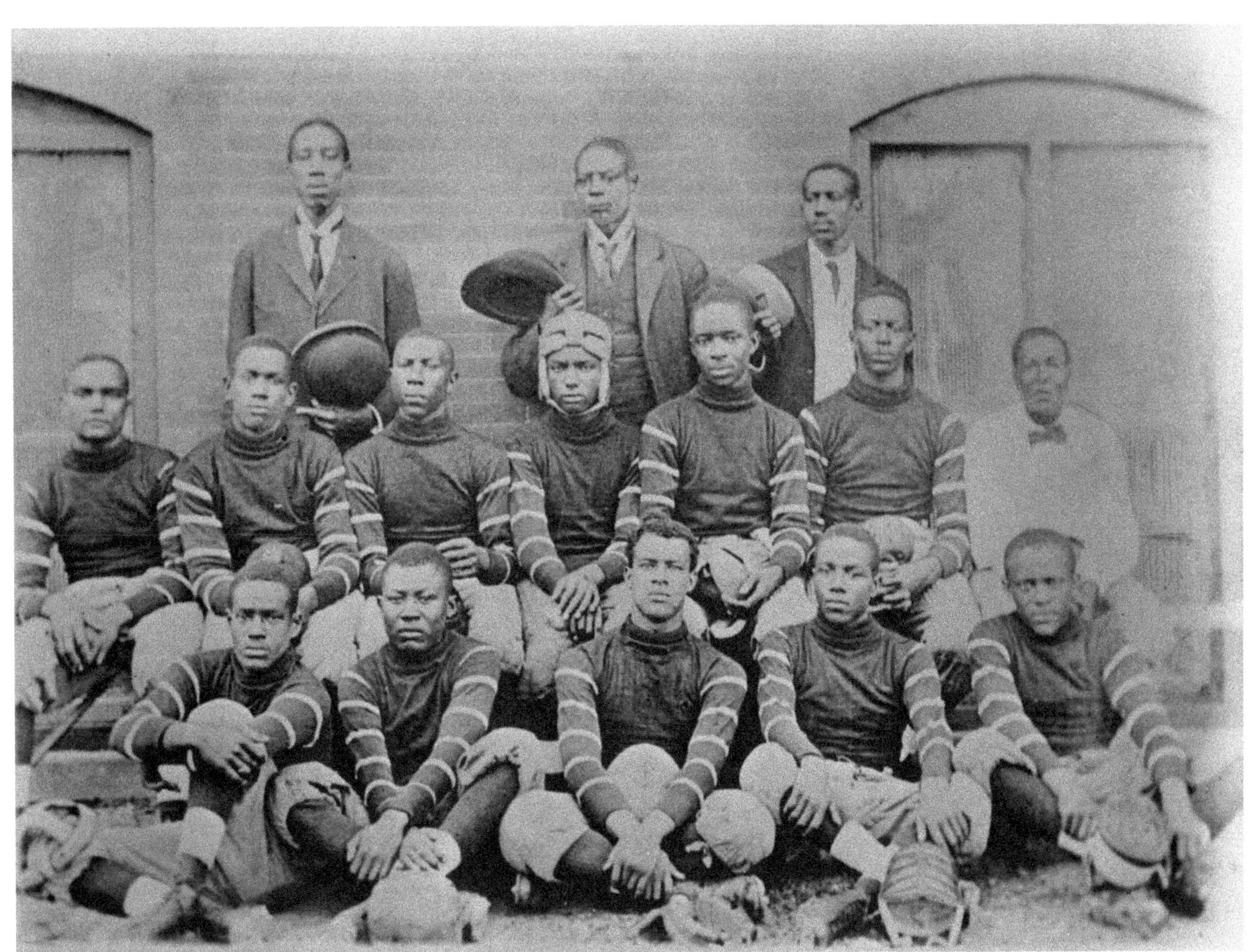

Dallas fielded the state's first high school football team in 1900. Within a few years, high school students throughout Texas were competing on the gridiron. Pictured here are the 1909 "Bulldogs," representing the Dallas Colored High School. Standing in the center of the back row is Dr. Norman Washington Harllee, a distinguished educator who doubled as school principal and football coach.

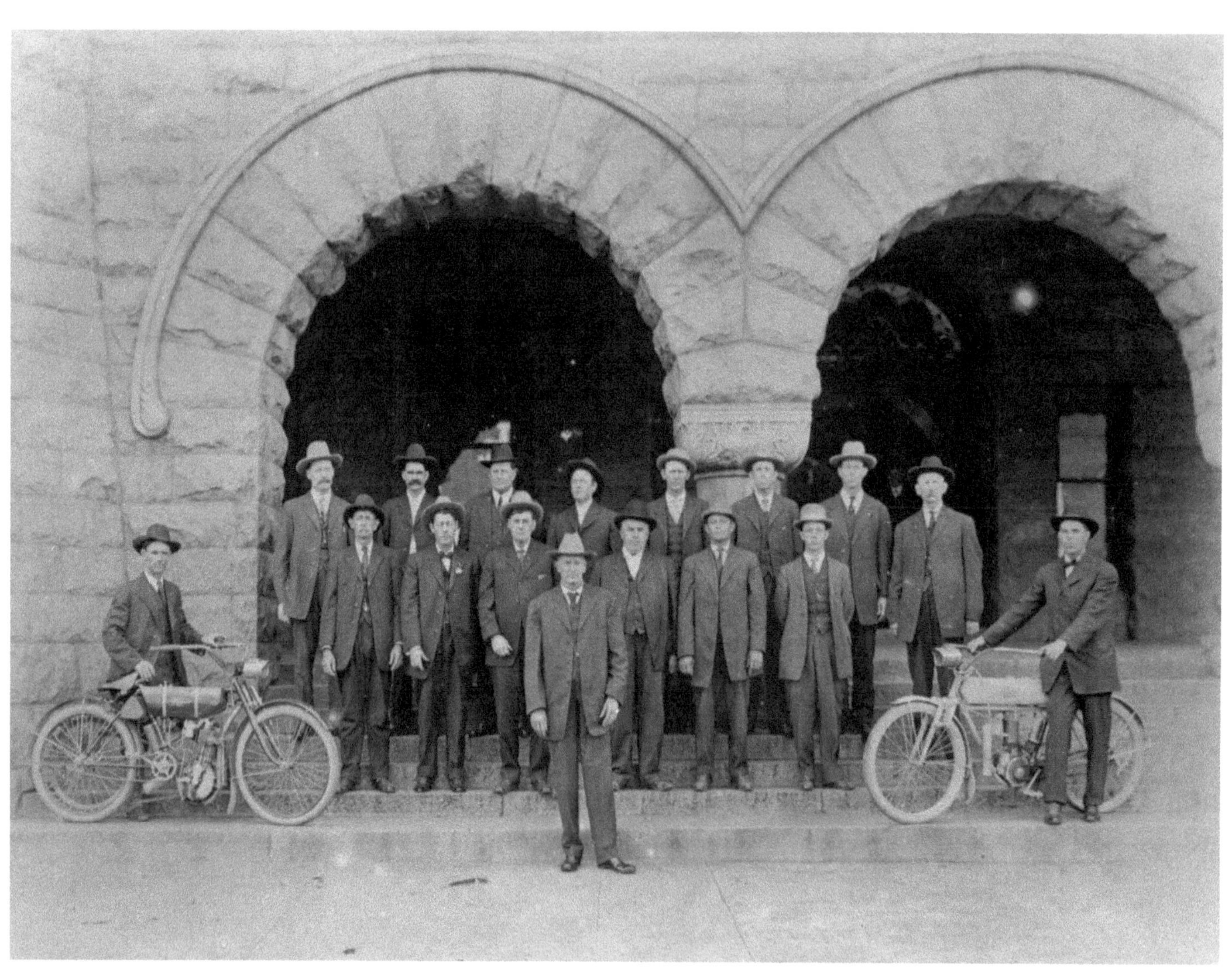

Sheriff Arthur Ledbetter served Dallas County during a time of rising racial tension. In 1910, a lynch mob forcibly seized an African American man from a courtroom in Old Red and killed him.

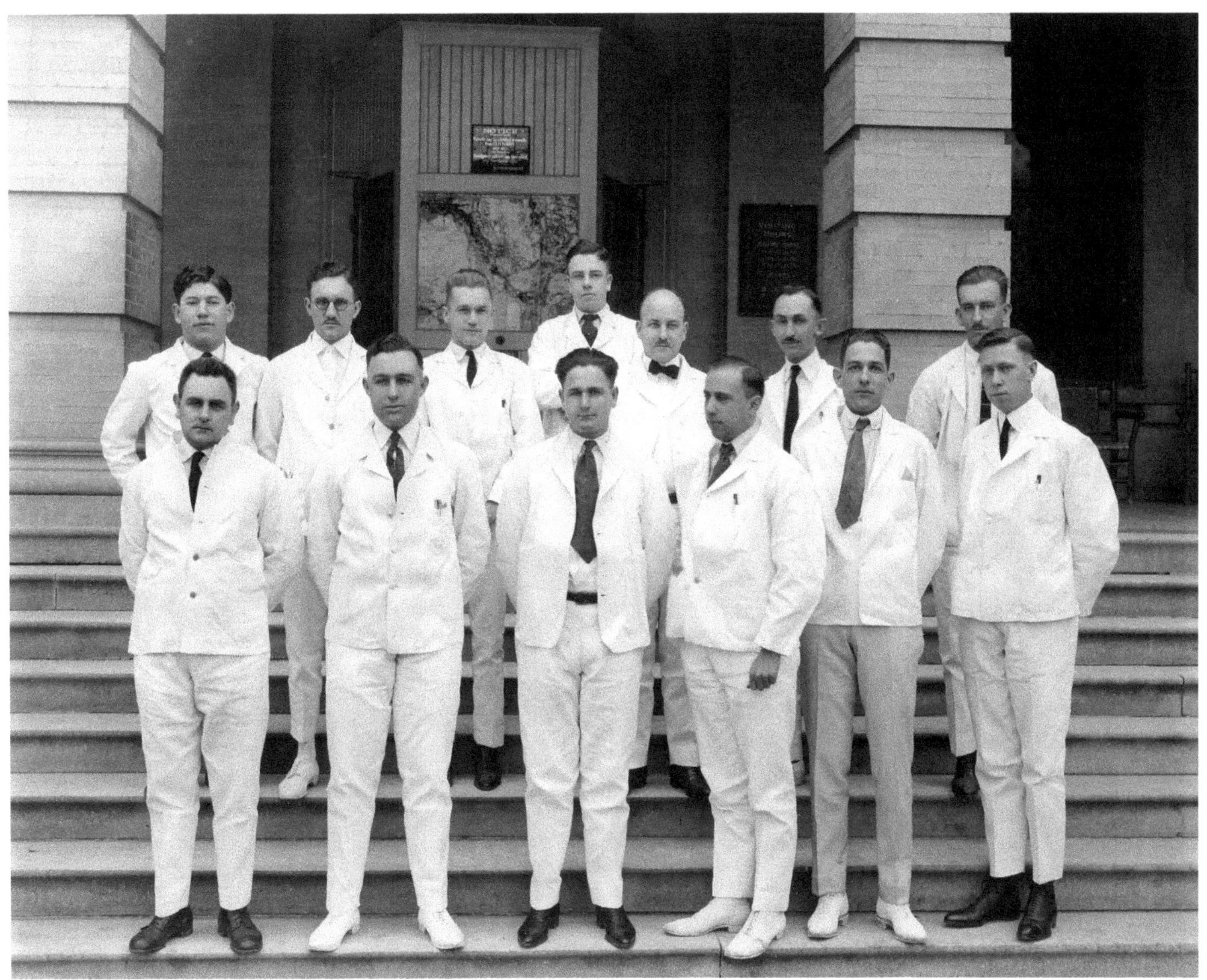

Baylor Medical School was founded in 1900 and developed in Dallas alongside Baylor Hospital, which opened in 1909 as the Baptist Memorial Sanitarium.

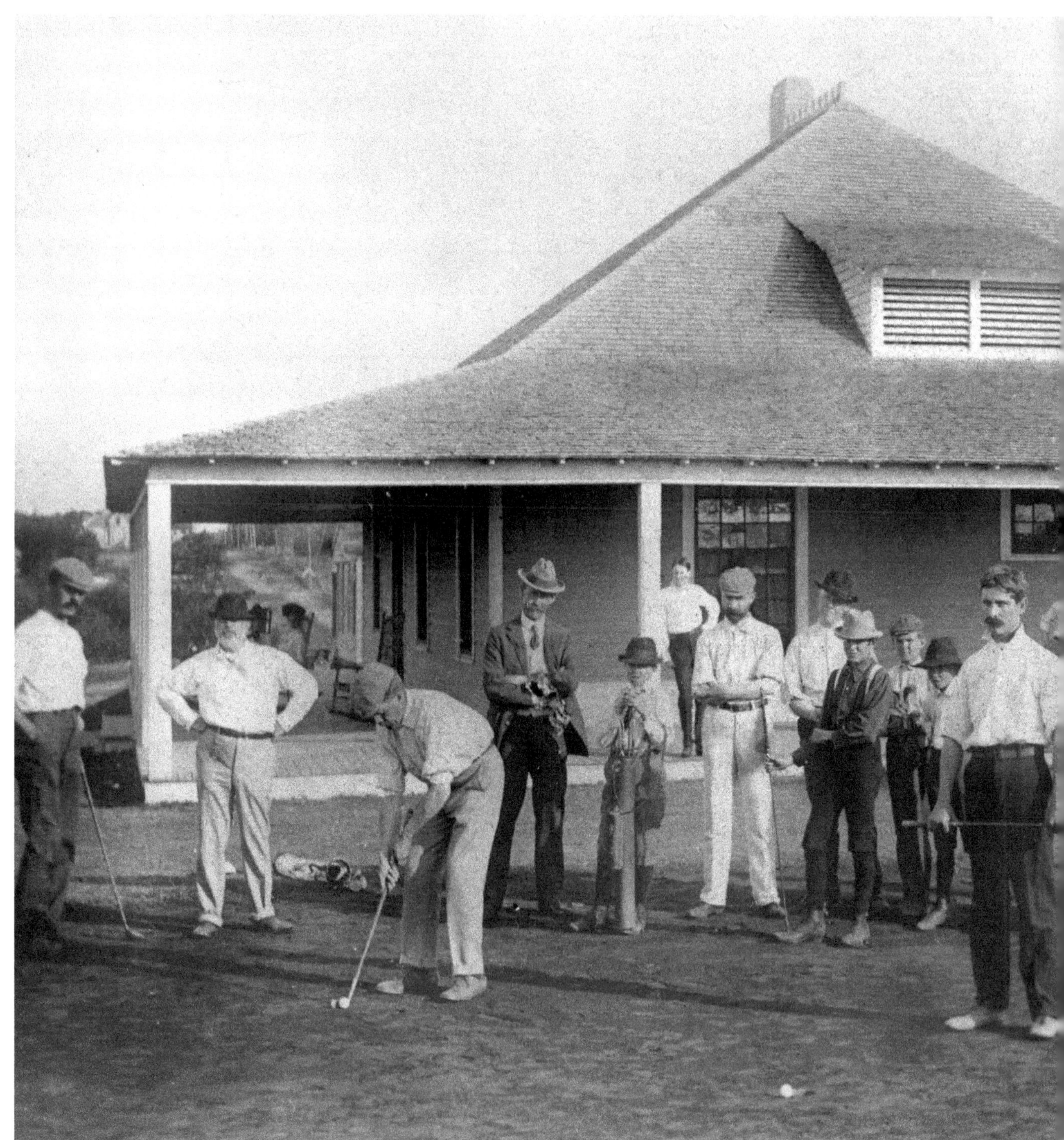

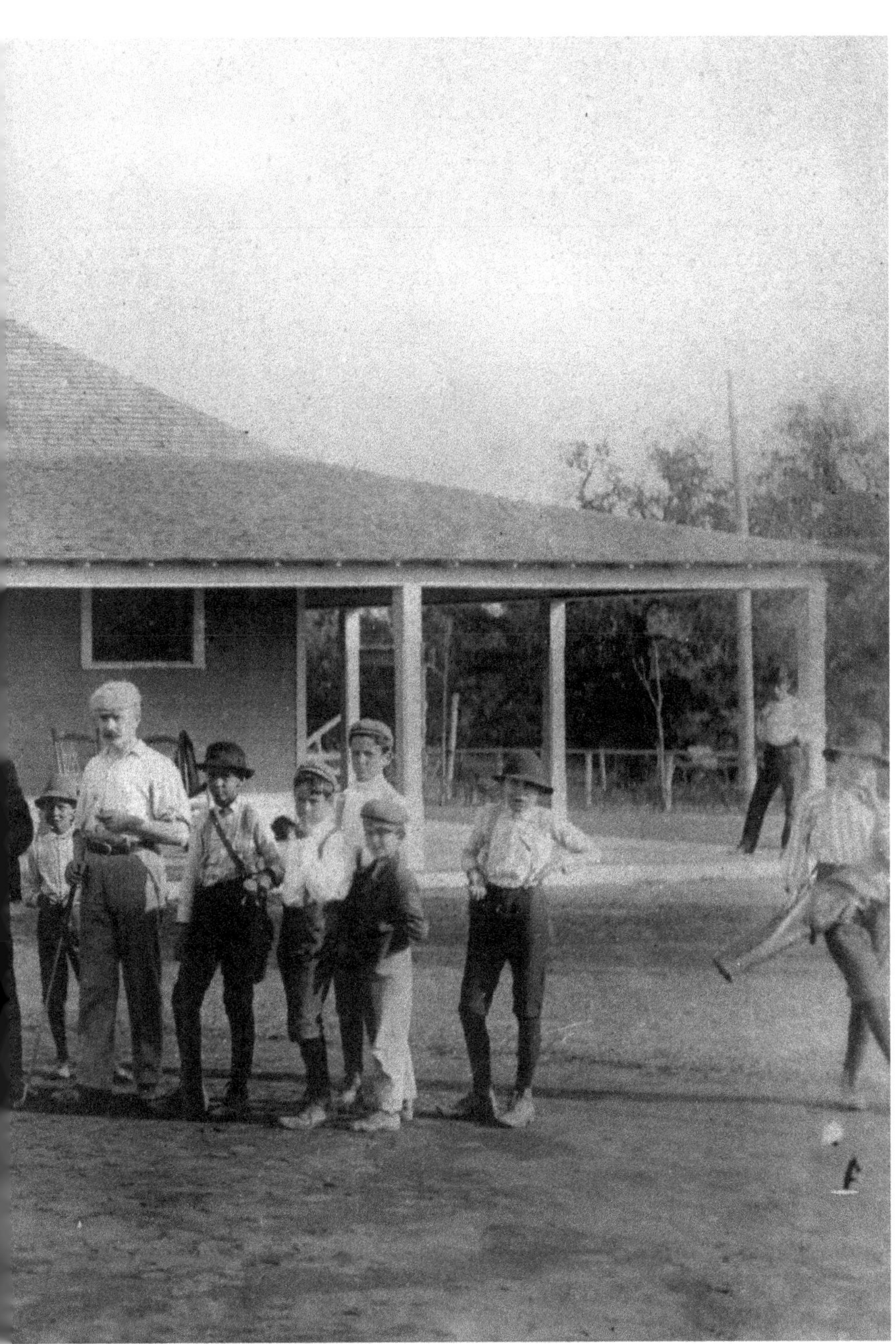

Two Englishmen introduced golf to Dallas in the 1890s, laying out a course on a cow pasture in Oak Lawn. The Dallas Golf and Country Club was organized there in 1899 (this is an early clubhouse) and moved to Highland Park in 1912.

Canny real estate developers built a streetcar line and a park as inducements to buy lots in their Oak Lawn project. The park was later renamed in honor of Robert E. Lee.

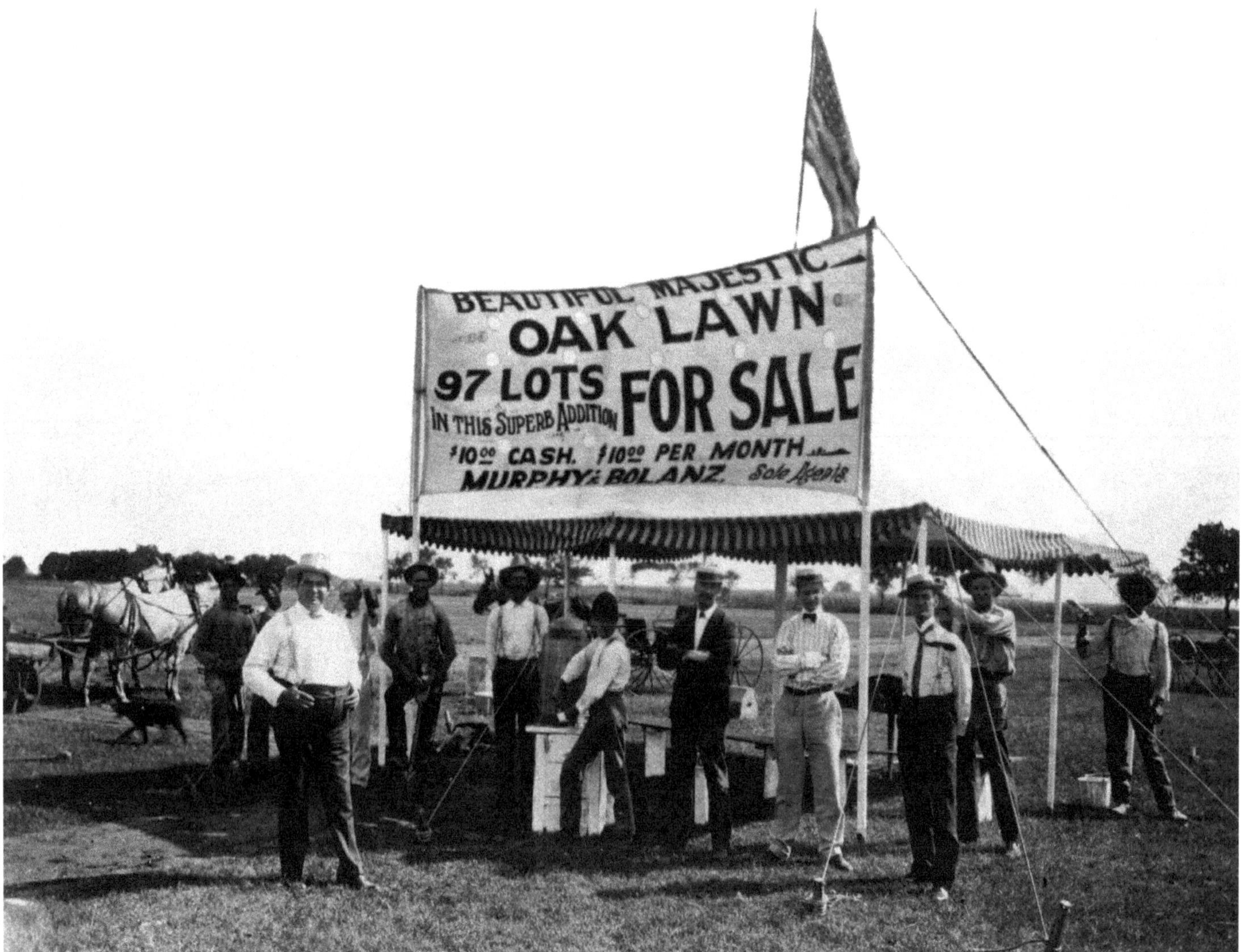

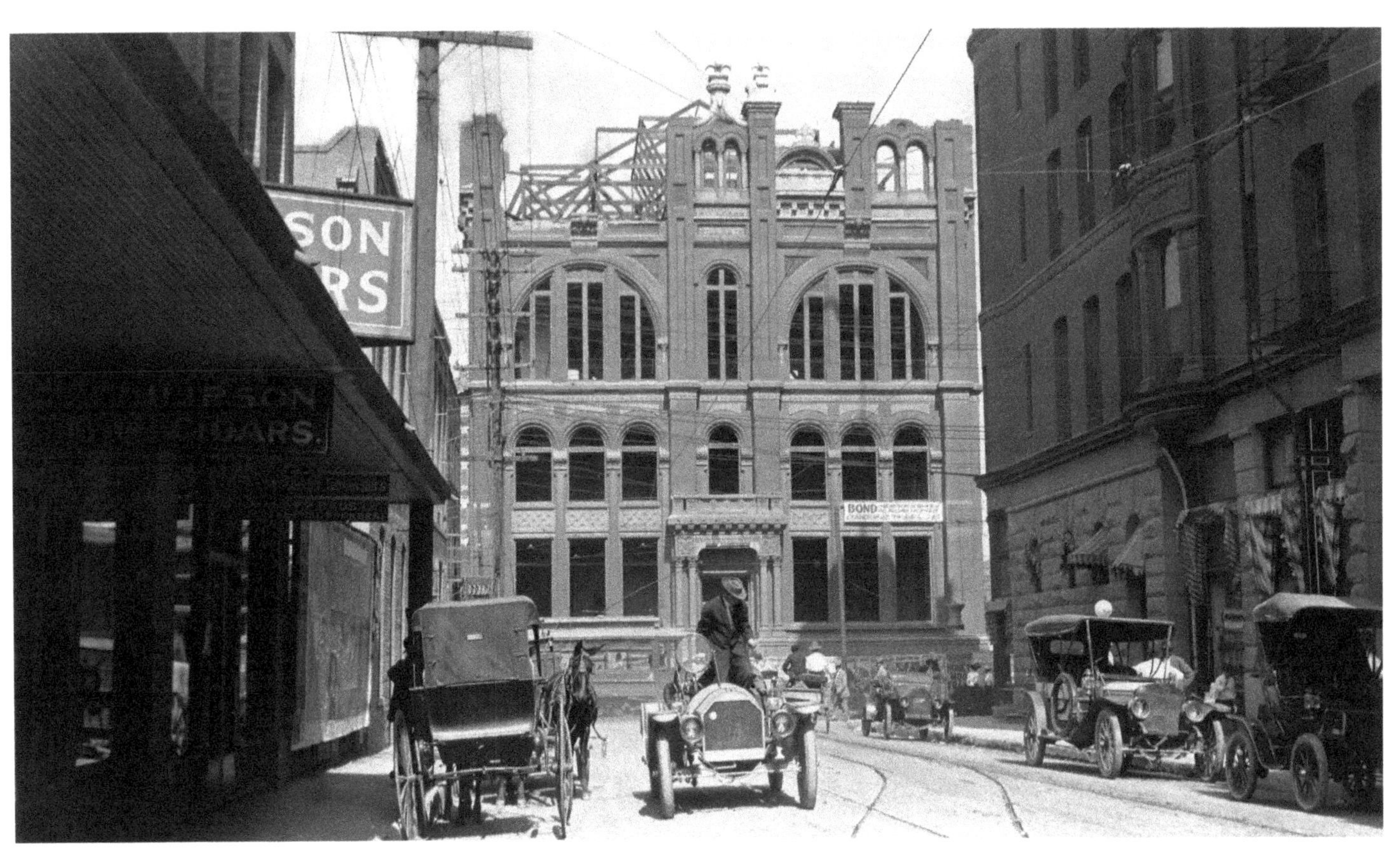

Although it was less than 25 years old, the Dallas City Hall at the northwest corner of Commerce and Akard was torn down in 1912 to make way for Adolphus Busch's luxury hotel.

In 1913, the Adolphus Hotel (seen in this shot taken from Main Street) was rising, as was the new Southwestern Life Building a block away. Insurance companies, banks, and hotels were the principal builders of "skyscrapers" in early twentieth century Dallas.

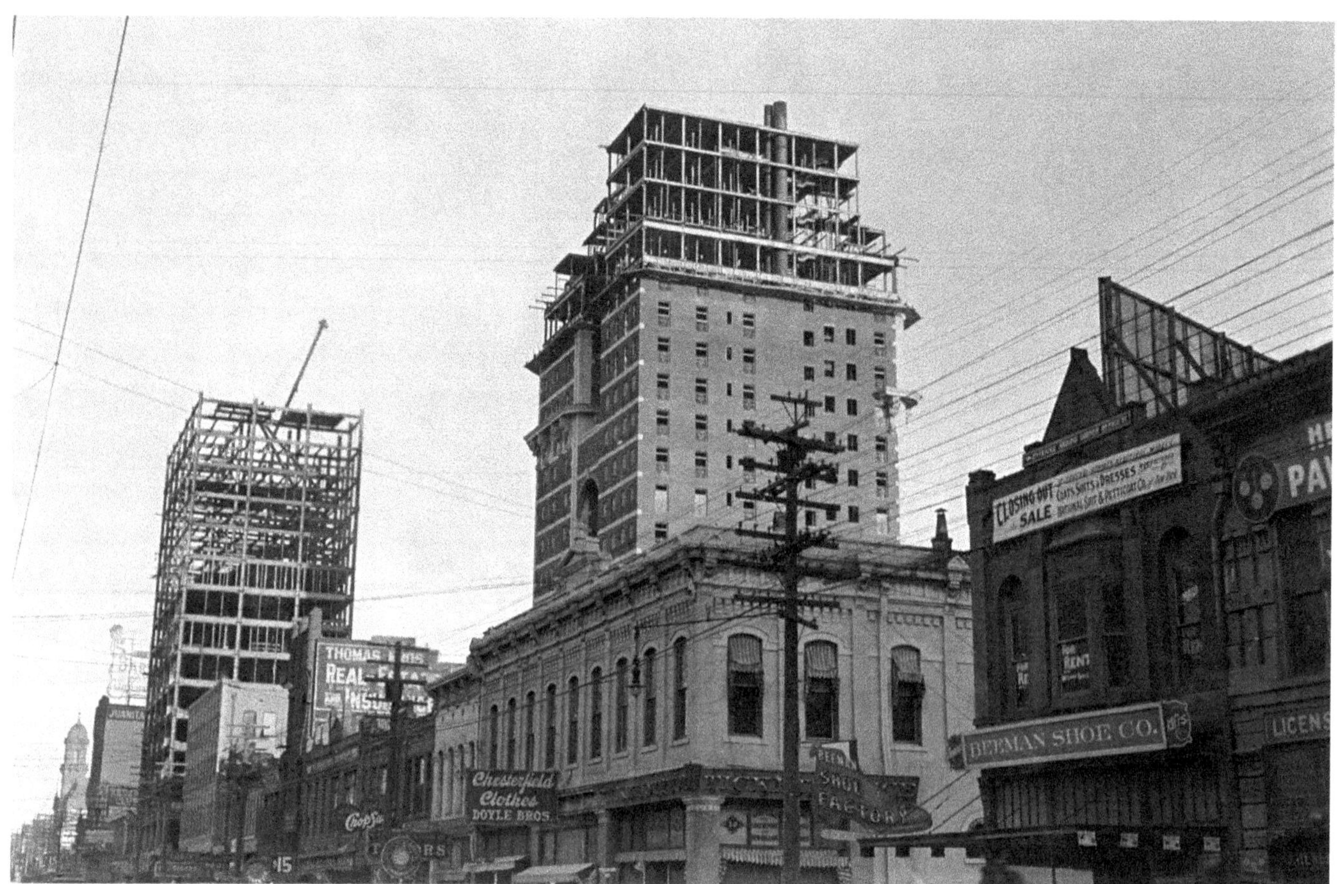

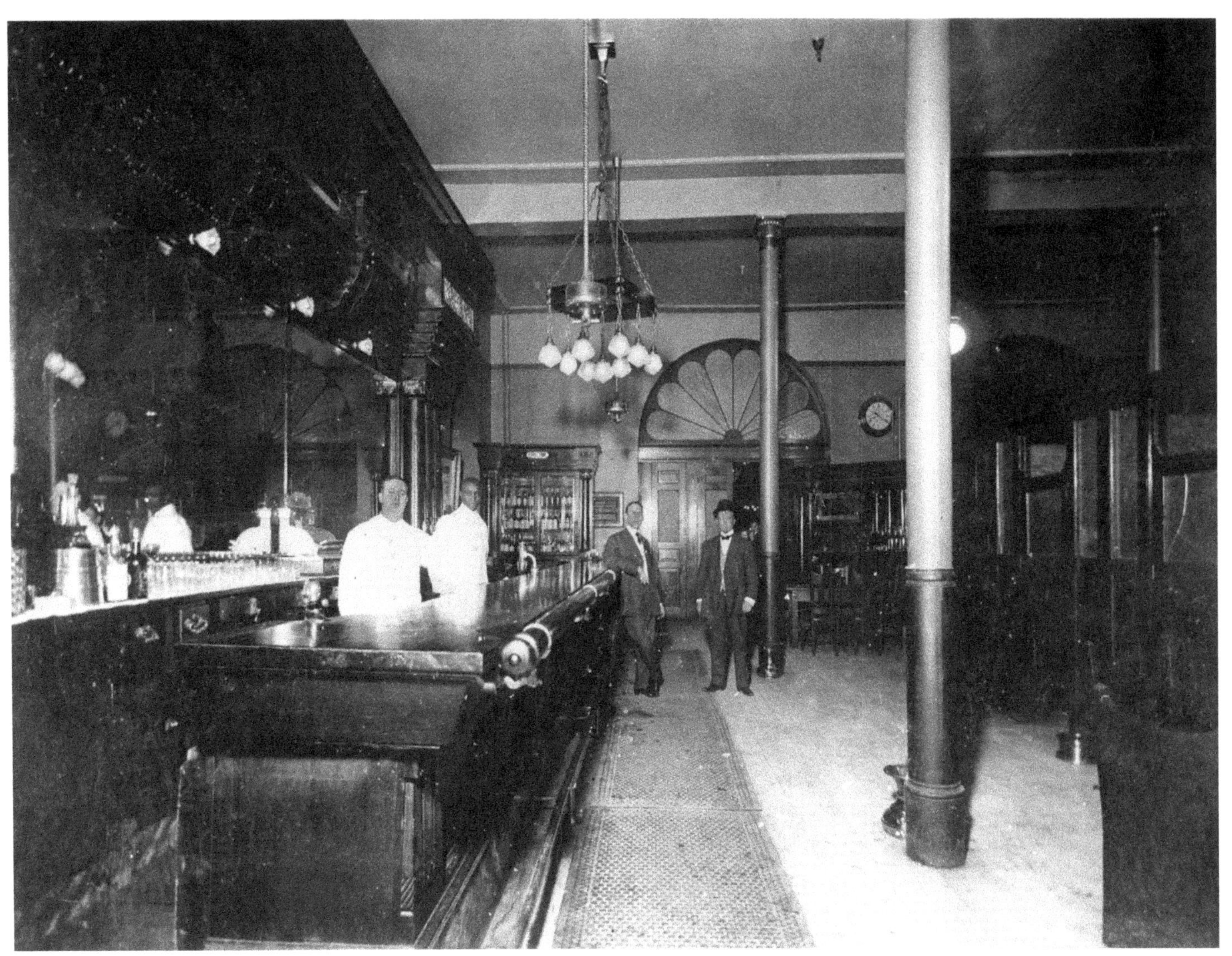

By the 1910s, hotels competed to offer the most luxurious bars and restaurants. This bar was in the Imperial Hotel on Main Street.

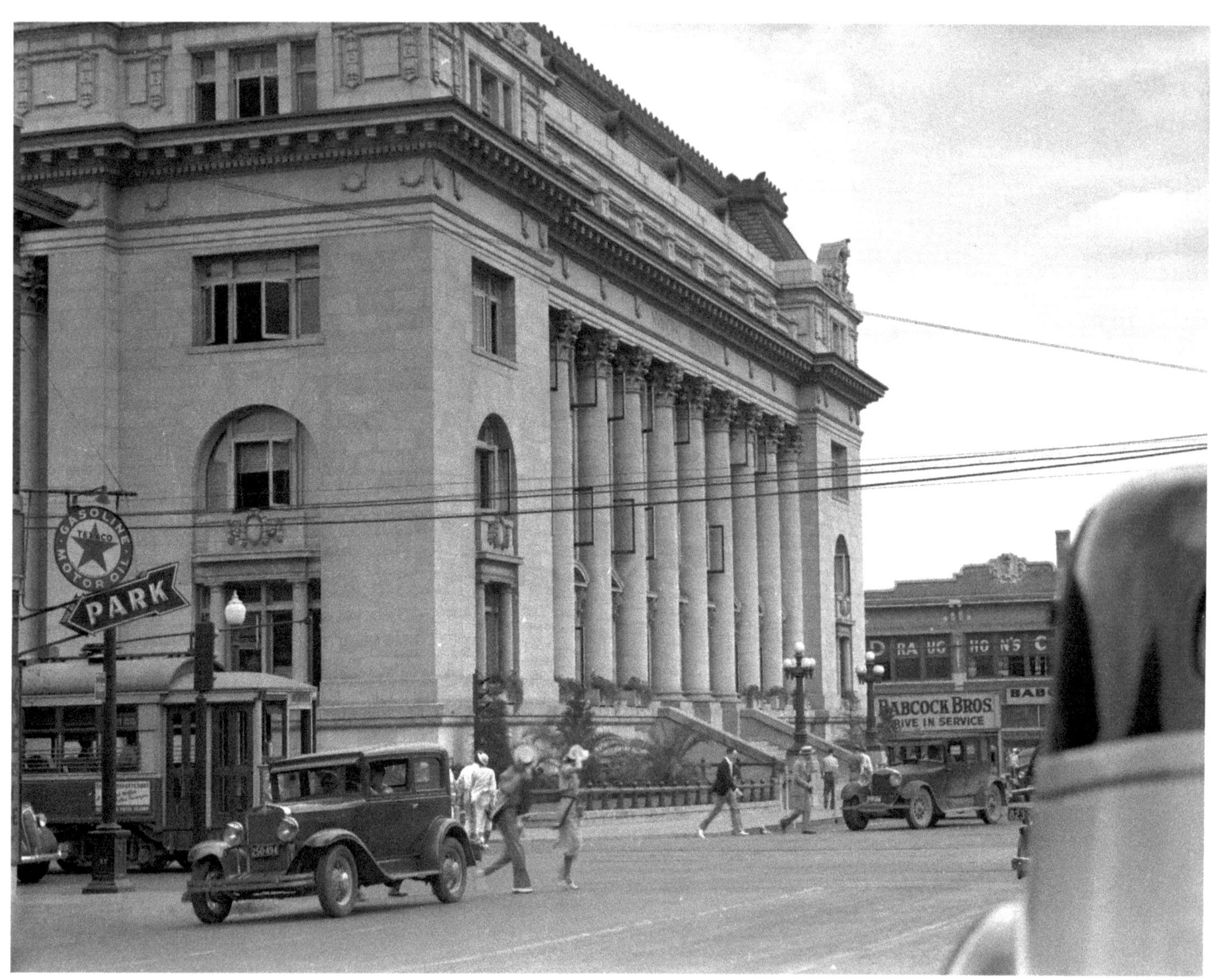

Local architect C. D. Hill designed a new Beaux-Arts city hall to replace the one on Commerce. Located on S. Harwood between Main and Commerce, it featured a pistol range for the police department, a city emergency hospital, and a 1,200-seat auditorium.

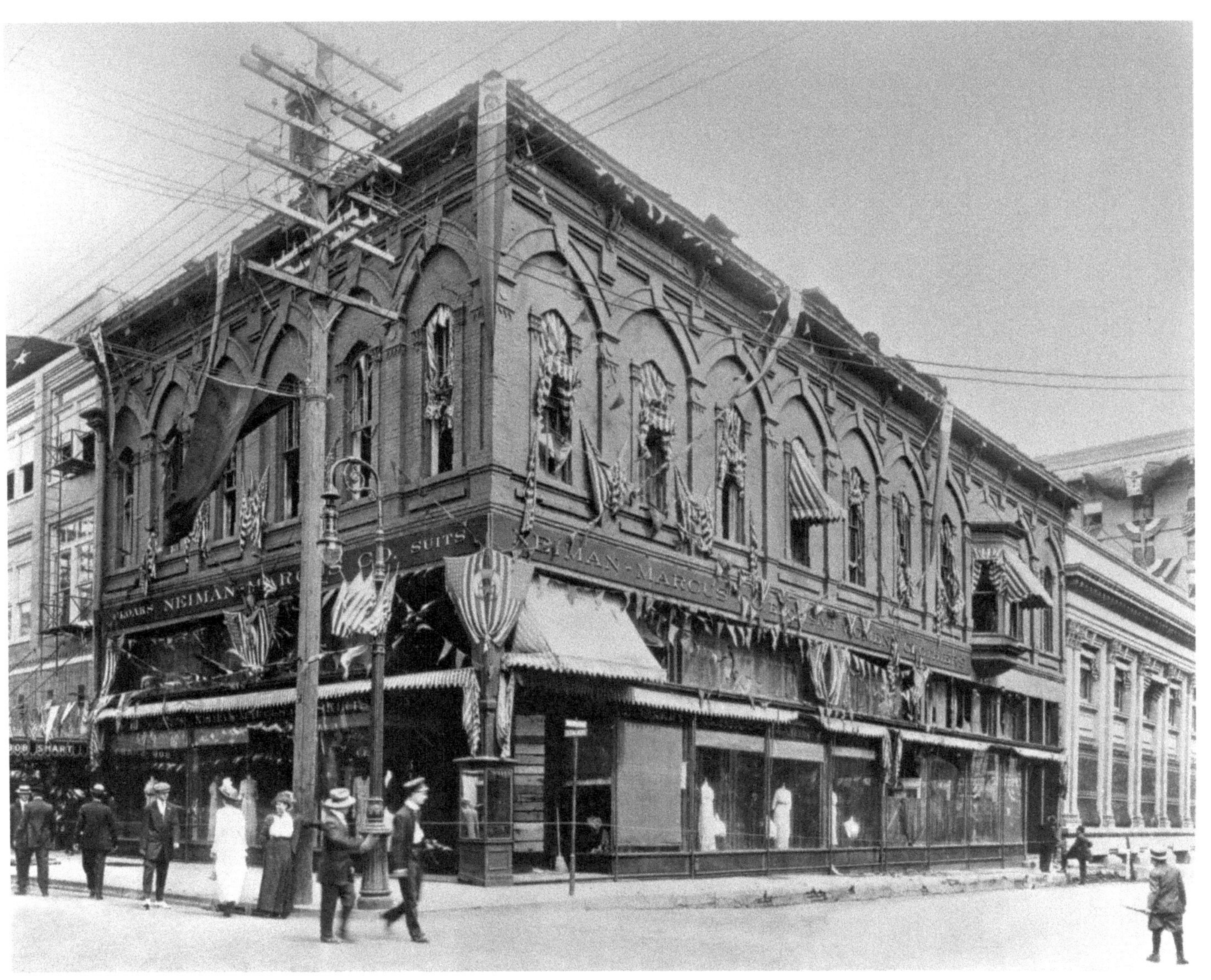

In 1907, Herbert Marcus and his sister and brother-in-law, Carrie and Al Neiman, opened a specialty women's clothing store, Neiman-Marcus, at Elm and Murphy, and quickly gained a reputation for carrying stylish merchandise of the highest quality. After the original building burned in 1913, they rebuilt on Ervay between Main and Commerce.

Hardware merchants Huey & Philp sponsored this amateur baseball club, pictured in 1915 at Fair Park, where baseball diamonds filled the infield of the racetrack.

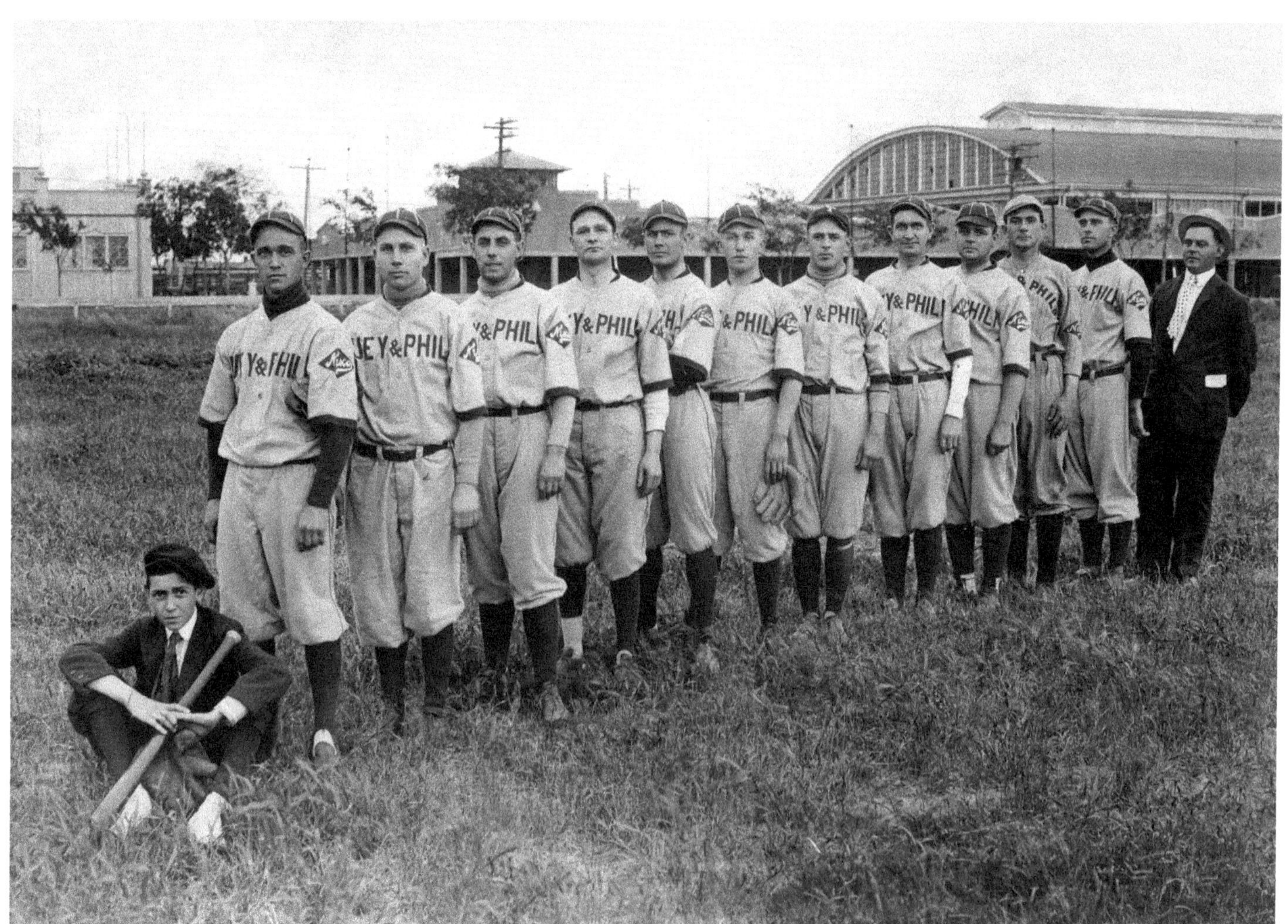

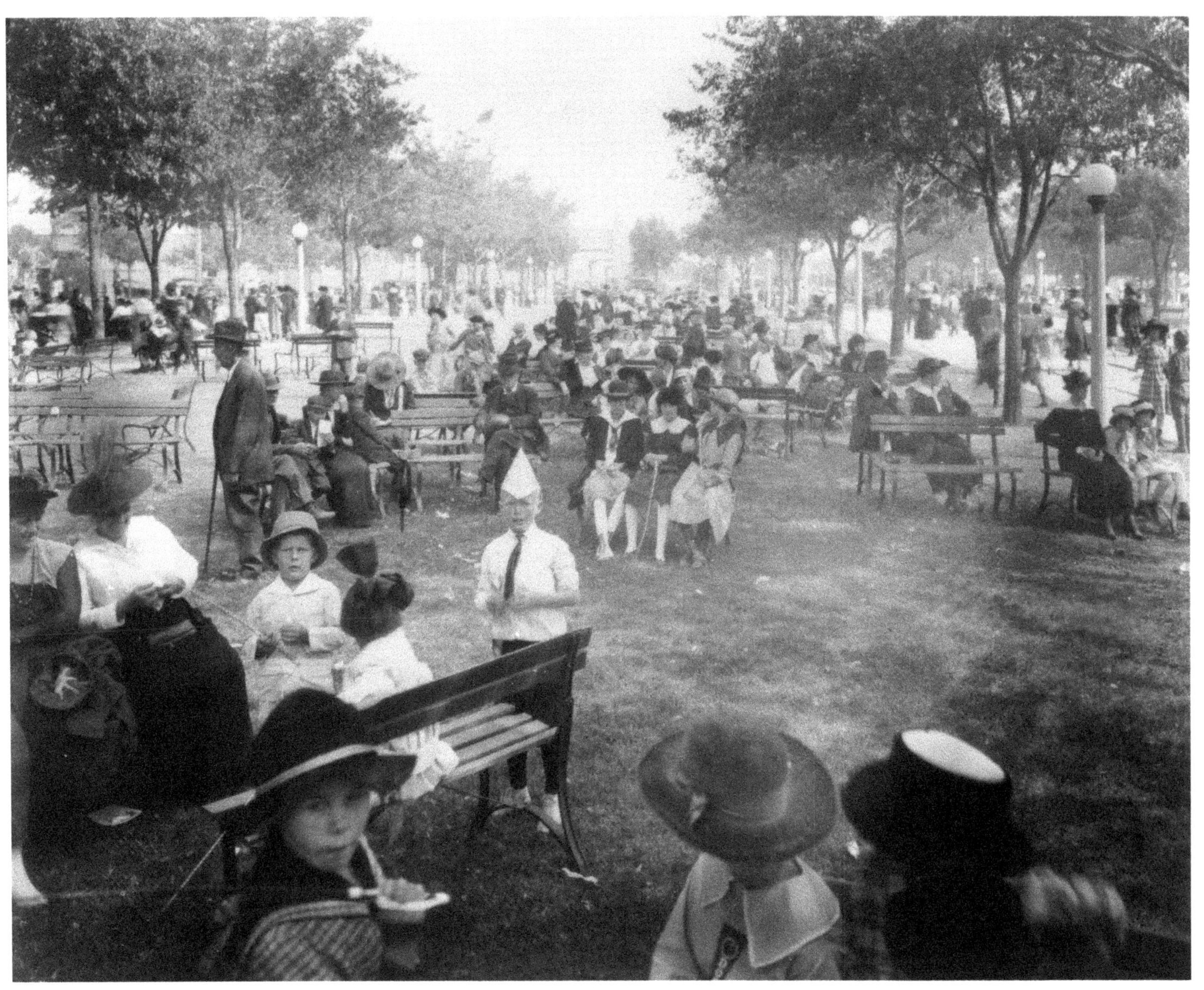

The annual State Fair of Texas has drawn thousands of people to Dallas each October since 1886. Family picnics have always been part of the tradition.

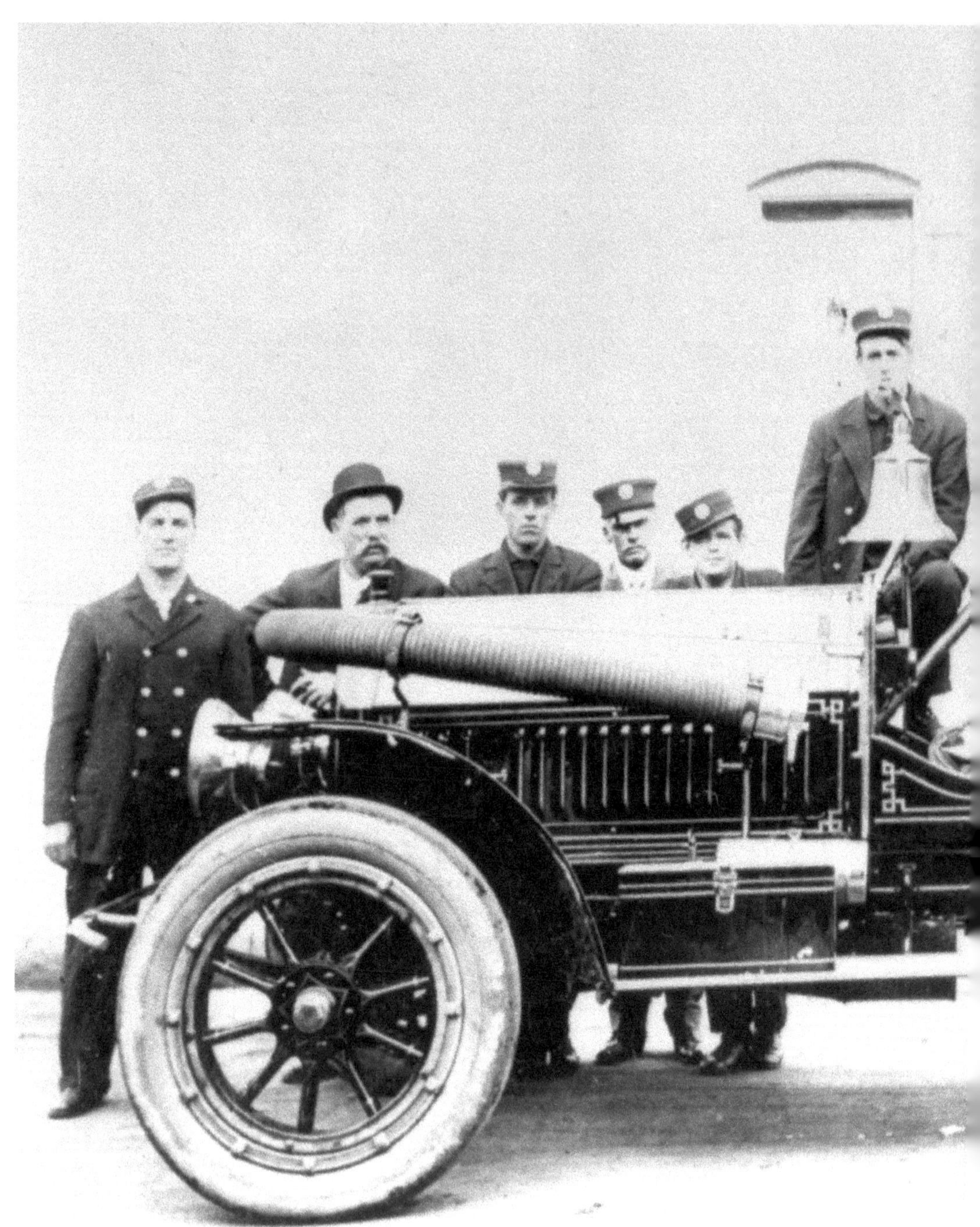

Organized as a volunteer fire brigade in 1872, the Dallas Fire Department gradually became a professional outfit. This was its first motorized pumper, ca. 1915.

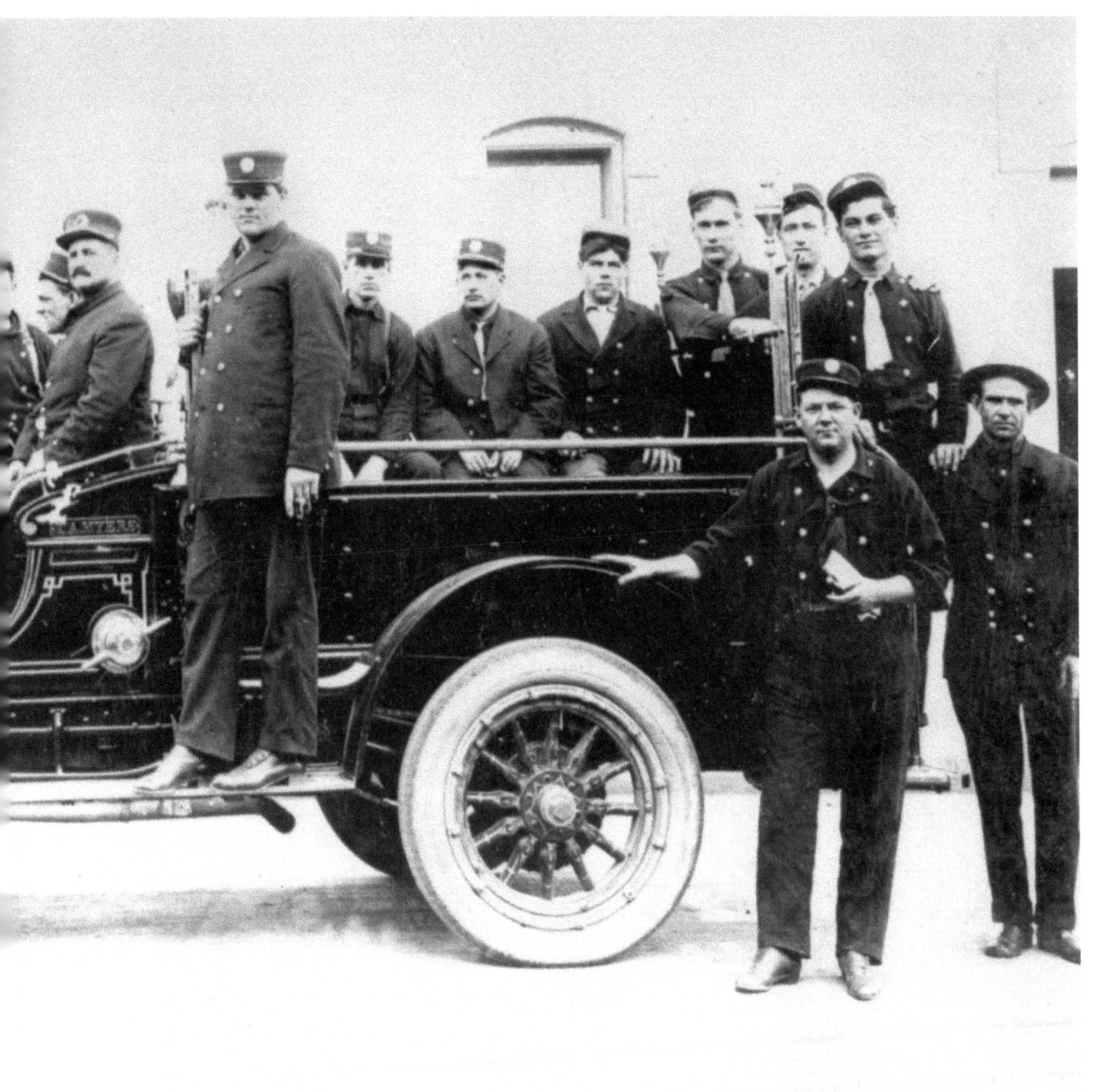

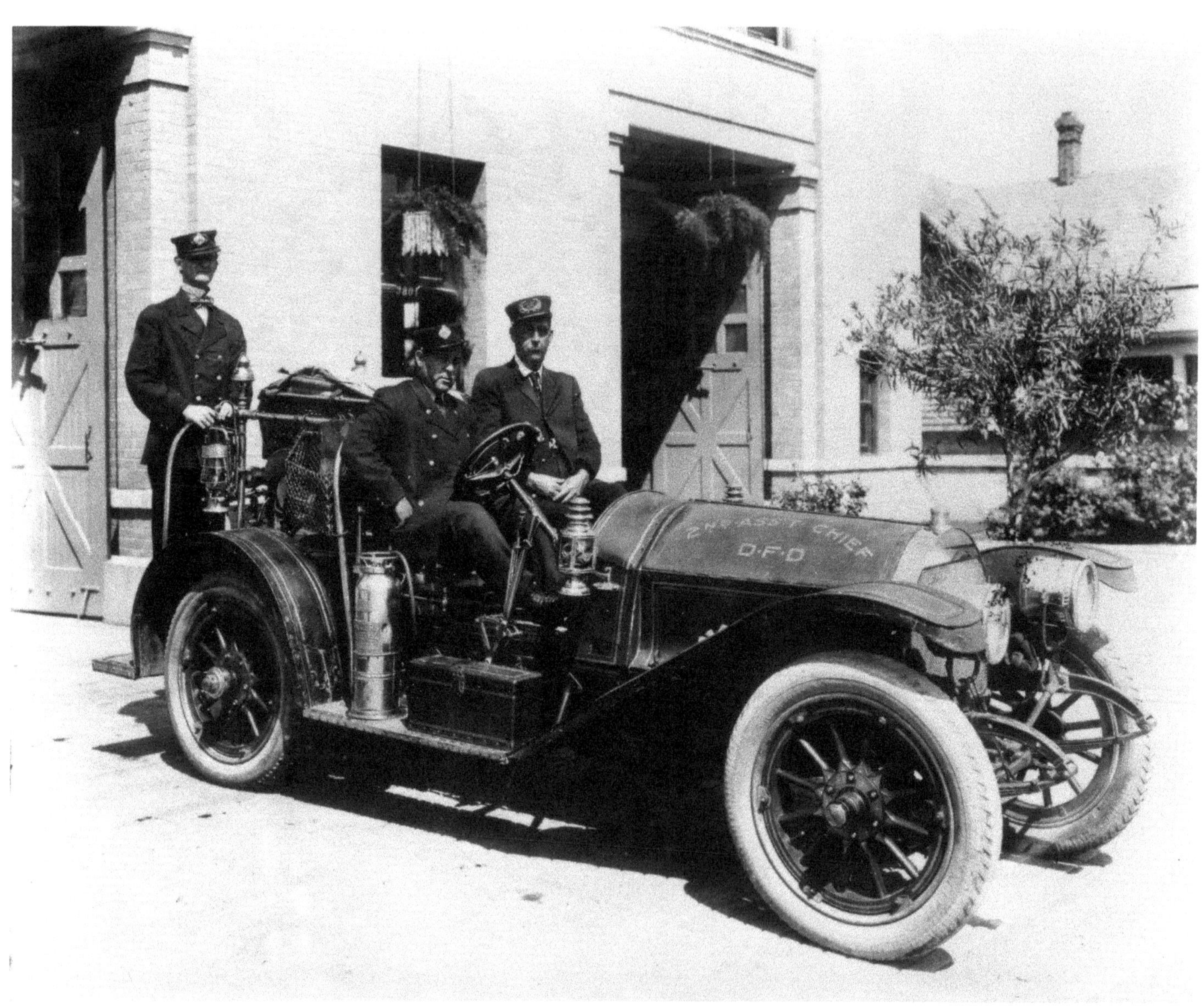

By 1911, the Dallas Fire Department was motorized. Here the second assistant chief proudly shows off his vehicle.

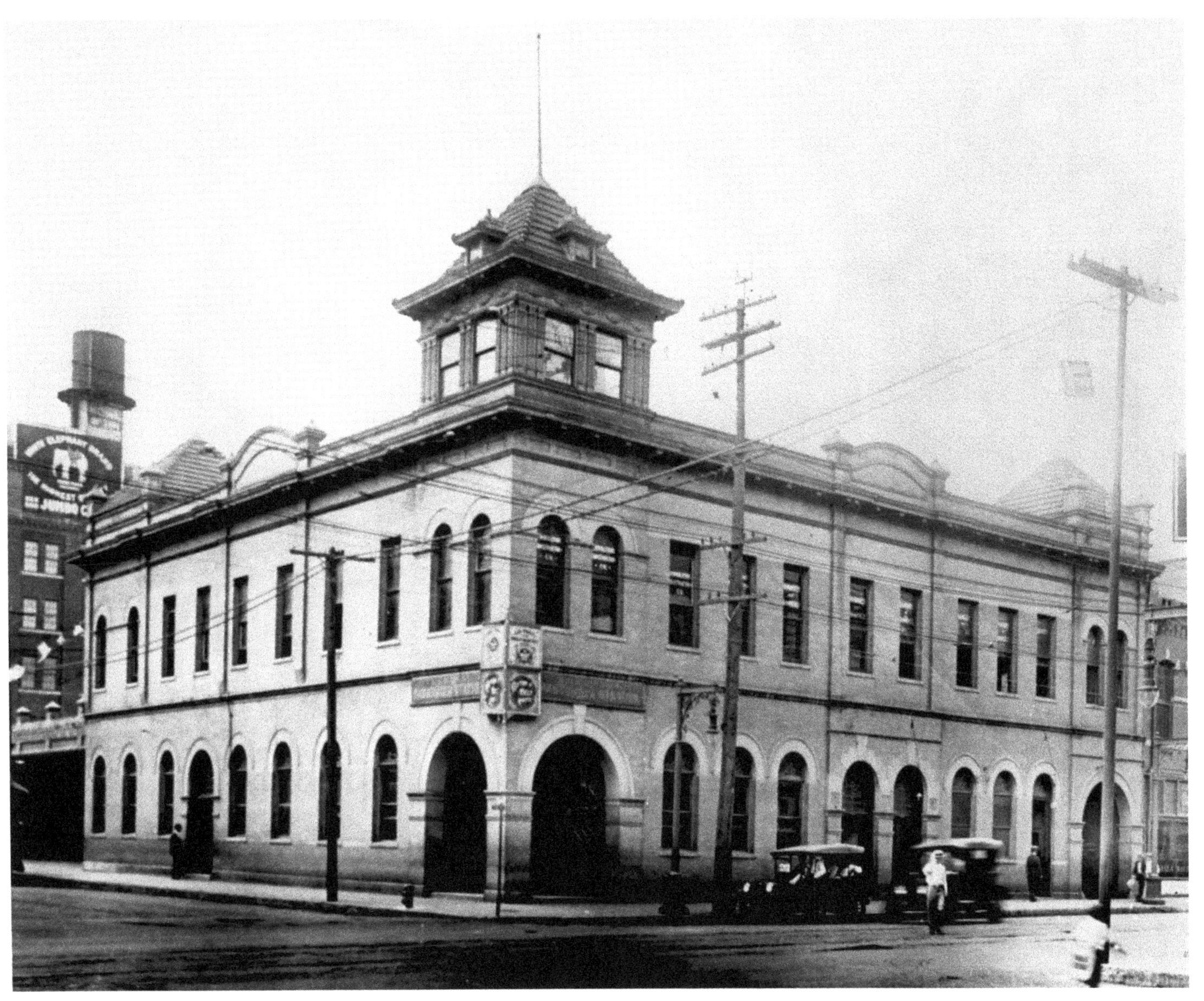

The Cotton Belt terminal, located at Commerce and Lamar, was one of several downtown railroad depots eventually replaced by Union Station.

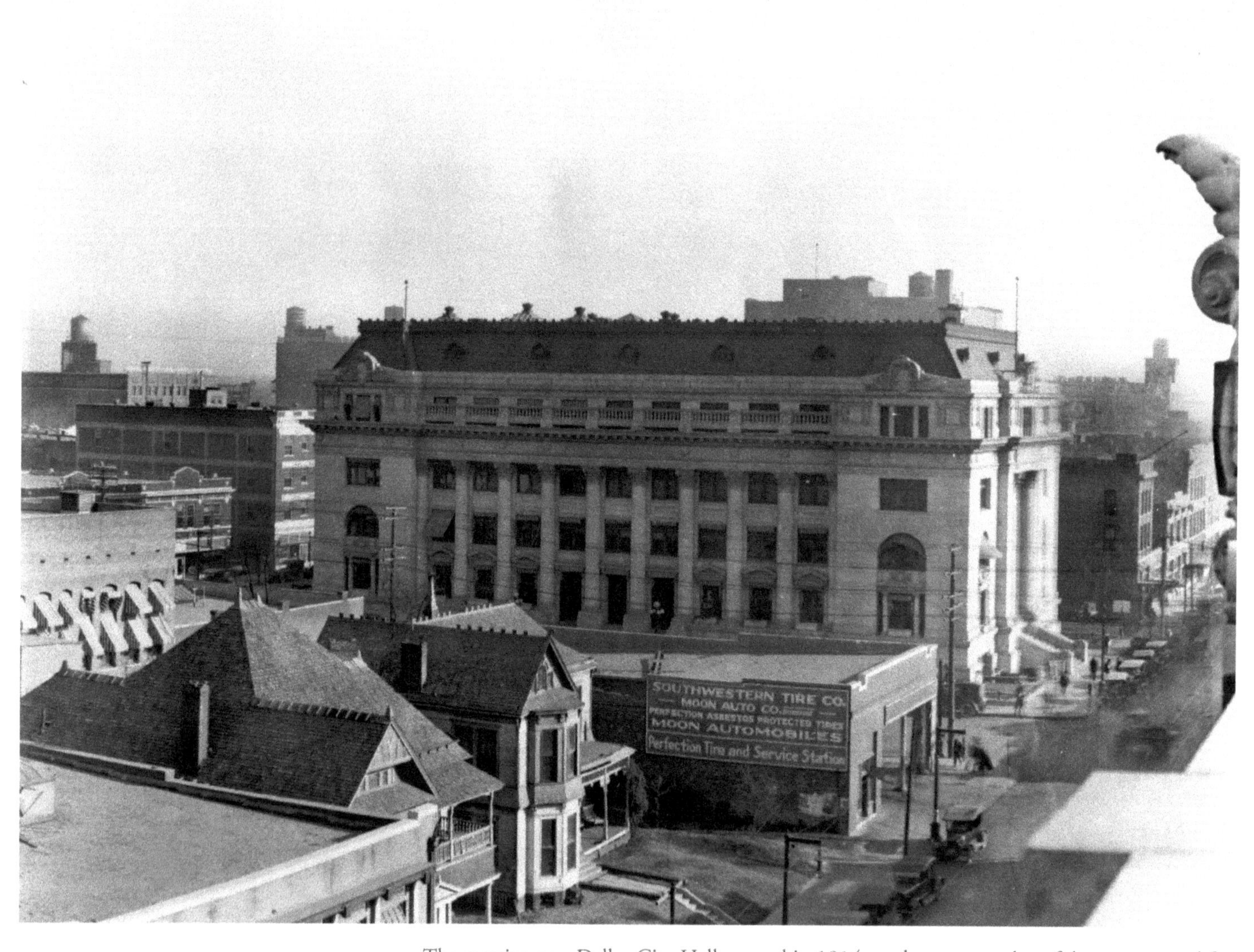

The massive new Dallas City Hall opened in 1914 on the eastern edge of downtown, and for many years remained surrounded by residences and small commercial buildings.

U.S. Army recruits lined up on Houston Street in 1918, headed toward Union Station to board a train for basic training before serving in World War I.

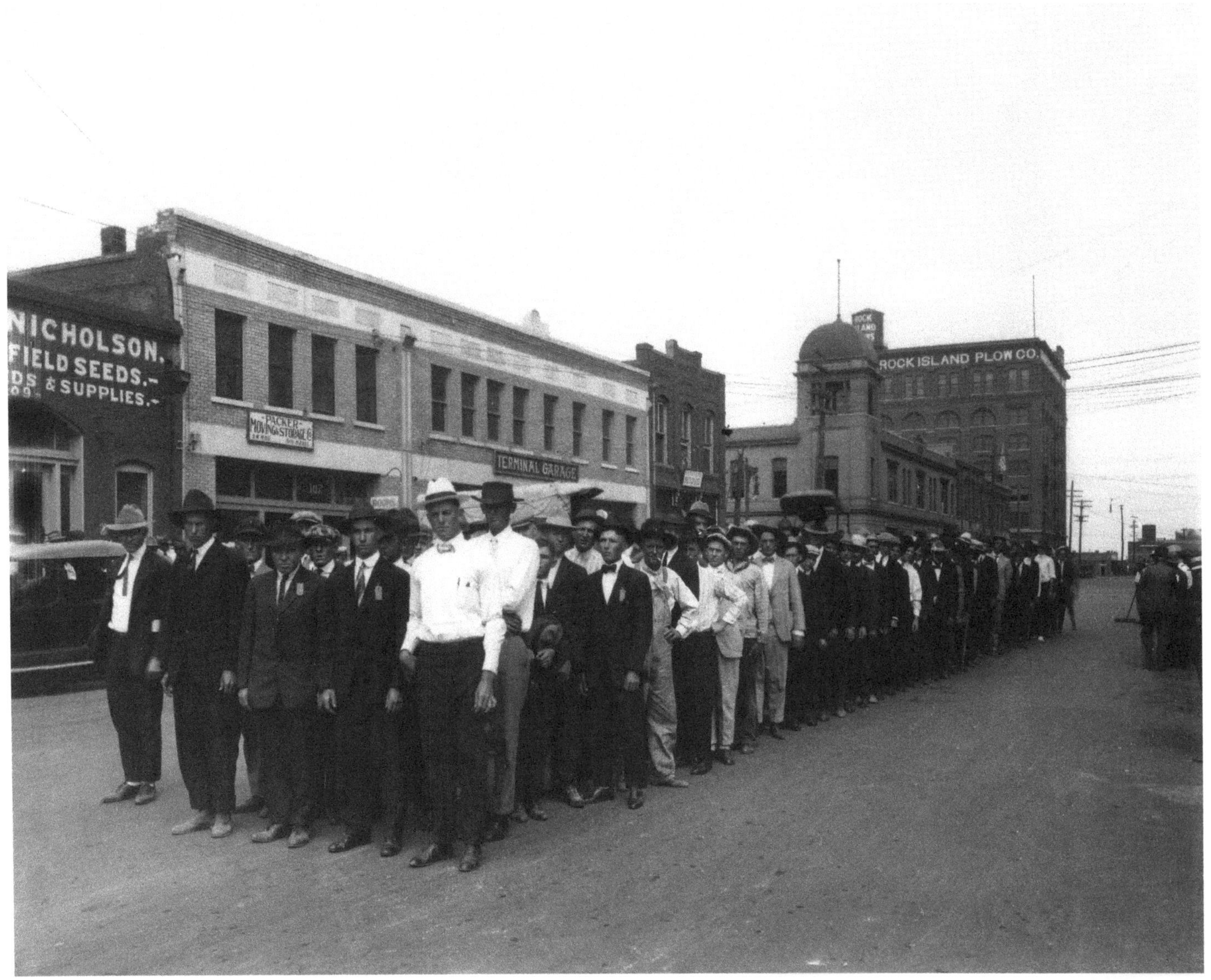

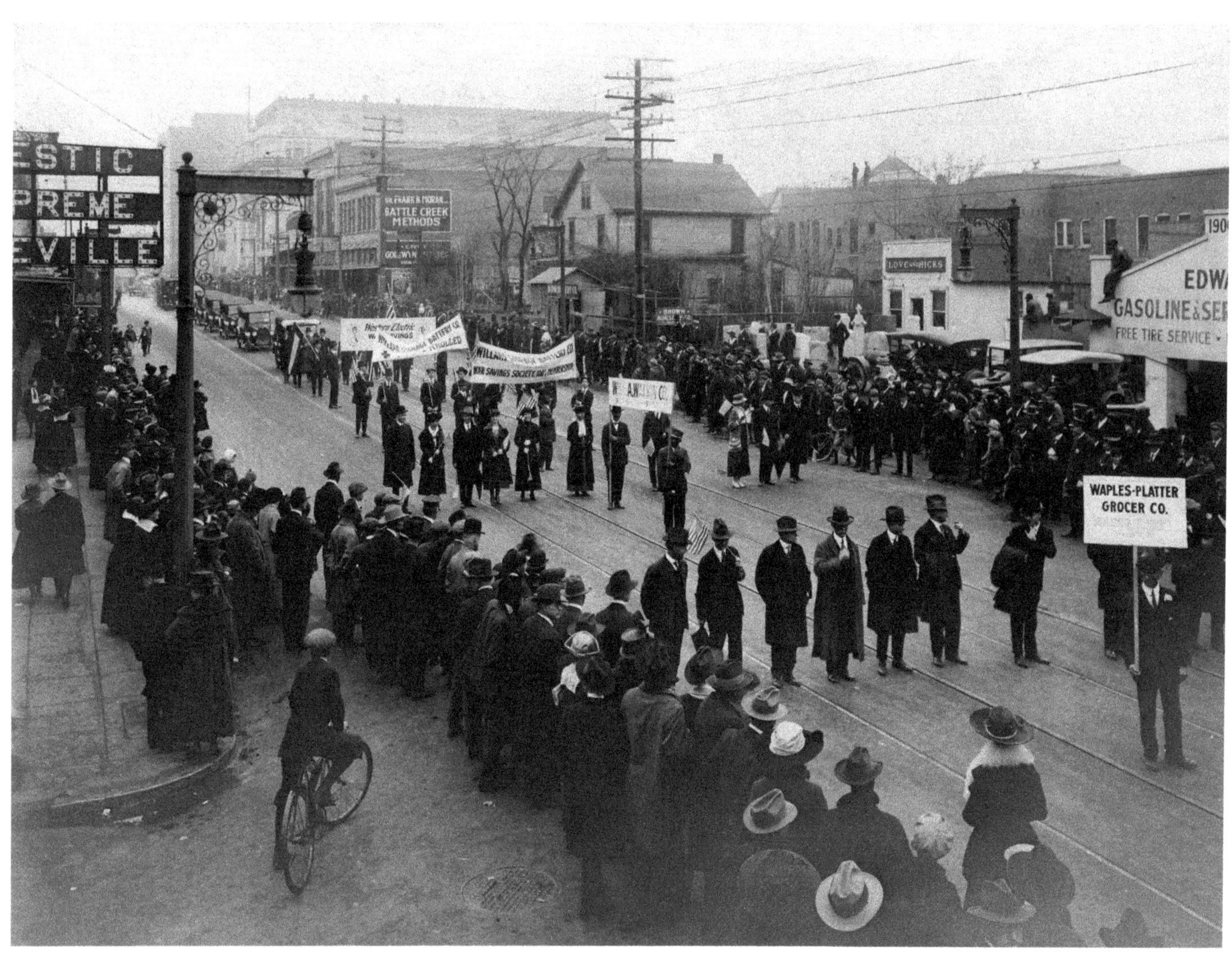

Communities throughout the nation observed Thrift Day during World War I. Marchers supported the purchase of savings bonds and thrift stamps to help the war effort.

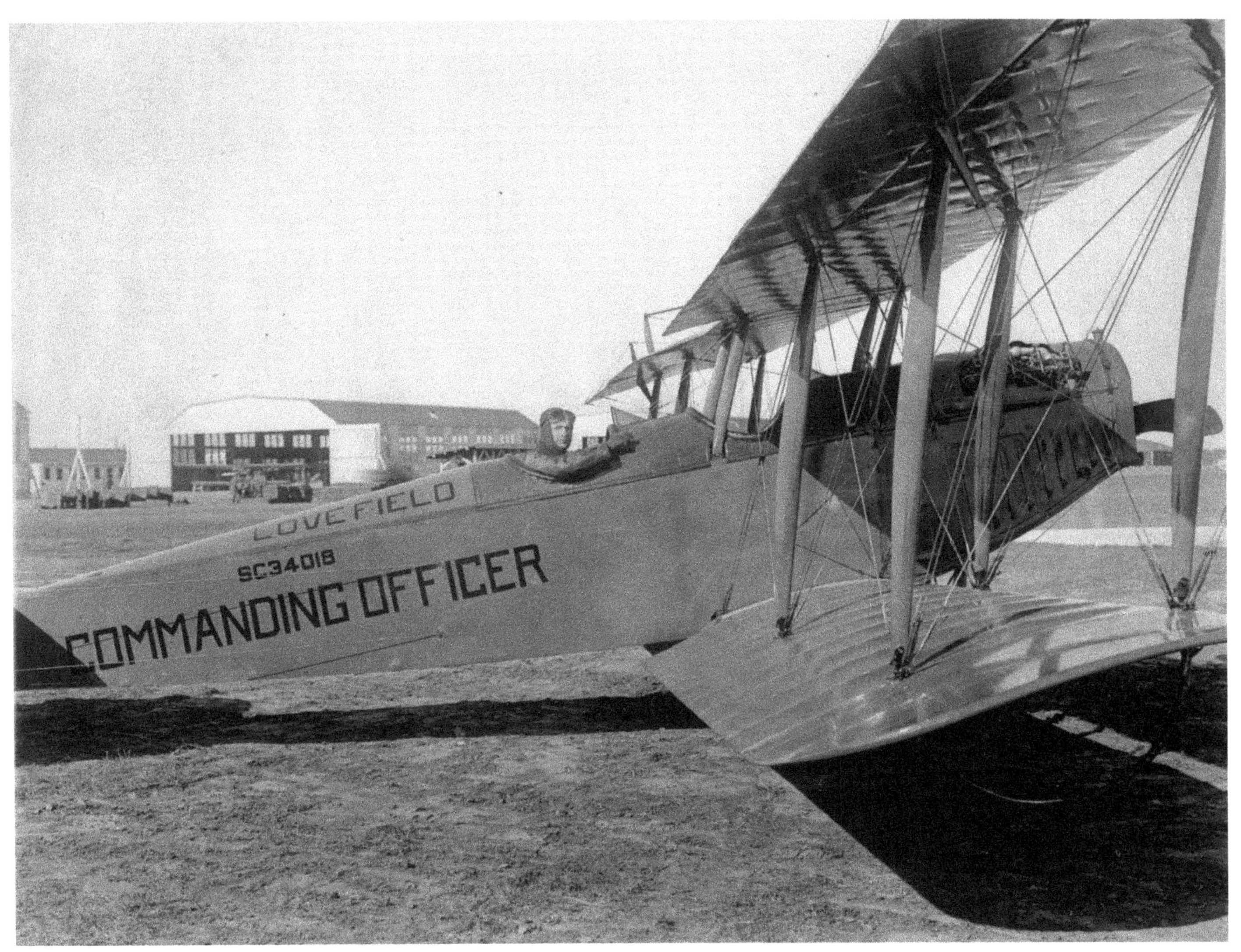

Love Field was built as a training base for army pilots during World War I. This is the commanding officer's plane.

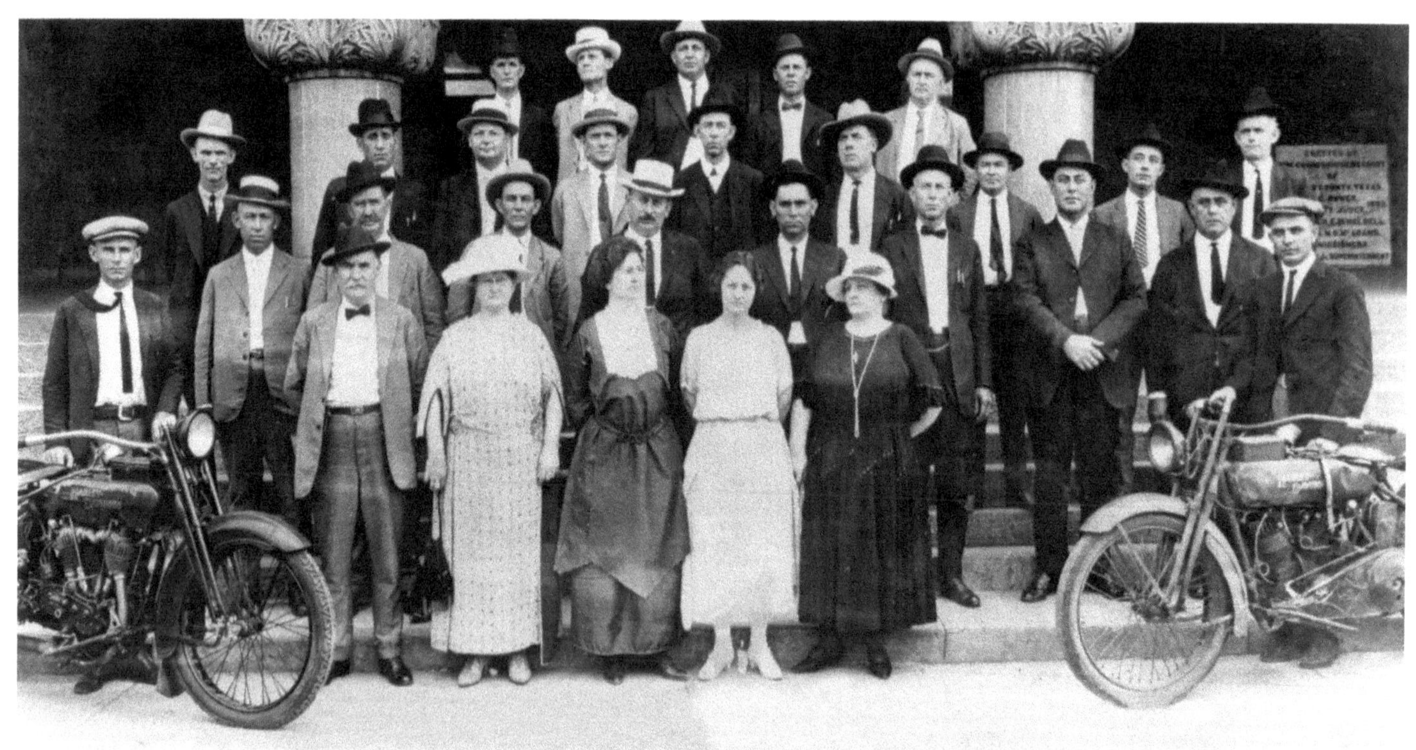

Dan Harston (second row with white hat and moustache) served as Dallas County Sheriff from 1919 to 1924, at a time when bootlegging was rampant.

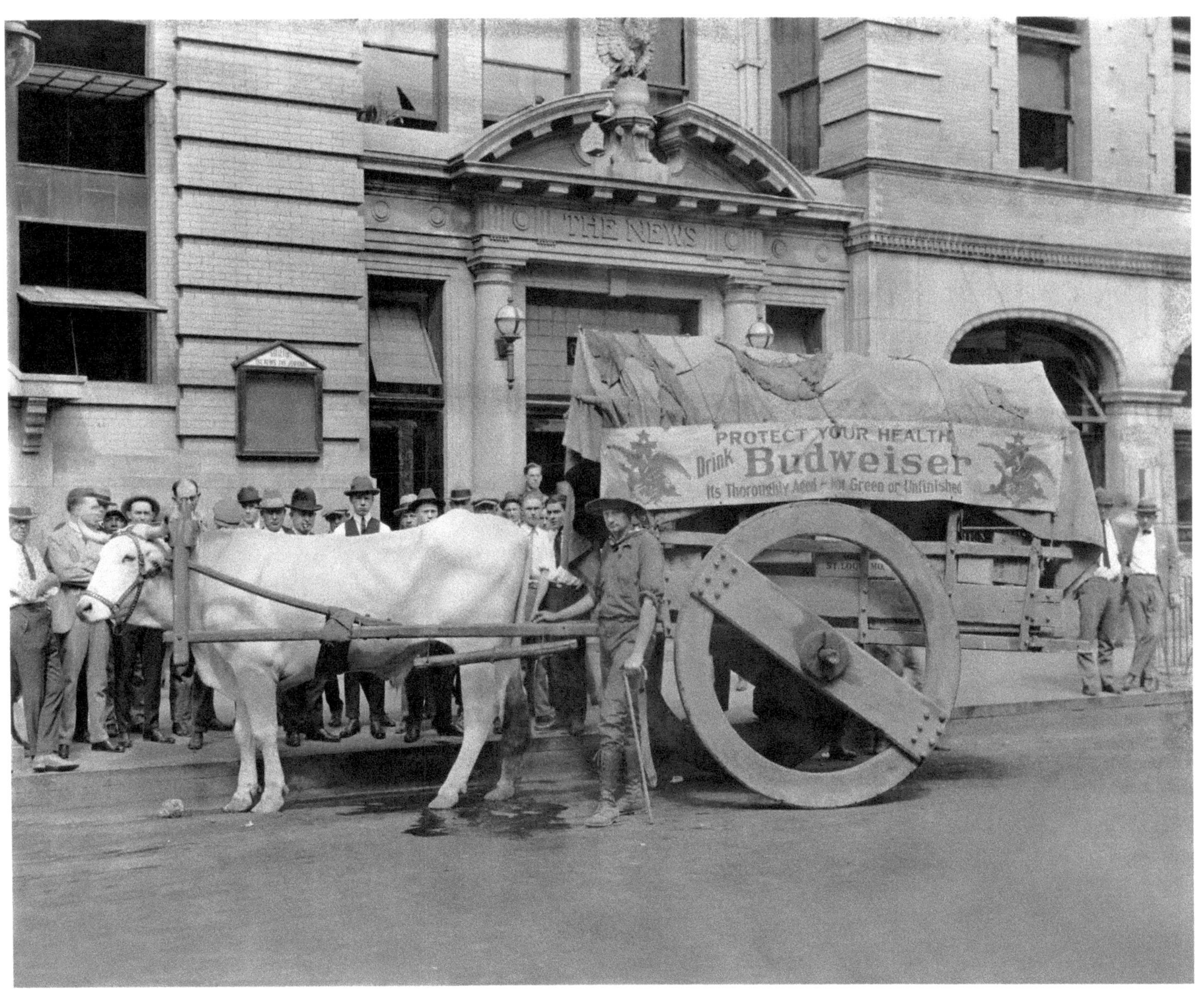

Why a Budweiser truck was parked in front of the *Dallas Morning News* building is unclear. But Dallas's large European immigrant population (especially Germans and Irish) supported numerous saloons and taverns.

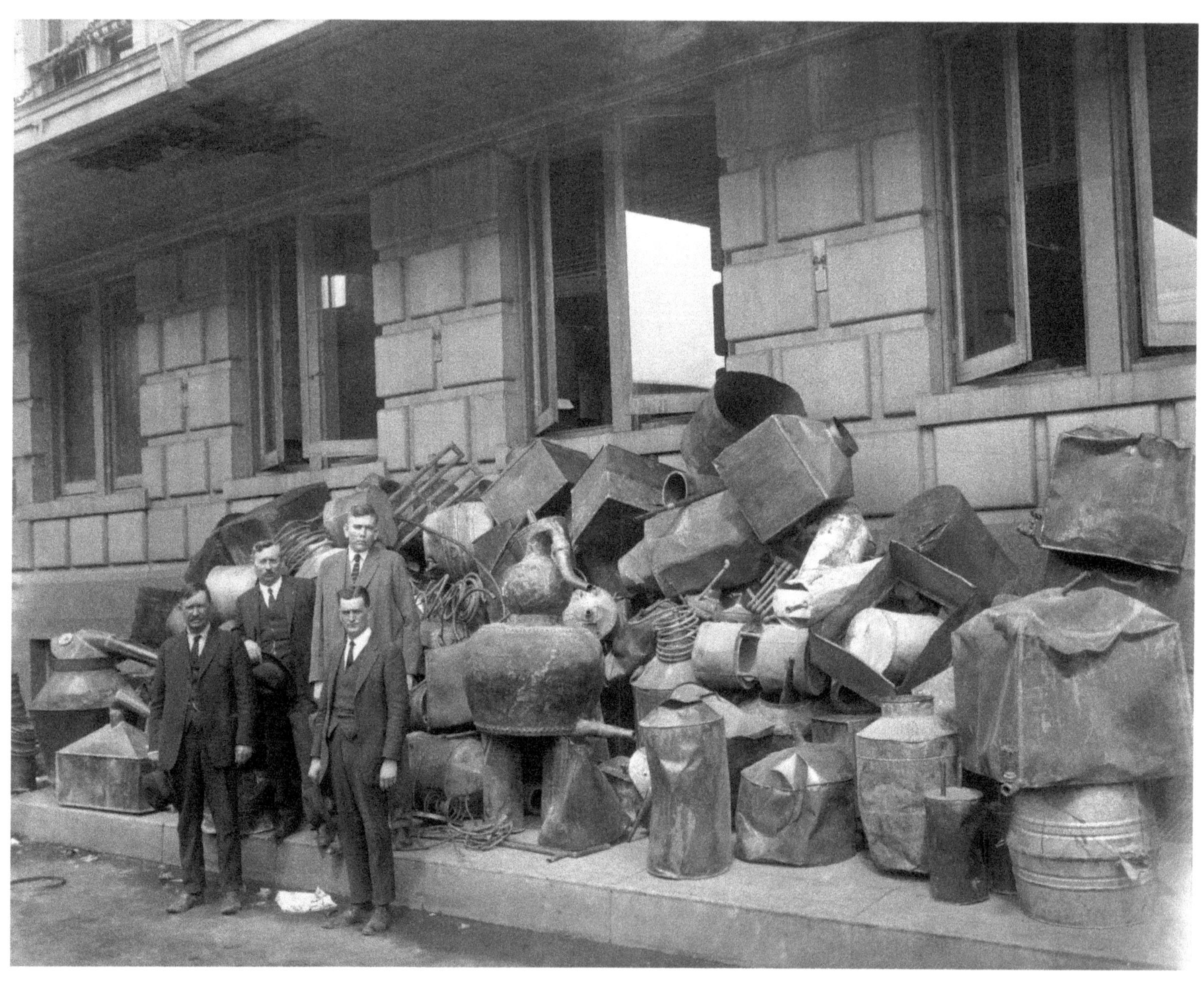

A national magazine described Dallas as "one of the wettest cities in the nation" during Prohibition, with more than its share of speakeasies and bootleg liquor. Sheriff Don Harston and his deputies were kept busy confiscating stills.

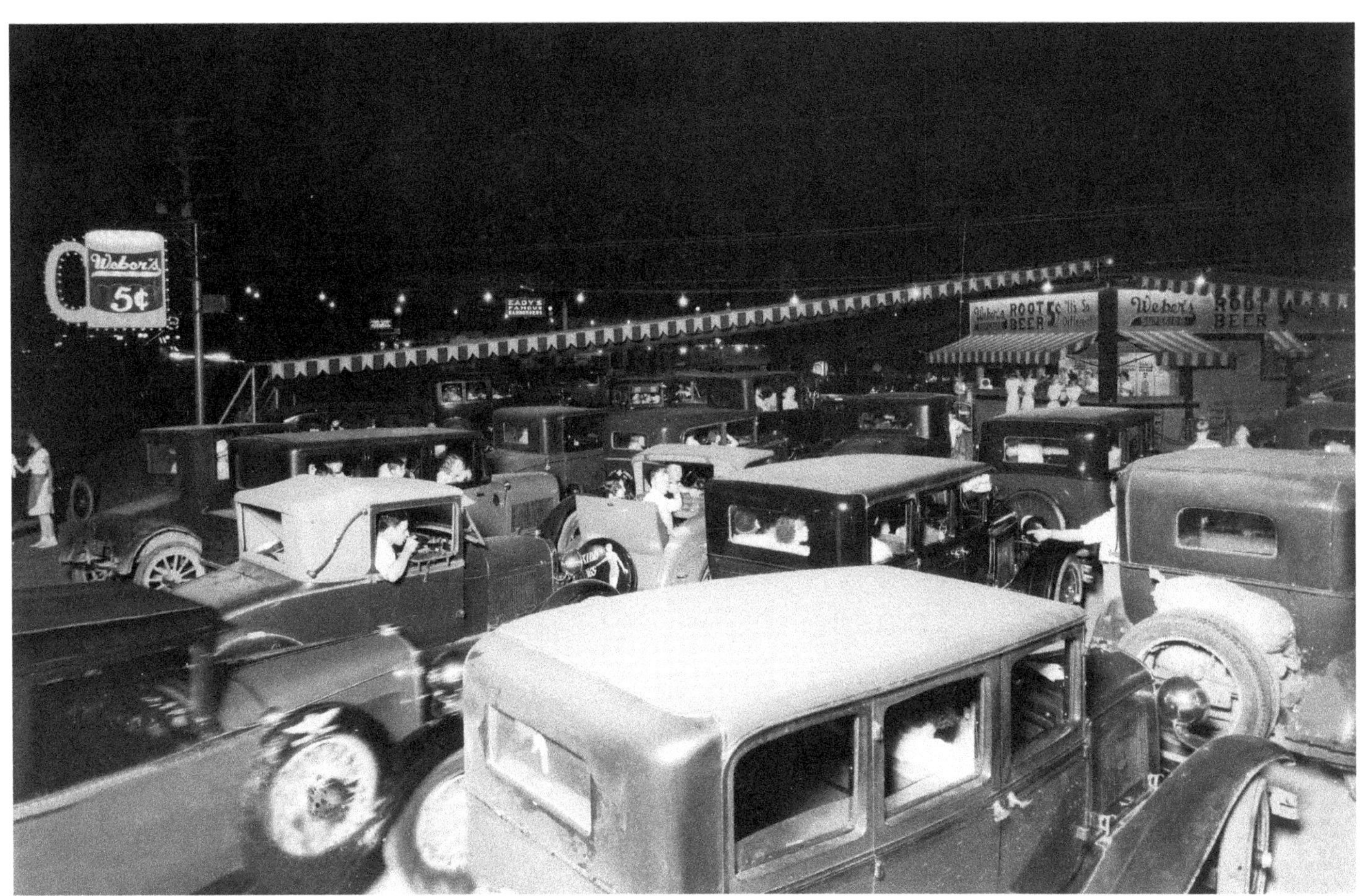

Weber's Root Beer stands, where aproned waitresses brought beverages to cars, were located throughout Dallas in the late 1920s and early 1930s. This one was at 1119 N. Zang in Oak Cliff.

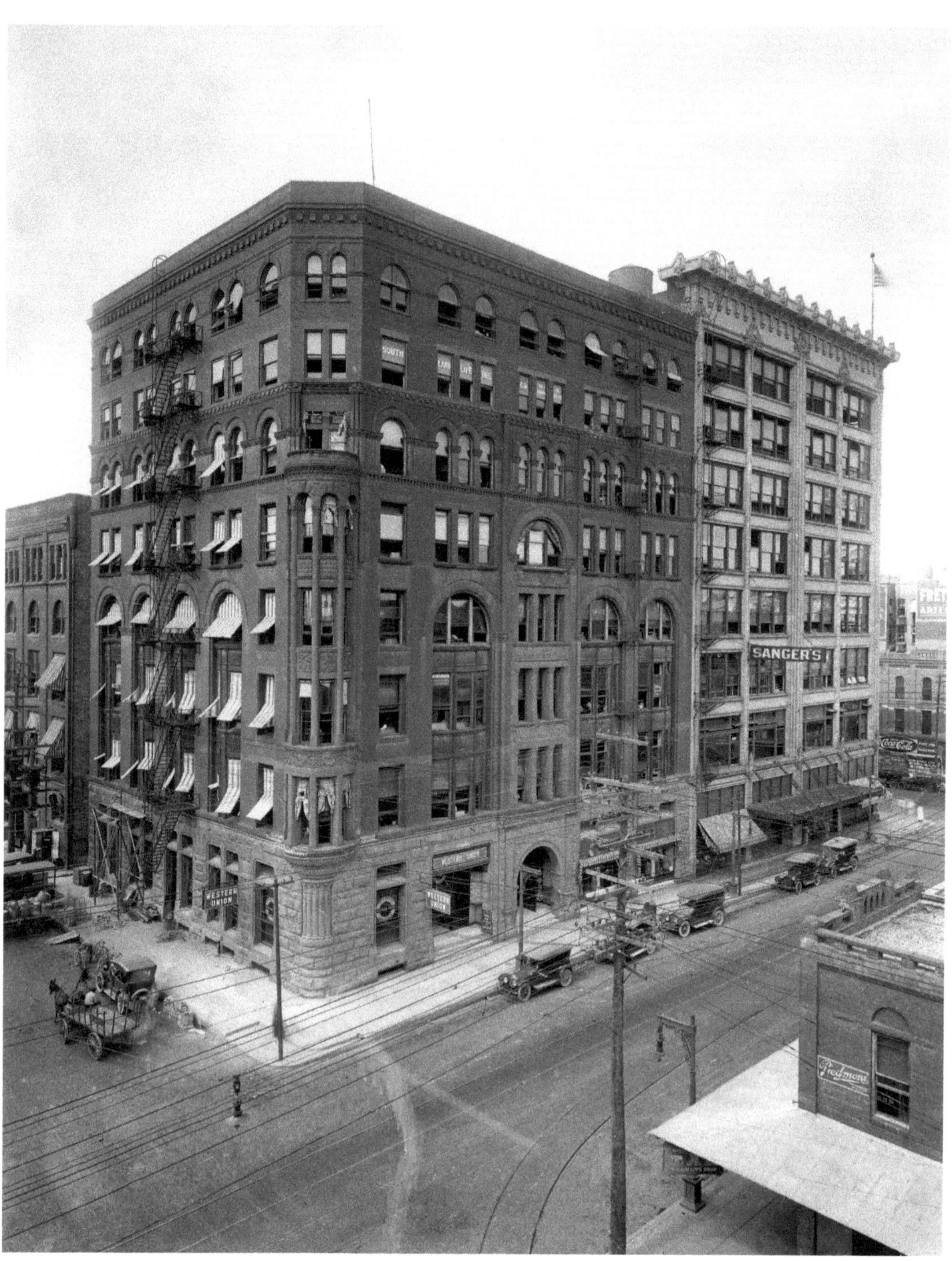

By the 1920s, Sangers Department Store encompassed the entire block bounded by Lamar, Main, and Commerce.

The first telephone in Dallas connected the fire station with the waterworks in 1880. Like the electric companies, telephone companies proliferated during the next few decades, before being consolidated into Southwestern Bell.

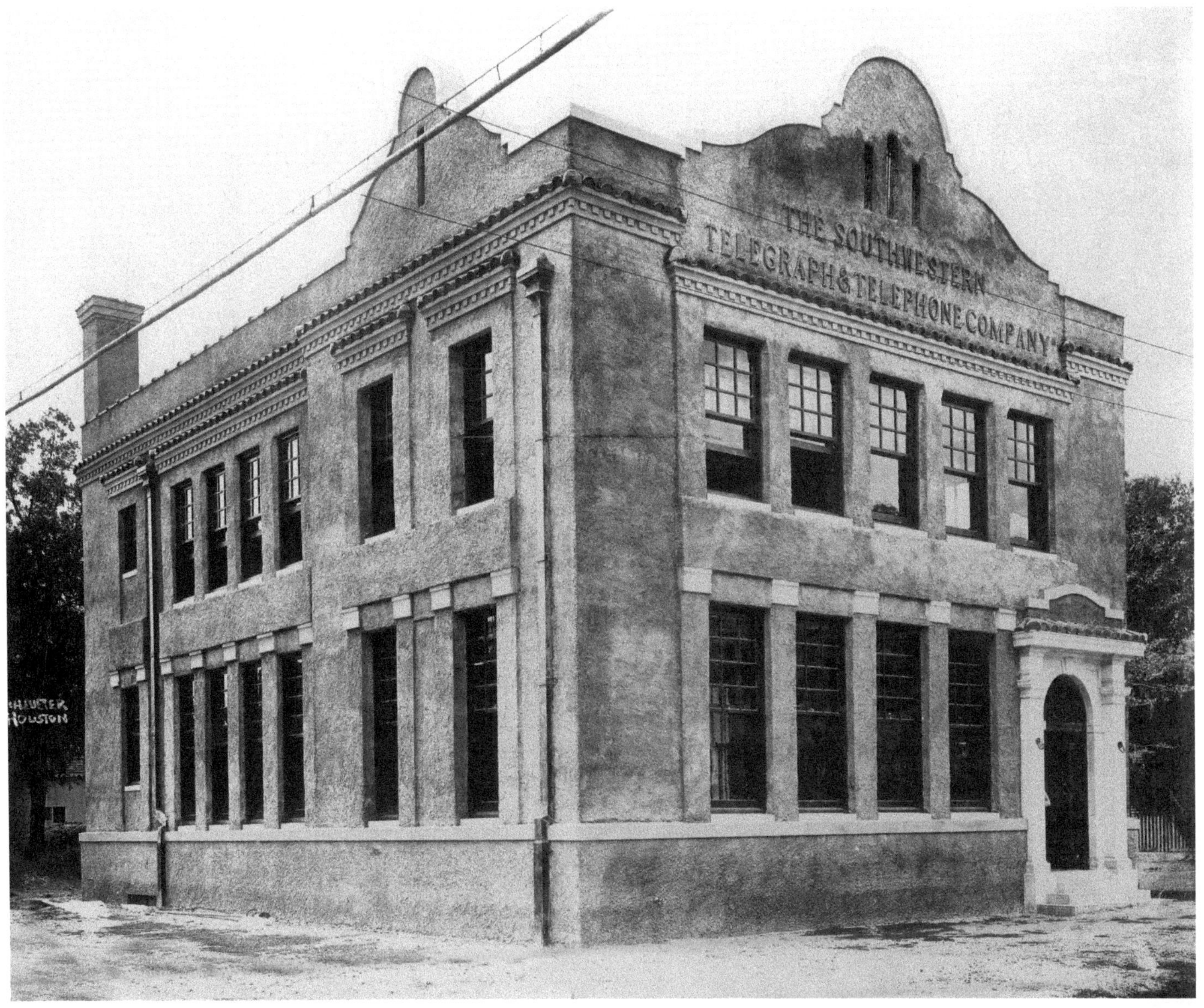

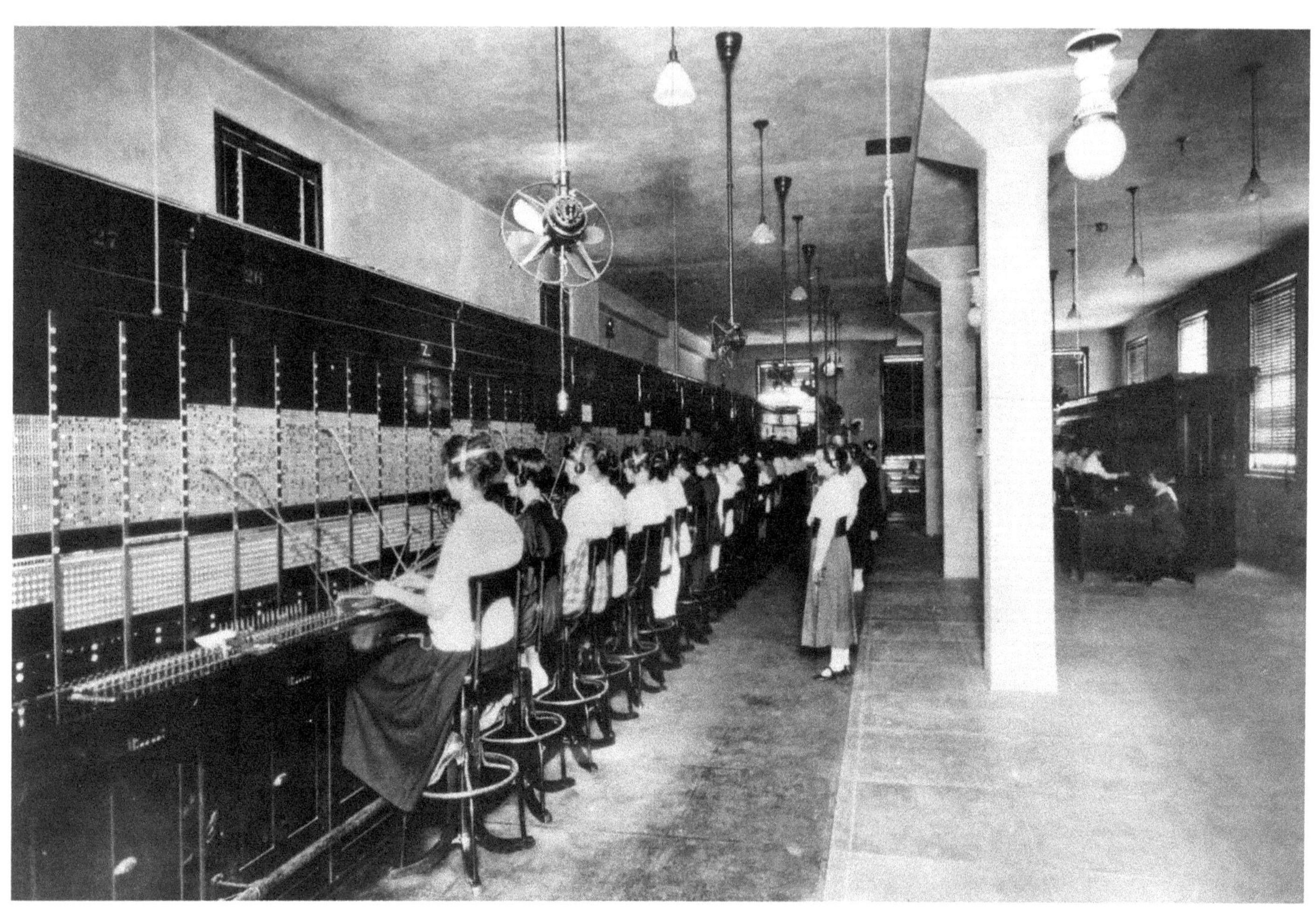

The development of the phone system created new jobs for women as switchboard operators. Early phone customers had to call "Central" to be connected to another number.

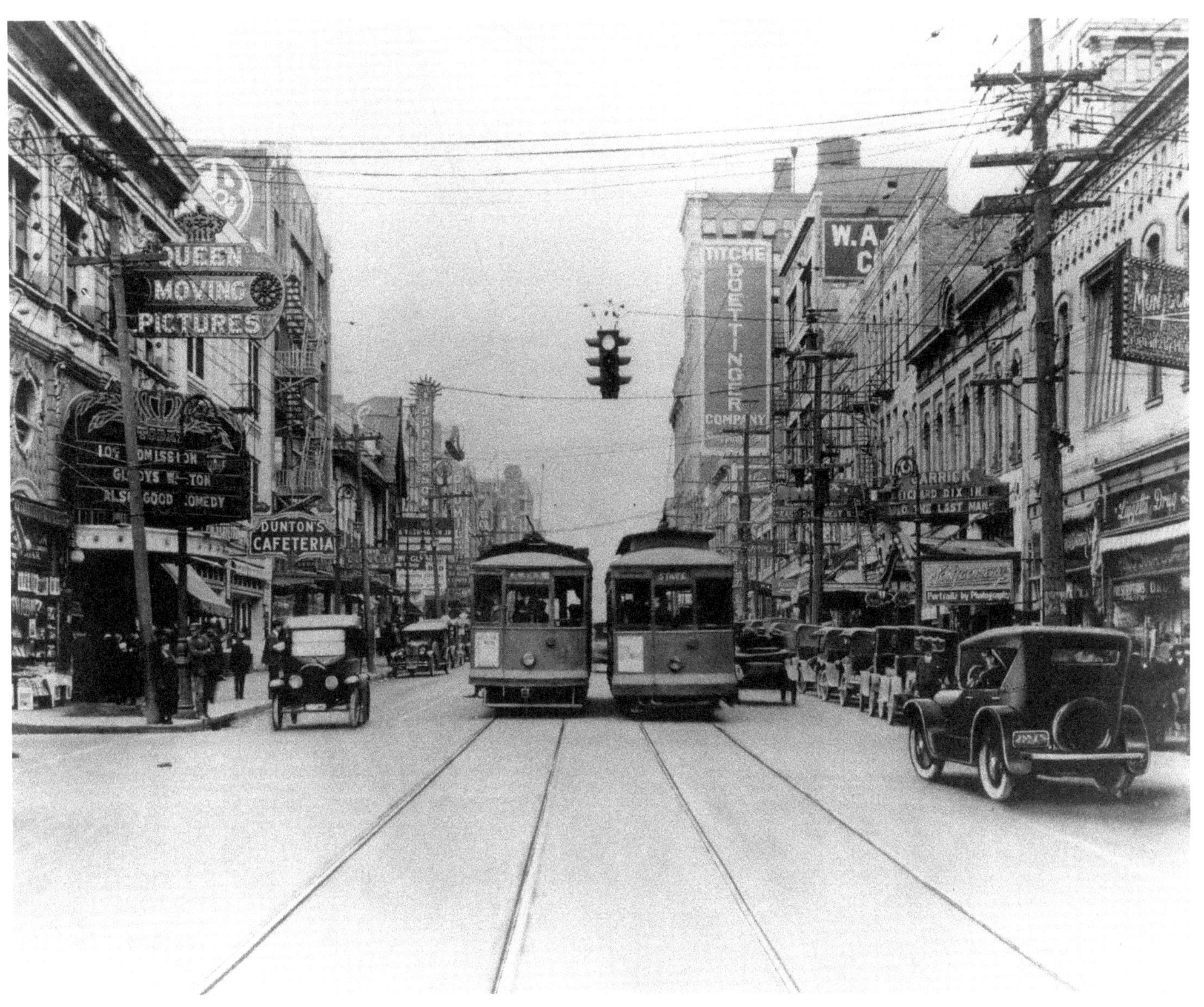

Elm Street was "Theater Row" in the 1920s, with dozens of vaudeville houses and moving picture palaces.

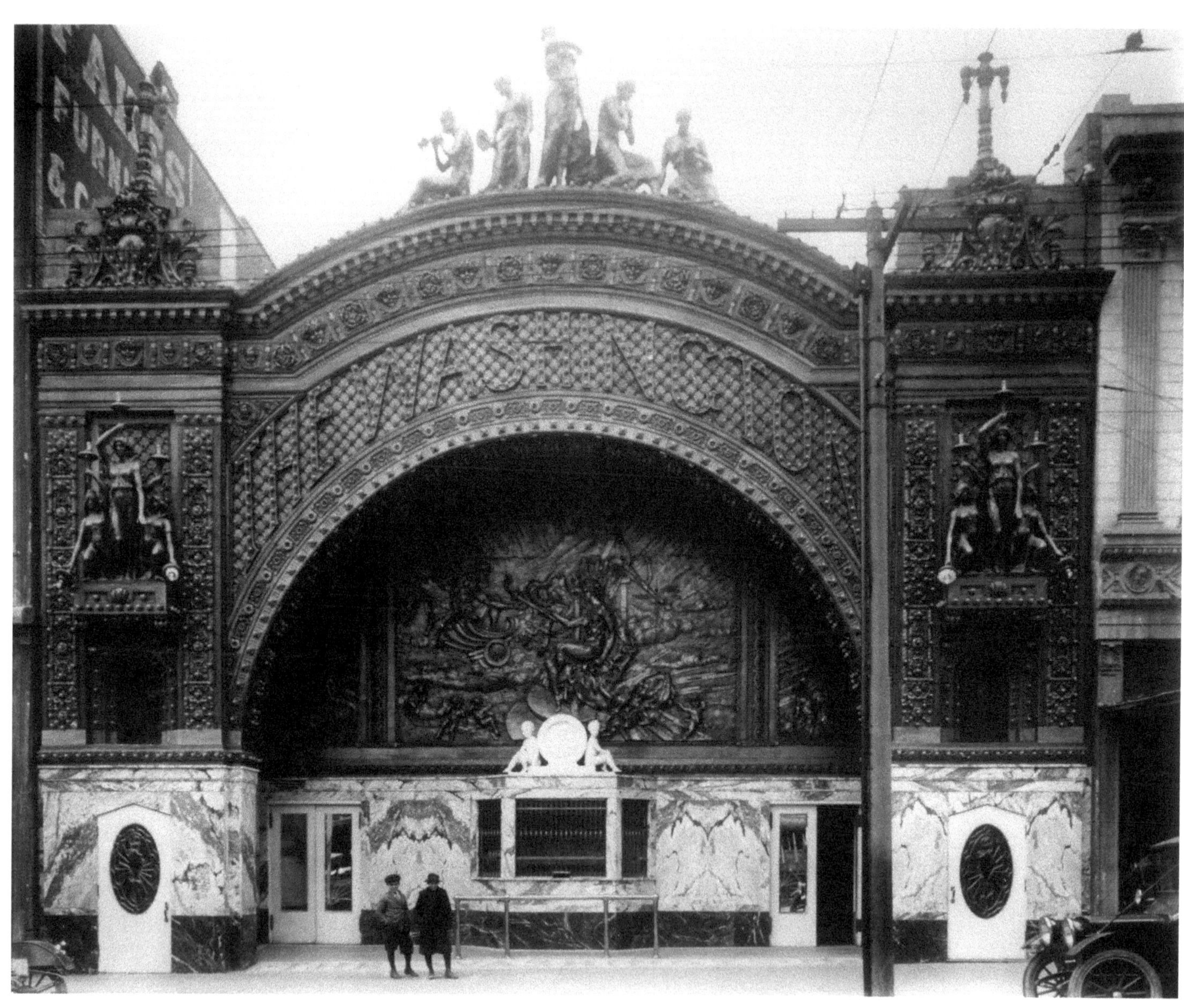

One of the most elaborate movie theaters on Elm, the Washington, featured films by Charlie Chaplin and Tom Mix, accompanied by organ music.

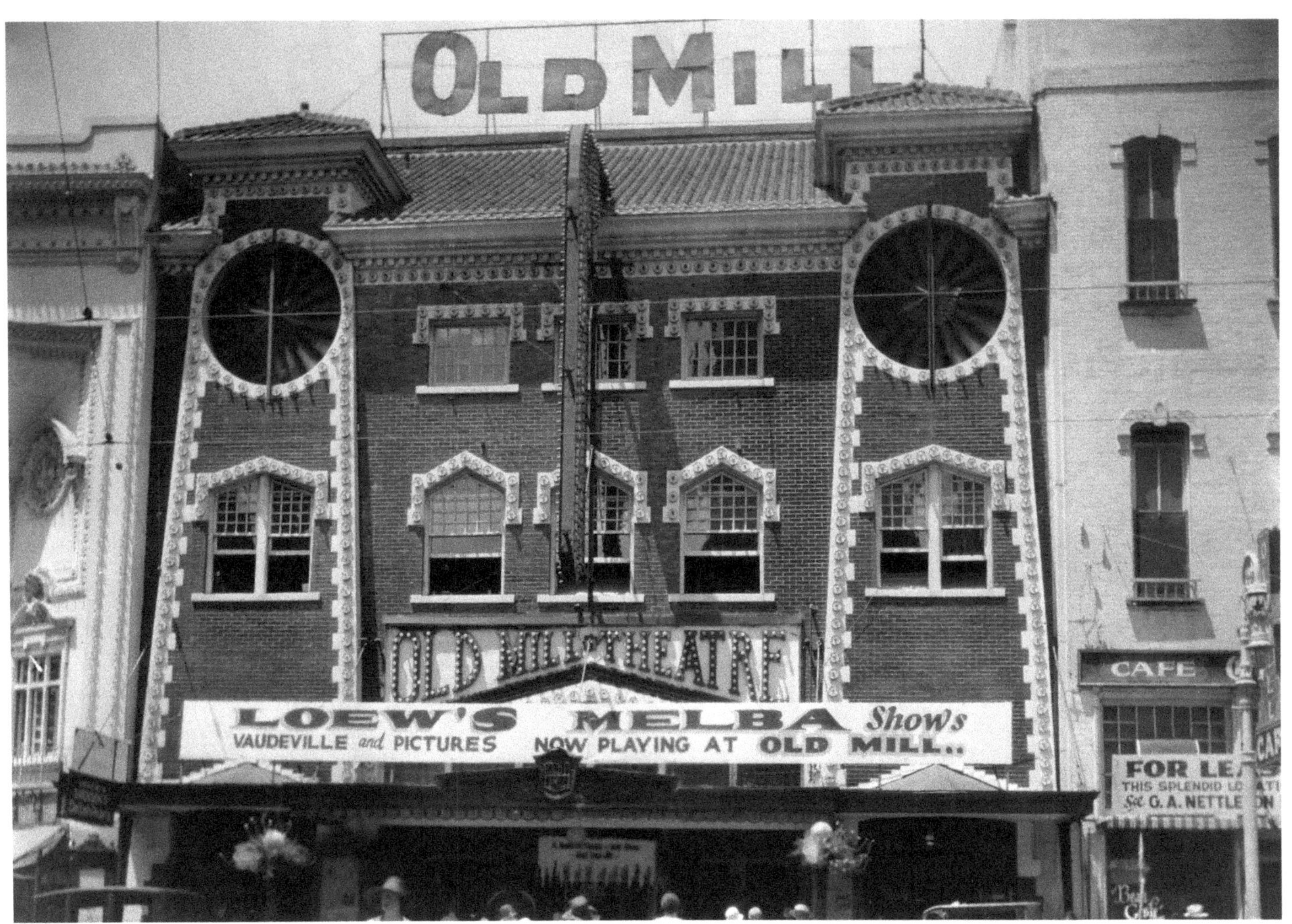

Yet another of the Elm Street theaters was the Old Mill, with a pseudo-Dutch facade.

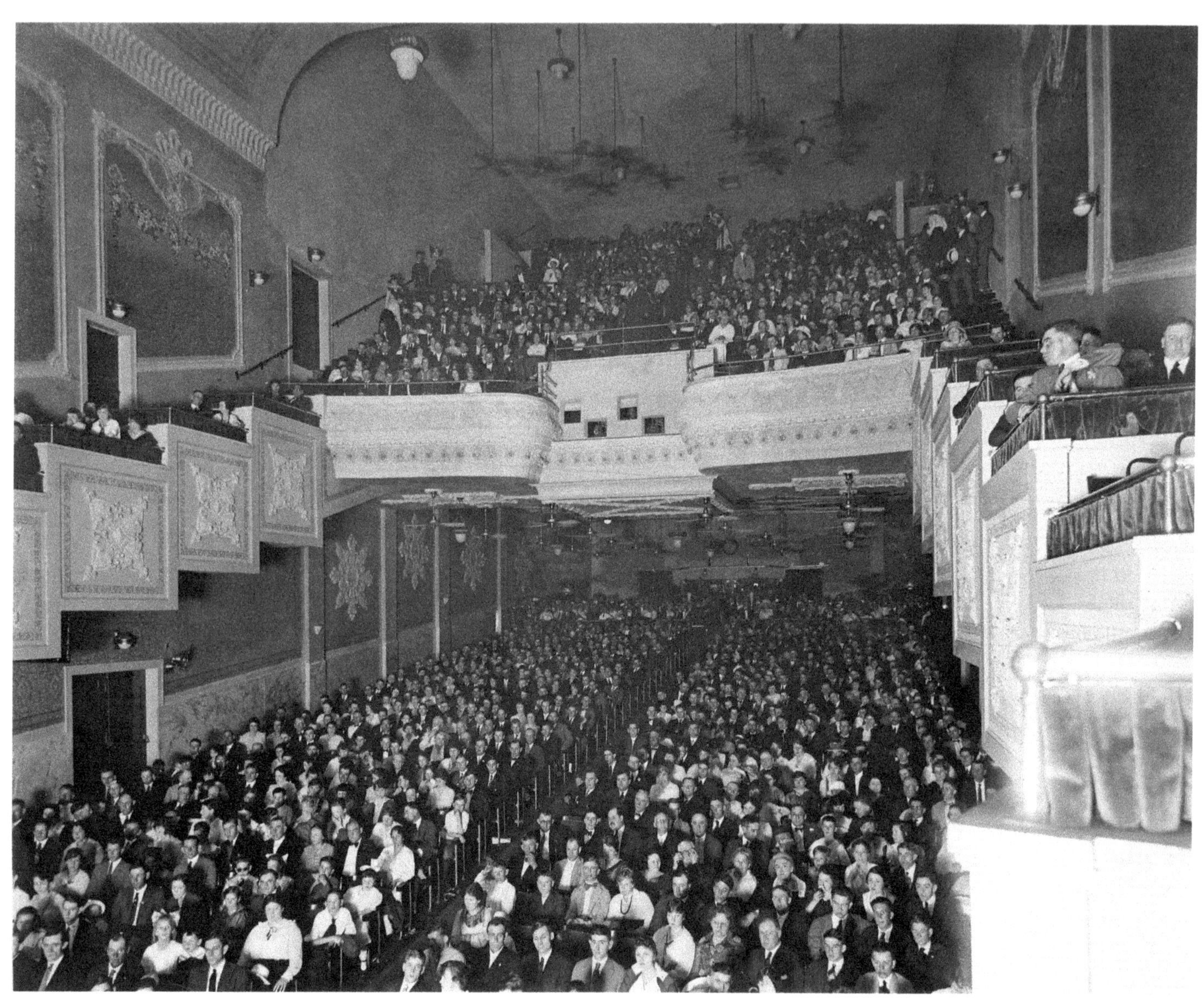

A packed audience inside the Old Mill waits for the show to begin.

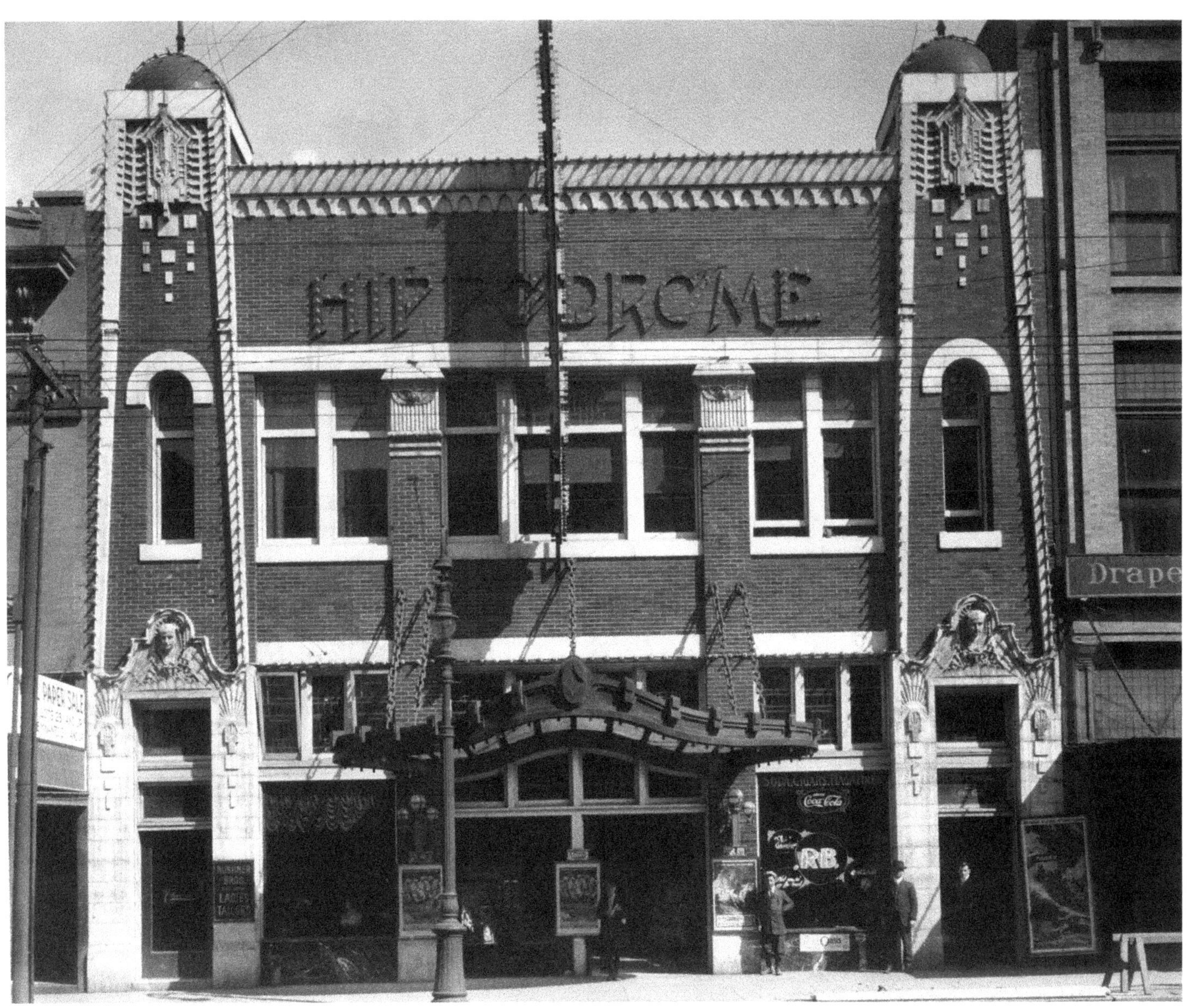

The Hippodrome featured an Egyptian Revival design. It survived until 1960.

After World War I, the Dallas Chamber of Commerce maintained Love Field as a private operation, renting space to flyer schools and airplane-related businesses. This aircraft was a Martin NBS-1, powered by two 420-hp Liberty engines.

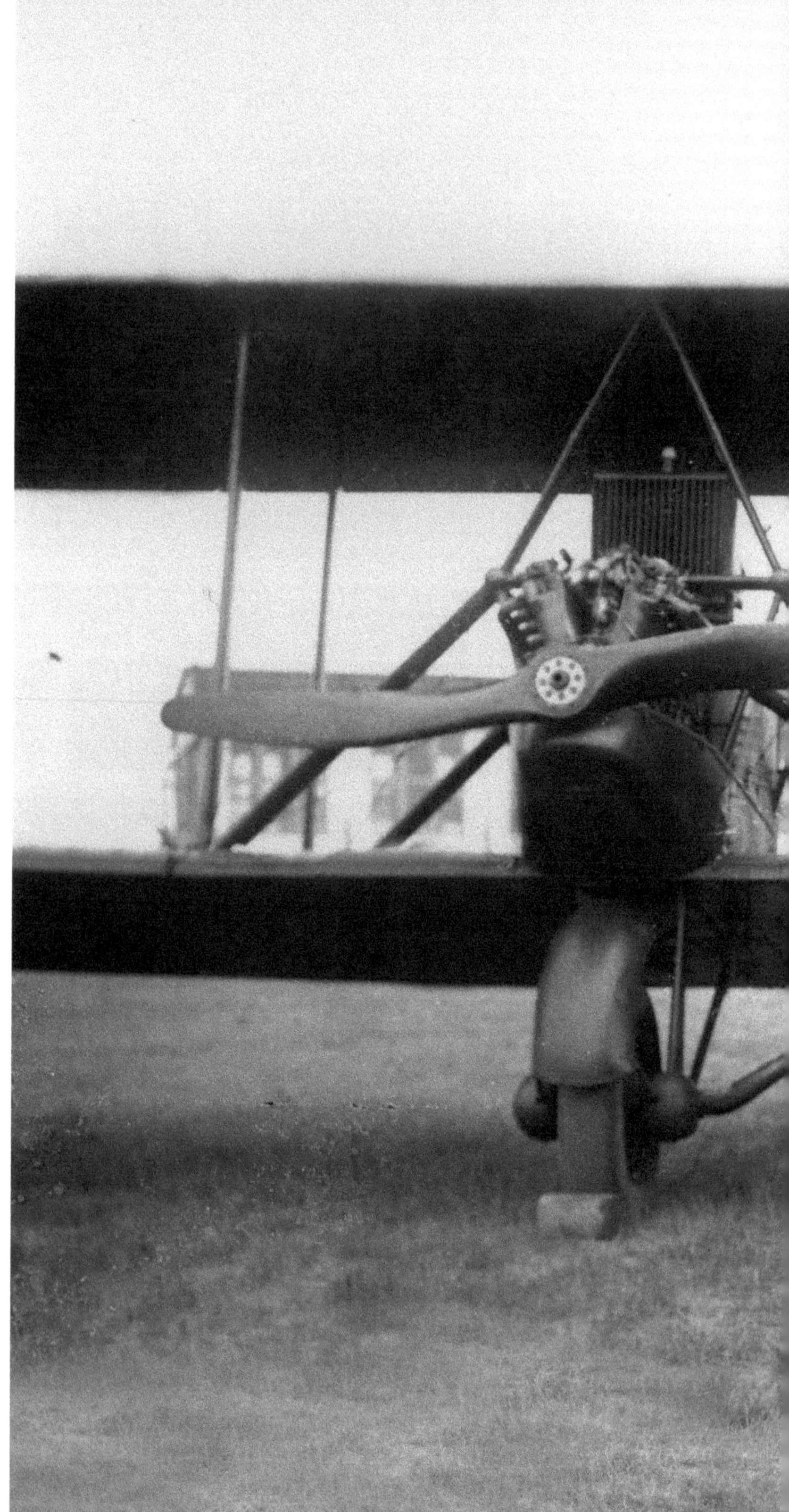

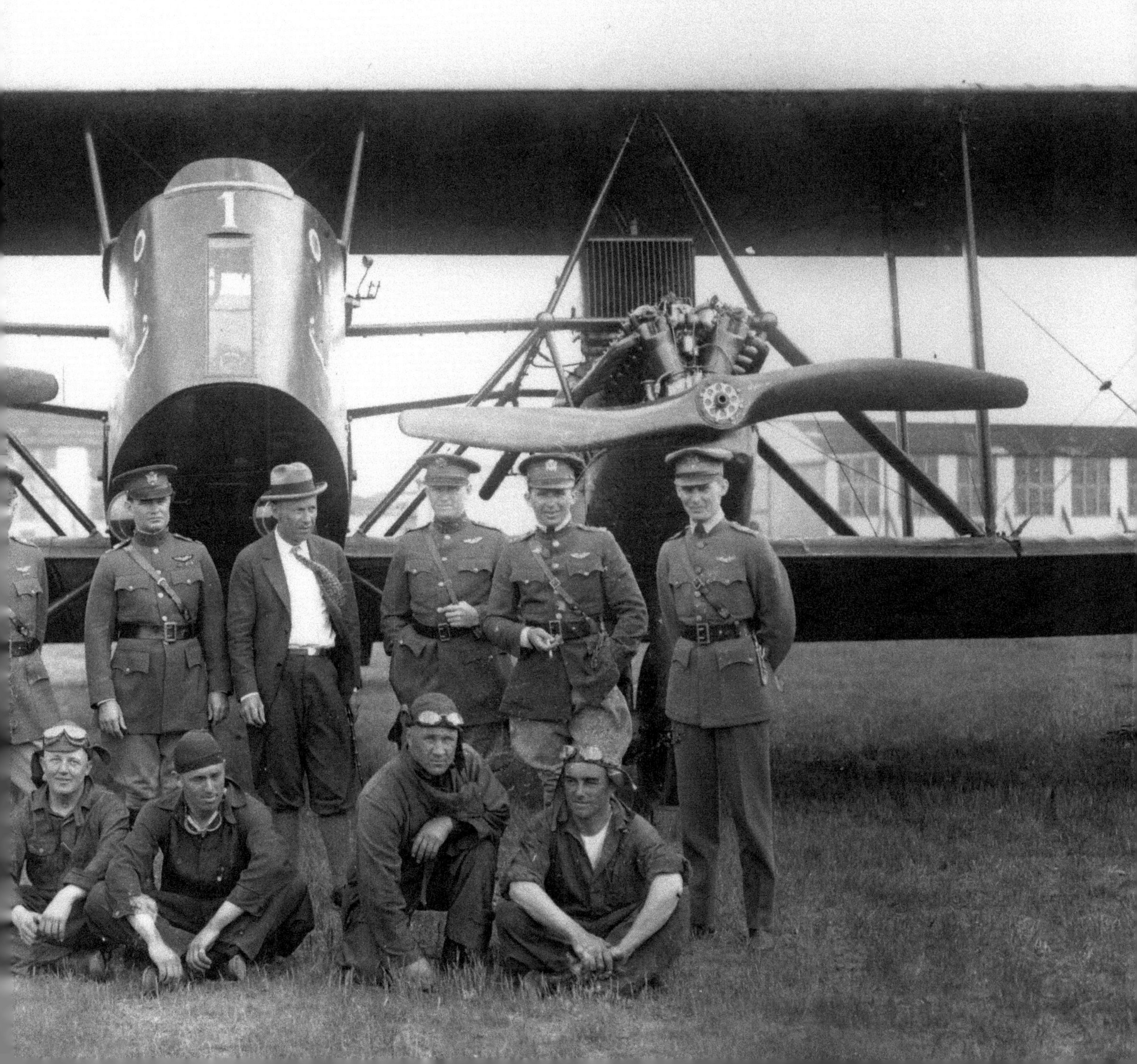
1

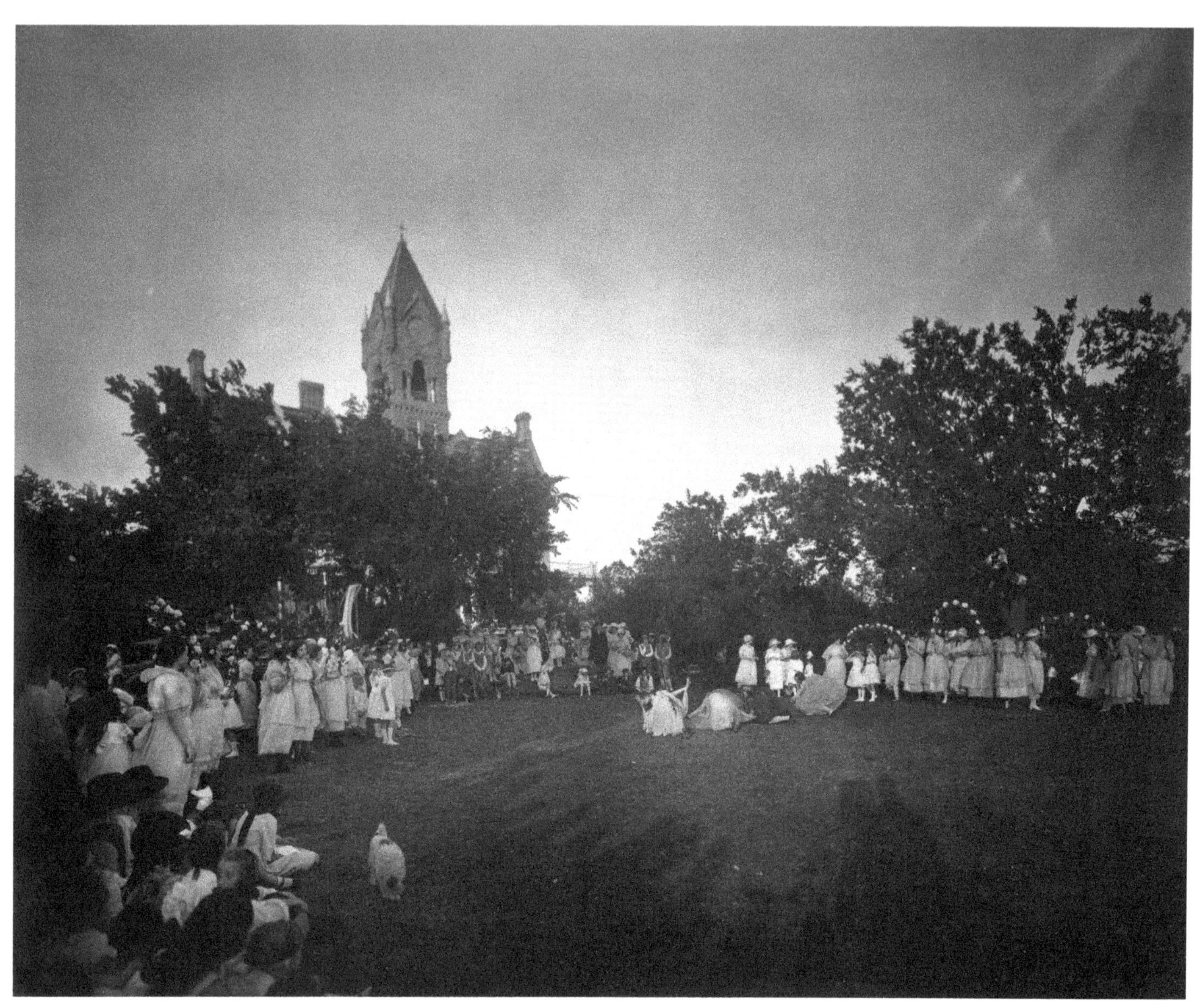

Students at St. Mary's College presented a May Day pageant in the 1920s. From 1889 until 1930, this Episcopal school provided higher education for young women.

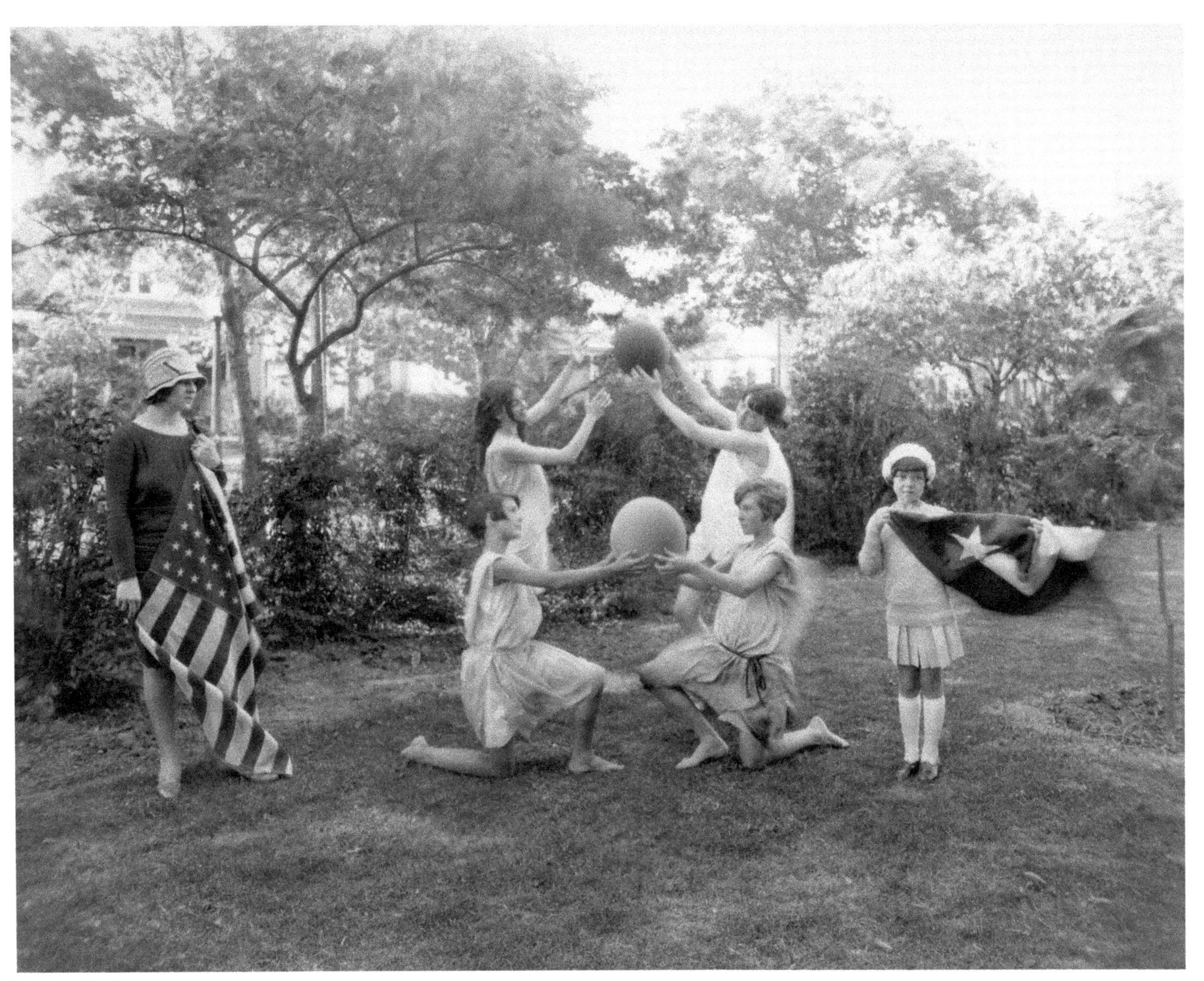

Several girls commemorate July 4 in the 1920s.

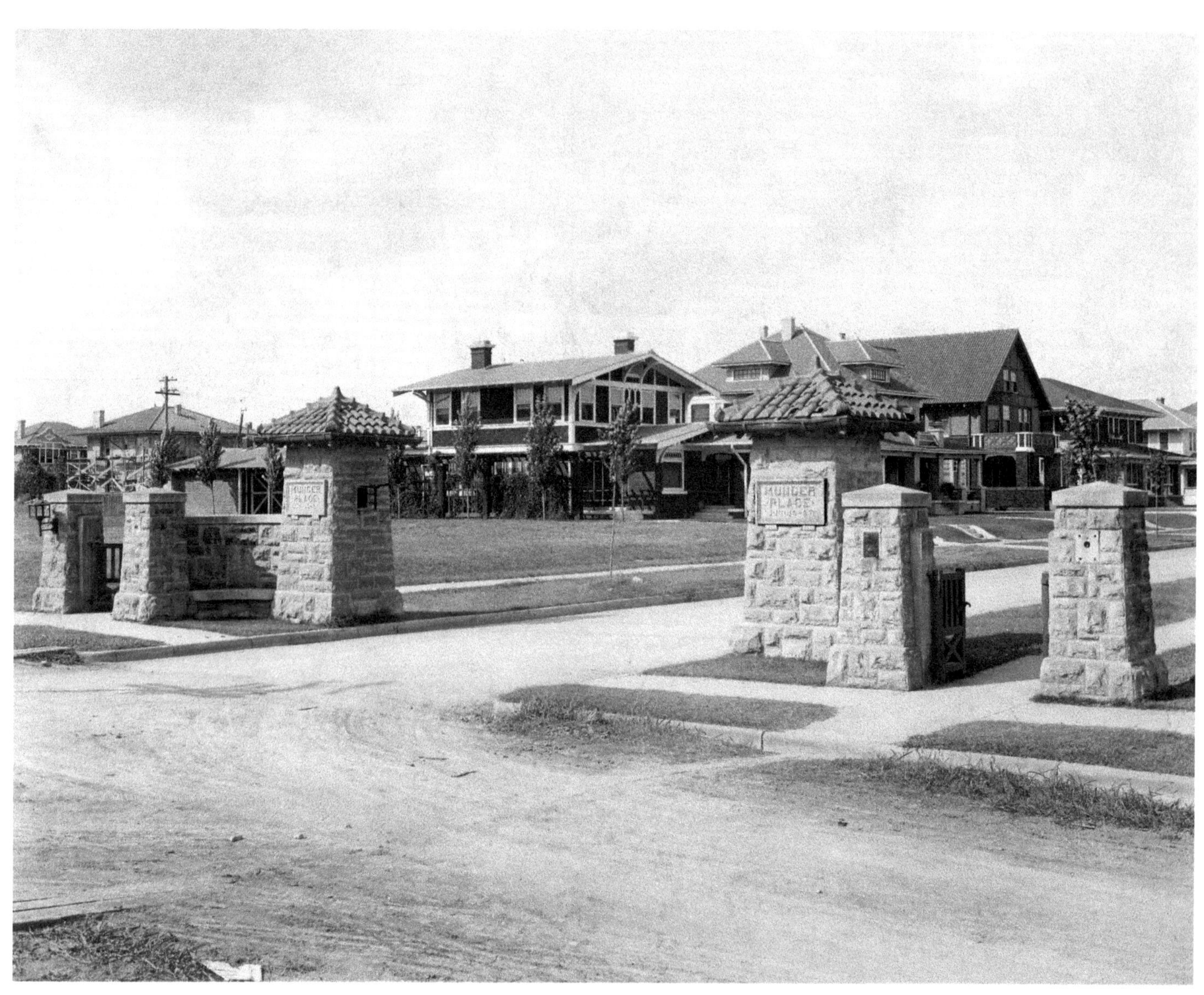

Beginning in 1905, cotton gin magnate Robert Munger began developing Dallas's first deed-restricted residential neighborhood in East Dallas, complete with utilities and paved streets. By the 1920s, Munger Place was filled with gracious arts-and-crafts homes.

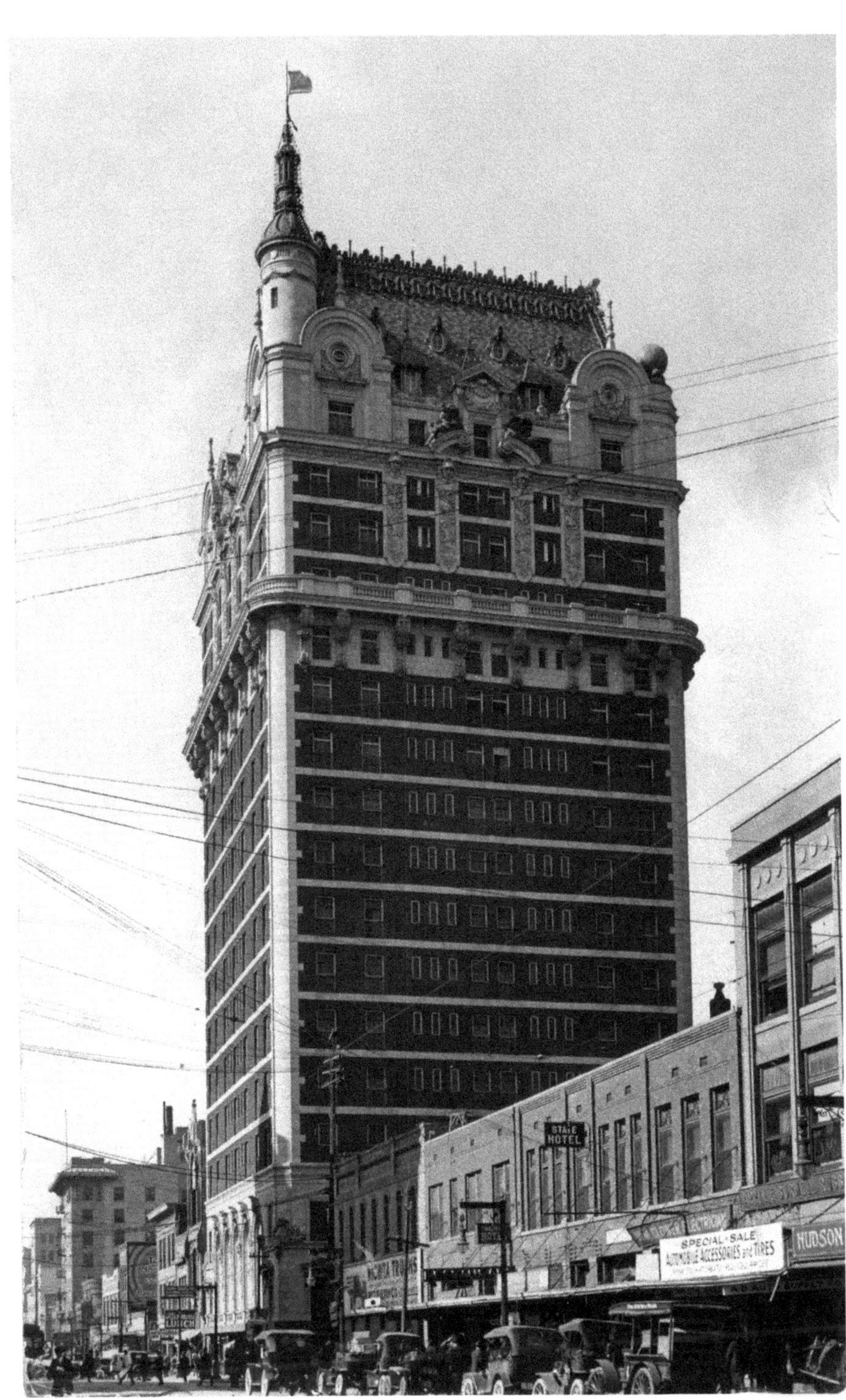

Before the construction of the Magnolia Building in 1922, the 21-story Adolphus Hotel soared over its stretch of Commerce Street.

Erected in 1924, the Baker Hotel blocked the south end of Akard Street, creating an urban canyon.

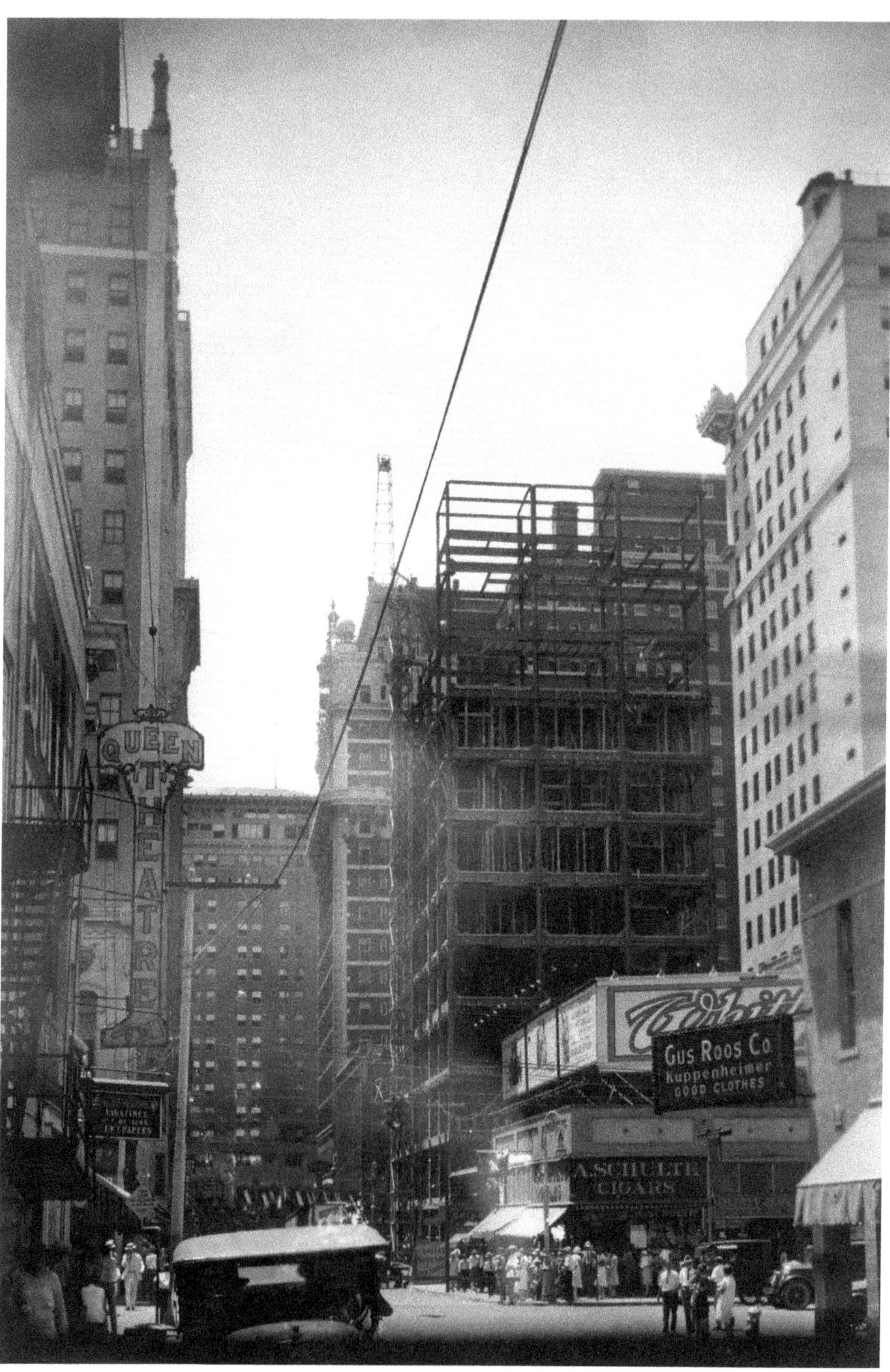

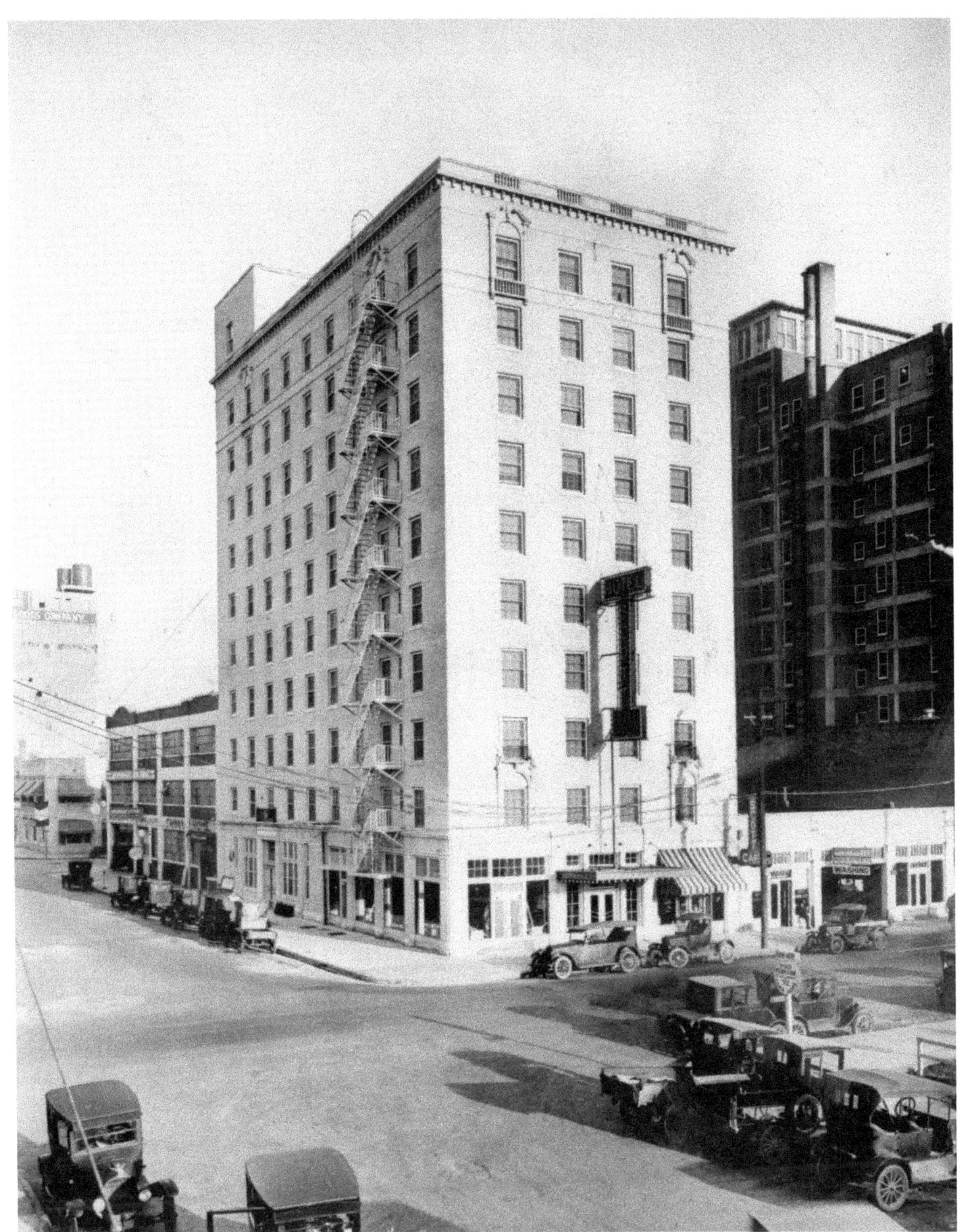

By World War I, Dallas was becoming a big convention city, and hotels sprouted up throughout downtown. The Scott Hotel was at the southeast corner of Houston and Jackson streets. It still stands as the Hotel Lawrence.

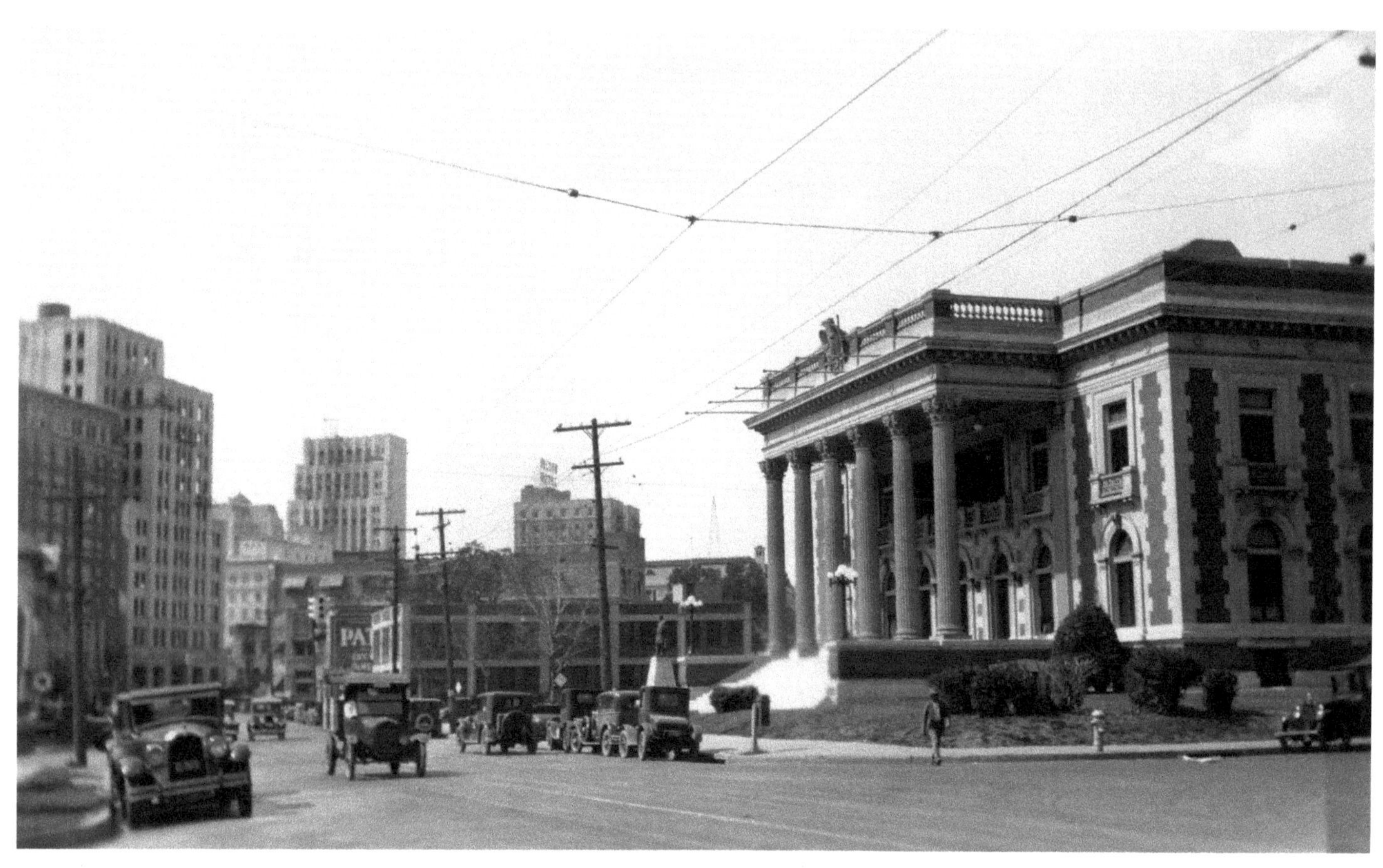

This 1920s view north along Harwood shows the Scottish Rite Cathedral on the right and the new Dallas Gas Company building on the left.

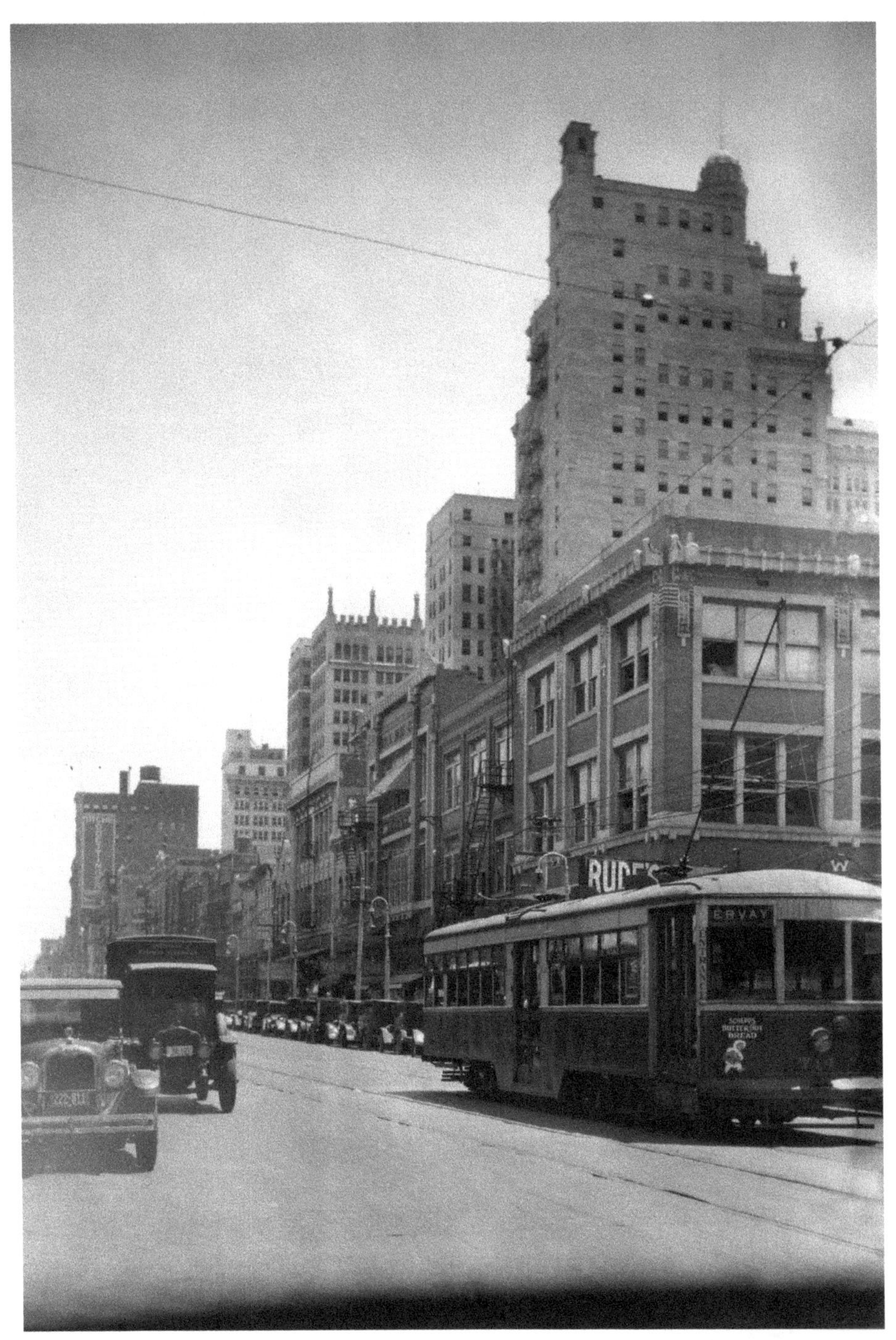

This view east on Elm in 1927 shows the street still mostly lined with old commercial structures, while the Main Street "skyscrapers" loom behind.

This view looking west on Main from Ervay shows Neiman Marcus on the left, before a 1929 remodeling added two floors and an annex.

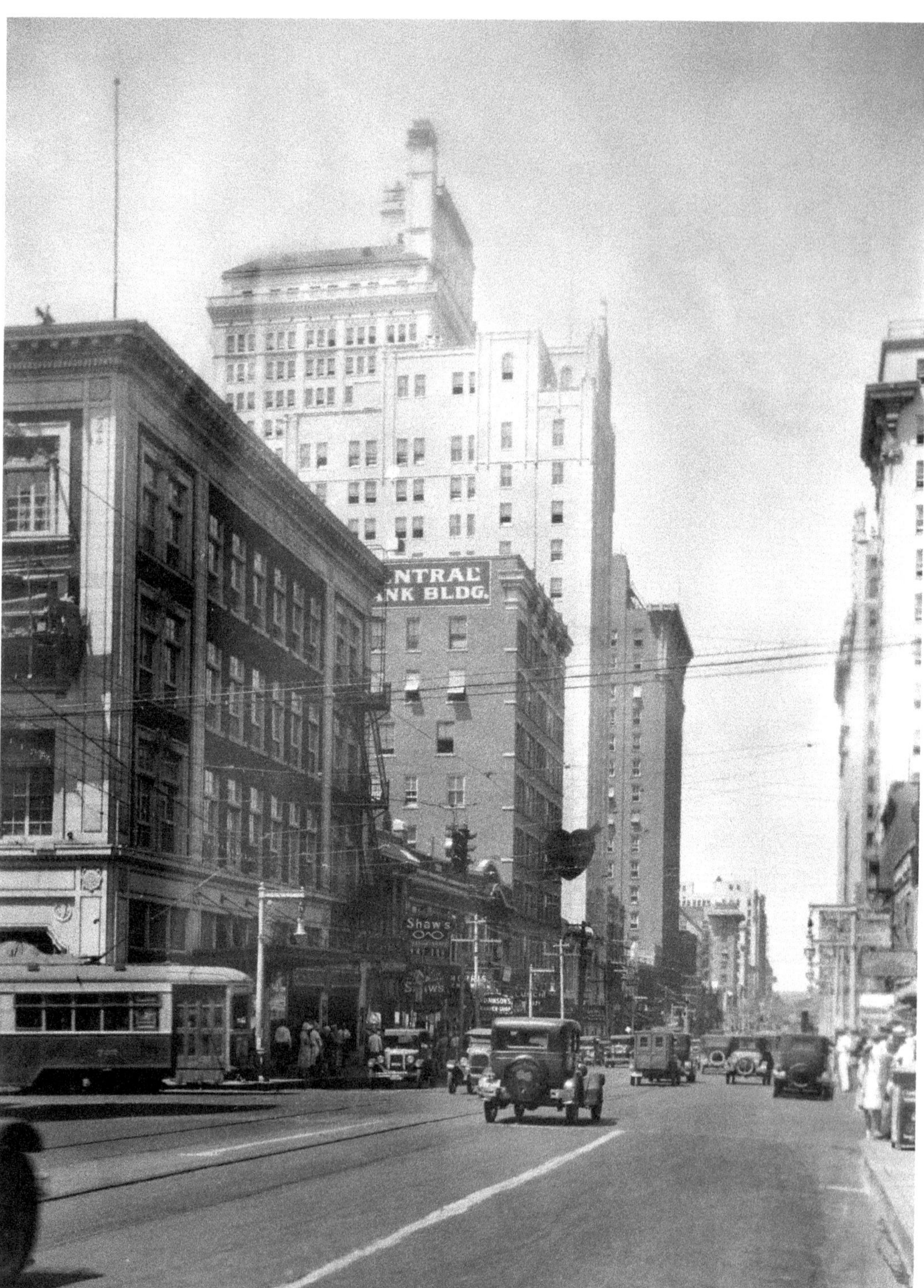

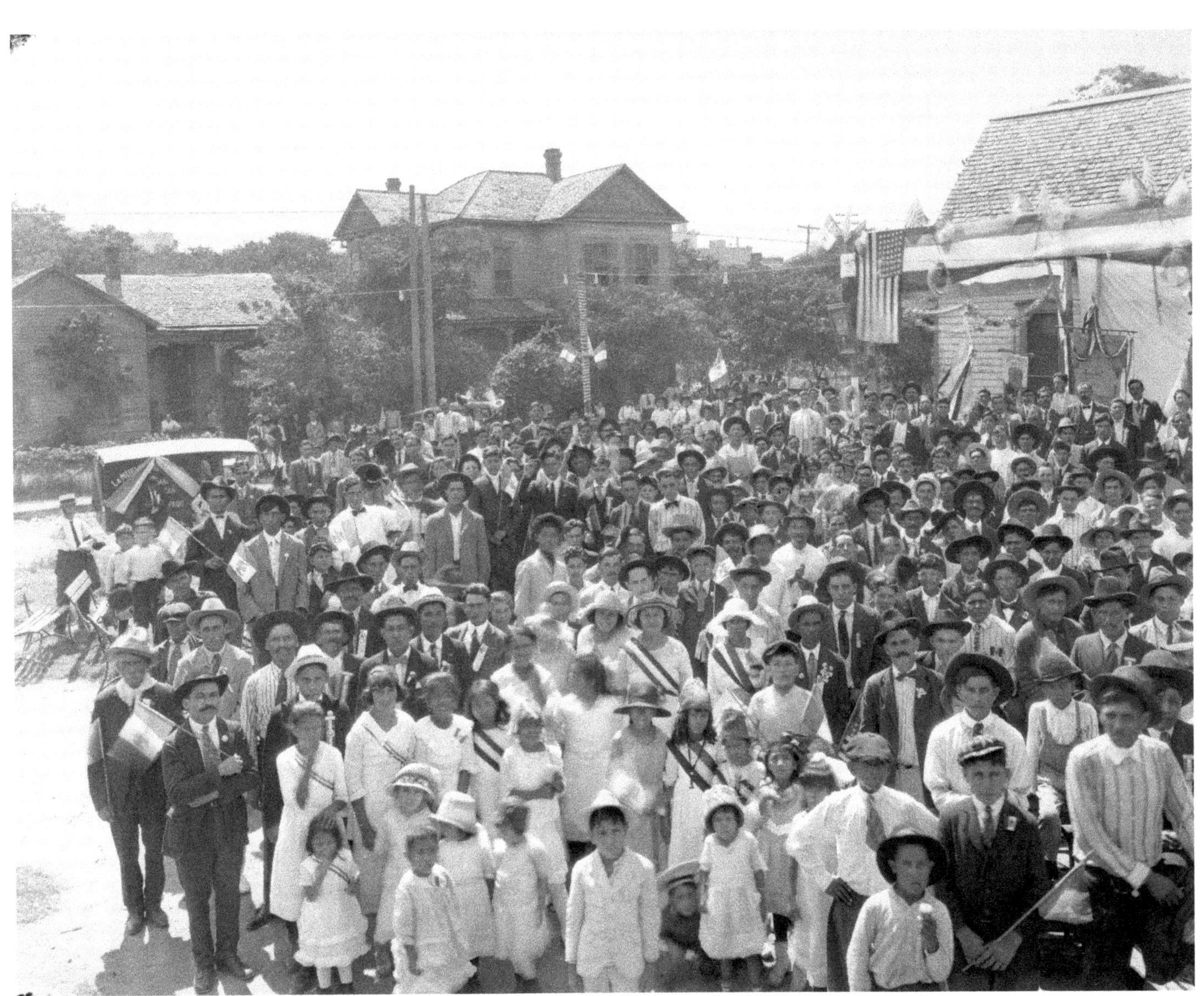

The Mexican American population of Dallas soared in the 1910s, as refugees fled revolution at home. The annual Cinco de Mayo celebration was a major event in the "Little Mexico" barrio just north of downtown.

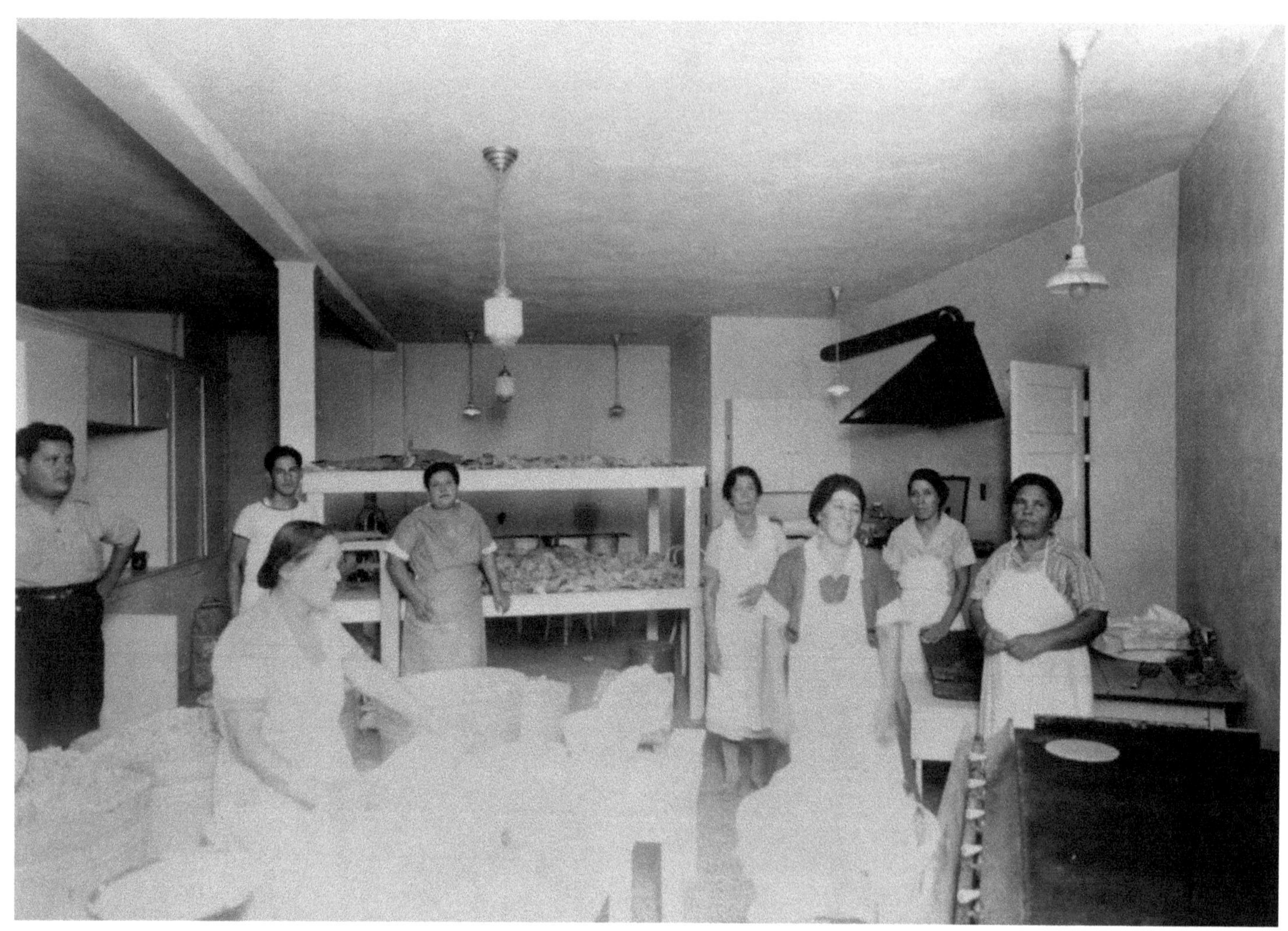

Maria Luna, a young widow, arrived in Dallas from Mexico in 1923. The next year she opened the city's first tortilla factory, gradually expanding until she was producing 100 dozen tortillas per hour in 1940.

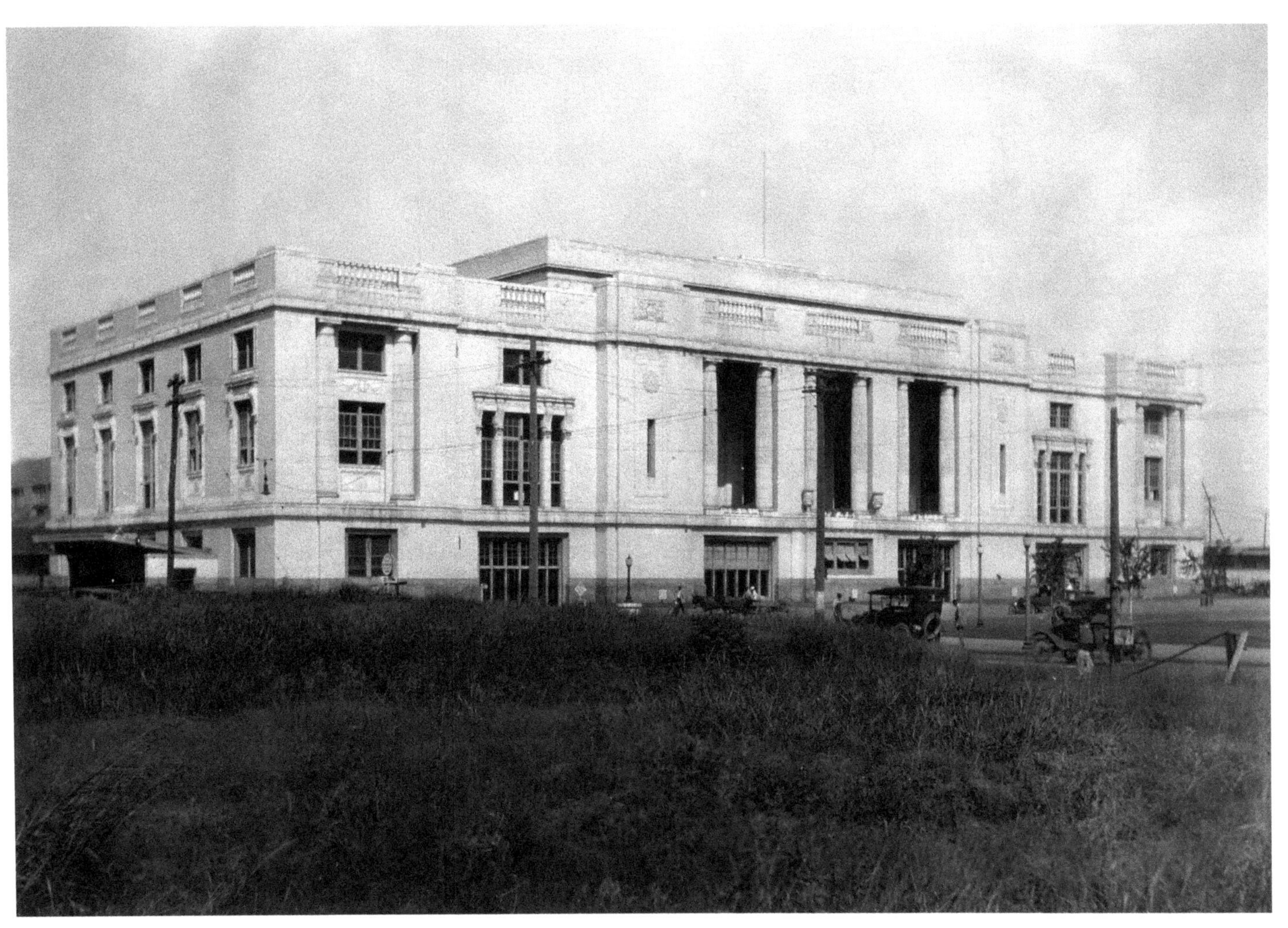

Union Station, which opened in 1916, provided a grand entrance to the city for the thousands of passengers who arrived by train.

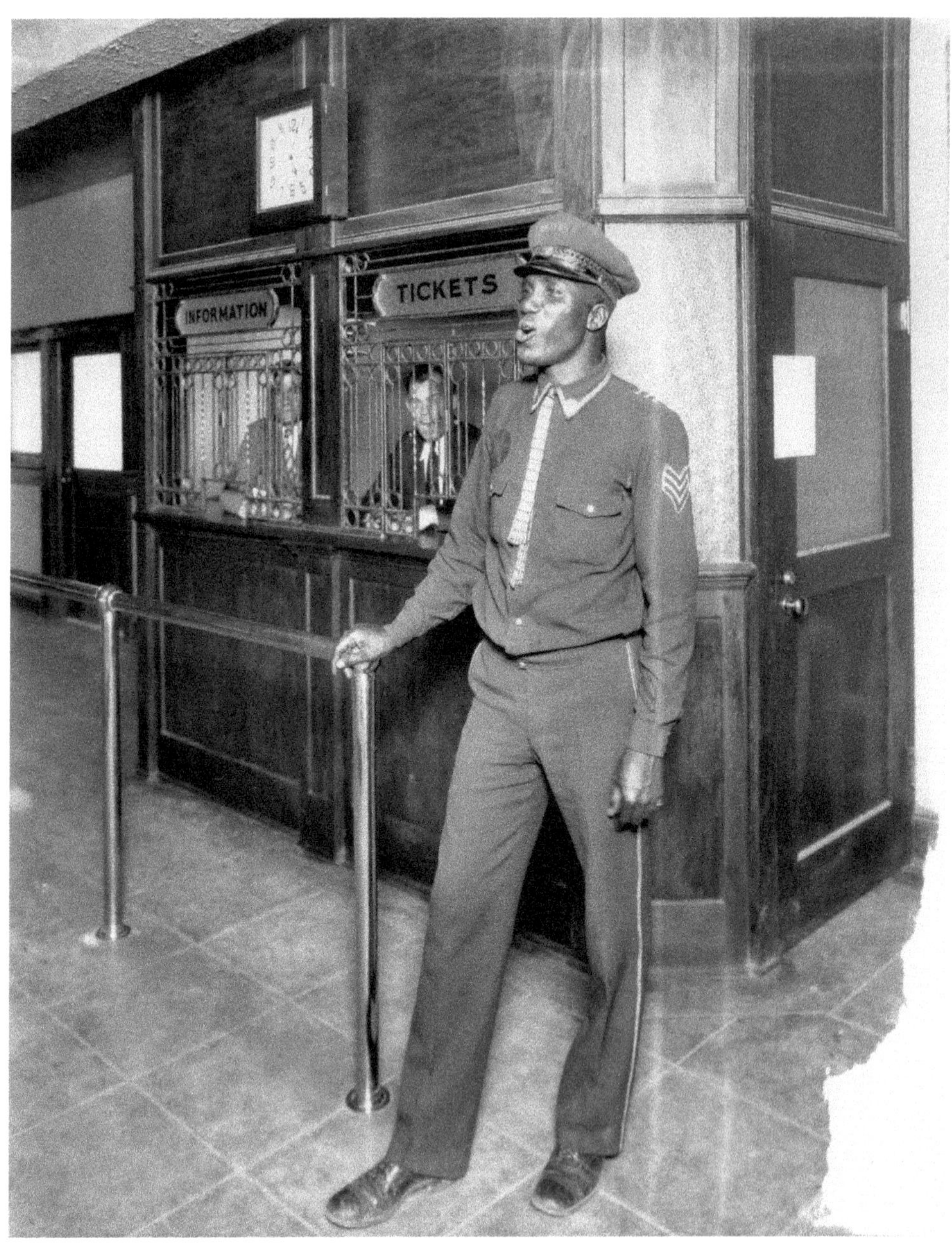

A porter calls "All Aboard" at Dallas's Union Station in the 1920s. The construction of Union Station simplified train service in Dallas for passengers, who previously might arrive or depart at any of five different depots.

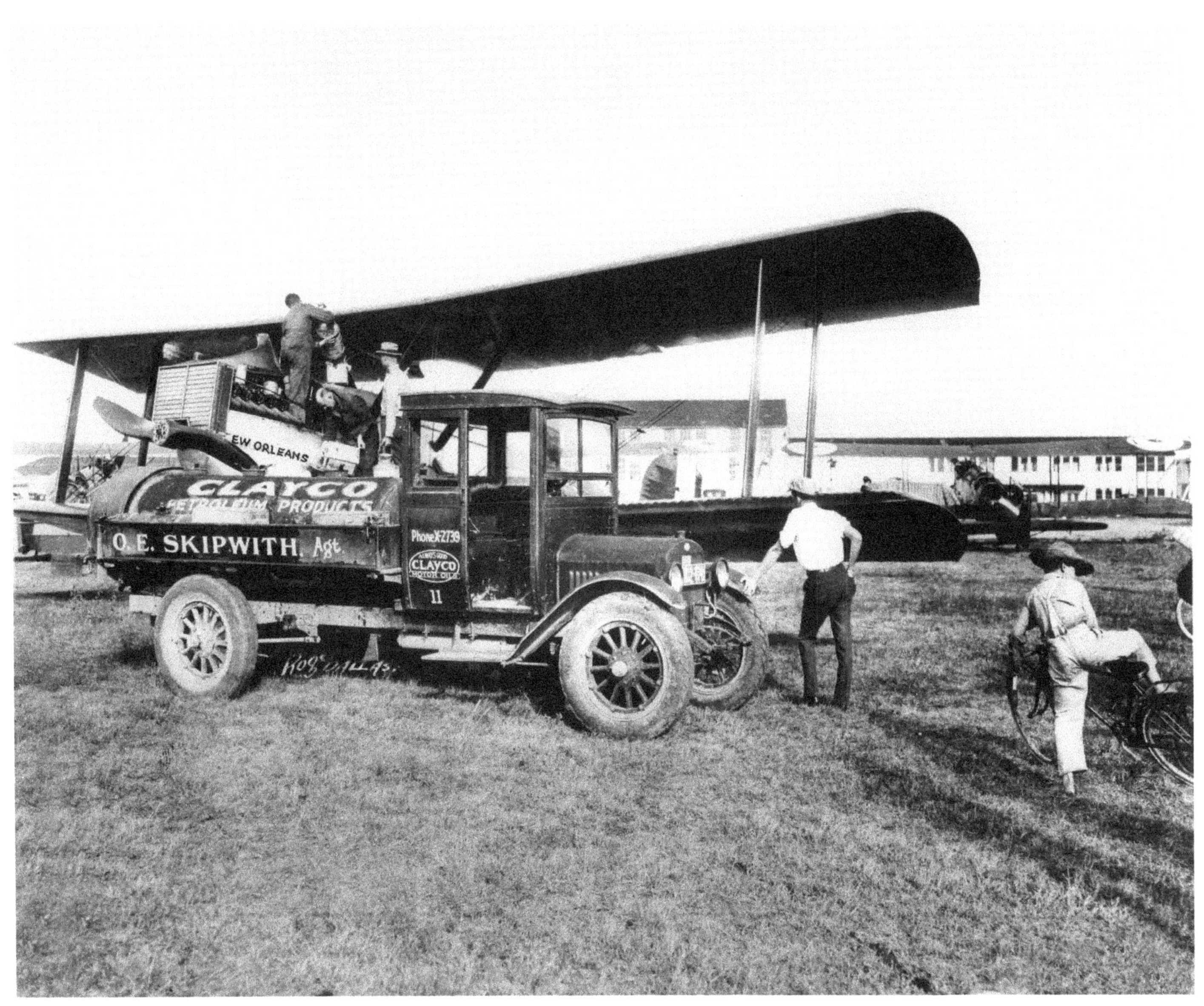

The *New Orleans,* one of the first three airplanes to circle the world in 1924, is being refueled at Love Field. Clayco was a local dealer in oil products.

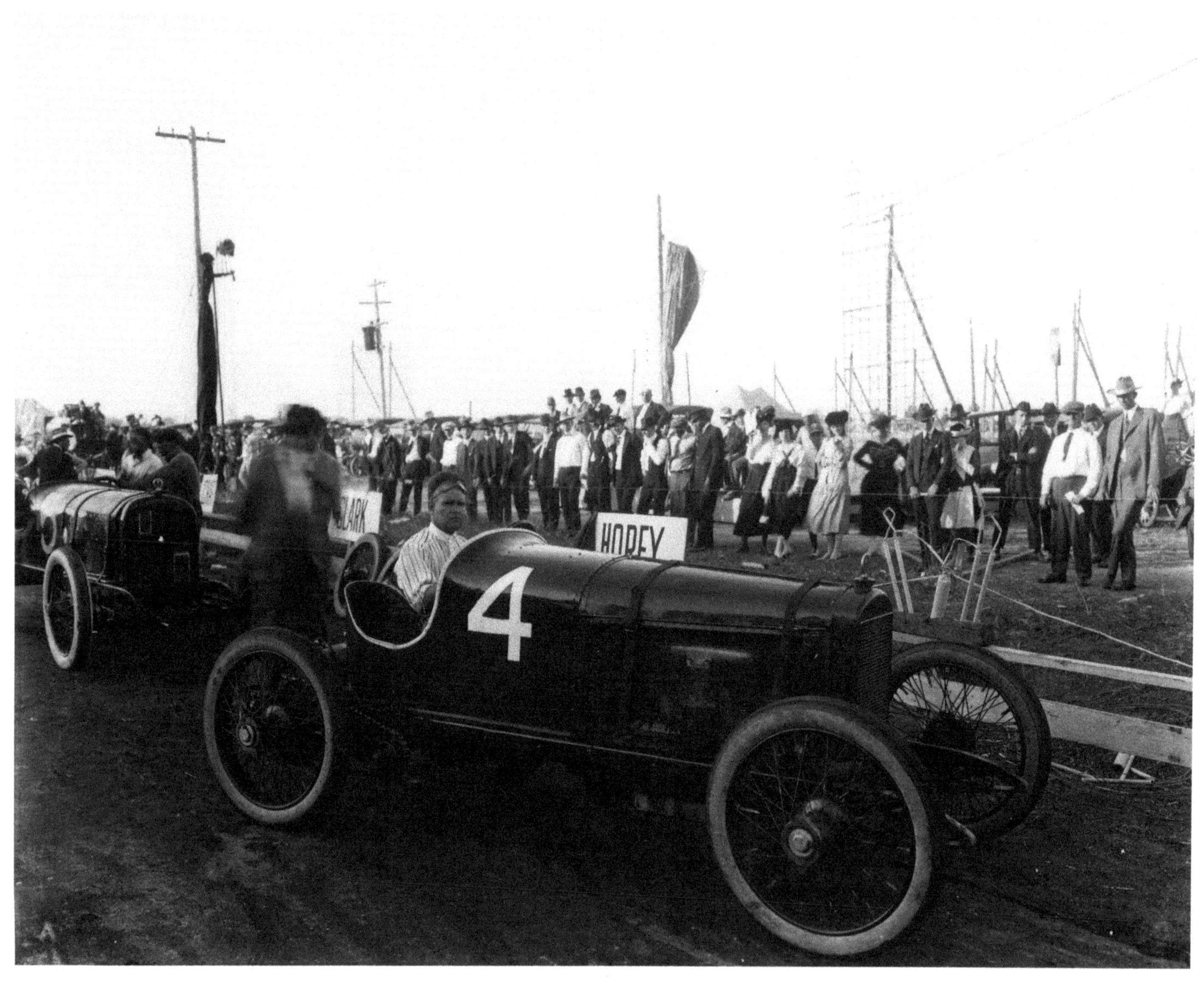

Just as automobiles replaced horses on Dallas streets, so too did they replace animals on the state fair racetrack.

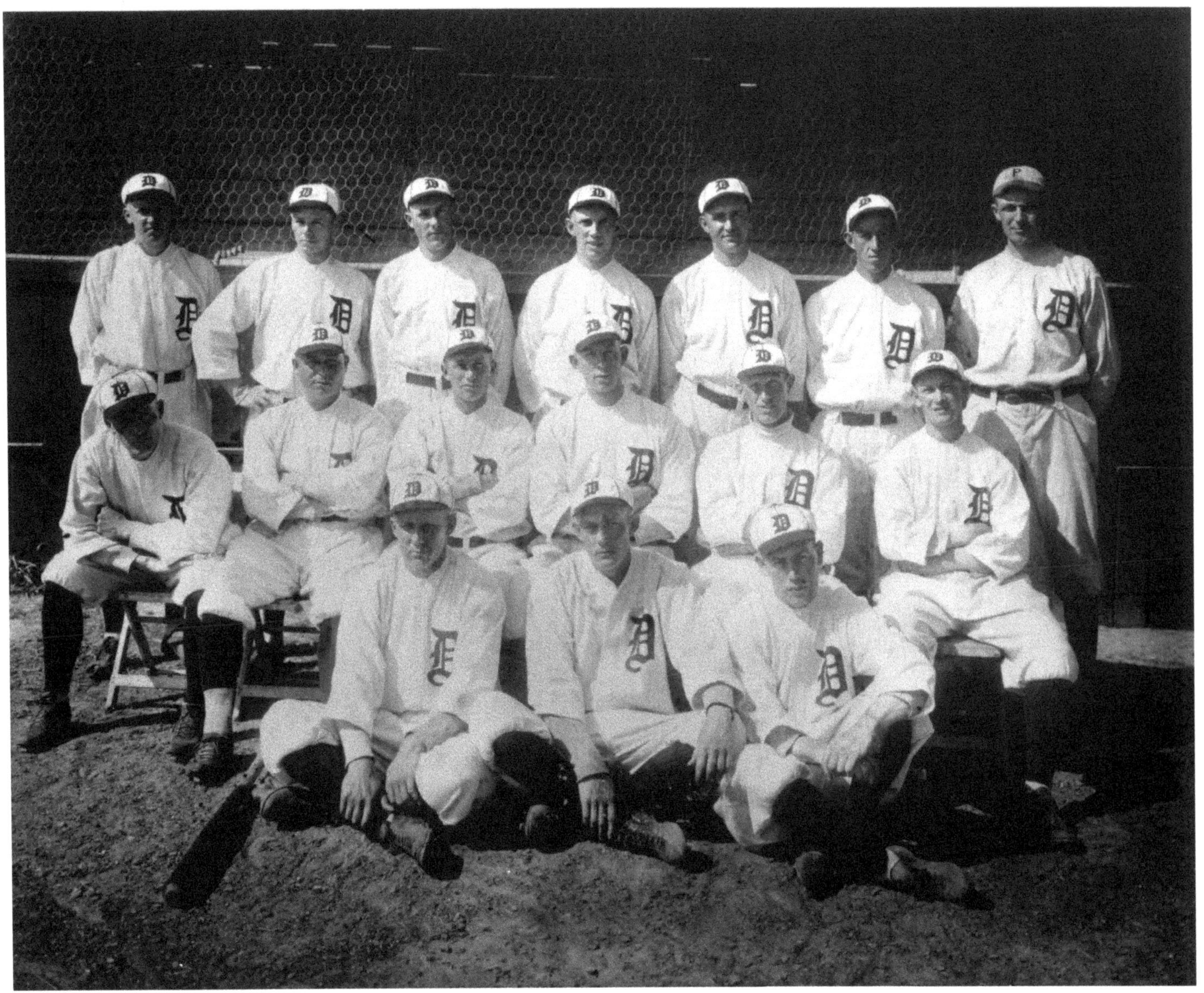

From 1884 until 1958, Dallas fielded Texas League teams, with nicknames including the Hams, Giants, Submarines, Steers, Rangers, and Eagles.

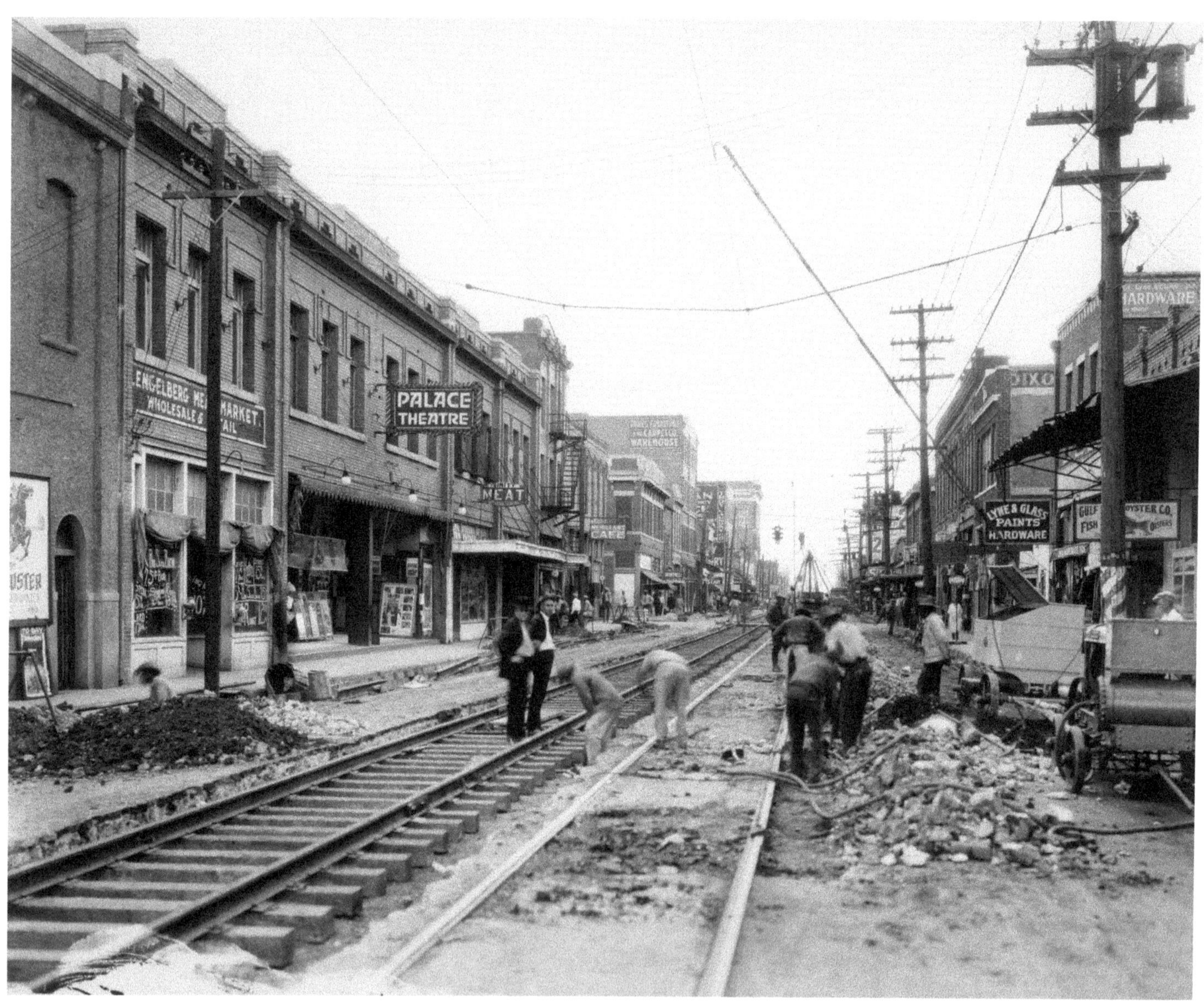

"Deep Ellum" was that portion of Elm Street east of the Central tracks, a colorful area of bars, jazz clubs, and pawn shops. Here a new streetcar line is being laid about 1927.

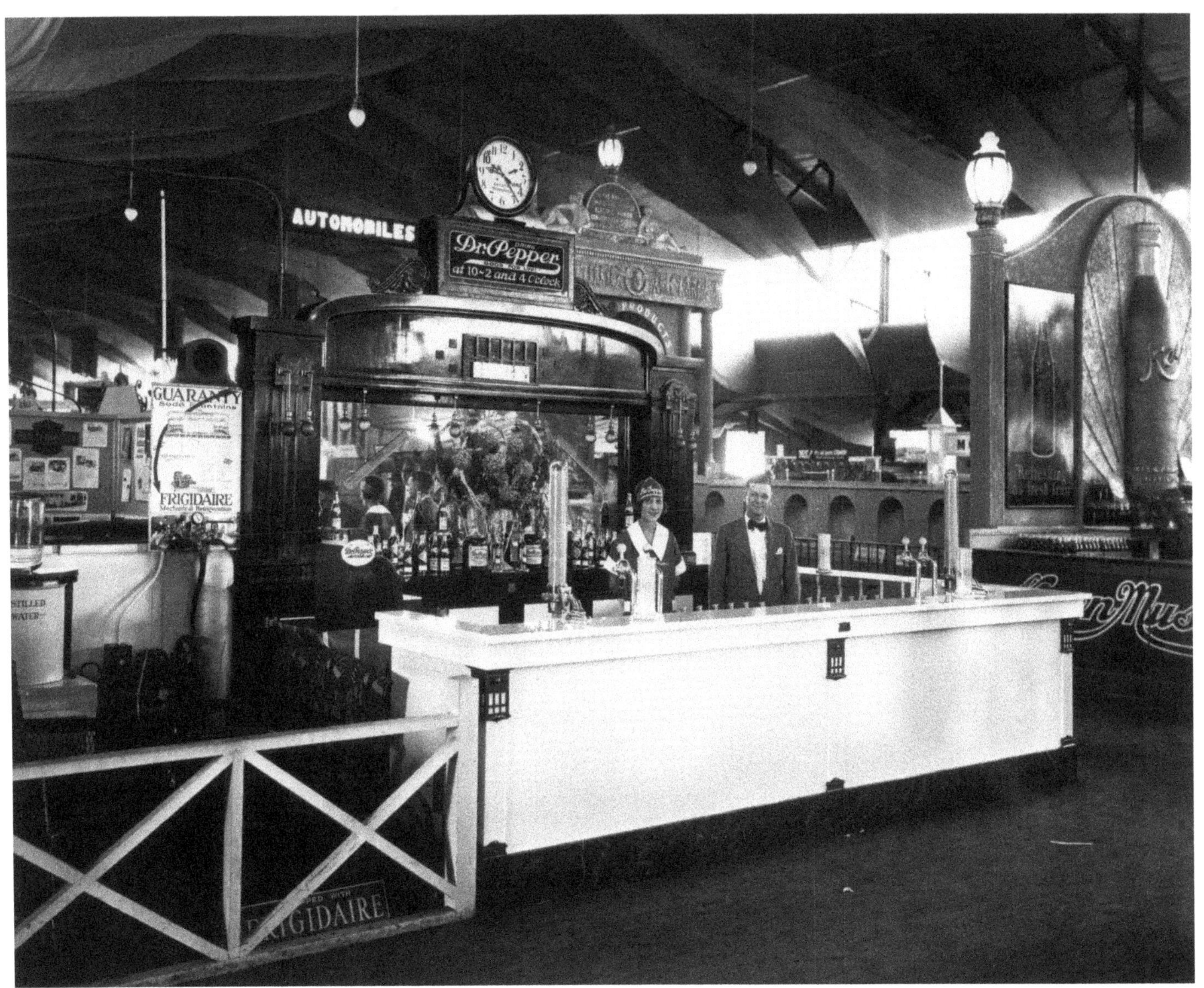

A popular exhibit at the annual state fair was the Dr. Pepper soda fountain, where visitors could sample various concoctions using the beverage.

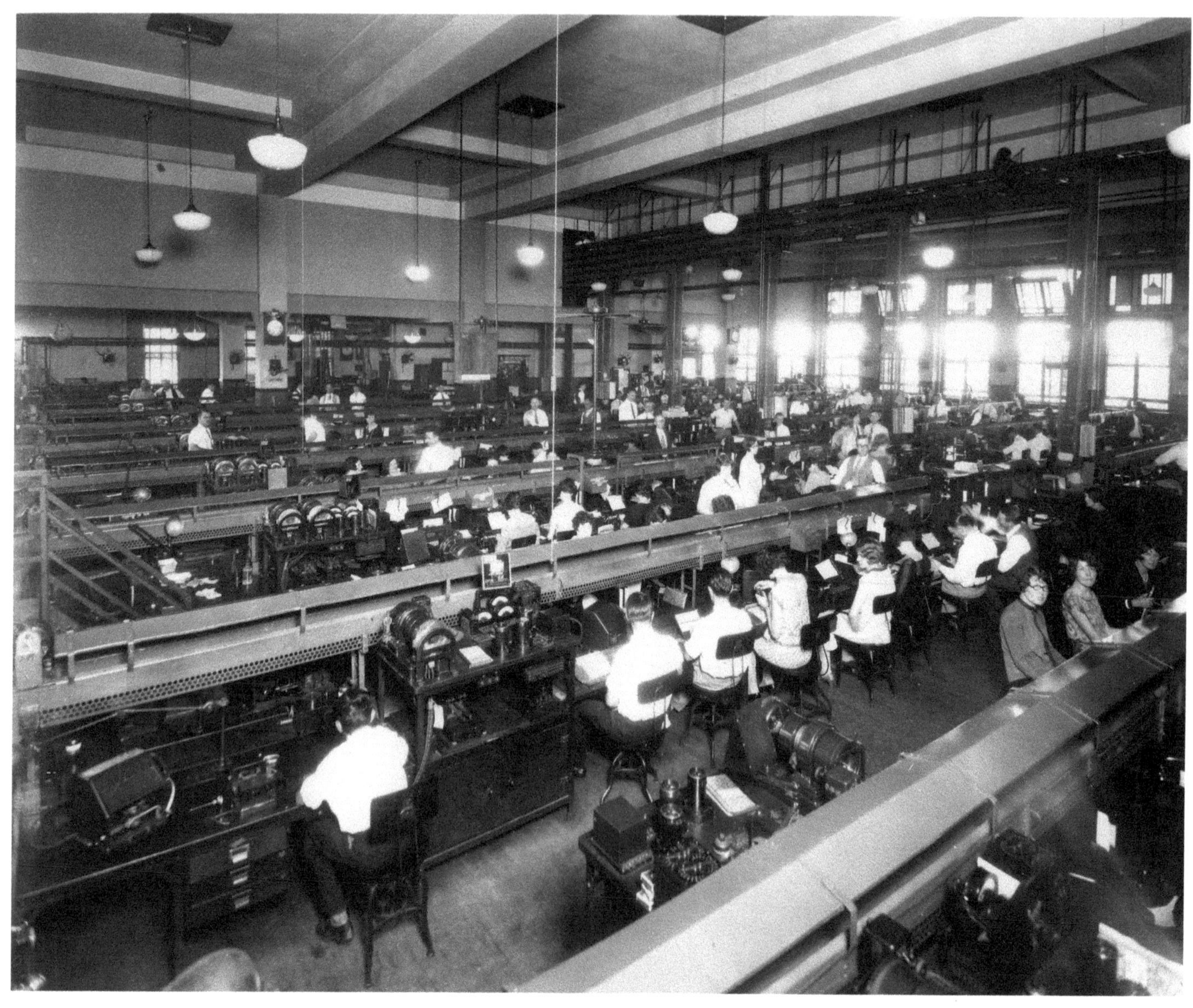

Western Union operators were still using Morse code equipment and early teleprinters when this photograph was taken in the 1920s.

George Bannerman Dealey, left, founded the *Dallas Morning News* in 1885 on behalf of his employer, Colonel Alfred H. Belo, publisher of the *Galveston Daily News*. In 1925, Dealey (left), T. R. Rinehart (center), and A. M. Allen, all surviving members of the founding staff, celebrated the newspaper's fortieth anniversary.

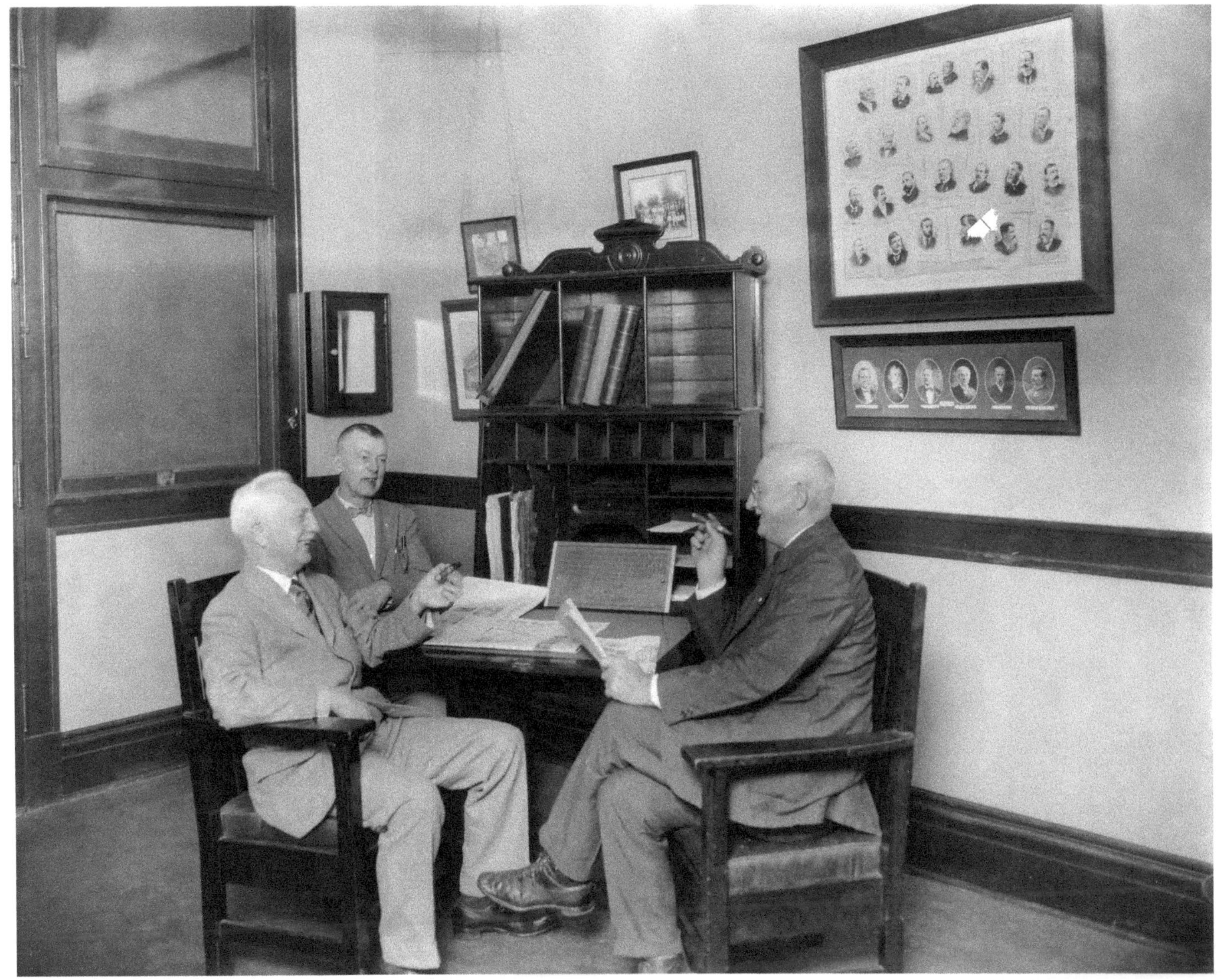

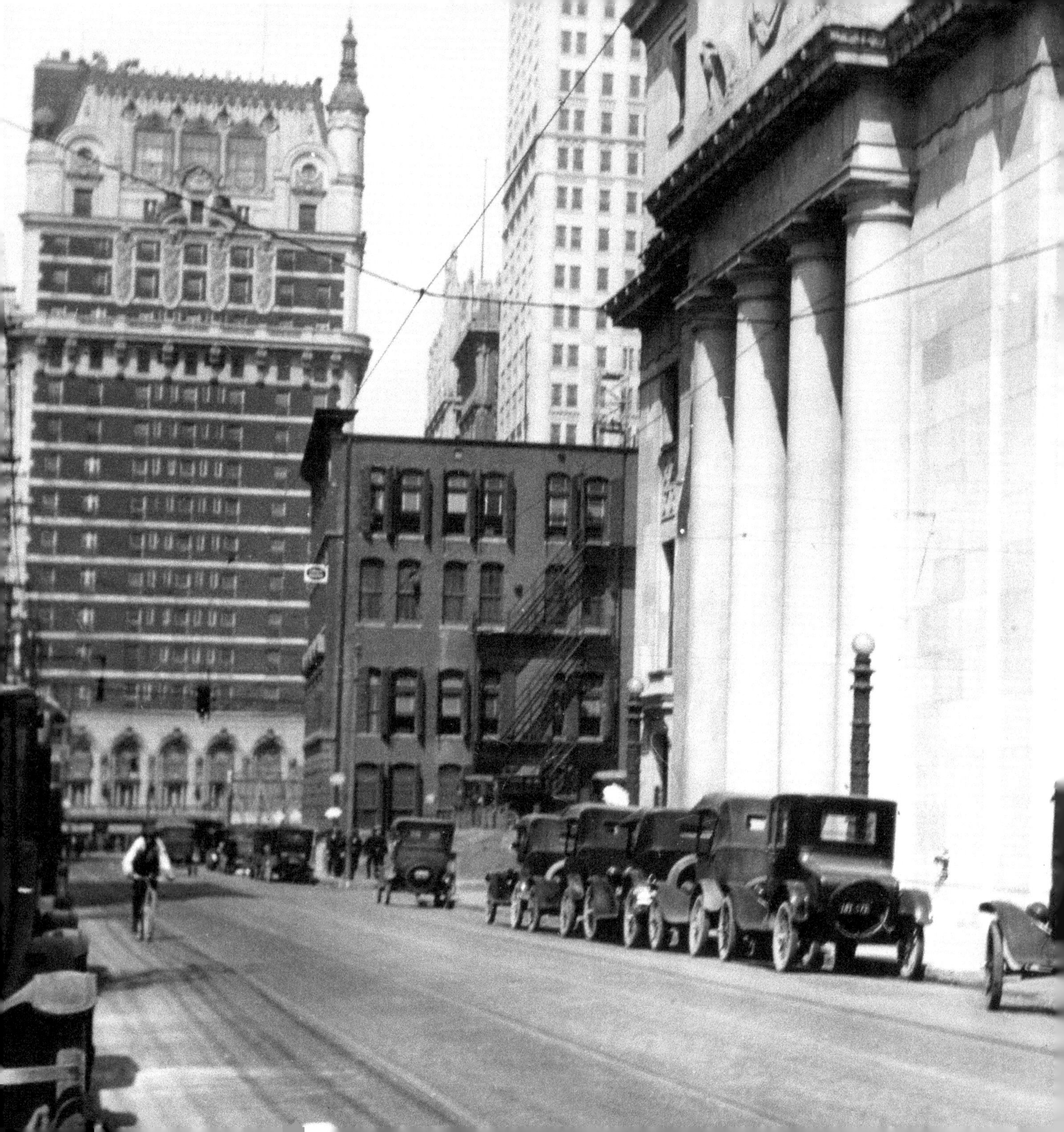

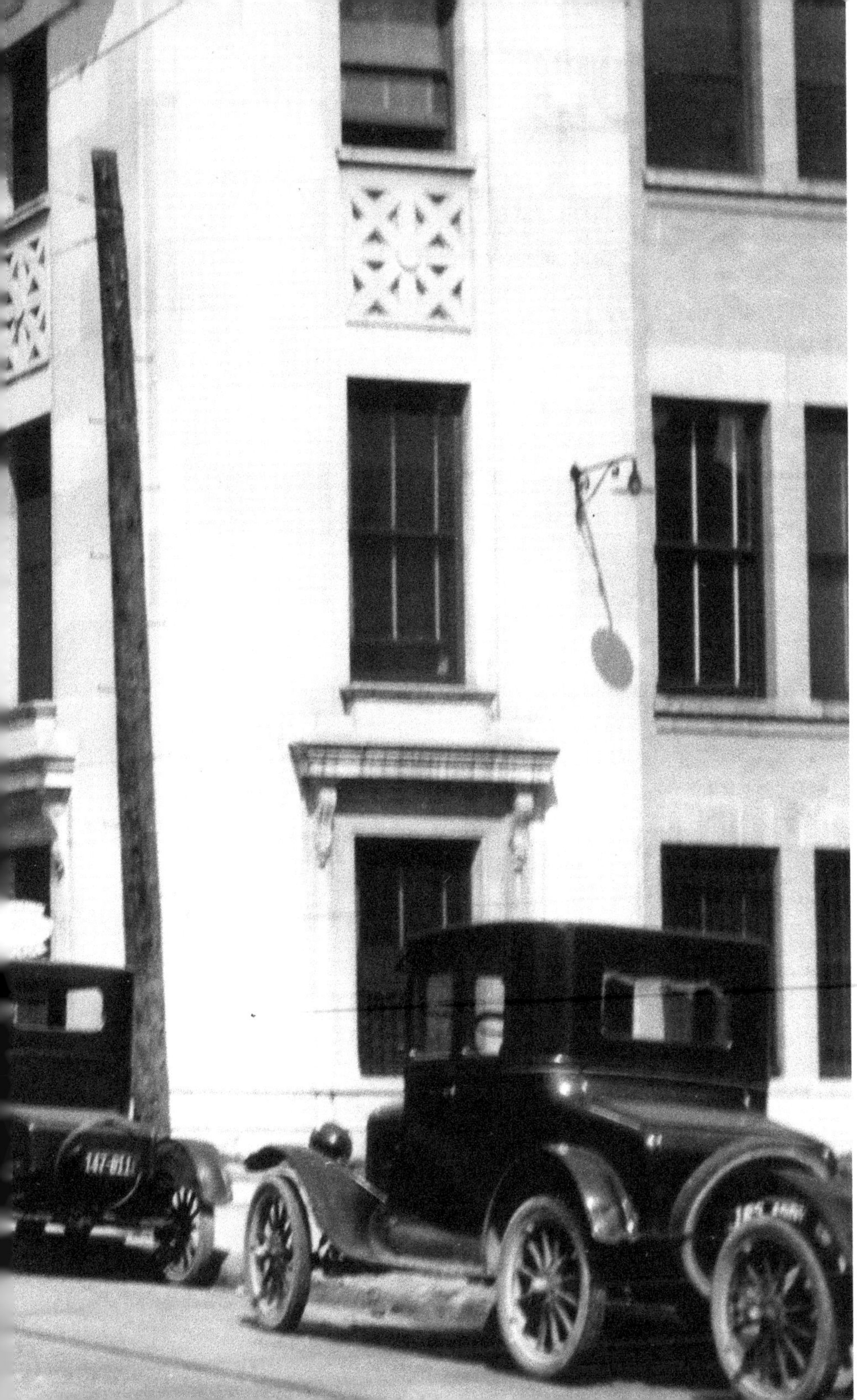

When Dallas was selected as headquarters for the 11th District of the Federal Reserve Bank in 1914, it was the smallest city in the nation to be so honored. But the selection ensured Dallas's position as the financial center of the Southwest. The Federal Reserve Bank building (right) anchored S. Akard Street for 75 years. The Adolphus Hotel is in the background.

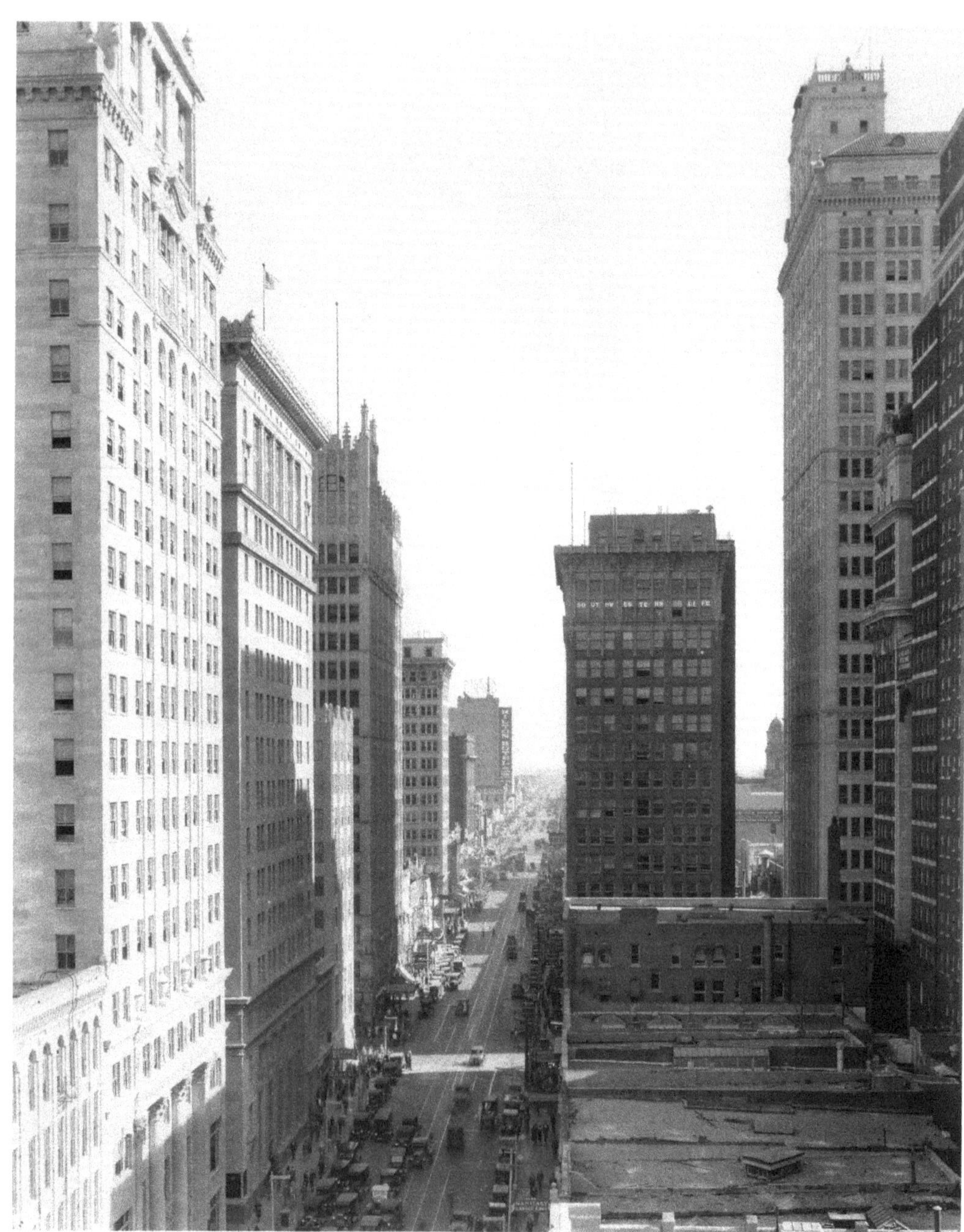

The Davis Building (left), now housing loft apartments, was built in 1926 as the headquarters for Republic Bank, which added the cupola on top to make the building taller than that of a nearby competitor.

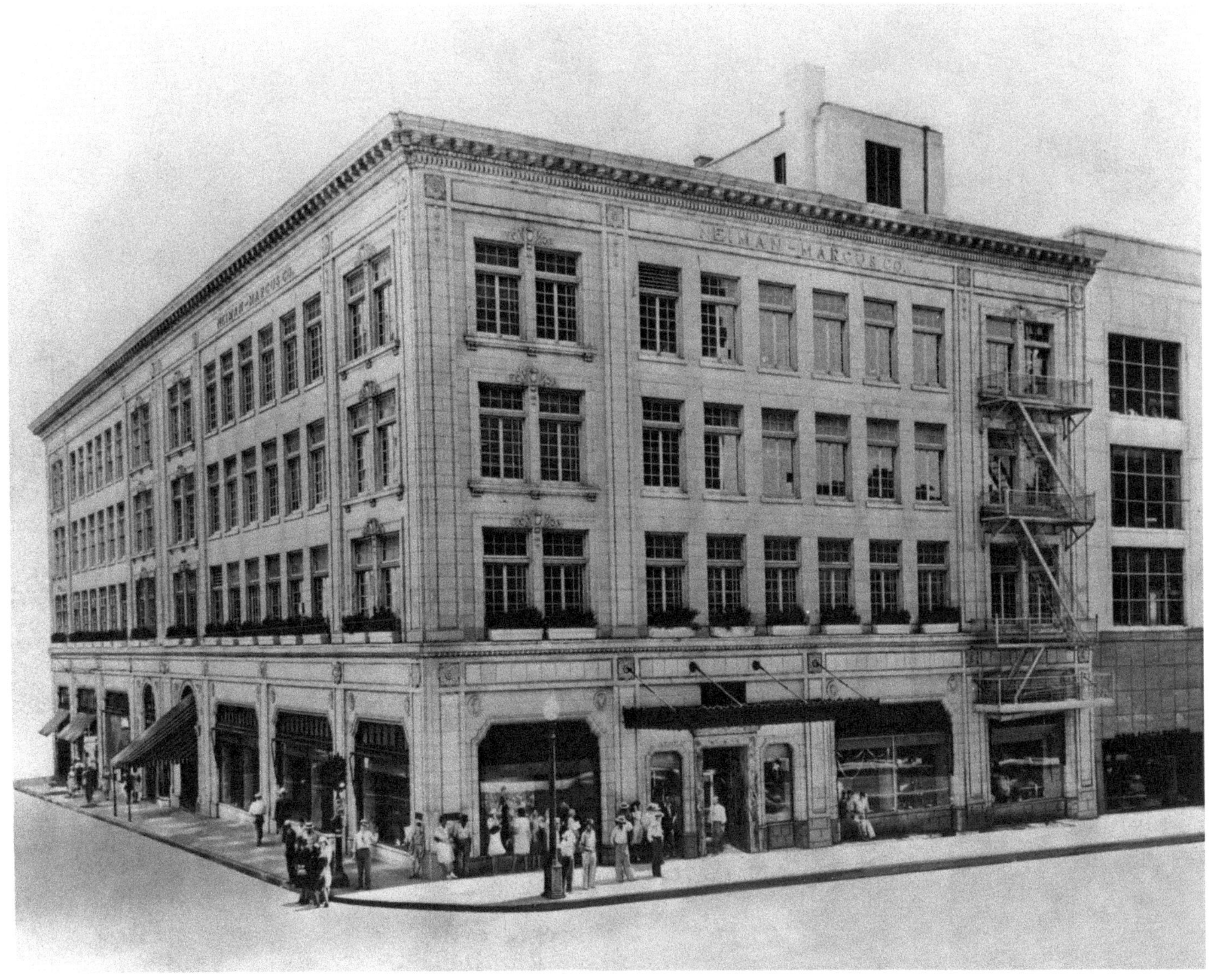

The Neiman Marcus store at the corner of Main and Ervay opened in 1913, replacing an earlier building on Elm that burned. This photo predates a 1929 expansion that added two floors.

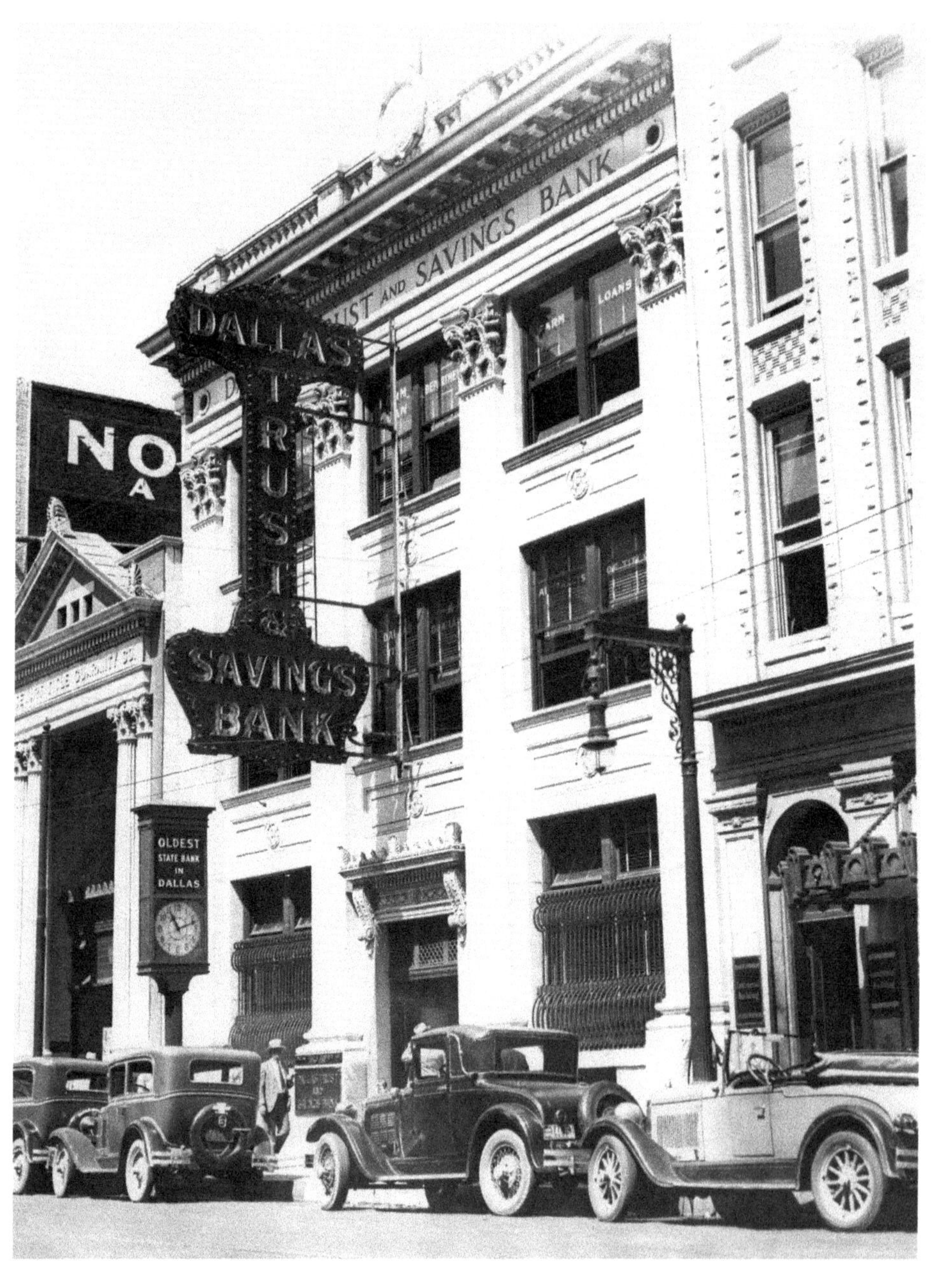

Before a 1905 state banking act provided safeguards, many Texans distrusted banks. After that point, banks proliferated and bankers became key civic leaders in Dallas.

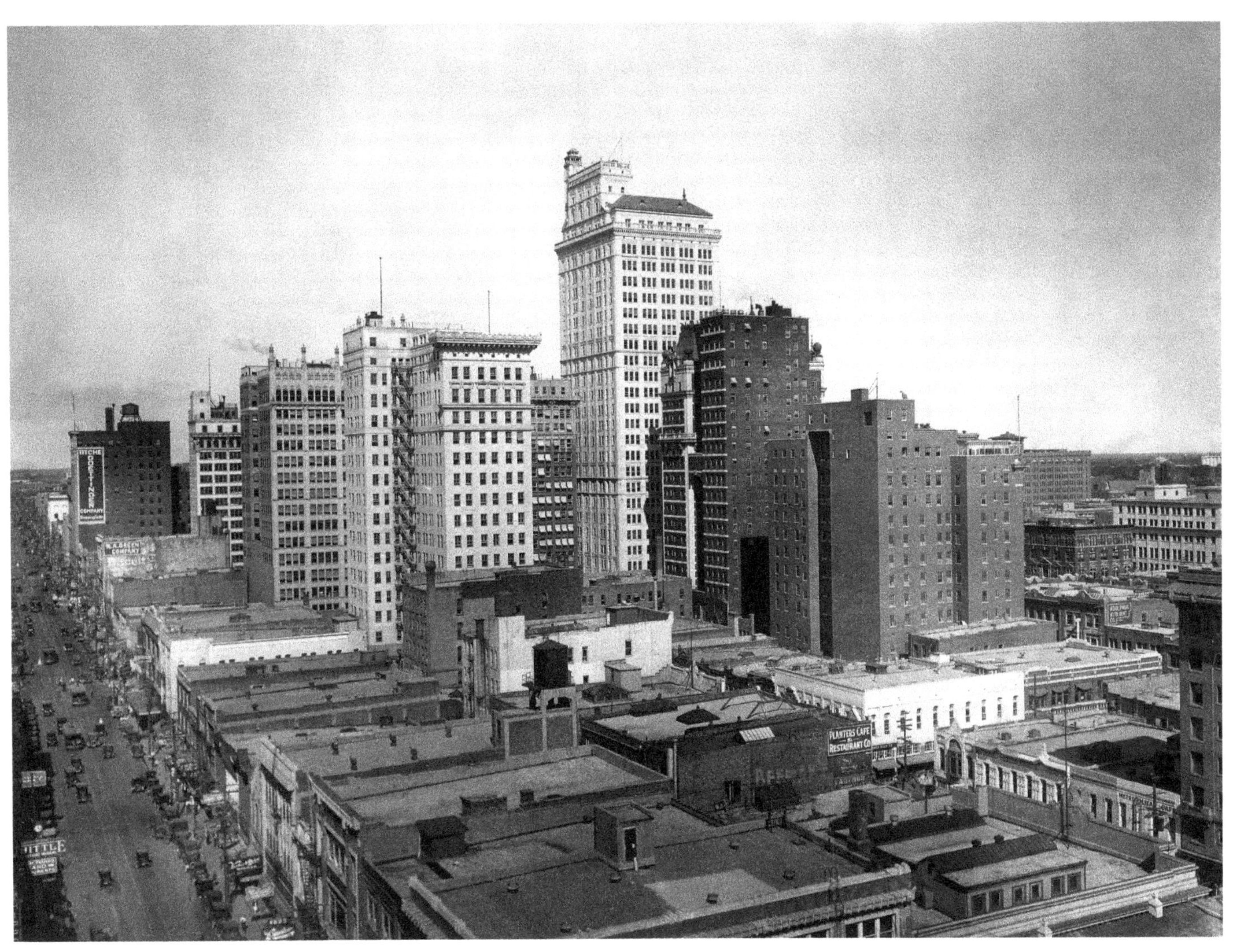

Although Main and Commerce were sprouting skyscrapers in the 1920s (dominated by the Magnolia Building, center), Elm Street (foreground) remained filled mostly with small two- and three-story commercial structures.

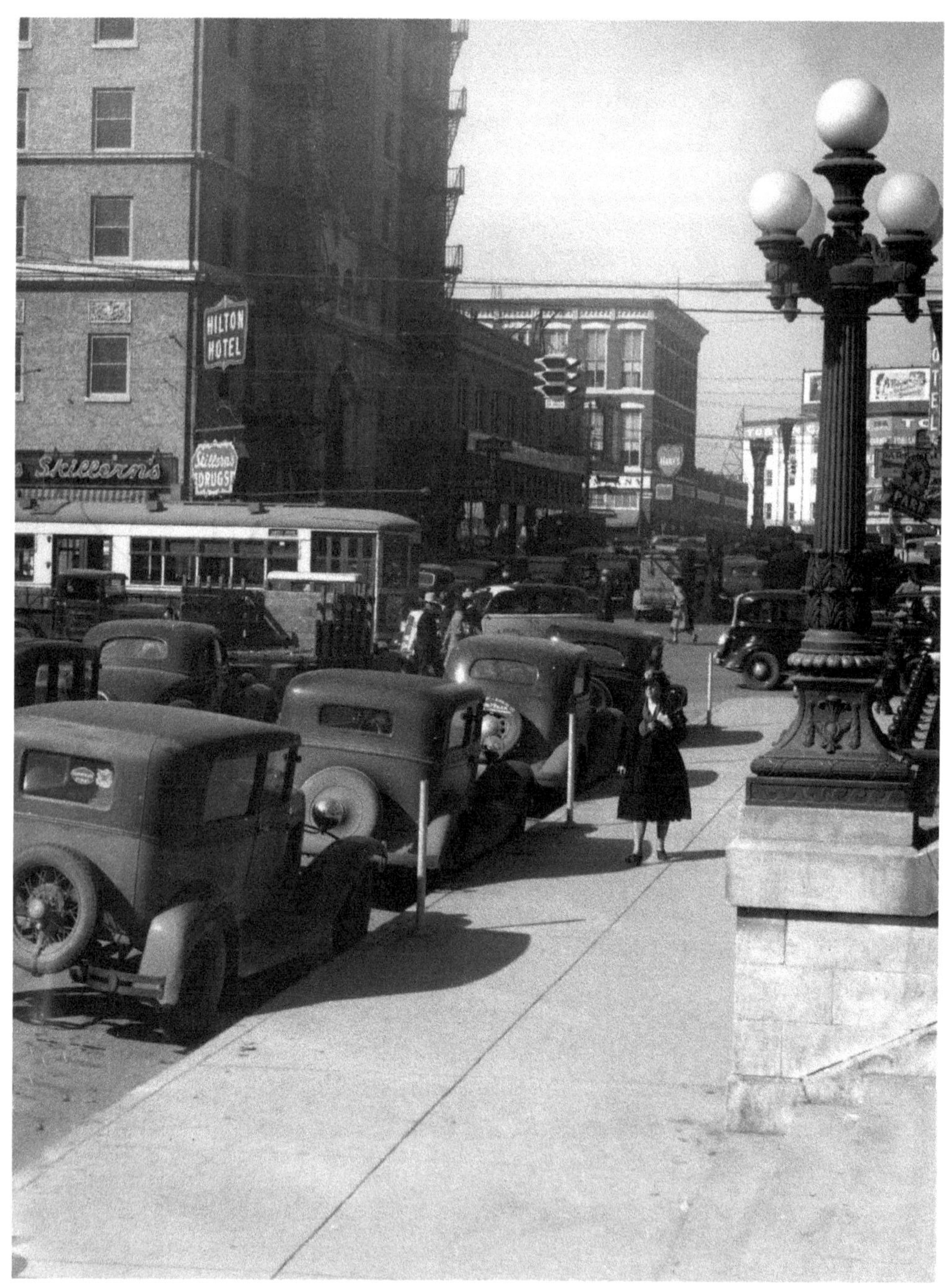

This view of Harwood Street looking north from the steps of the Municipal Building shows the Hilton Hotel at the left. Opened in 1925, this is often cited as Conrad Hilton's first high-rise hotel, and was the first with the Hilton name on it.

From the Great Depression to Postwar Metropolis

(1930–1949)

By 1930, the population of Dallas exceeded 260,000. A majority of county residents were now in the city. The city was transformed from an agricultural to an urban economy.

The 1930s opened in the shadow of the Great Depression. By 1931, 18,500 Dallasites were unemployed. The city's suffering was eased by the discovery of oil in East Texas. Oil producers, investors, equipment manufacturers, and geologists all found Dallas convenient for their headquarters. Dallas bankers, willing to accept underground oil reserves as collateral, profited, as did home builders, upscale stores like Neiman Marcus, and others prepared to cater to the newly rich.

Civic leaders seized the opportunity to host the 1936 Texas Centennial Exposition, celebrating the state's 100th anniversary of independence from Mexico. Dallas had no historic rights to host since no one had lived in the area in 1836. With a financial package of nearly $8 million, however, Dallas overwhelmed Houston, San Antonio, and other older communities vying for the honor.

Within 18 months, Fair Park was expanded and transformed. Hundreds of workers, ranging from laborers to artists, began remodeling or constructing 77 buildings, including fine arts and history museums. More than 250,000 people lined up to watch the opening parade on June 6, 1936. Inside the grounds, they found theatrical shows, historical pageants, music, corporate exhibits, and more. Six million visitors from every state and around the world attended the six-month exposition. The local economy soared. The next year saw the Greater Texas and Pan American Exposition.

"The year America discovered Texas" was 1936. It was the same year Dallas became "Big D." The national media now viewed it as a sophisticated, modern metropolis.

World War II dominated the first half of the 1940s. More than 58,000 Dallas County residents served in World War II. Some 10,000 men and women helped with civil defense efforts. Many local plants converted to wartime production and began hiring women. These included Ford Motors on East Grand Avenue and Continental Motors in Garland: first for tanks and later for aircraft. North American Aviation was the first airplane plant built under the National Defense Program. By war's end, 55,000 Dallas residents worked in war industries, laying the foundation for future manufacturing plants.

The Adolphus became the first hotel in the world to be fully air conditioned in 1940, the Starlight Operettas premiered in the Fair Park bandshell in 1941, Southwestern Medical School opened in 1943, and in 1943 the Mercantile Bank Building surpassed the Magnolia as the tallest building in town.

After the war, Dallas enjoyed rapid growth, former farmland quickly becoming residential subdivisions. By 1950, the city limits encompassed 147 square miles. The construction of new highways and shopping centers aided this process, encouraging families to live farther from the central business district. In 1949, Frigikar became the first mass manufacturer of automobile air conditioners due to the increased reliance on cars.

Margo Jones opened her trend-setting theater-in-the-round at Fair Park in 1947, and Dallas got its first television stations in 1948-49. Southern Methodist University's Doak Walker won the Heisman Trophy in 1948, and the Cotton Bowl was expanded to accommodate crowds coming to see him play. As the city's population crept toward 450,000, the future looked bright.

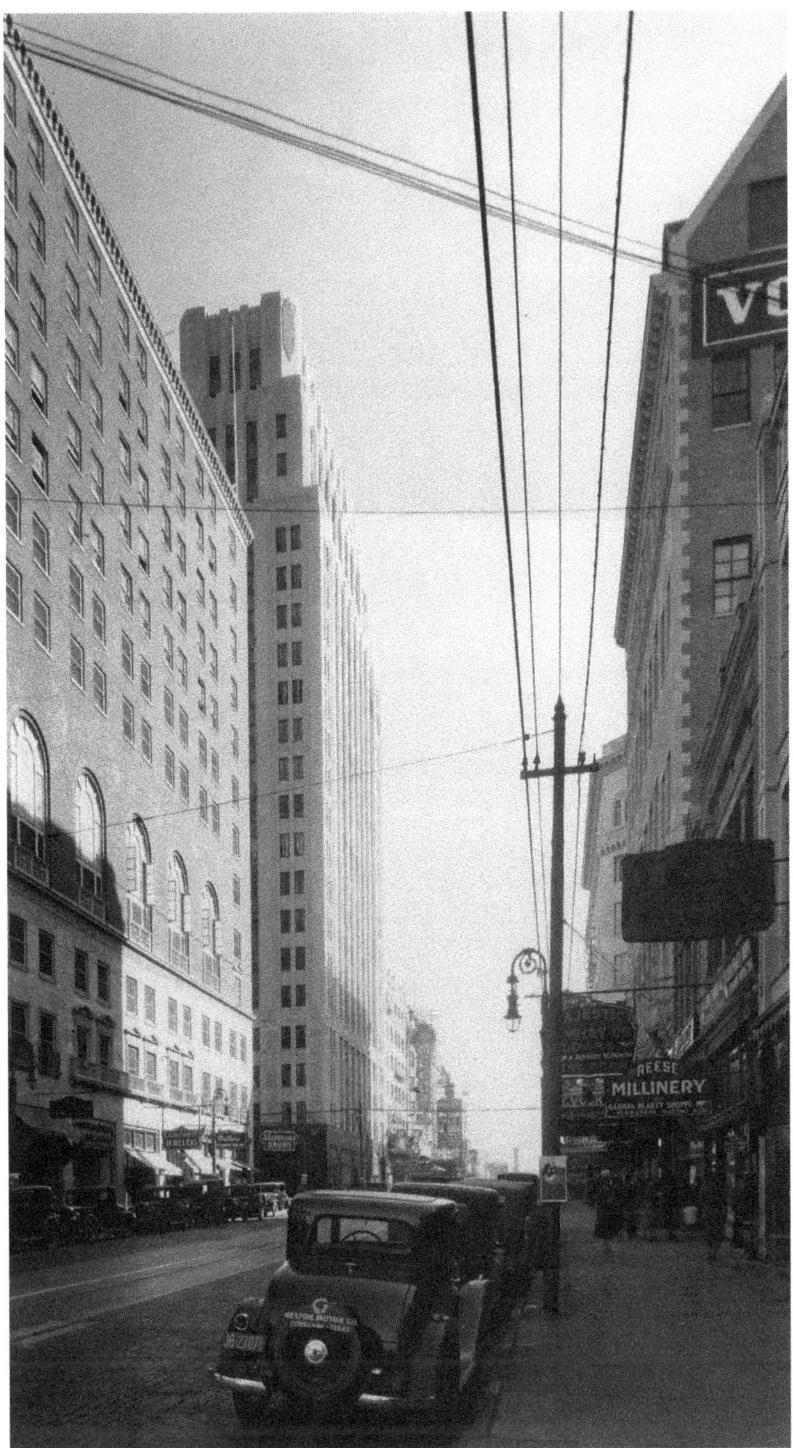

Theaters were still prominent on Elm Street in the 1930s, although high-rise office buildings, such as Tower Petroleum (center-left), were beginning to line the street.

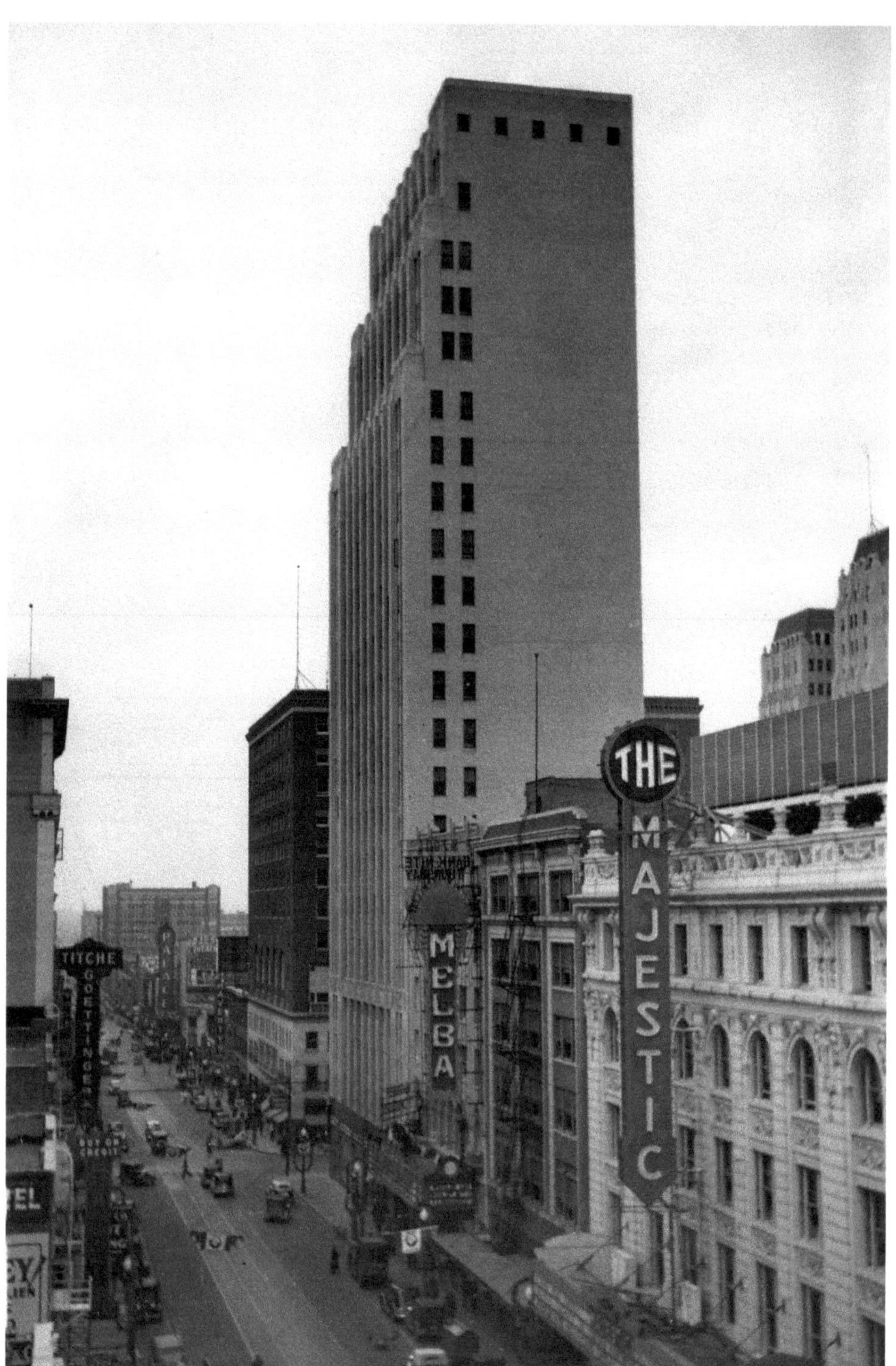

Dallas architect Mark Lemmon designed the high-rise Tower Petroleum Building in 1931, taking his inspiration from "Moderne" buildings in Chicago and New York City.

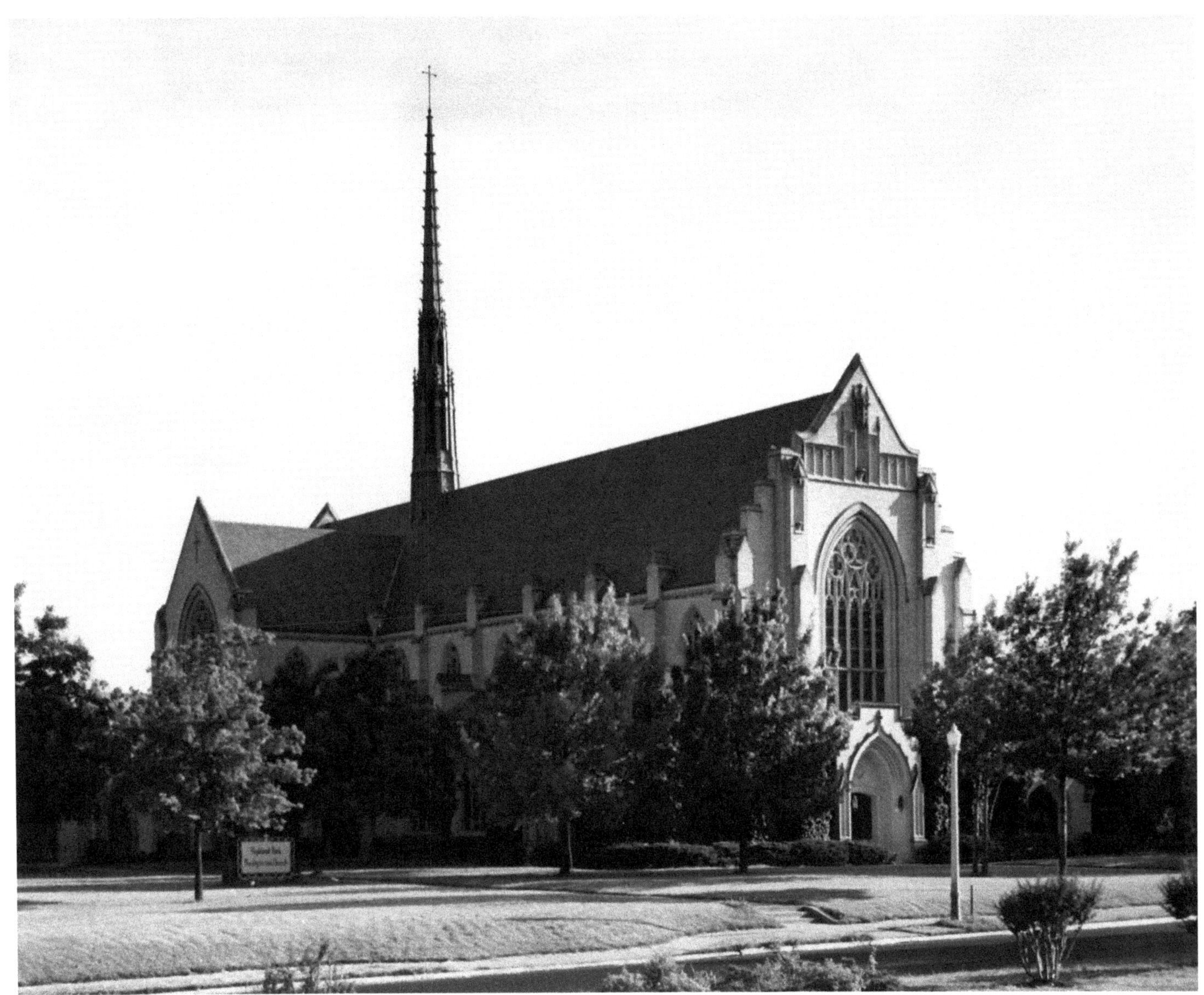

Mark Lemmon also designed many churches, including the campus for Highland Park Presbyterian Church, which was built in stages between 1927 and 1975. The central sanctuary opened in 1941.

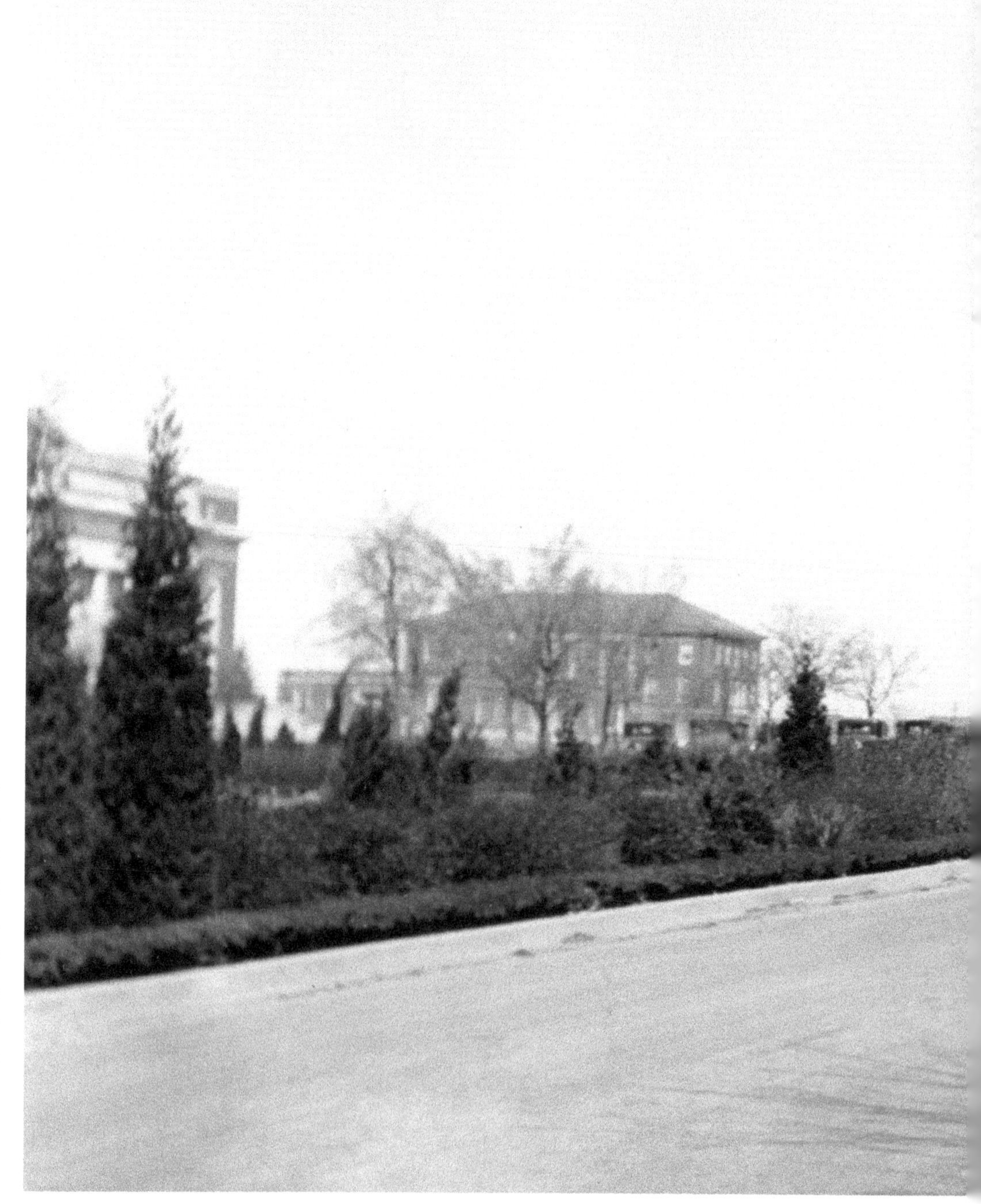

Southern Methodist University opened in 1915 with two buildings—a women's dormitory and Dallas Hall, a domed structure inspired by Thomas Jefferson's centerpiece for the University of Virginia. By the 1930s, the campus in University Park boasted a dozen more buildings.

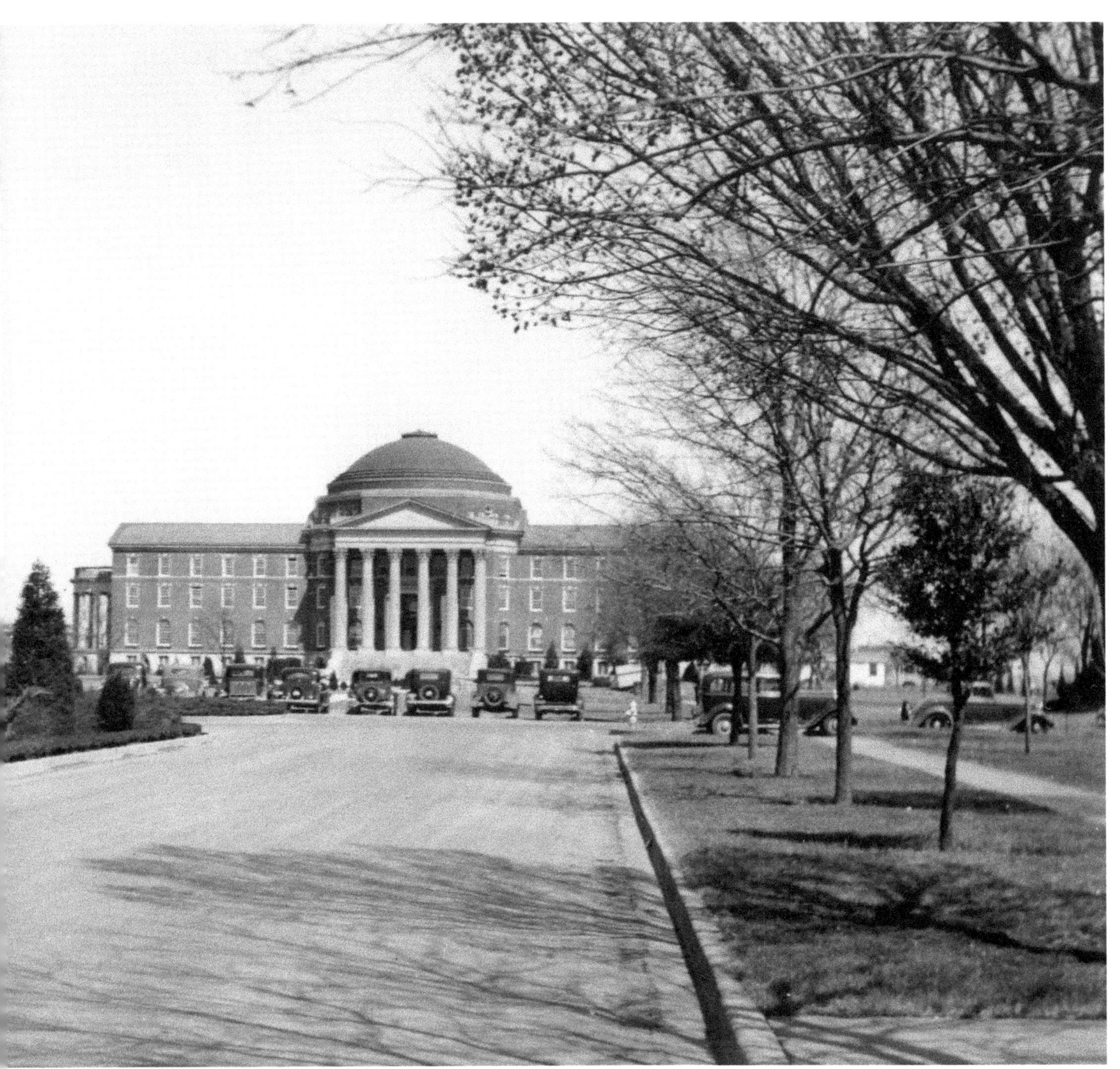

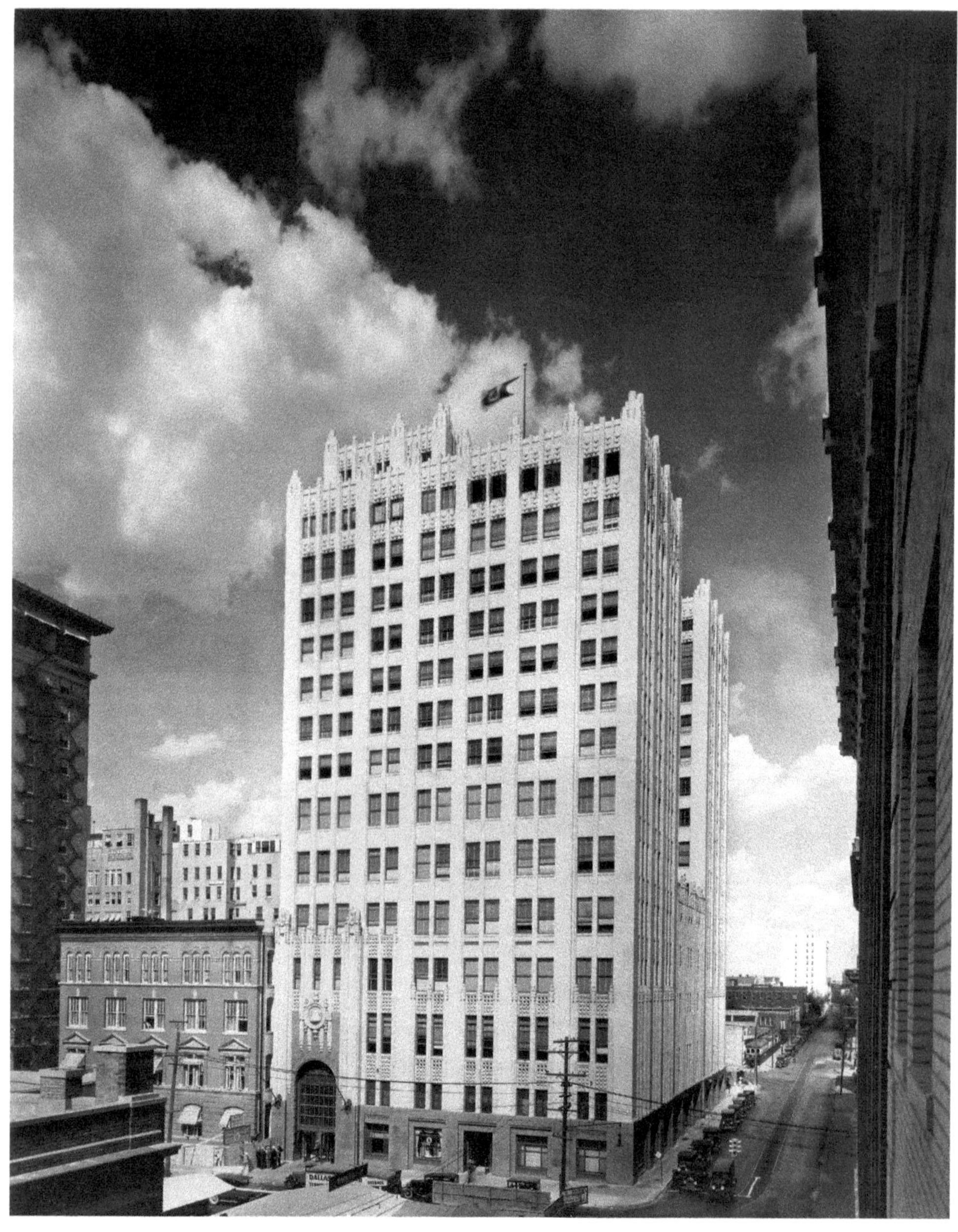

The modern, art deco facade of Southwestern Bell's office building on Akard Street was designed to reflect the advanced technology of the telephone company. Constructed in the early 1930s, it's now part of a multi-structure AT&T complex.

Lloyd Long's dramatic night view of downtown Dallas about 1935 shows an urban skyline dominated by the Magnolia Petroleum Building (the tallest west of the Mississippi) and its rooftop neon sign of Pegasus, "the flying red horse."

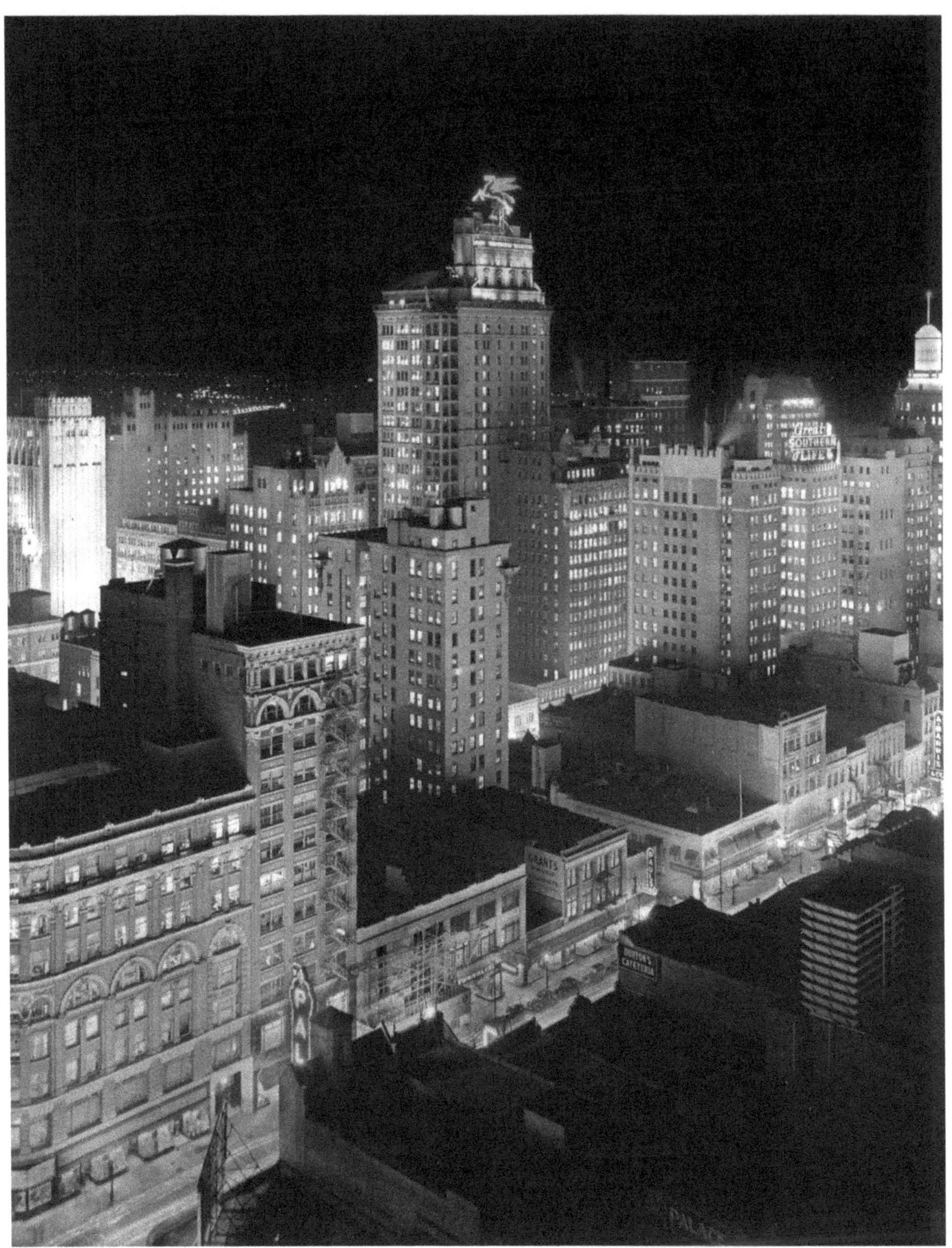

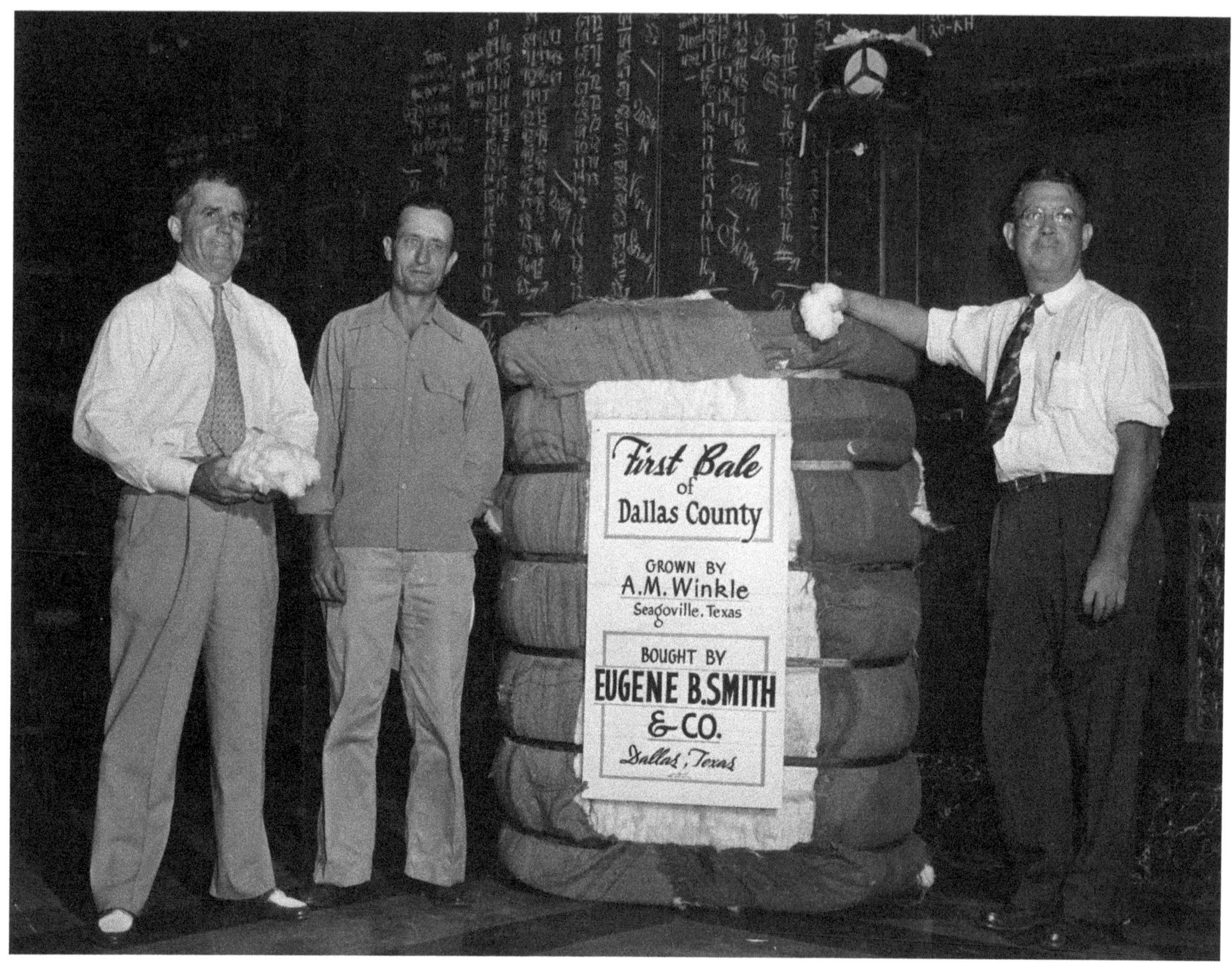

Cotton remained "king" of North Texas agricultural products until World War II. By 1940, brokers at the Dallas Cotton Exchange were handling 2.5 million bales each year.

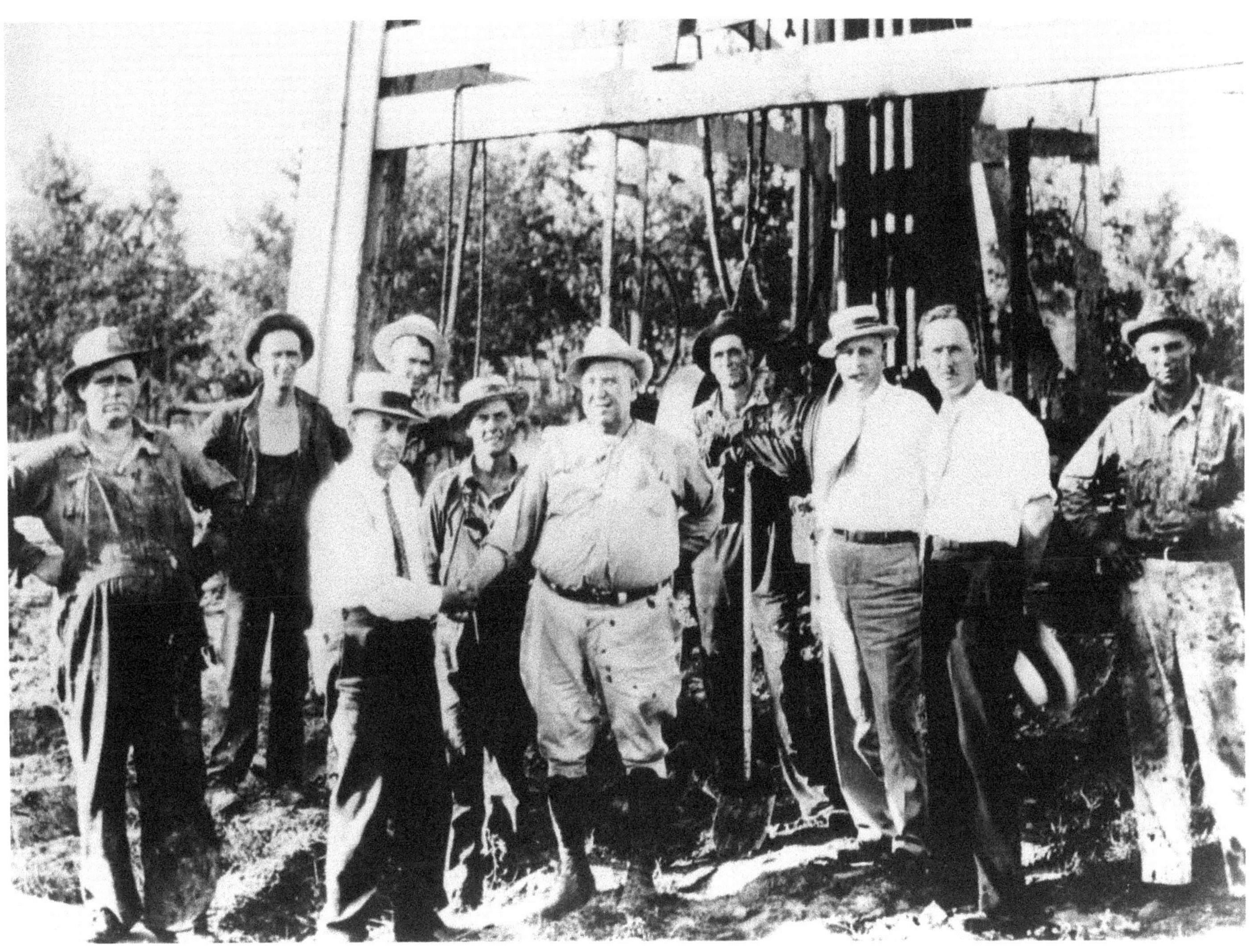

The discovery of oil in East Texas in 1930 made a fortune for H. L. Hunt (third from right, in front of "Daisy Bradford No. 3") and others, many of whom established their business headquarters in Dallas.

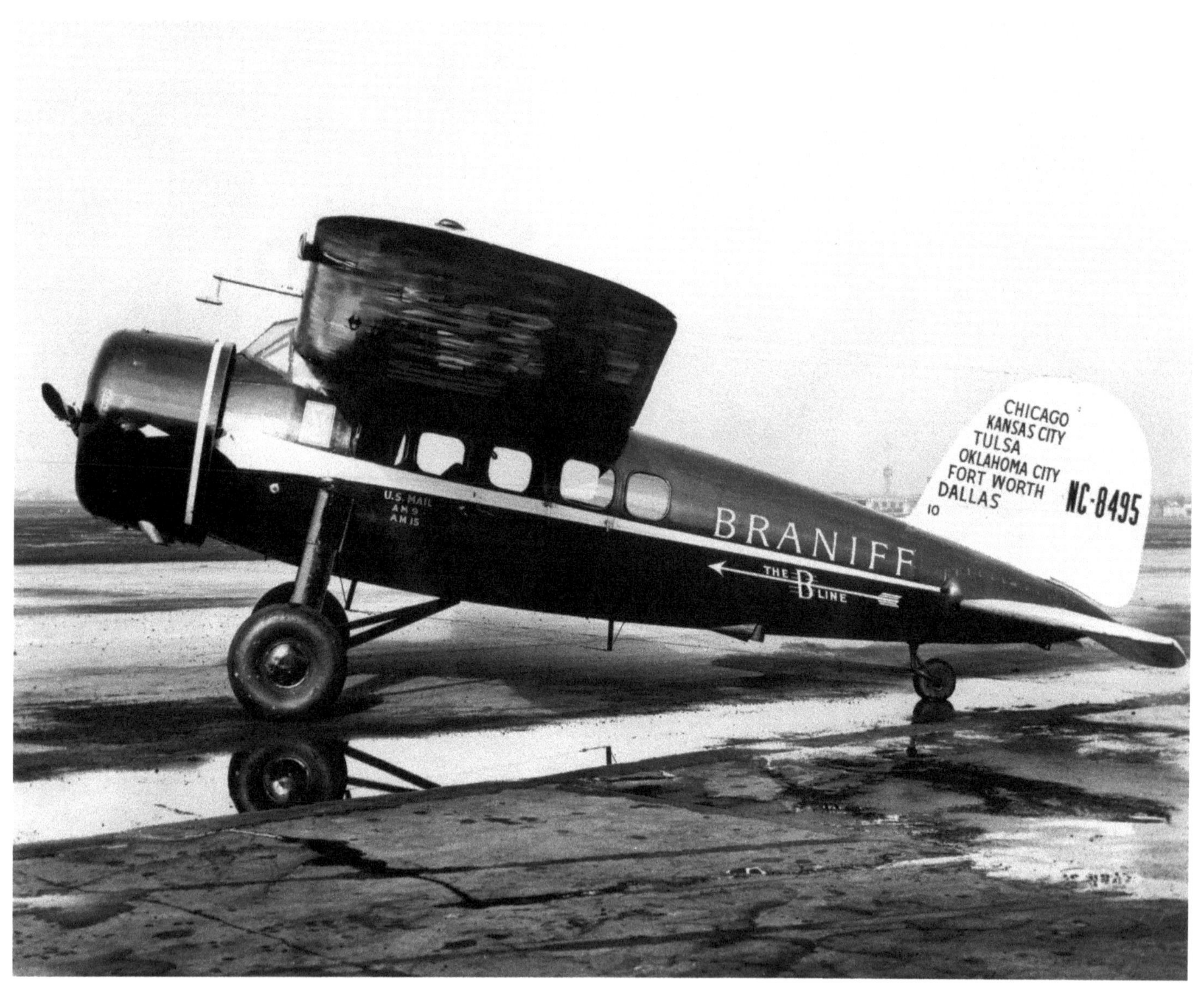

Oklahoma-based Braniff Airlines moved its company operations and maintenance facilities to Love Field in 1934 after the U.S. Post Office awarded it an airmail route between Dallas and Chicago.

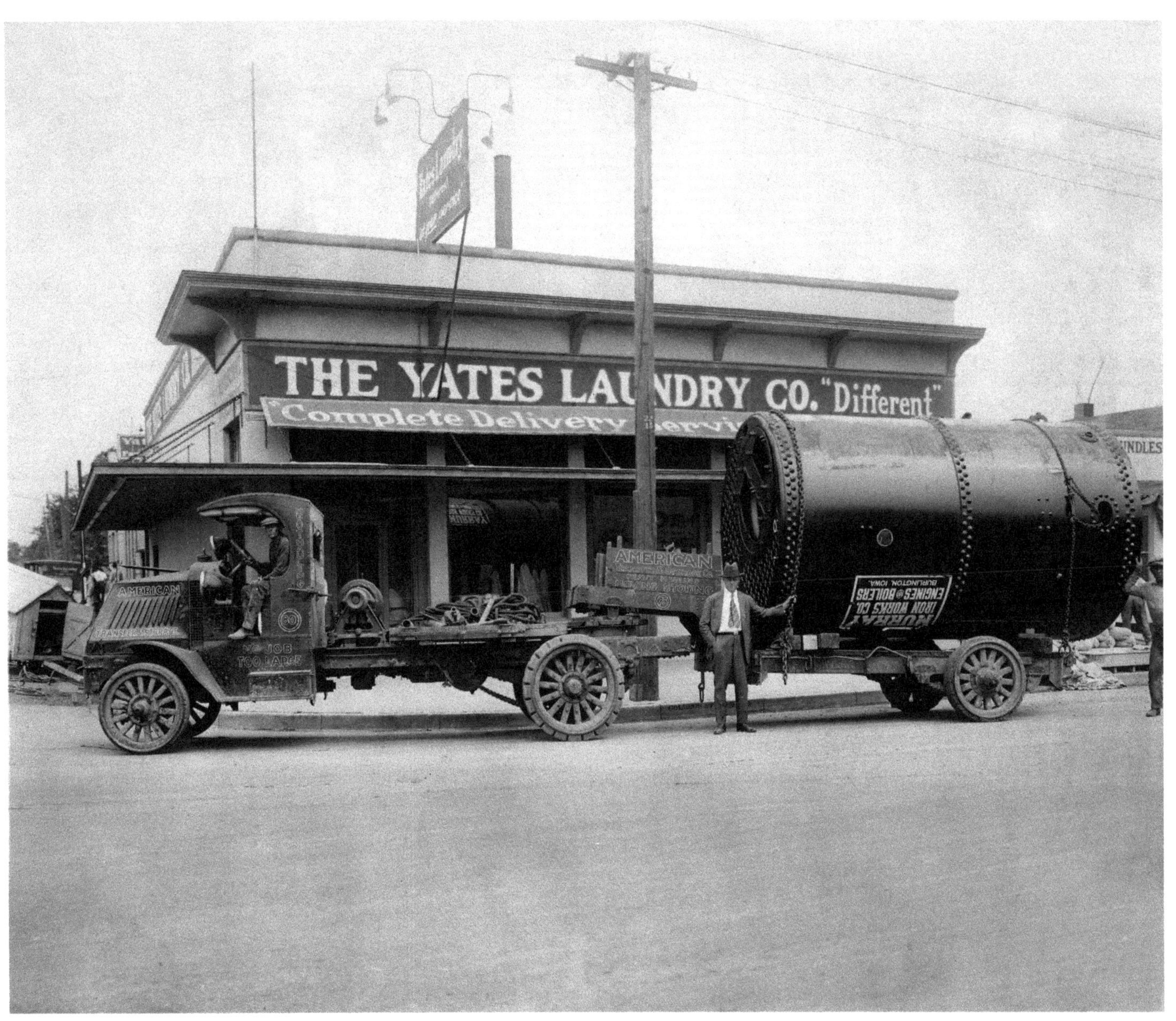

The American Transfer and Storage Company, founded in 1912, specialized in moving large and heavy items. This boiler must be destined for the Yates Laundry Company in East Dallas, which advertised "clean washing, careful finishing, courteous service."

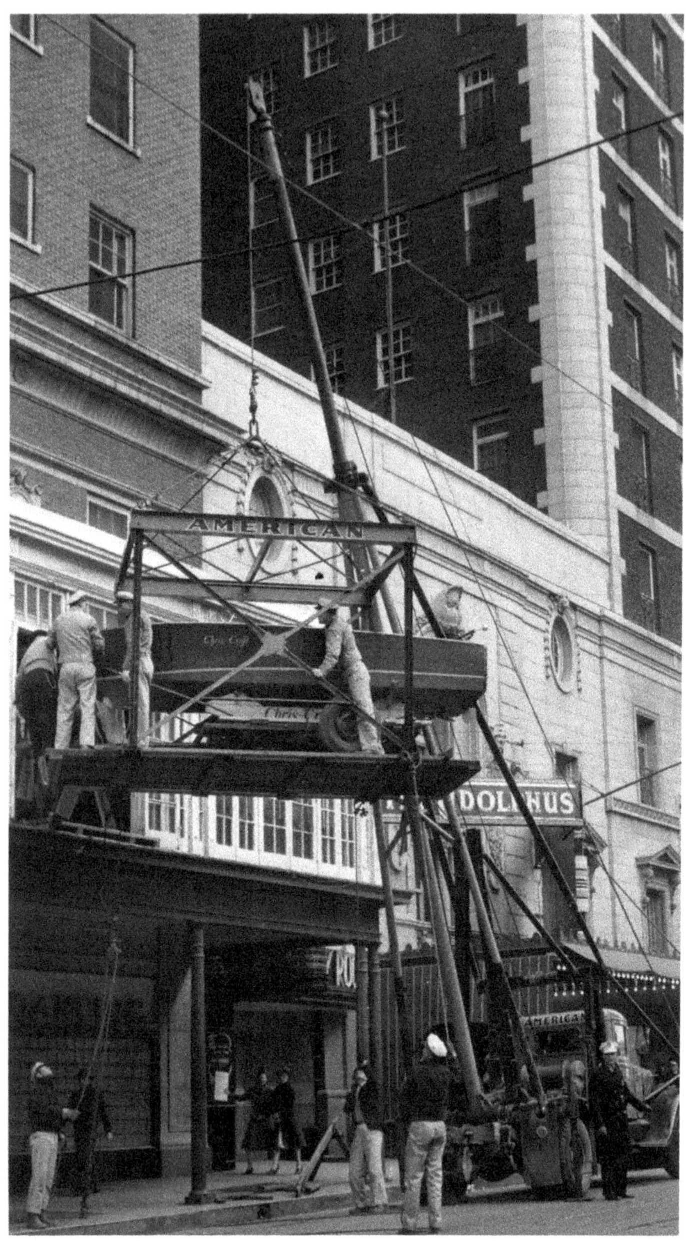

The American Transfer and Storage Company appears to be hoisting a Chris-Craft boat into the Adolphus Hotel in this photo. The company, founded in 1912, advertised "heavy hauling."

The Libecap Electric Company was so proud of its status as a state fair contractor that it hired professional photographer George McAfee to record its crews installing lights at the Grand Avenue entrance to the fairgrounds about 1934.

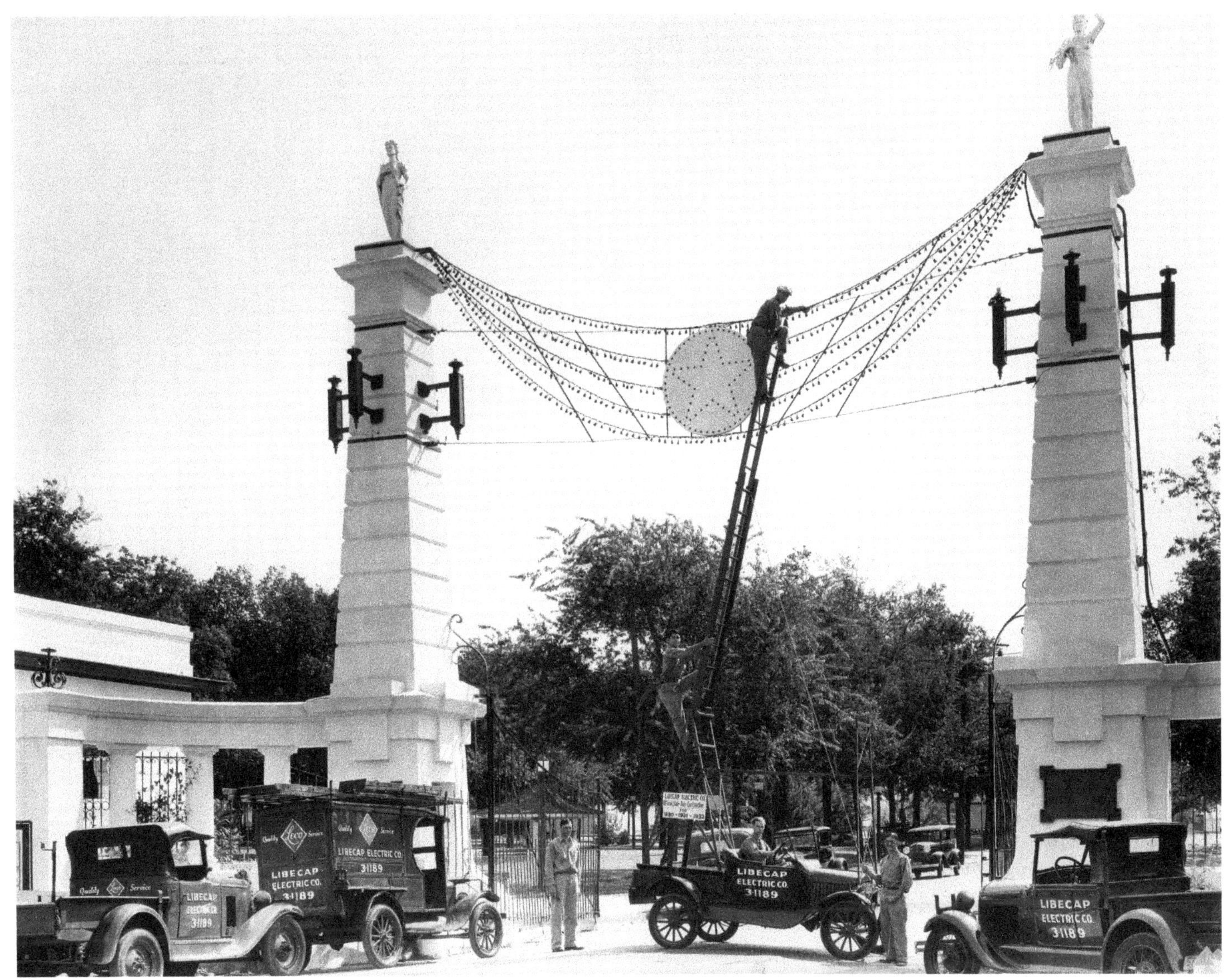

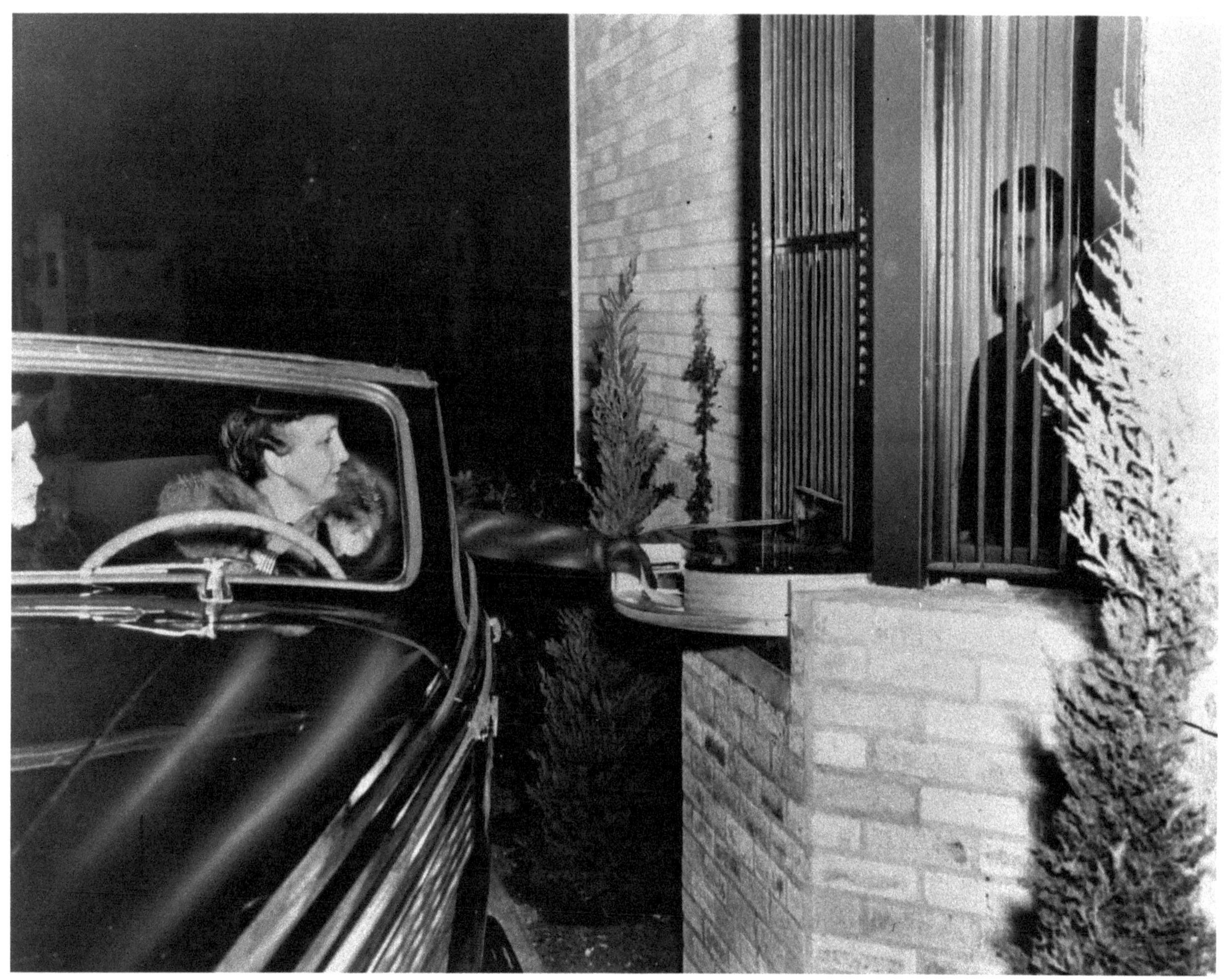

In 1938, architect George Dahl designed the first drive-through bank window in the world for the Hillcrest State Bank in University Park across from Southern Methodist University.

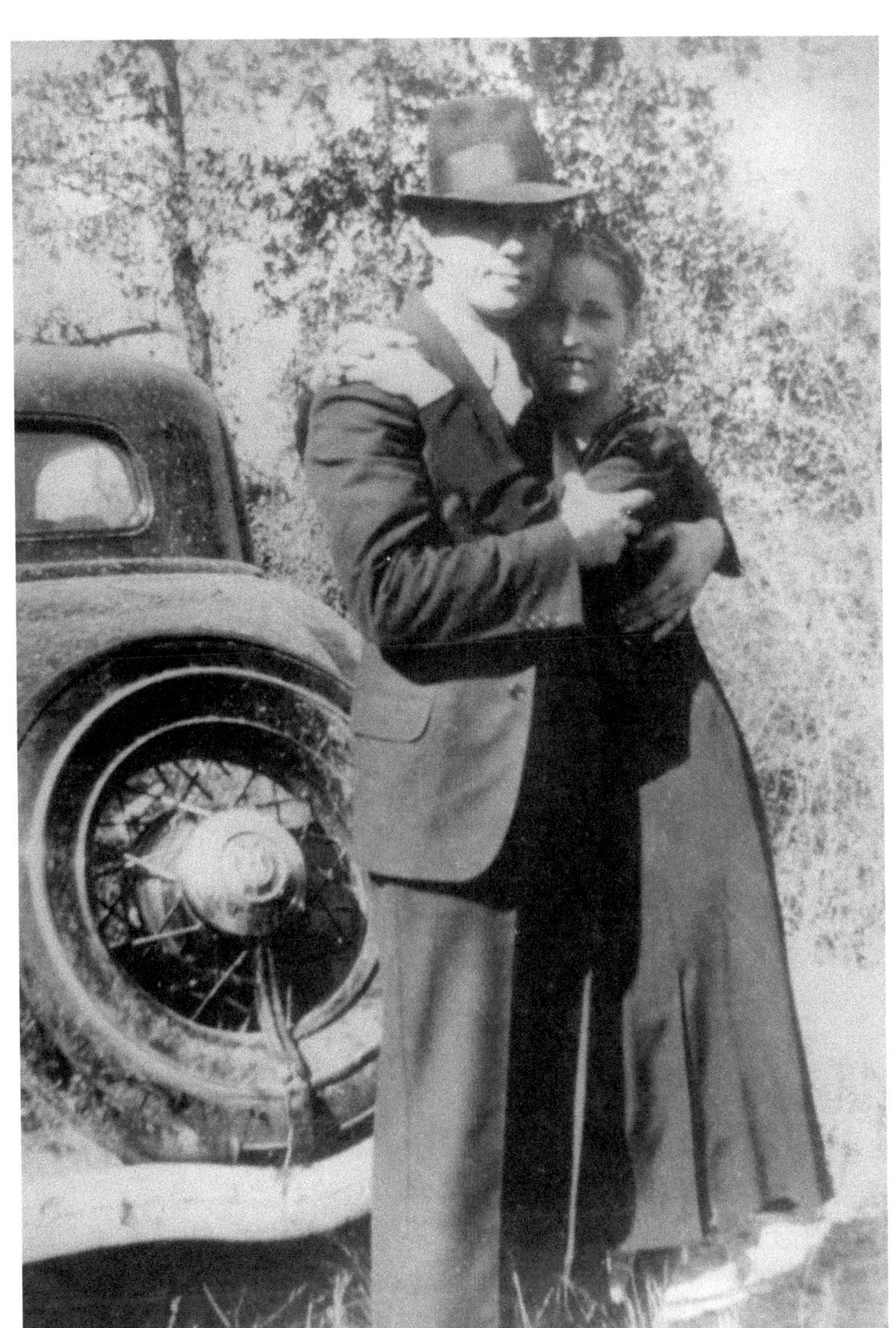

Clyde Barrow, whose family lived in unincorporated West Dallas, and Bonnie Parker terrorized Texas and nearby states for several years with their bank robberies and murders before being gunned down in Louisiana in 1934.

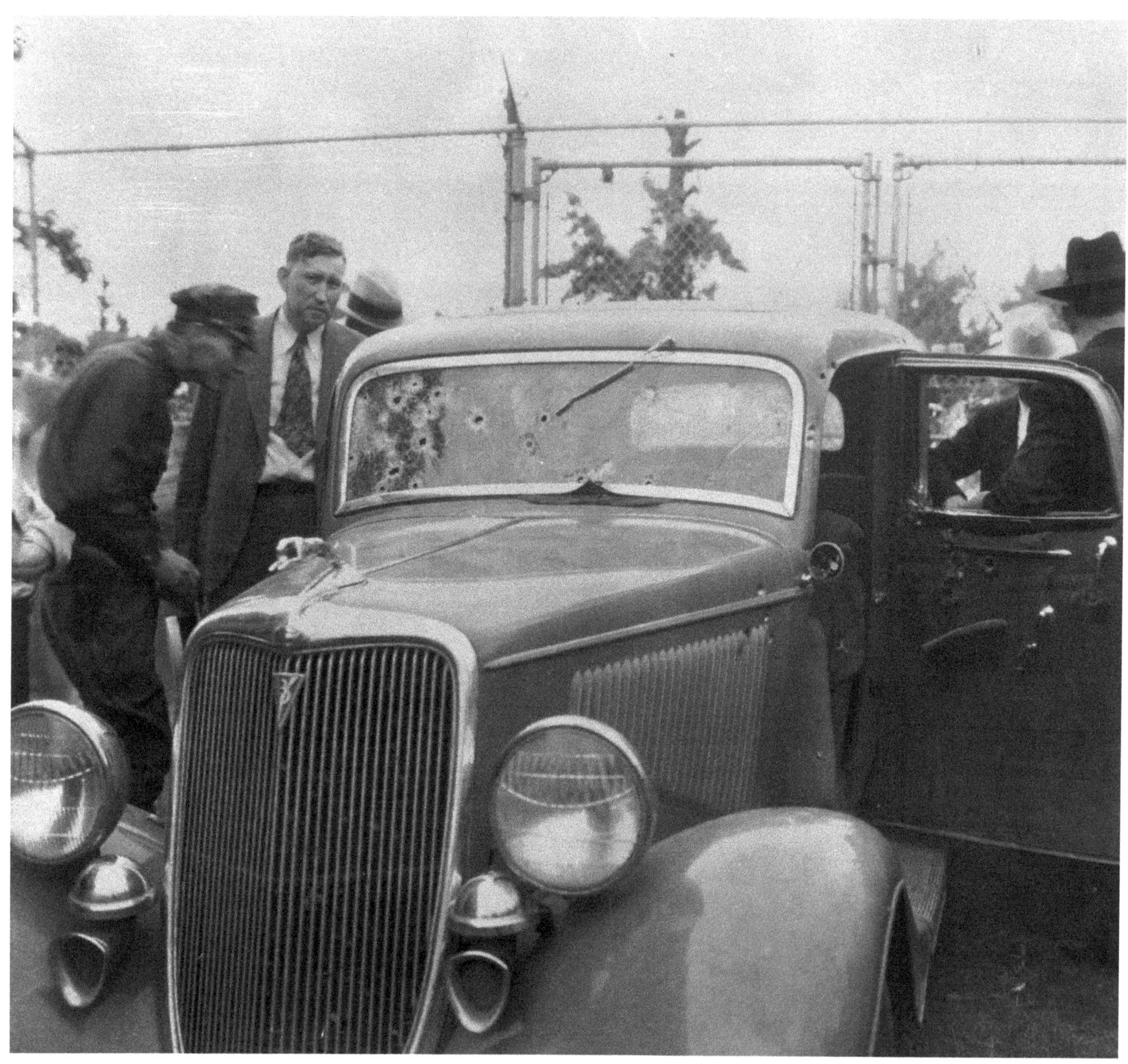

Lawmen inspect the bullet-riddled car in which Bonnie and Clyde were killed near Gibsland, Louisiana, in May 1934.

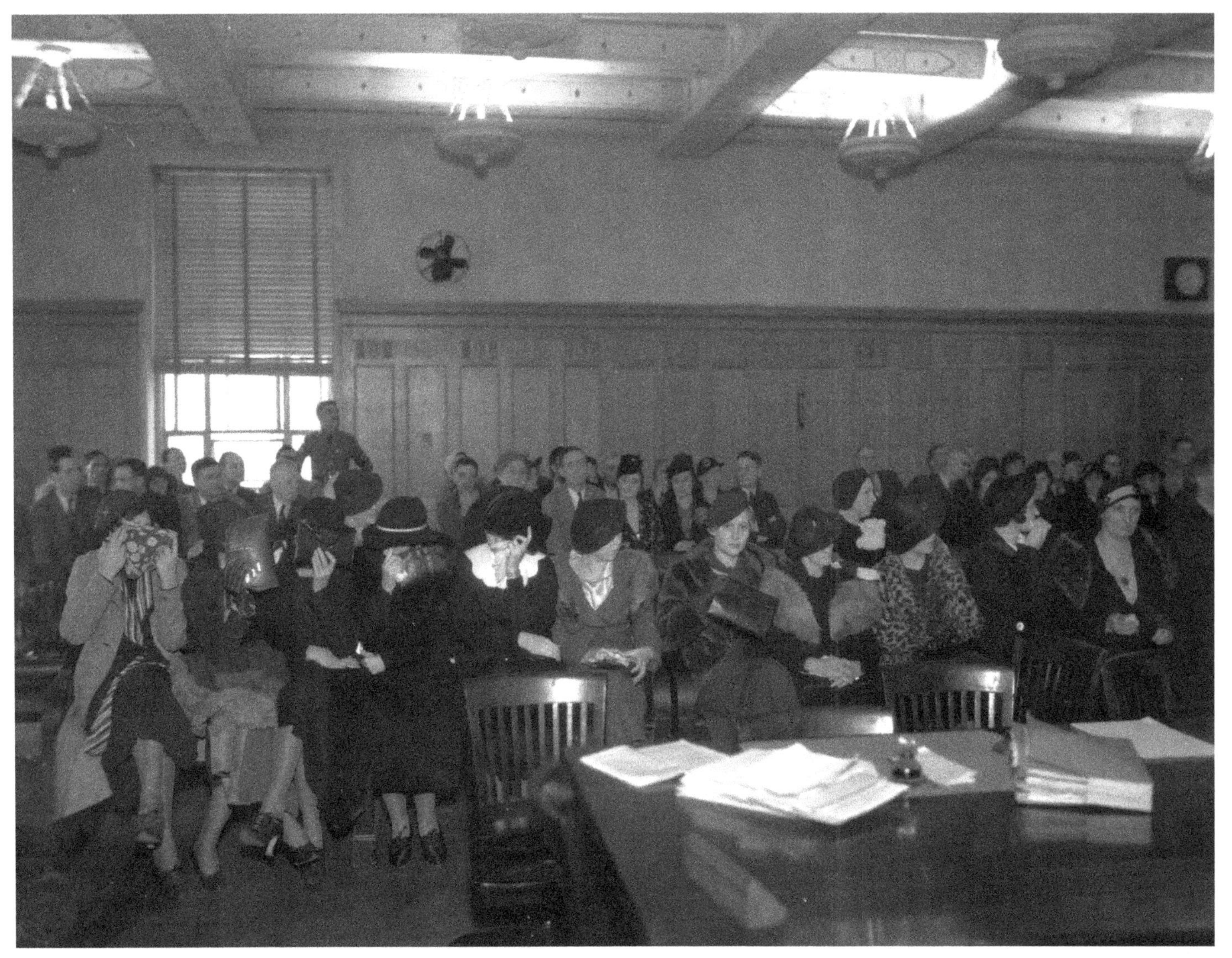

Members of the Barrow and Parker families were among those who stood trial in 1935 for harboring the outlaws.

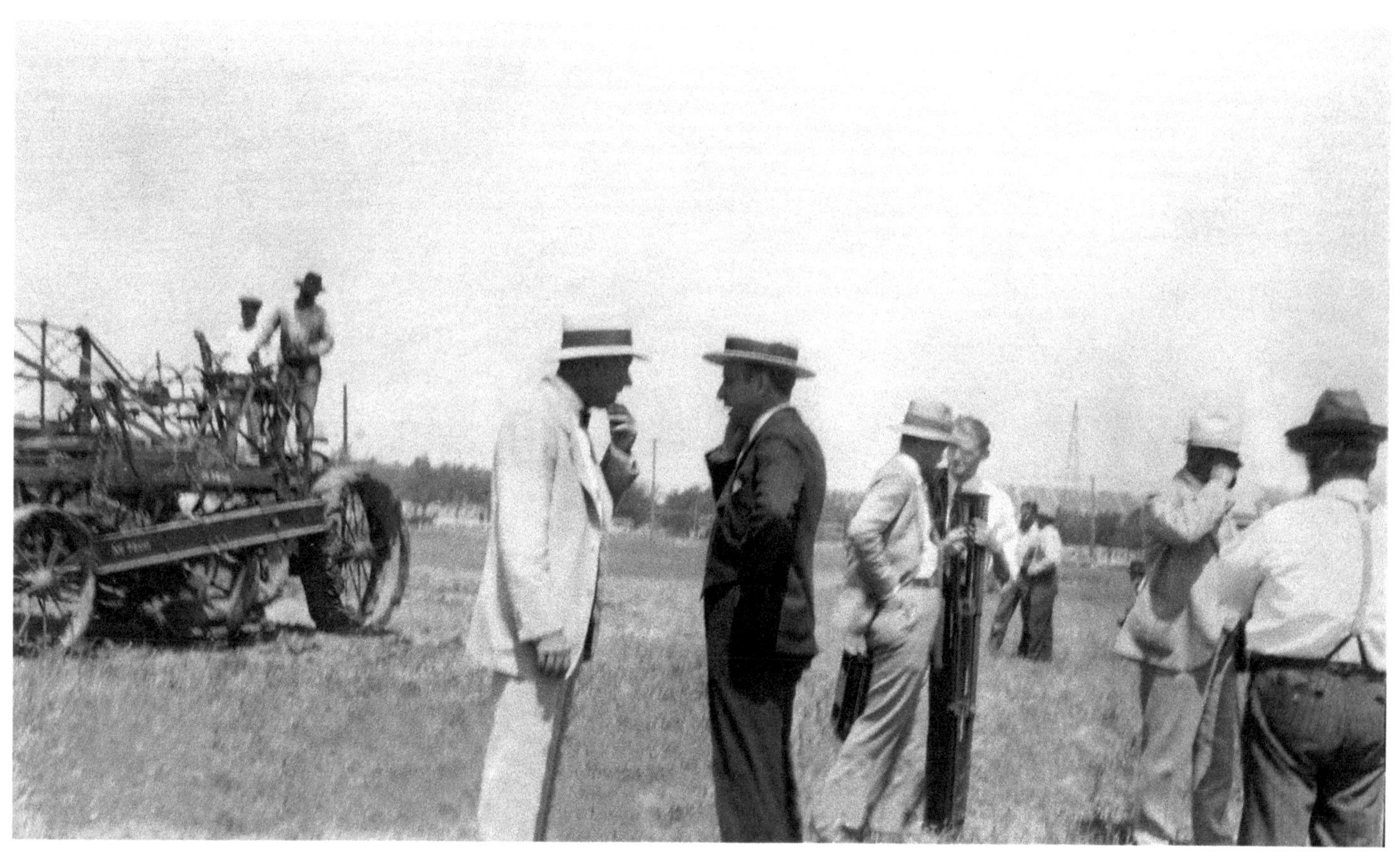

A new football stadium—soon known as the Cotton Bowl—was constructed at Fair Park in 1930. The playing surface was located 18 feet below ground, and a 46-foot embankment was built up from the field. Seating 46,200 people, it was the largest such facility in the South.

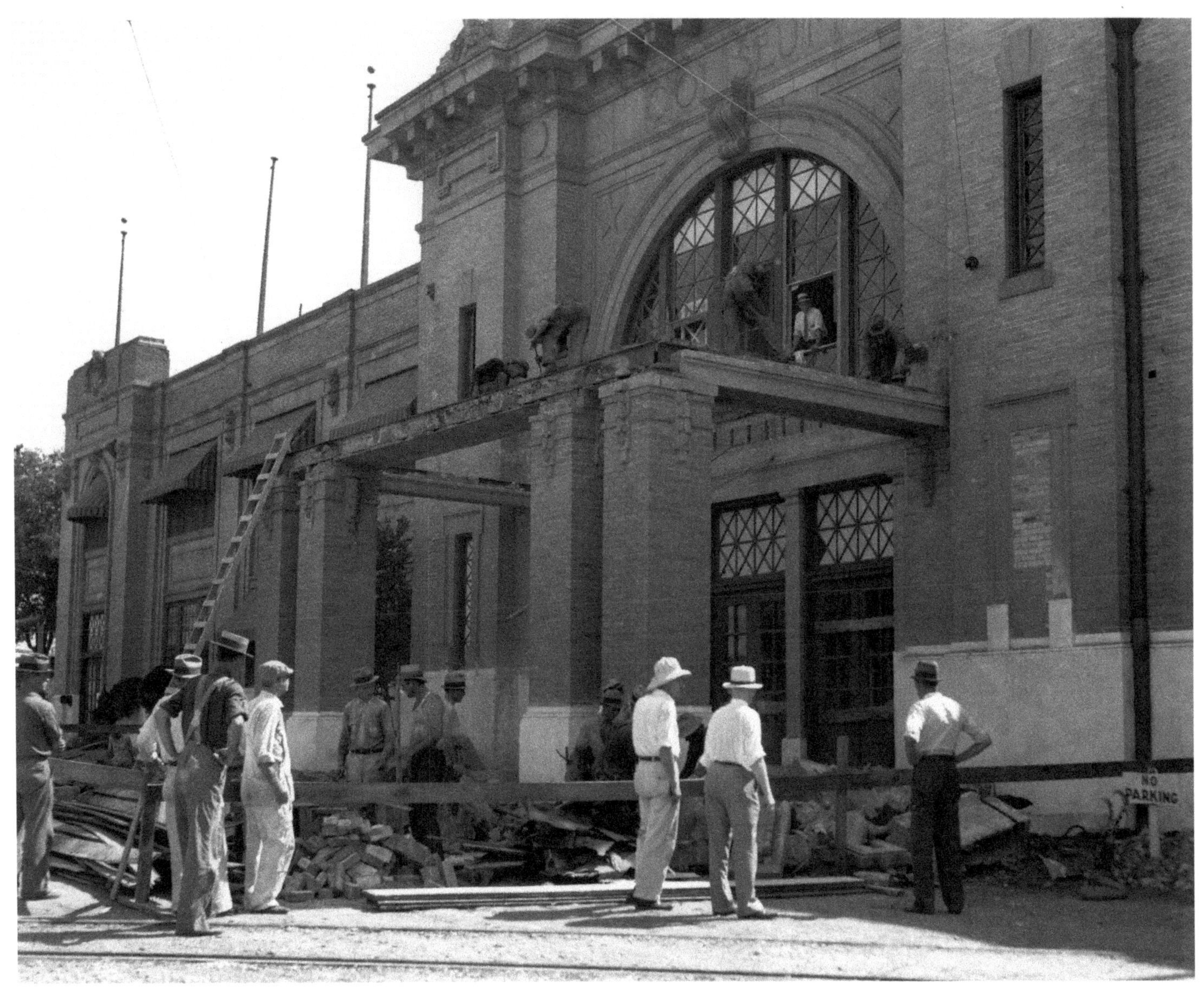

The old Fair Park Coliseum (1910) received a facelift in preparation for the 1936 Texas Centennial Exposition, blending it with the new art deco structures designed for the event. Today it houses the Women's Museum: An Institute for the Future.

Most visitors approached the Centennial Exposition from Parry Avenue, where architect George Dahl's 85-foot-tall pylon at the entrance was topped with a gold star representing the lone star of Texas.

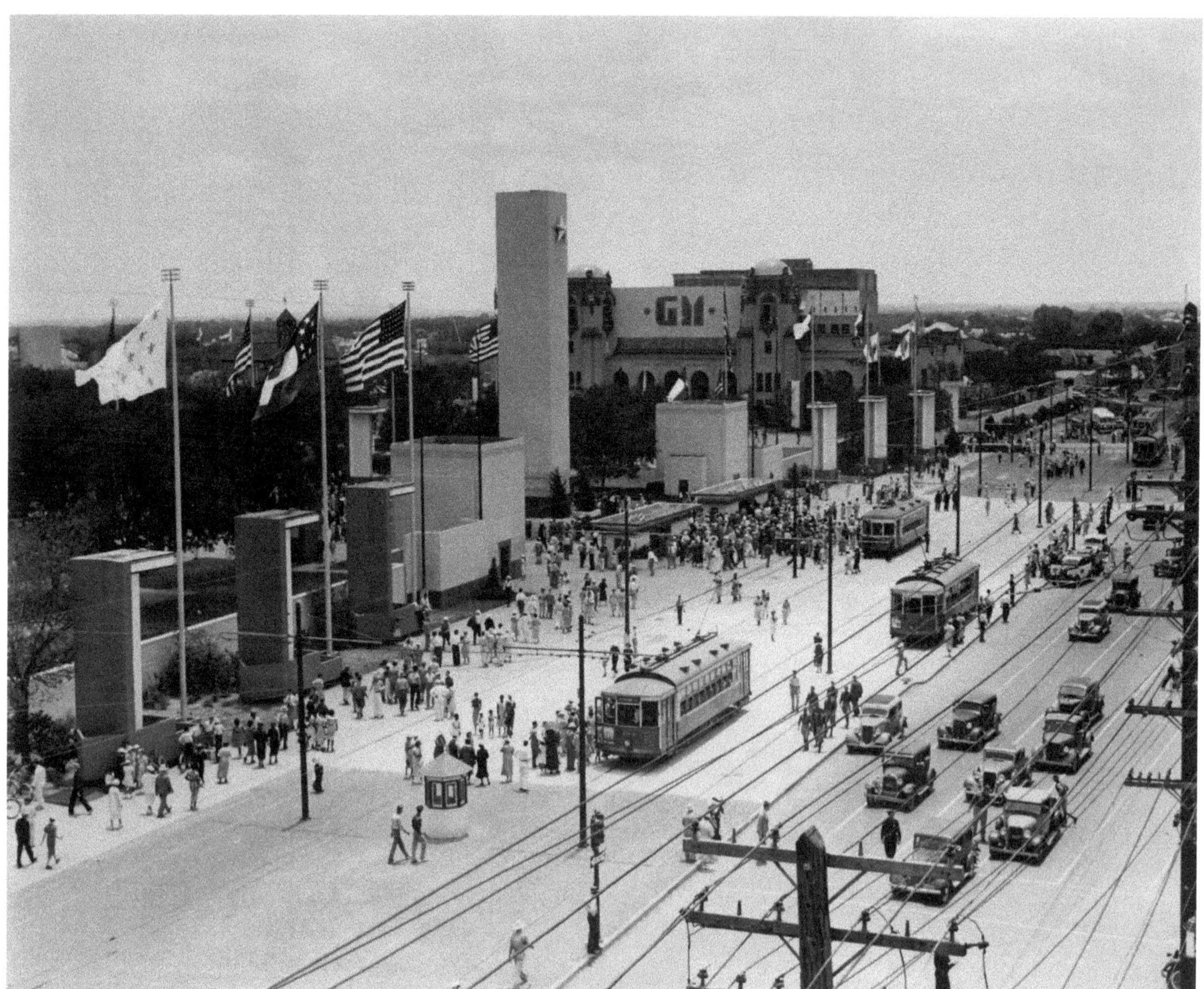

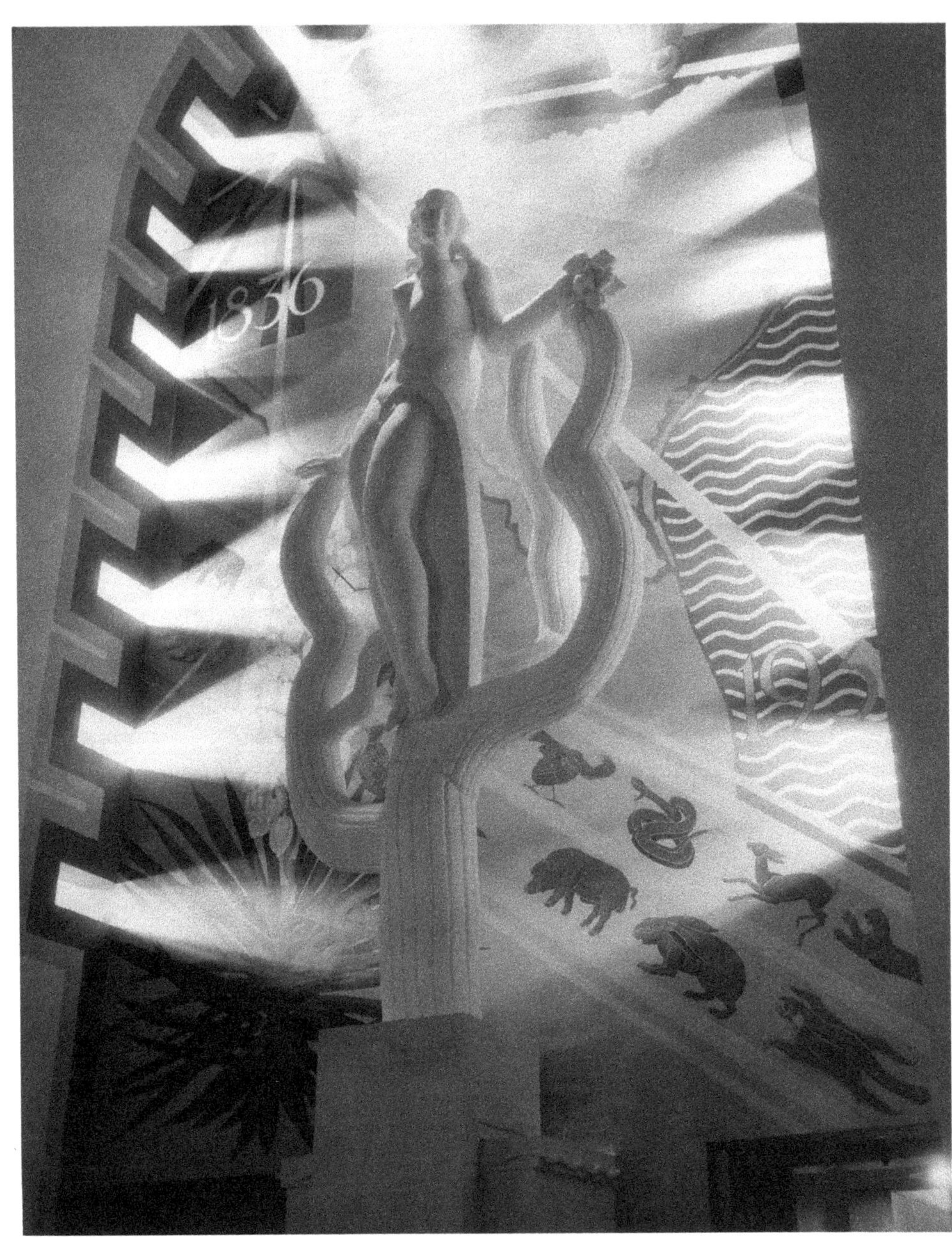

Raoul Josset's sculpture, *Spirit of the Centennial*, greeted visitors outside the Administration Building near the main entrance.

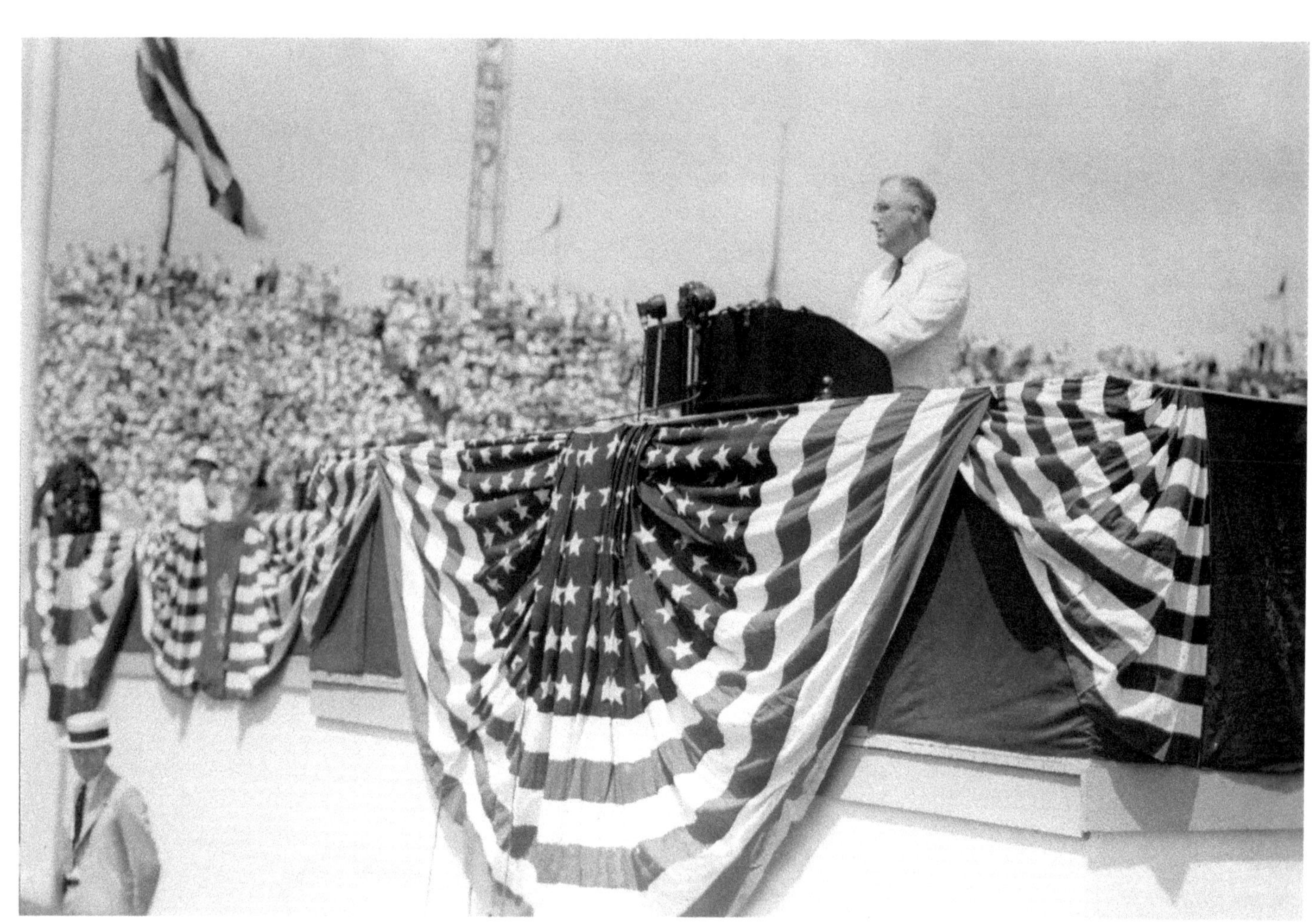

President Franklin D. Roosevelt visited the Texas Centennial Exposition at Fair Park on June 12, 1936, and spoke to a huge crowd in the Cotton Bowl. Texas, he told his audience, was "100 years young."

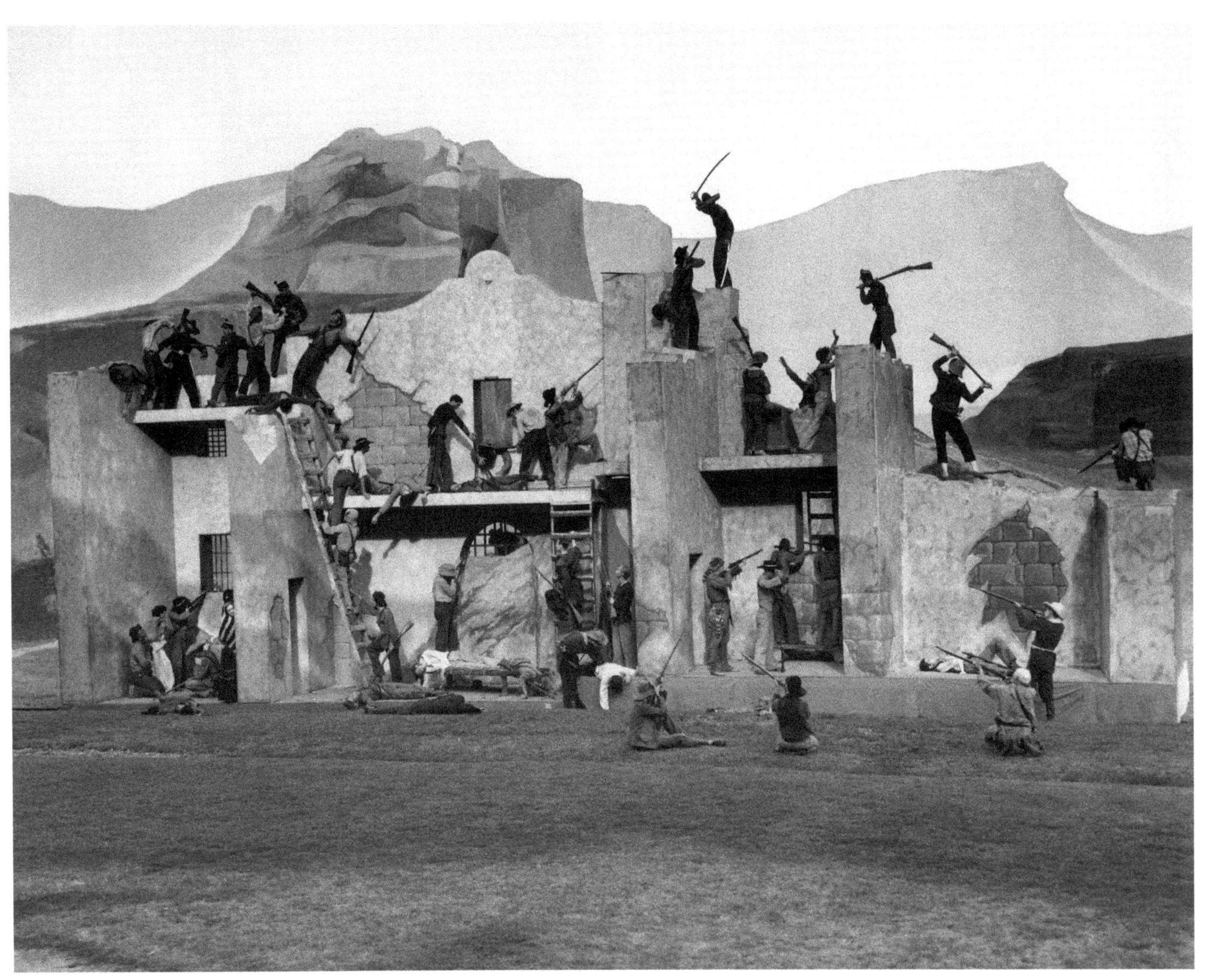

Among the highlights of the Texas Centennial Exposition was the Cavalcade of Texas, an outdoor historical pageant featuring cowboys and horses.

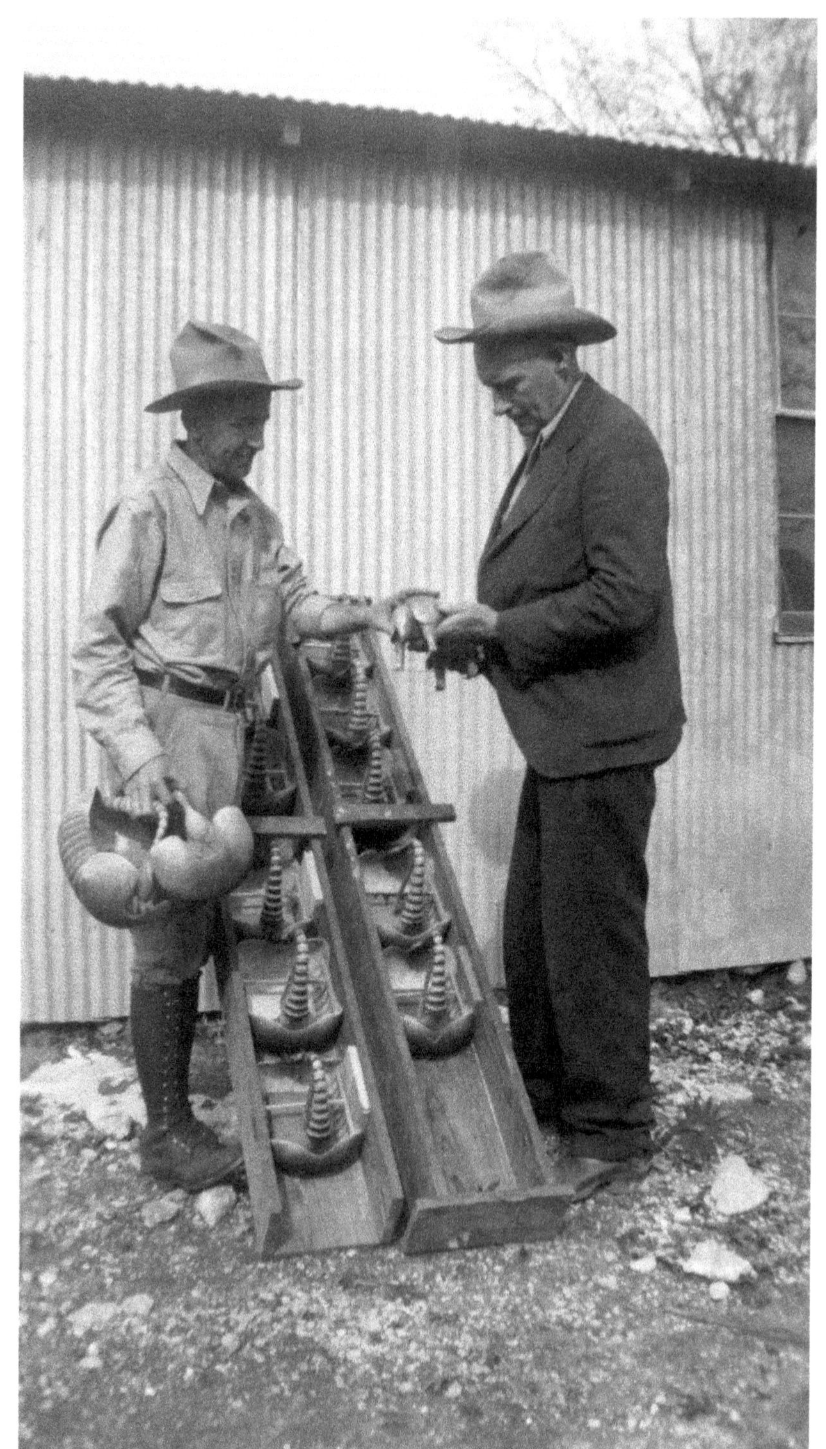

Among the many human interest stories relating to the Centennial Exposition was that of armadillo hunter Noel Insall, right, and armadillo basket "king" Joe D. Johns, left. Insall, a former deputy sheriff, gave up the pursuit of criminals to follow the more lucrative hunt for armadillos. In this photo, he bargains with Johns for 1,000 shells.

Crowds fill the plaza in front of the Federal Building during the Texas Centennial Exposition. An estimated six million people visited Dallas during the six-month spectacle.

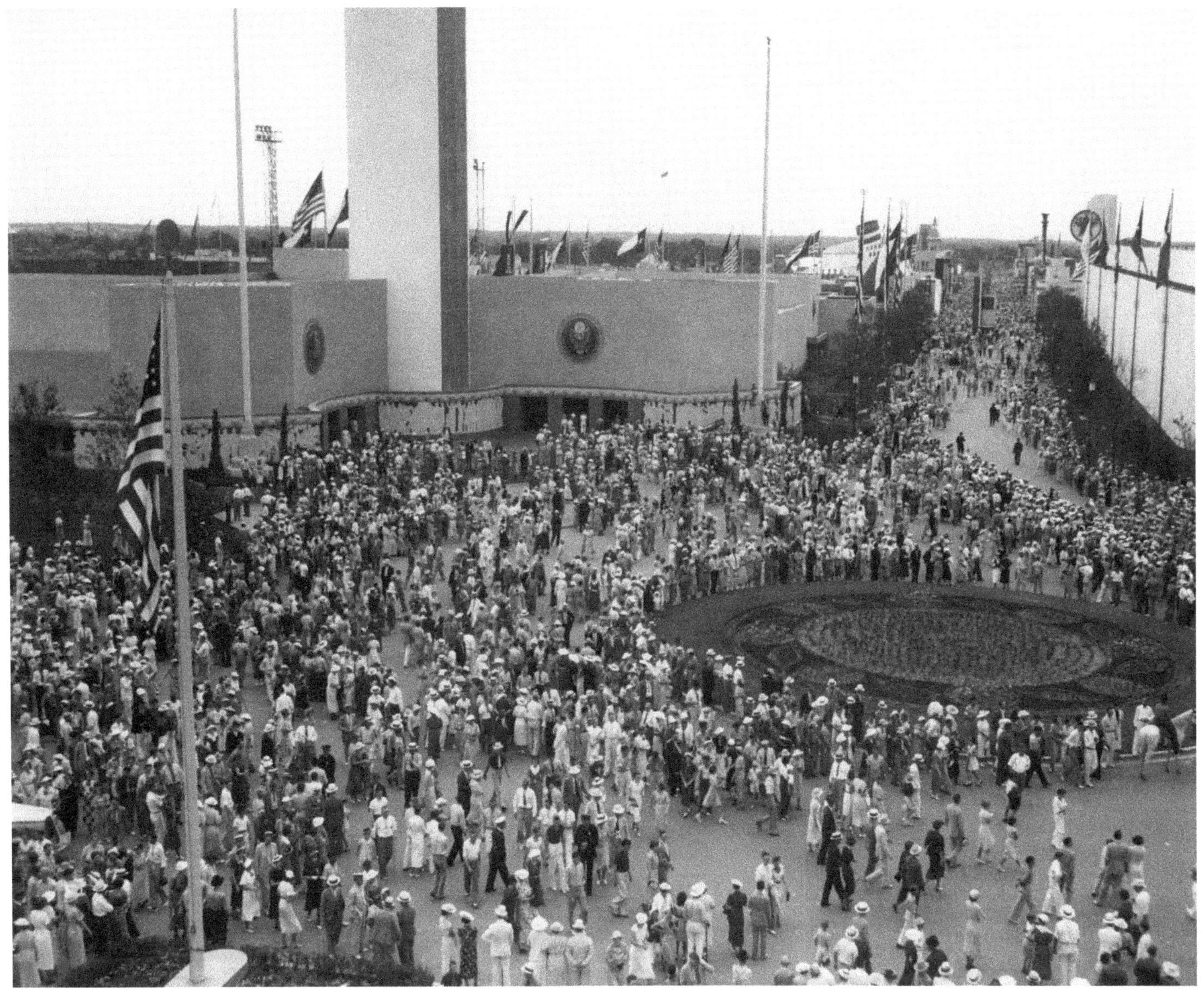

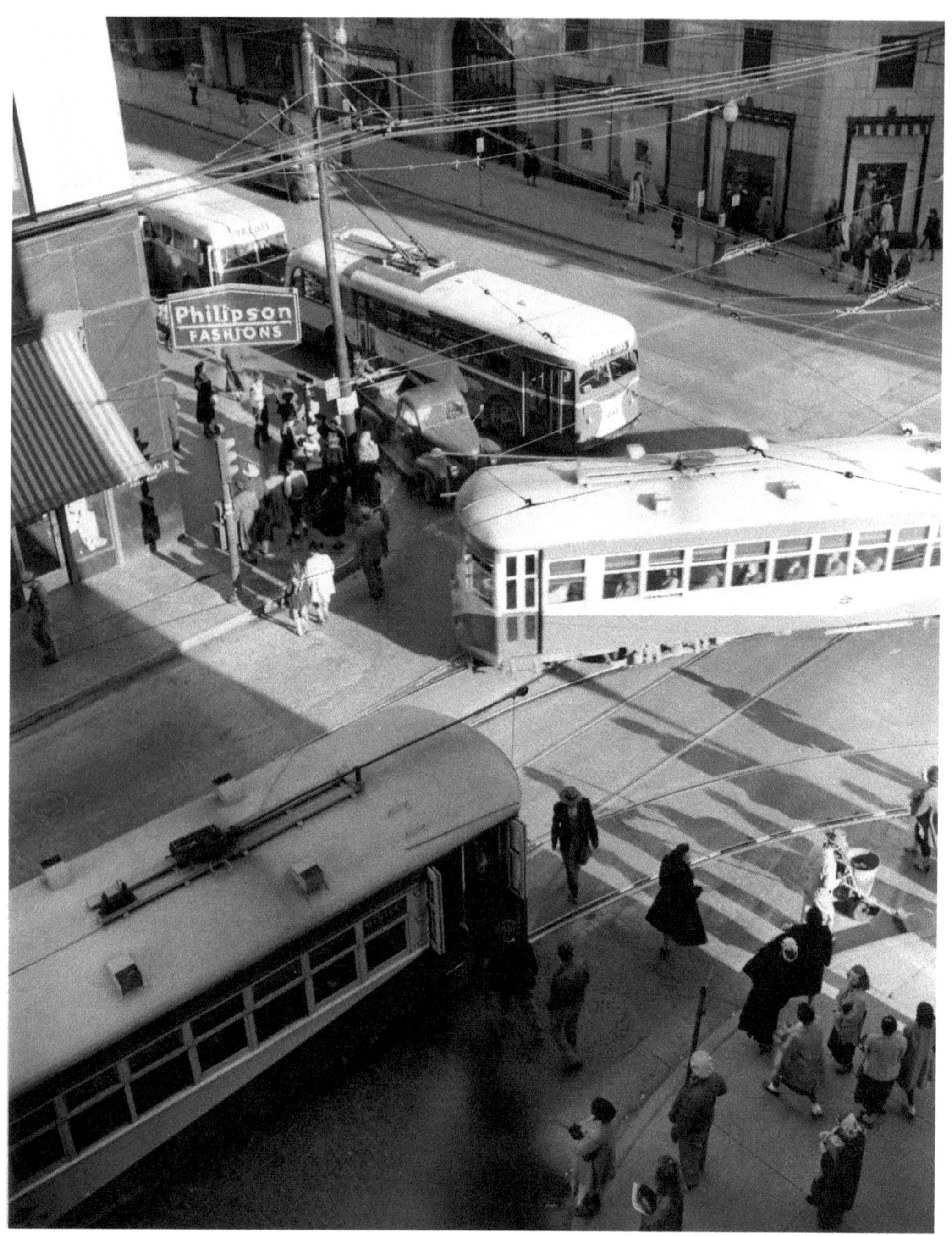

During World War II, when gasoline was strictly rationed, streetcars became an even more important form of urban transportation in Dallas, as in other cities. This view is at Elm and St. Paul streets.

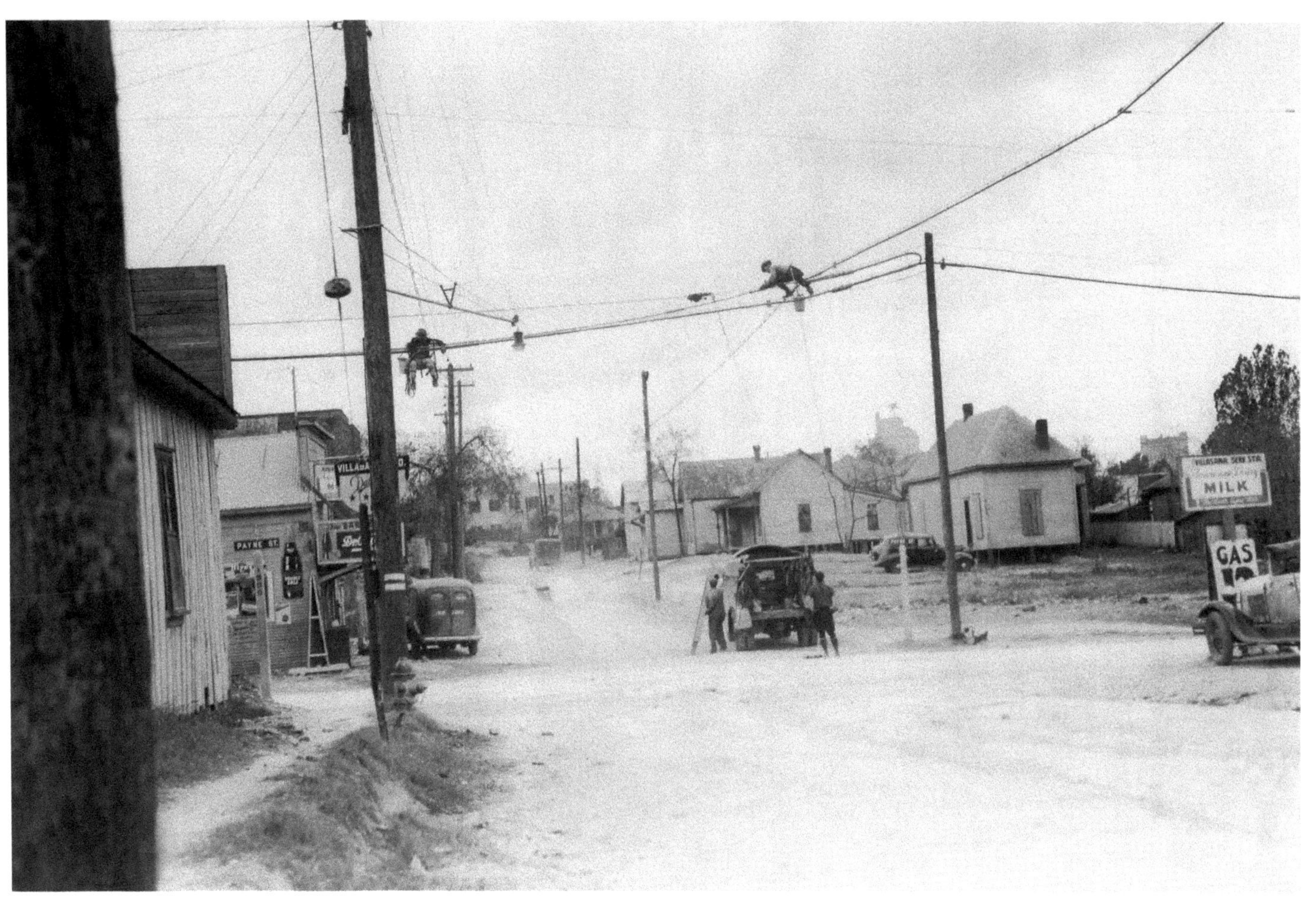

Some streets in the Little Mexico barrio north of downtown remained unpaved into the 1940s. The tightly knit community supported a variety of stores and several churches.

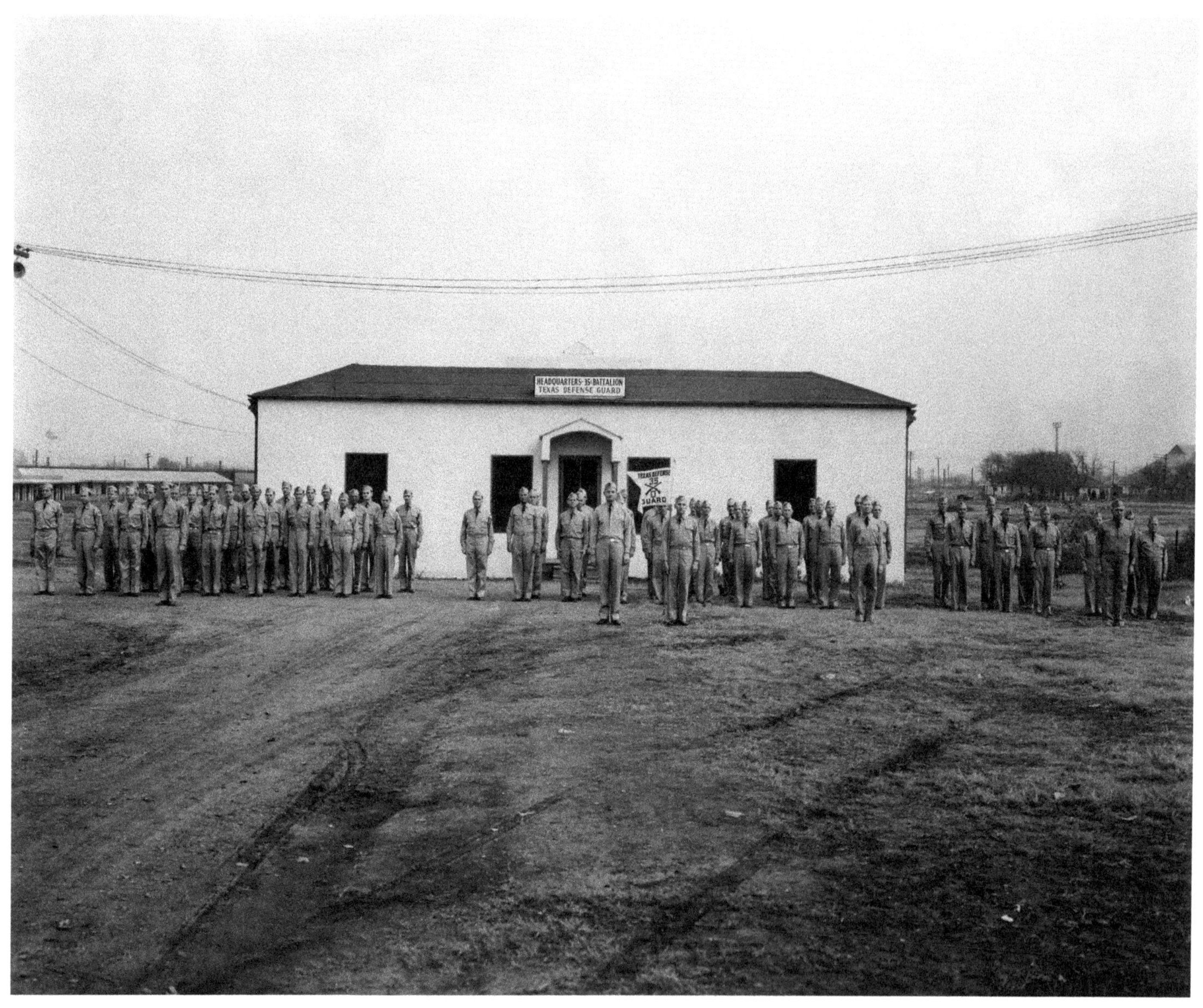

More than 52,000 Dallas County residents served in the armed forces during World War II. This is Company "D," 35th Battalion, of the Texas Defense Guard.

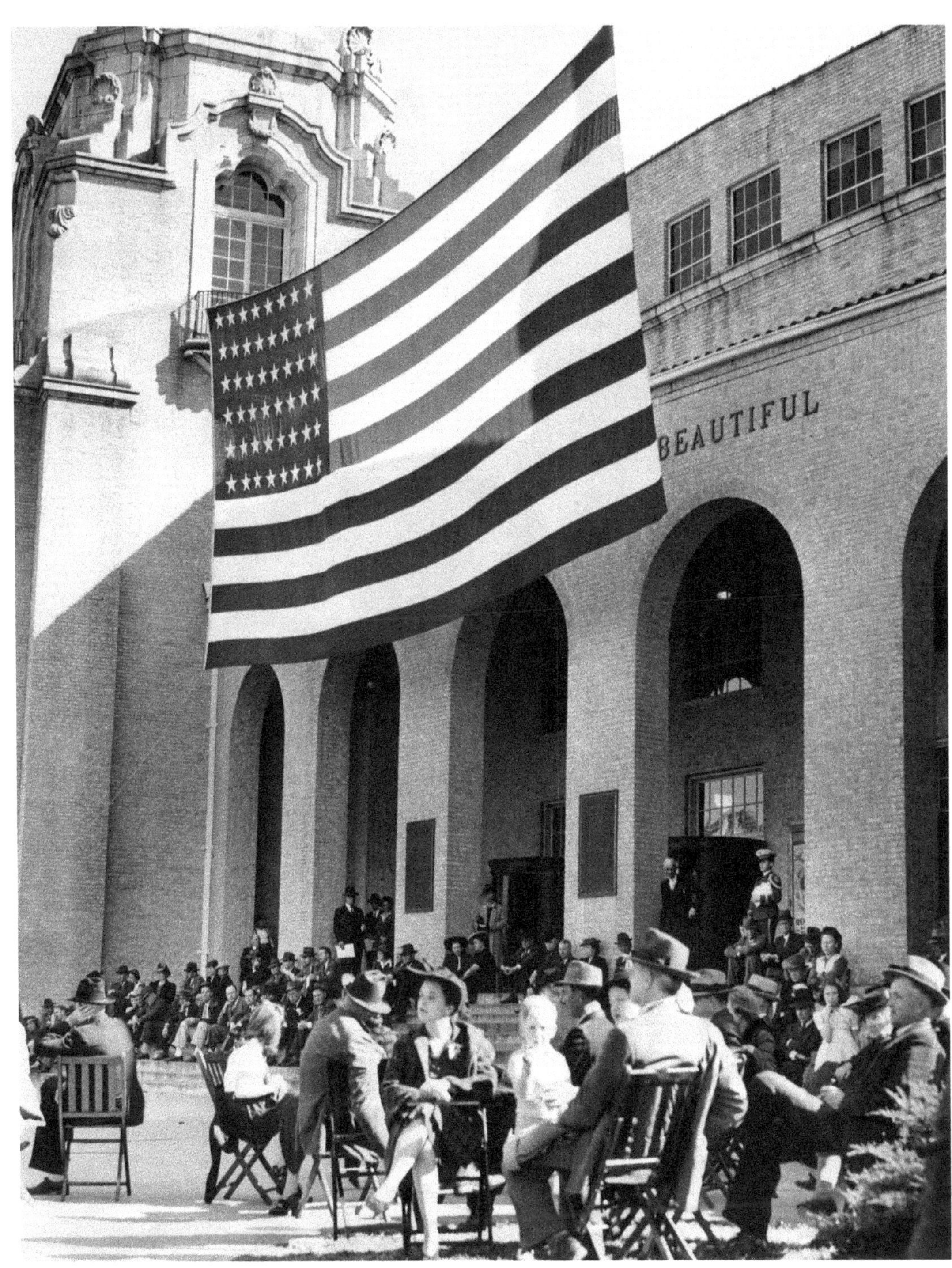

On March 23, 1942, several hundred people gathered at Fair Park for a rally urging more active involvement in World War II. These people are sitting outside the Music Hall.

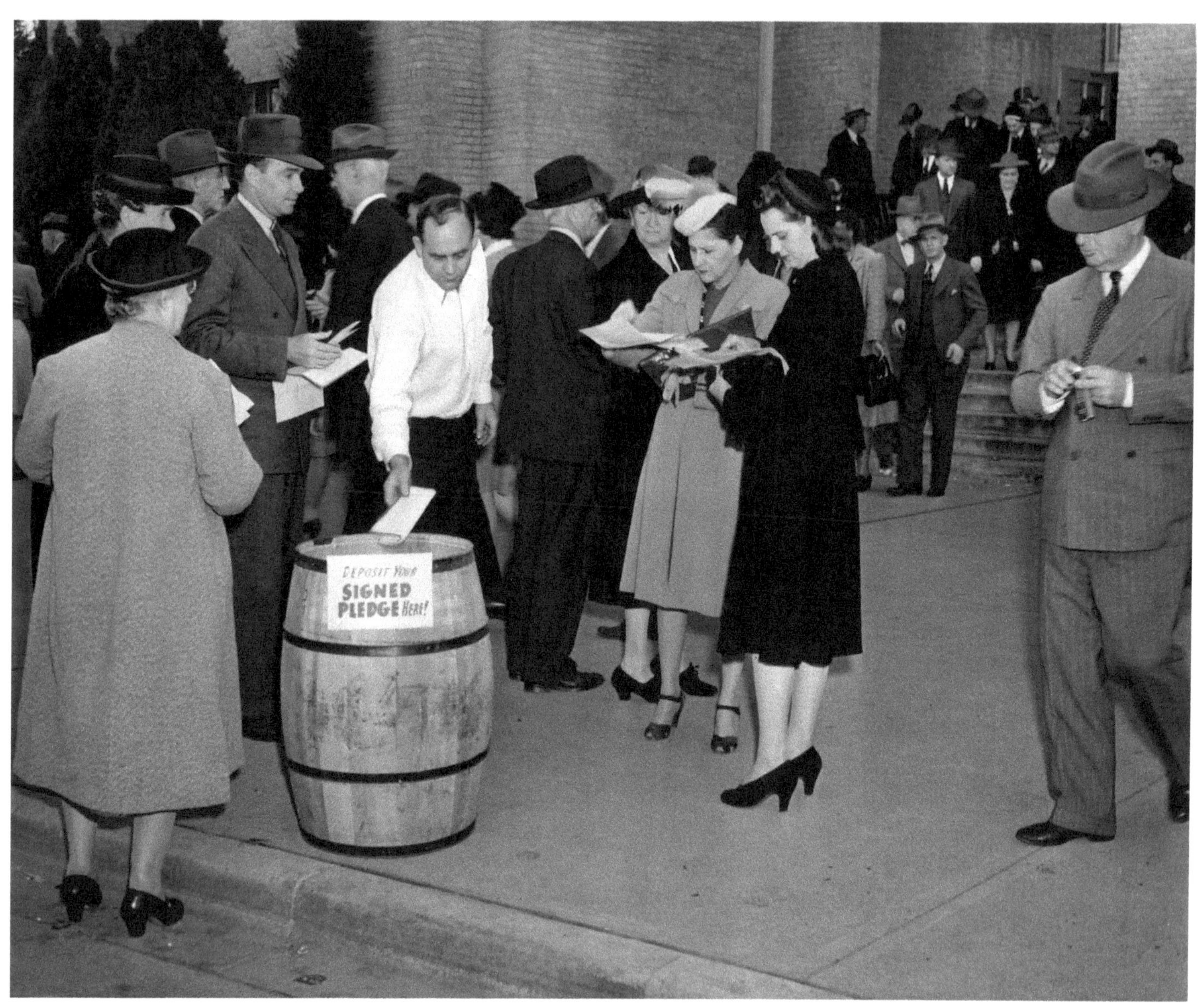

Participants in the "We Want Action" rally at Fair Park in March 1942 deposited signed pledges into barrels.

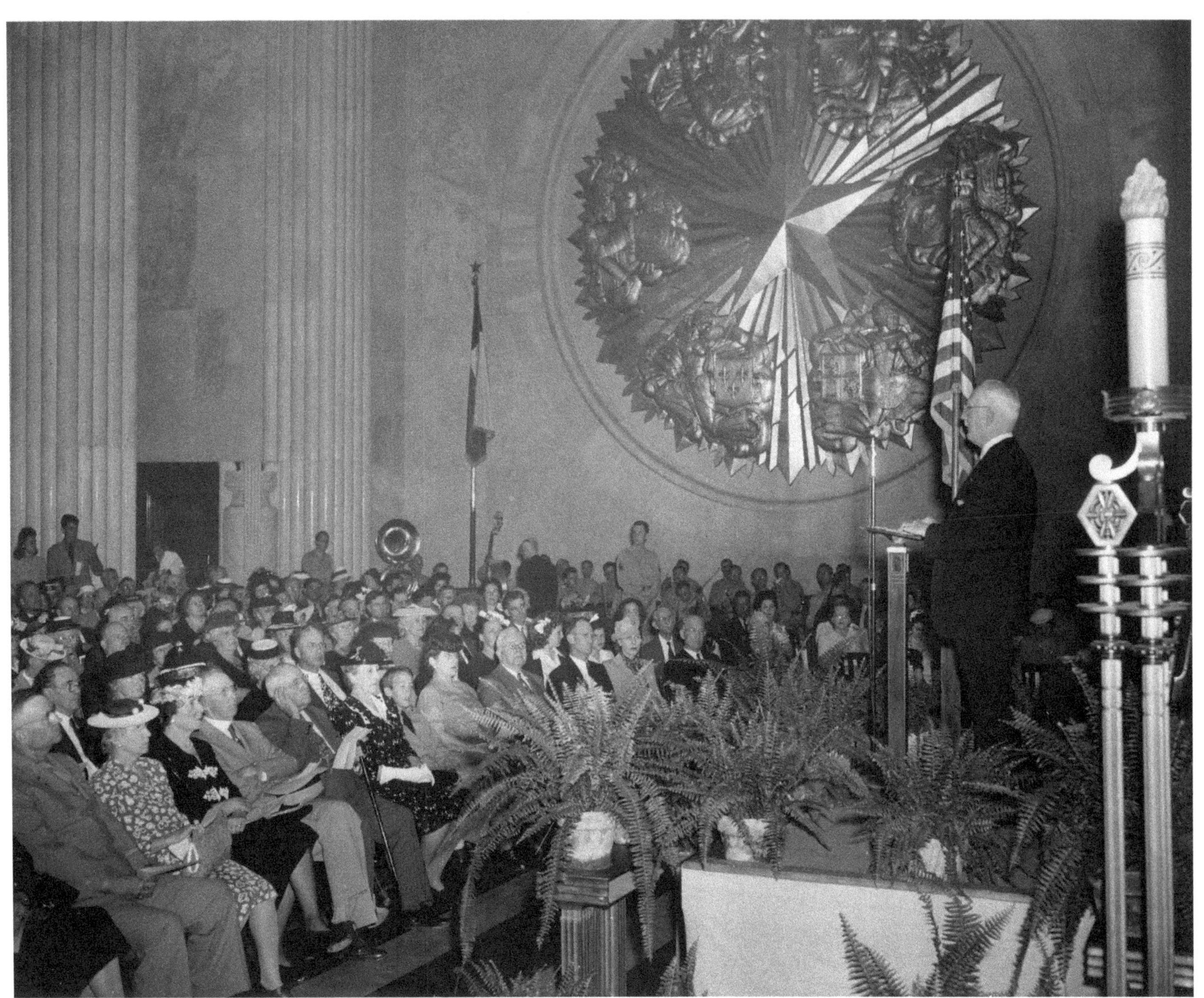

As president of the Dallas Historical Society, the elderly G. B. Dealey spoke to a crowd at the third annual "I Am an American Day" ceremony in May 1945 at the Hall of State.

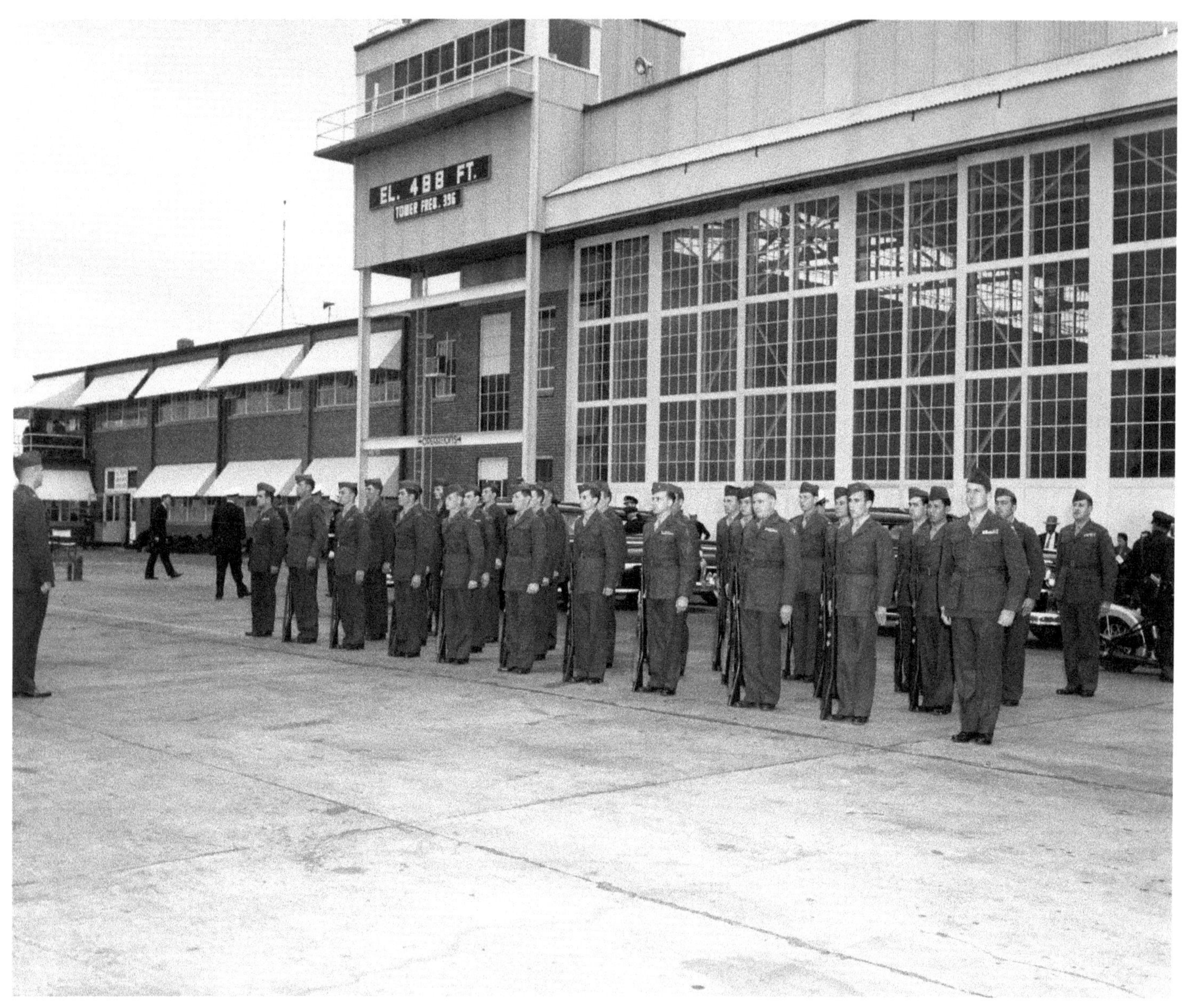

A Marine Honor Guard lined up at the Naval Air Station to welcome Admiral Chester Nimitz on his arrival in Dallas on October 12, 1945. It was the admiral's first Texas appearance since accepting the surrender of the Japanese. His parade through downtown Dallas attracted 300,000 spectators.

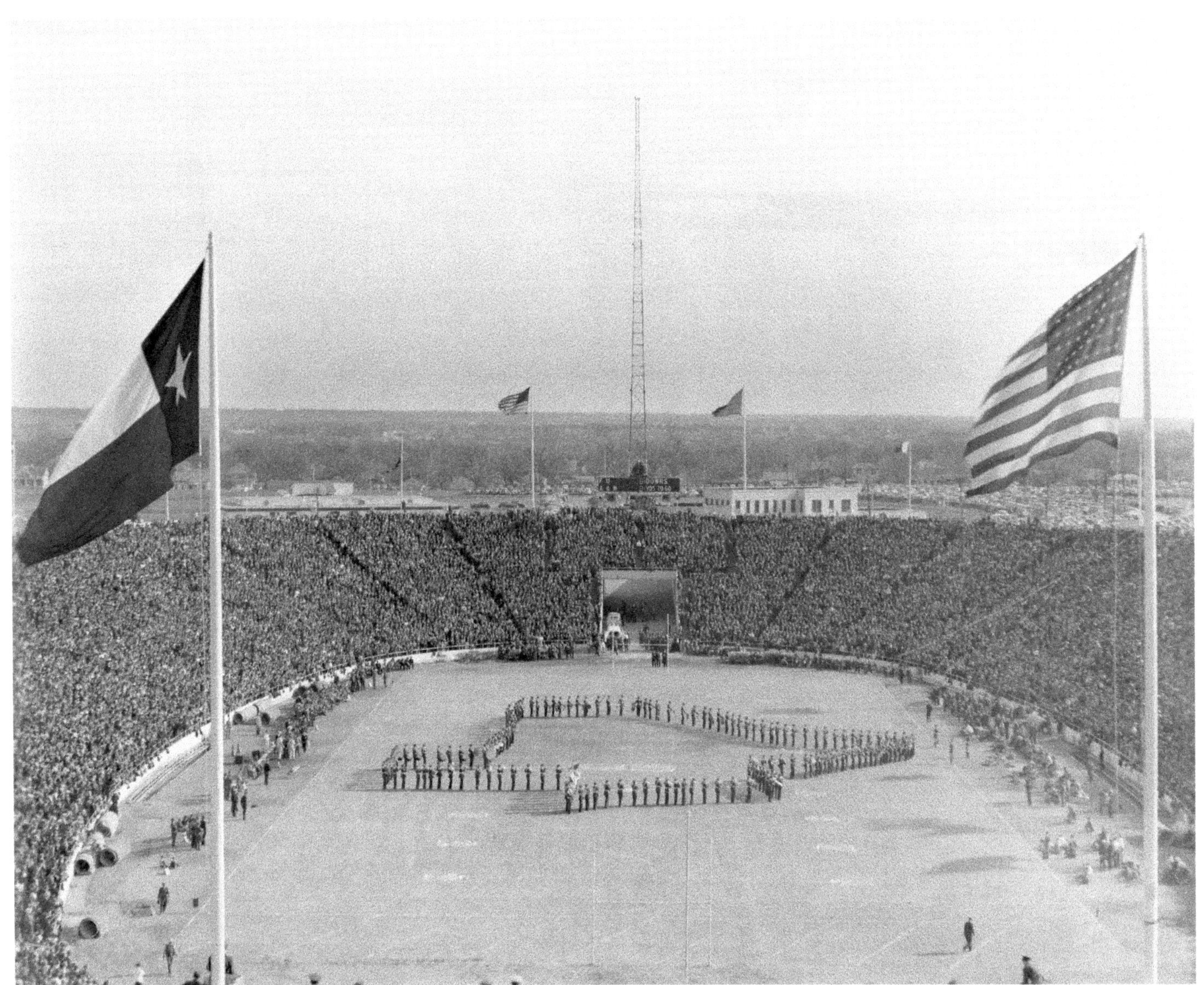

Two hundred cadets with the Texas A&M University marching band form the shape of the state of Texas during halftime at the New Year's Day Cotton Bowl game in 1941. A&M defeated Fordham 13–12 before a crowd of 47,000.

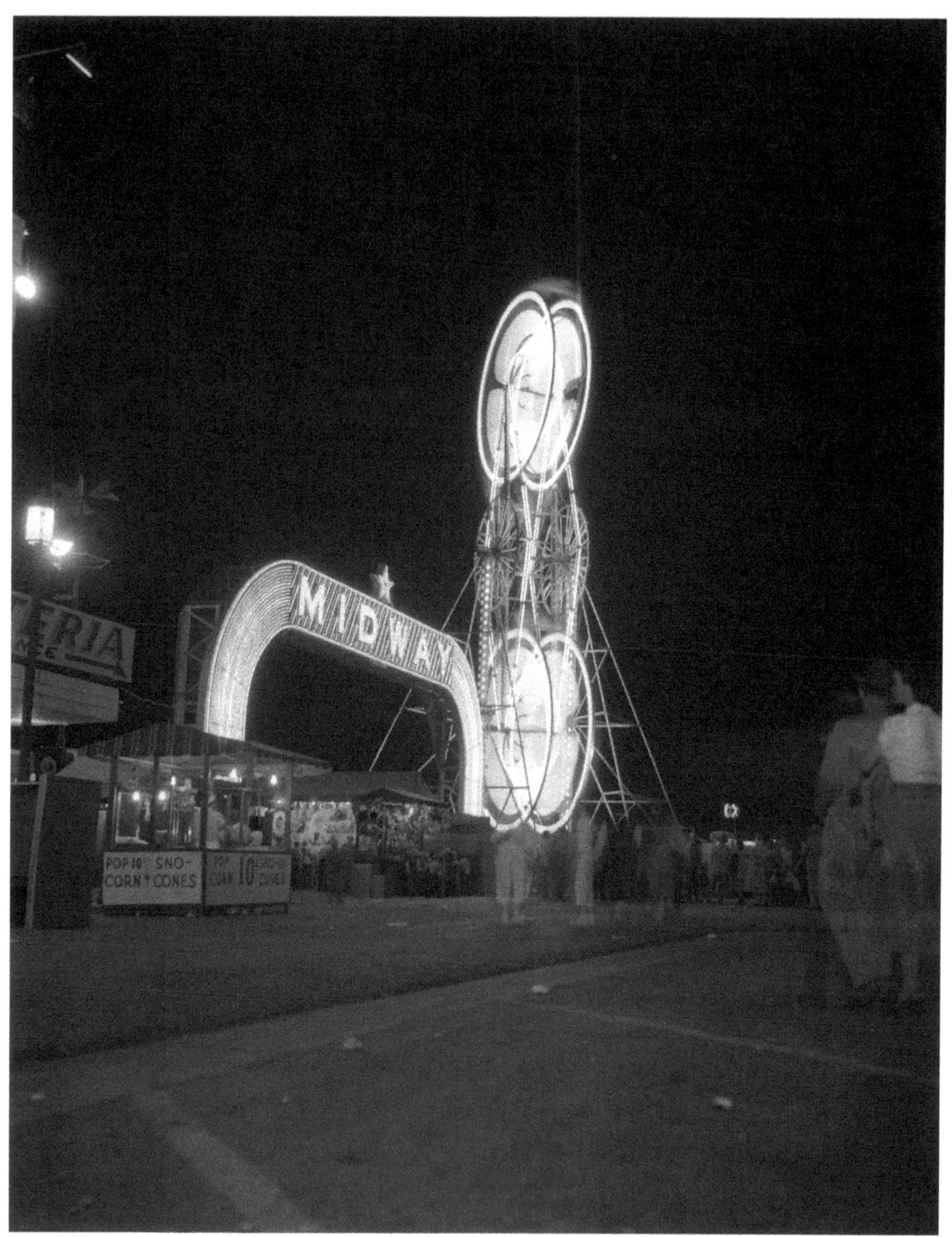

The Fair Park Midway was continually improved, with new and exciting rides.

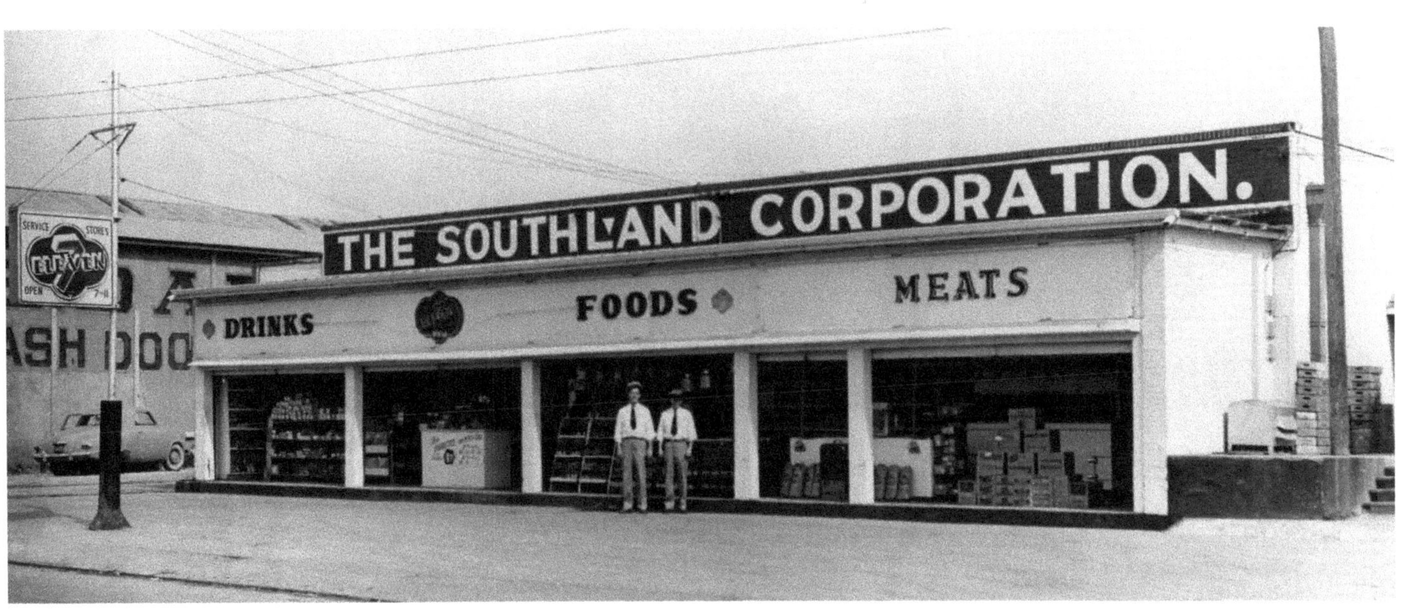

In 1927, an enterprising ice dock employee at the Southland Ice Company in Oak Cliff began offering milk, bread, and eggs on Sundays and evenings when grocery stores were closed. The new business idea proved so popular that Southland soon opened outlets known as Tote'm stores, since customers "toted" away their products. In 1946, Tote'm became 7-Eleven to reflect the store's new, extended hours, 7 A.M. to 11 P.M., seven days a week.

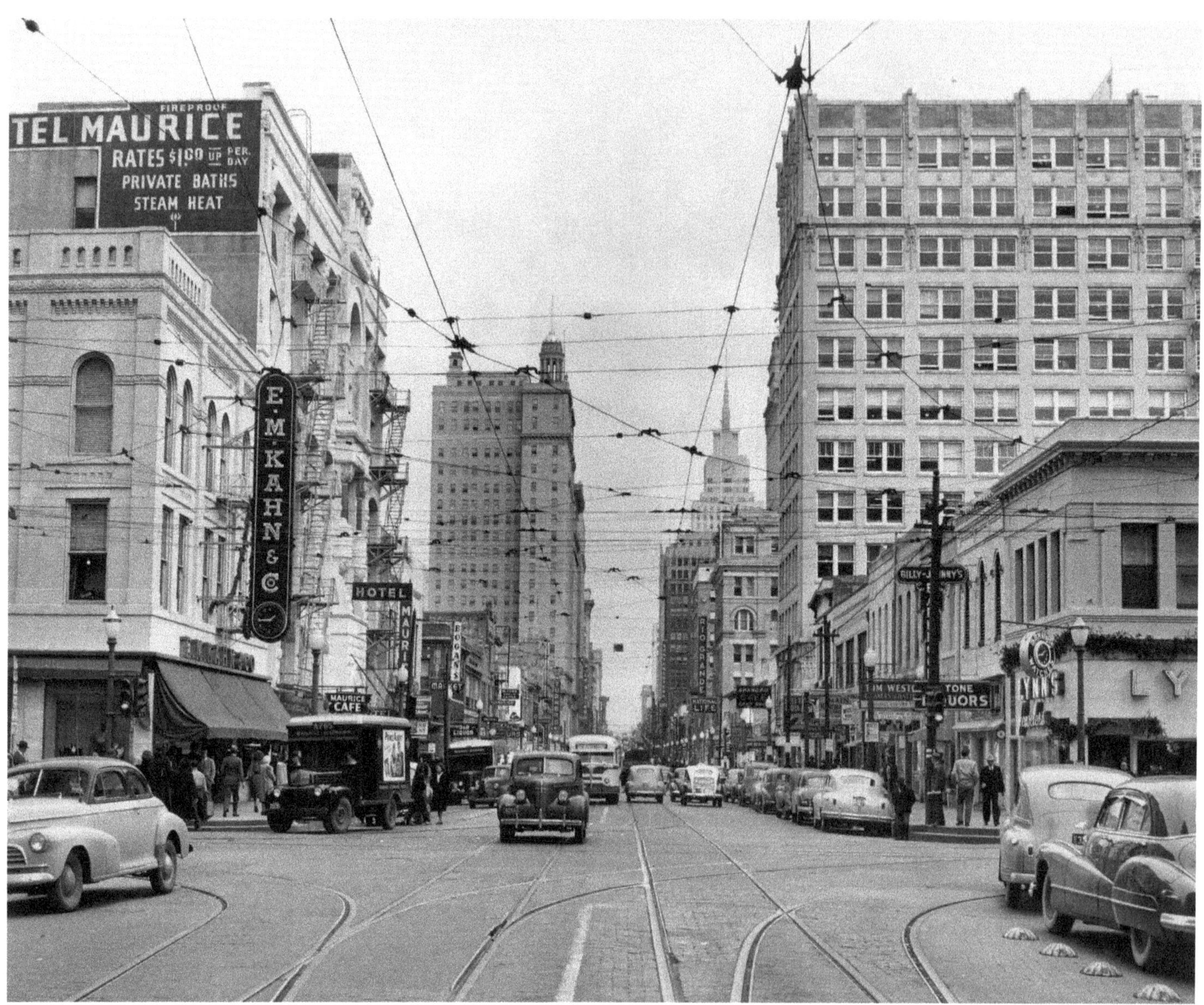

Main Street, looking east from Field in 1947, was dominated by skyscrapers such as the Republic Bank with its cupola (center-left) and the Mercantile Bank with its clock (center-right). But it still had its share of two- and three-story commercial buildings, some of which dated to the nineteenth century.

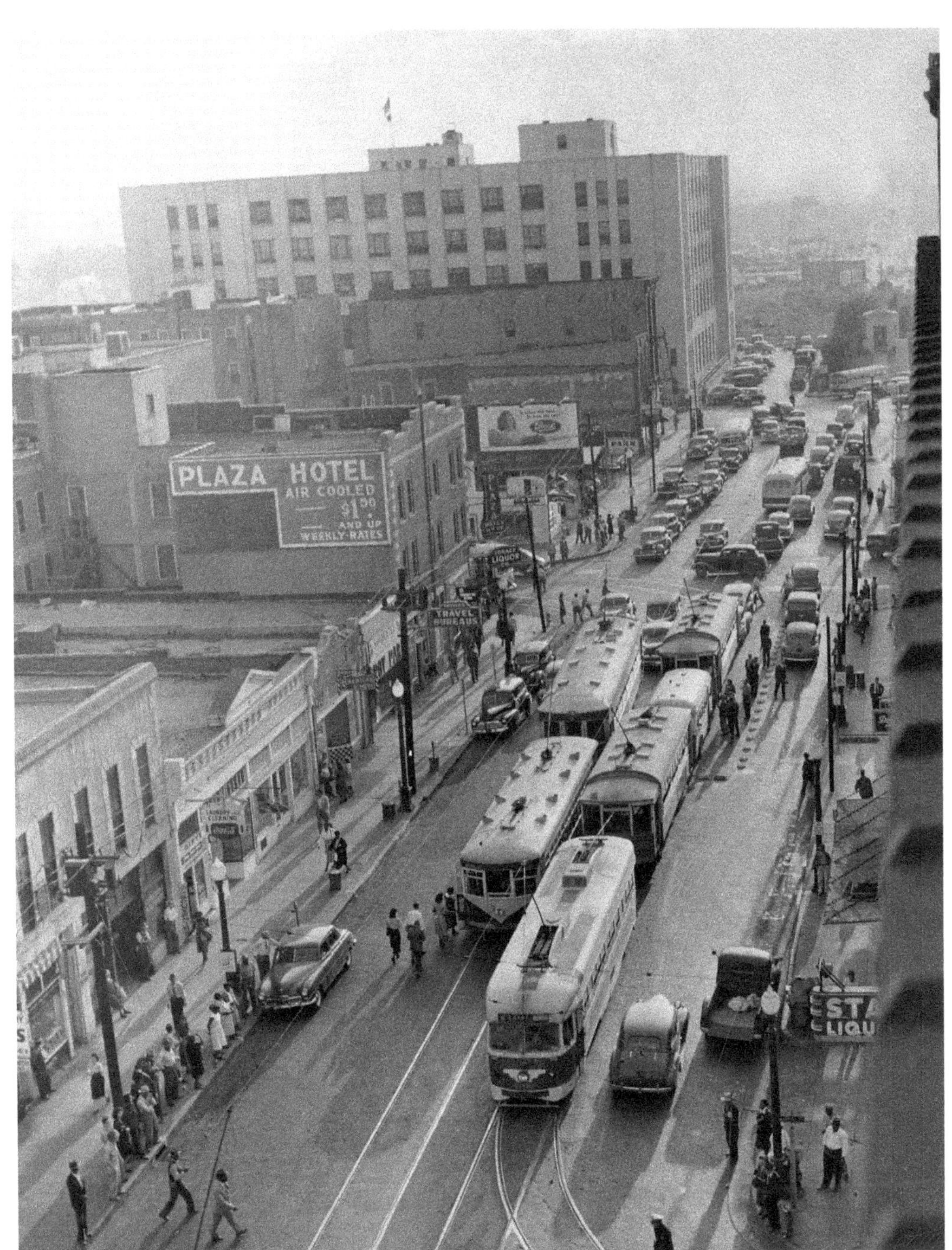

This view of S. Ervay Street was taken on September 27, 1948, when President Harry Truman visited Dallas.

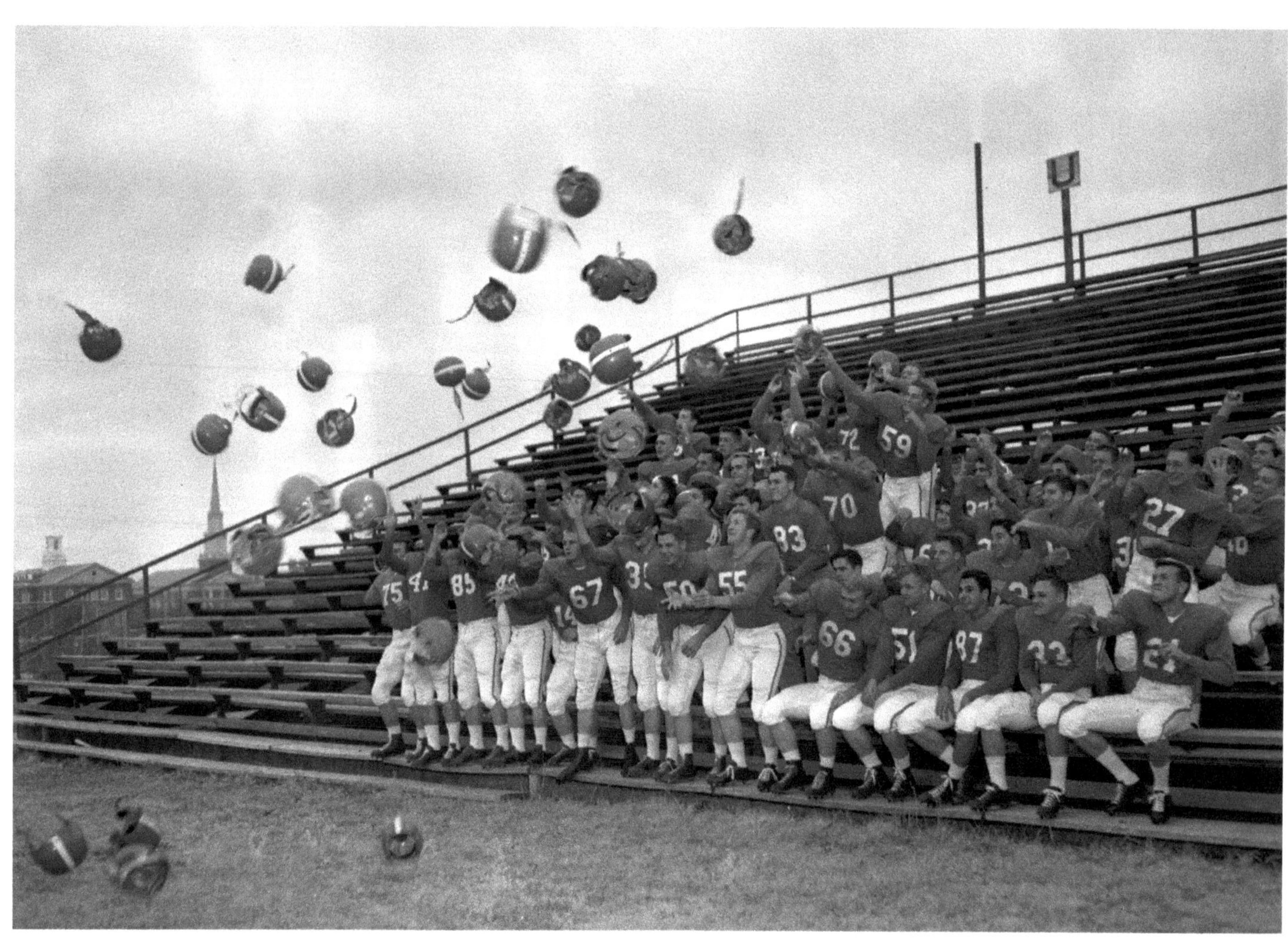

The popularity of Southern Methodist University's Doak Walker led to an expansion of the Cotton Bowl in 1948 and 1949, bringing seating capacity to more than 75,000. SMU continued to play its home games at the Cotton Bowl until the 1970s. Here the players toss their helmets for a photo shoot on the SMU campus. Here the players toss their helmets for a photo shot on the SMU campus.

The Modern Age

(1950–1969)

In the last half of the twentieth century, Dallas became an international city. High-tech industries like Texas Instruments (inventor of the computer chip) affected lives everywhere. Scientists and researchers (including five Nobel Prize winners at Southwestern Medical School) transformed medical science. Major corporations such as American Airlines, Exxon-Mobil, and J. C. Penney chose to locate their headquarters here. These businesses were enticed by business-friendly tax programs, an educated, non-unionized labor force, and a modern airport with worldwide connections.

Led by professional teams such as the Dallas Cowboys, Dallas Mavericks, and Texas Rangers, sports gained larger media coverage and popular patronage. By the 1960s, Dallas boasted the nation's largest congregations in the Southern Baptist, Methodist, and Presbyterian denominations. The arts flourished, with new concert halls, art museums, and theaters. For the first time, citizens began to prize and preserve reminders of the city's architectural heritage.

The city suffered its most traumatic moment in 1963, when President John F. Kennedy was assassinated while riding in a motorcade through downtown Dallas. But its citizens managed to pull together and, through the Goals for Dallas program, create a more tolerant, open community. Their efforts were rewarded with *Look* magazine's All-American City honor less than a decade later.

The city's population soared past one million in the late 1980s. Dallas became more culturally and ethnically diverse, with people of differing backgrounds moving into the region, taking advantage of the ever-expanding economic opportunities. With civil rights legislation, African Americans, the county's earliest minority group, gained new visibility and assumed leadership roles. The Mexican American population increased dramatically. And newer ethnic groups from Asia, the Middle East, and Central America arrived, retaining their native languages and cultures while interacting with the local society.

By 2000, Dallas had grown from the one square mile of John Neely Bryan's township to comprise more than 400 square miles. But like its founder, it continues to look to the future.

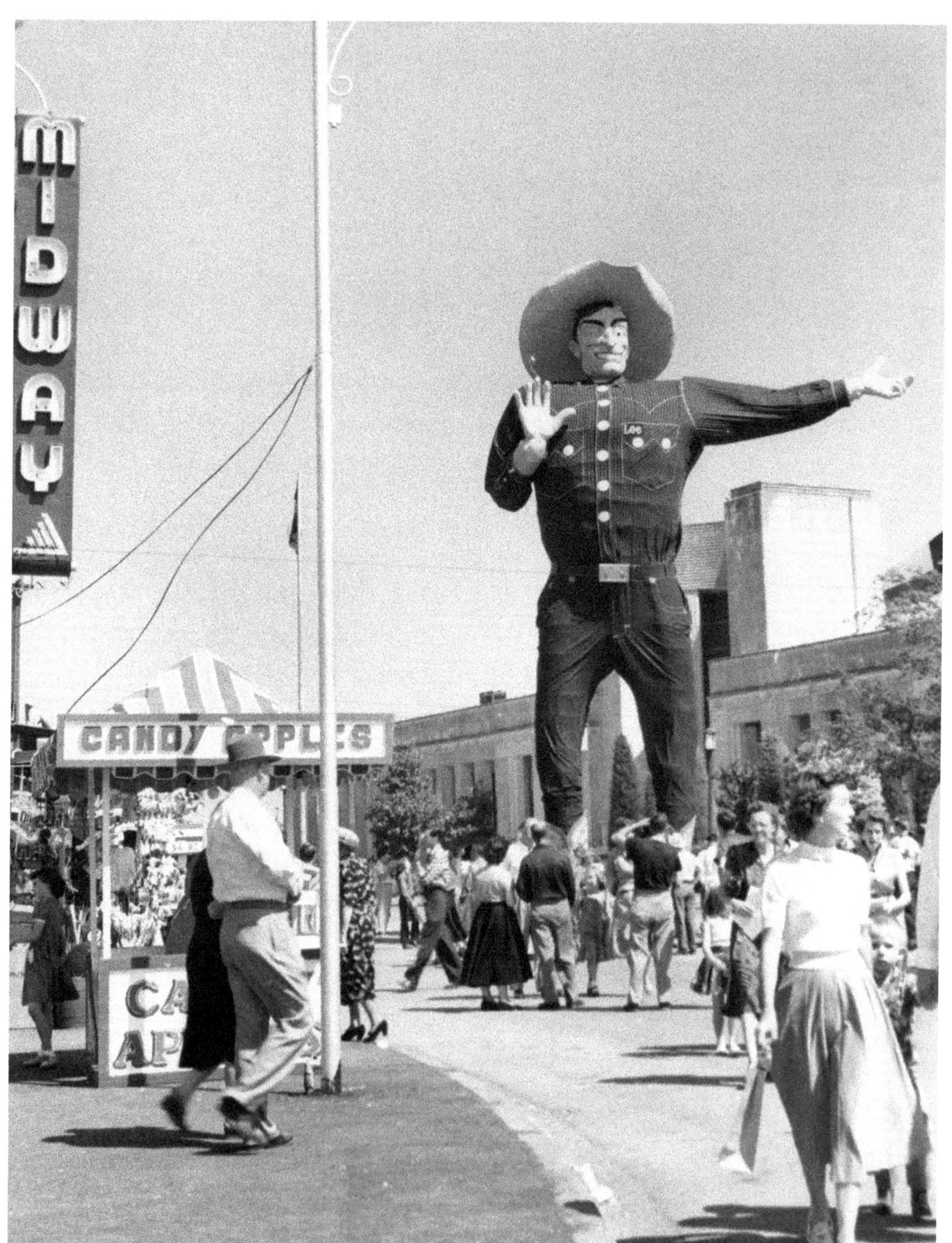

A former Santa Claus, the 52-foot-tall "Big Tex" made his debut at the state fair in 1952 wearing size 70 boots and a 75-gallon hat. He quickly became the fair's most recognizable symbol.

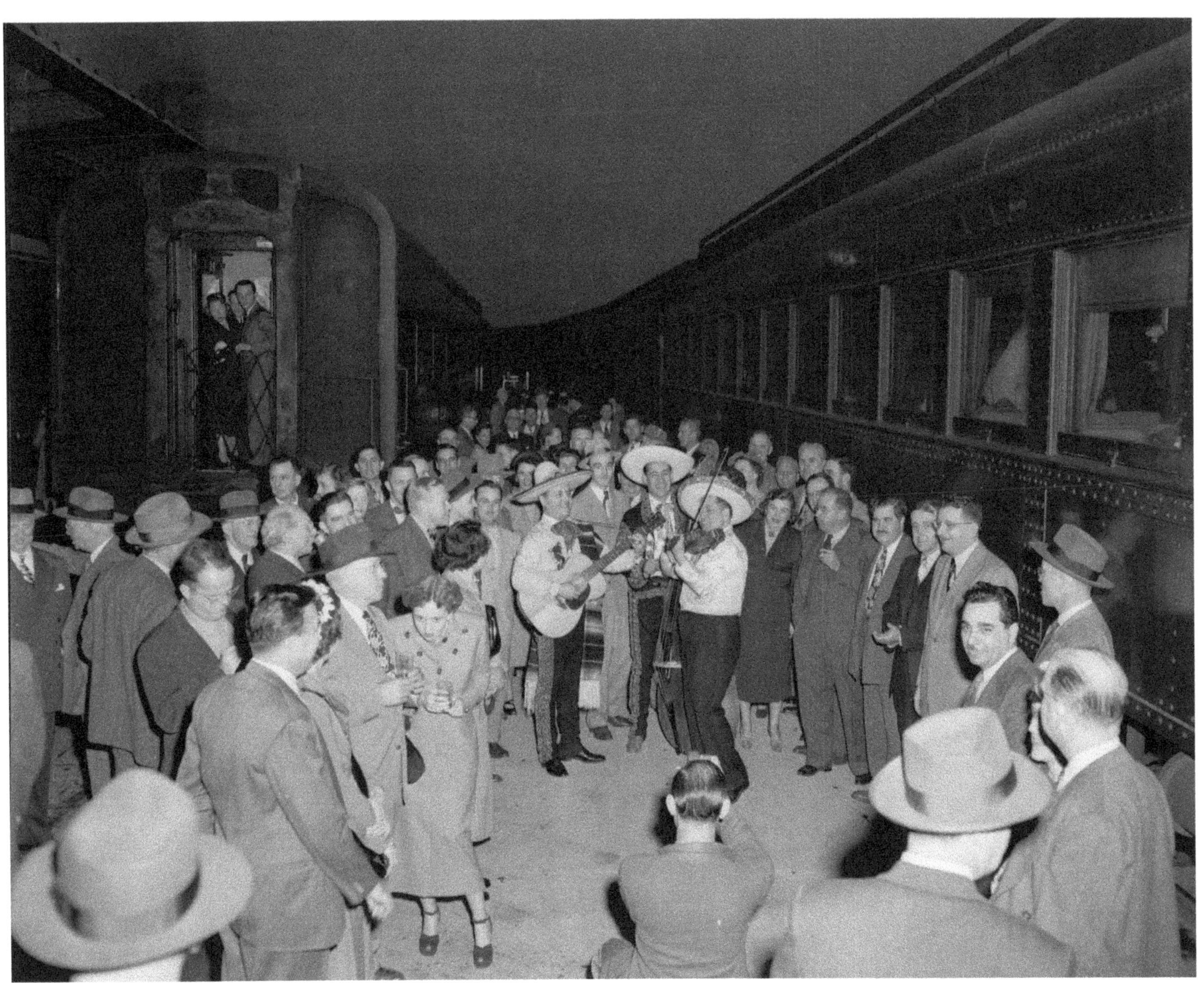

A mariachi band serenades passengers about to board an MKT train bound for San Antonio.

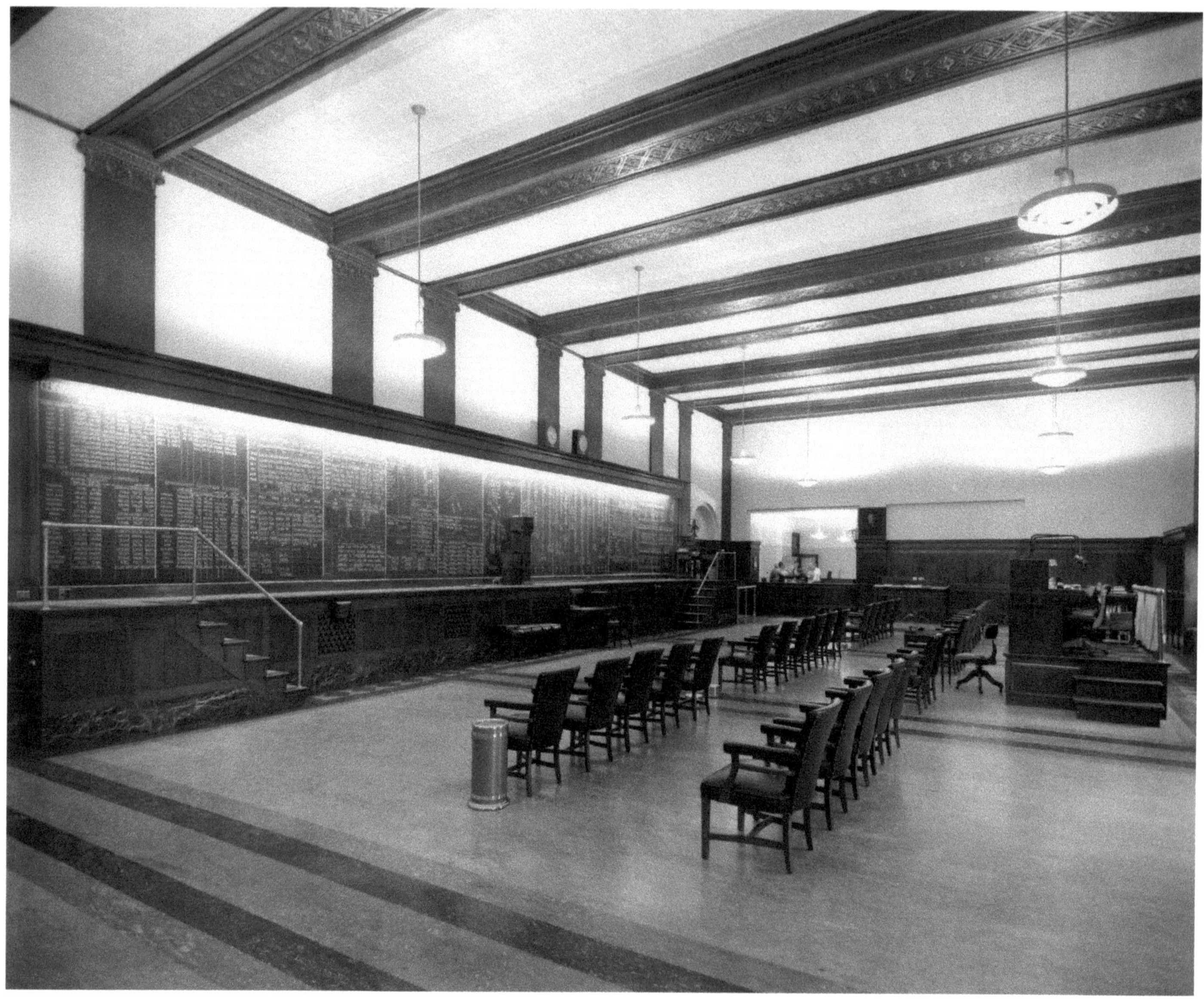

The Dallas Cotton Exchange was beginning to decline by 1951, when this photo of its trading room was taken. From 60,000 bales ginned in Dallas County during World War II, the number slid to barely 10,000 in 1950, as synthetic fabrics and foreign competition cut into the market.

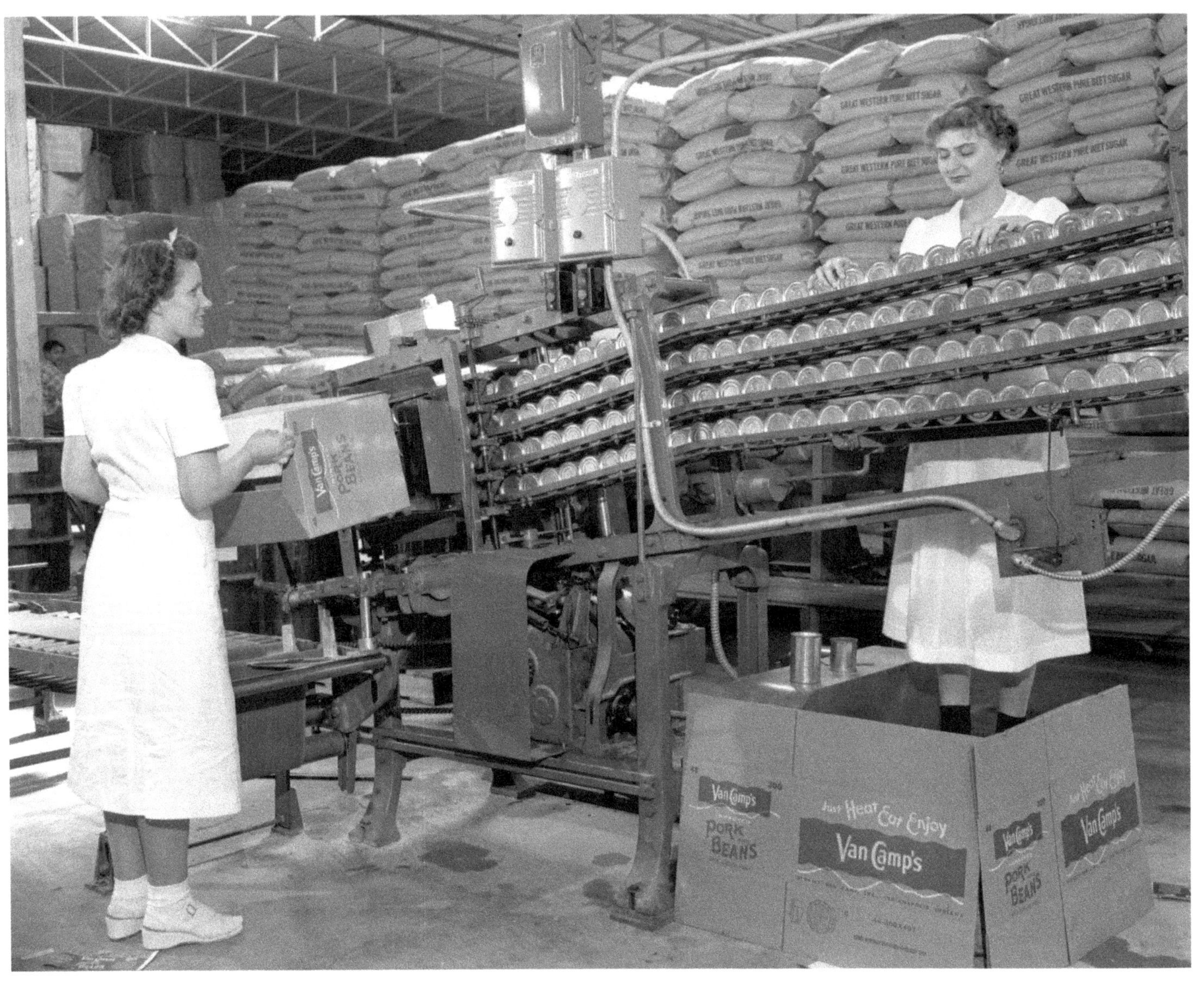

In the postwar years, small manufacturing and food processing plants proliferated throughout Dallas County. Stokeley–Van Camp operated a food distribution center at 2822 Glenfield Street for more than 30 years beginning about 1952.

First step in clearing the way for erection of Southland Center in 1954 was demolition of a two-story building at the northwest corner of Live Oak and Pearl. Officials included (left to right) Dan C. Williams, president; James B. Goodson, assistant vice-president; William H. Oswalt III, vice president; John L. Briggs, vice-president; and Ben H. Carpenter, executive vice-president.

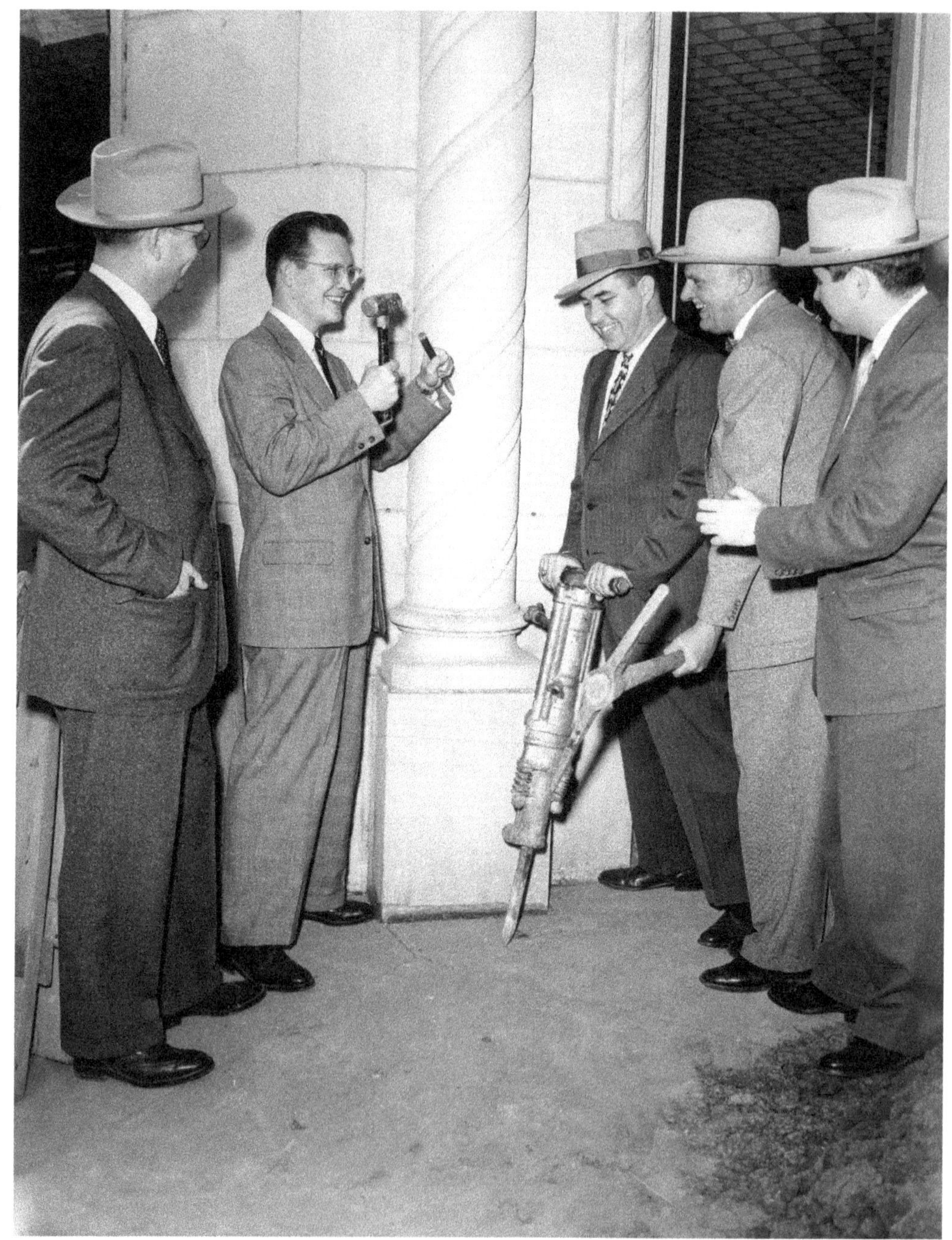

"The Texas Special" transported passengers on the MKT Railroad between St. Louis and San Antonio. It introduced an air-cooled dining car in 1931. Note the photos of downtown Dallas in the background.

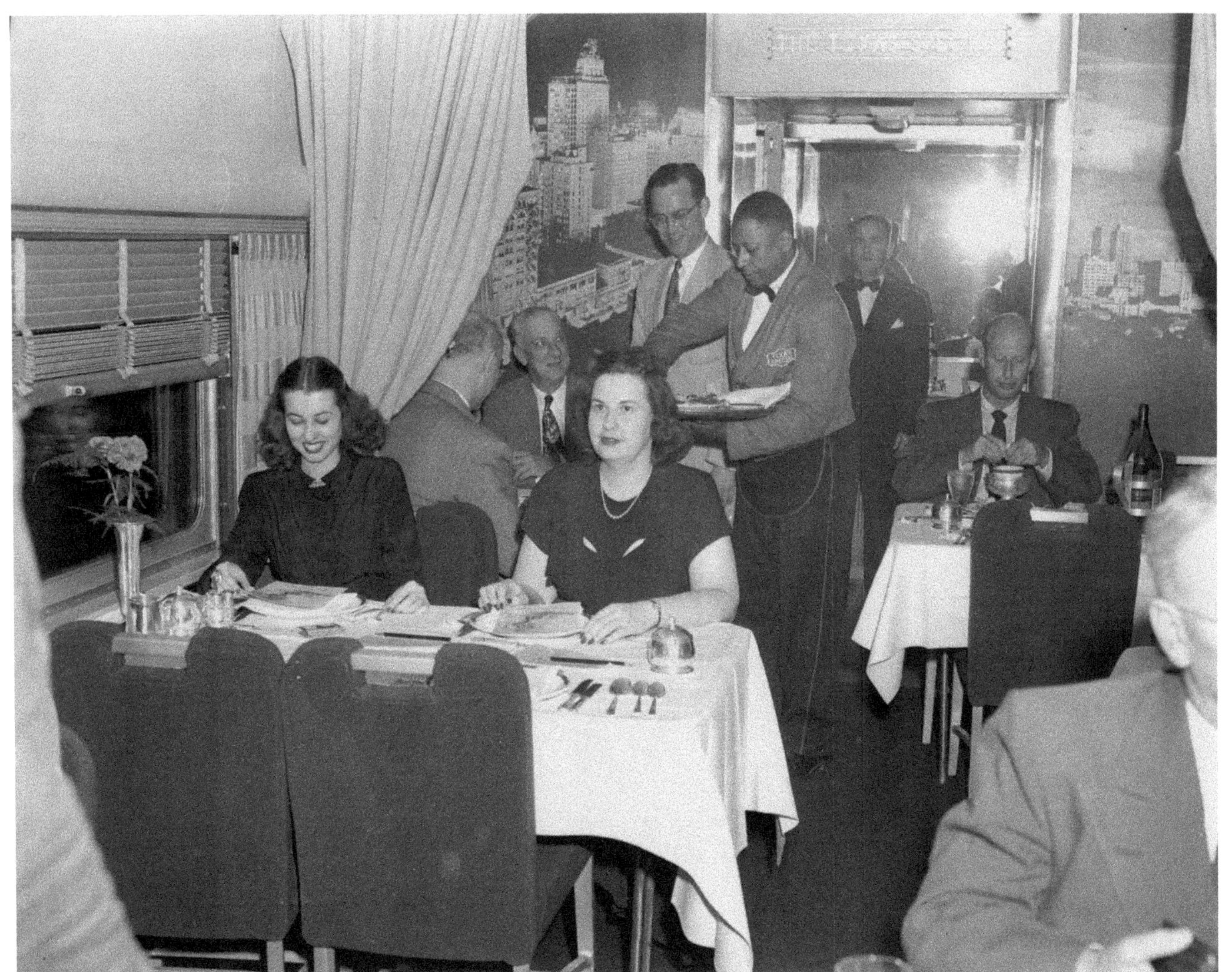

Dallas Mayor R. L. Thornton greets Texas Senator Lyndon B. Johnson on a visit to Dallas in 1952.

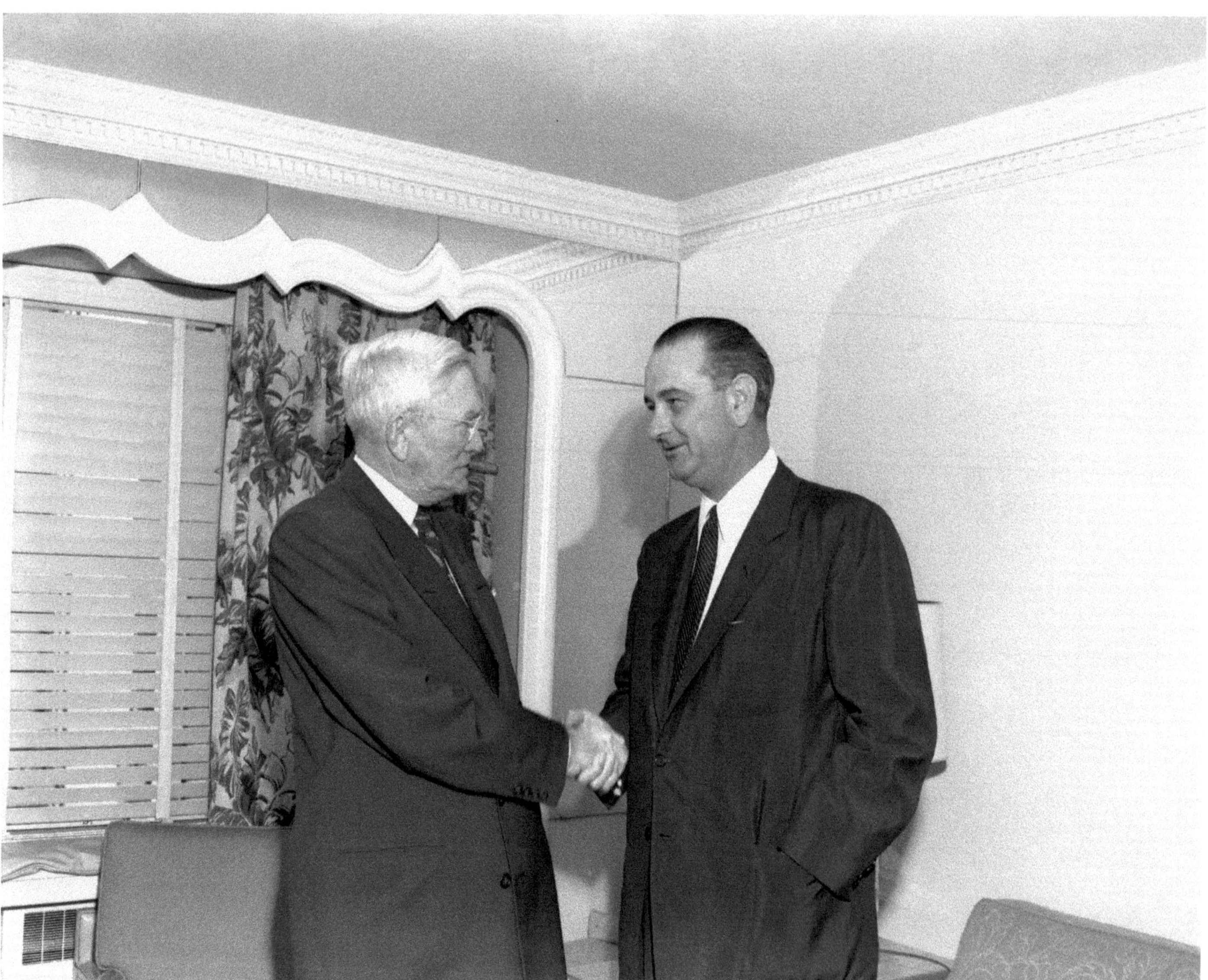

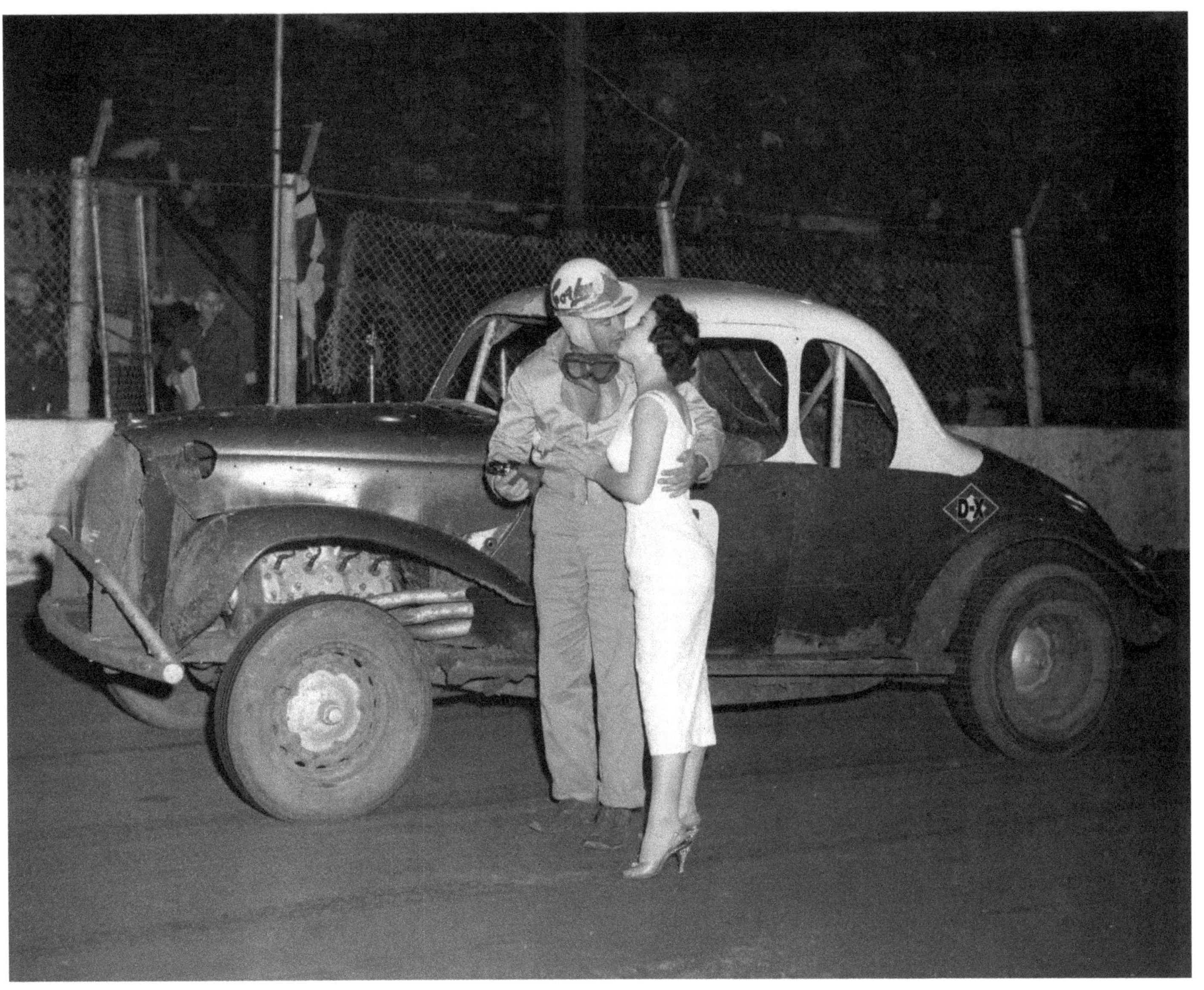

In the 1950s, auto racers competed each Saturday night at Fair Park Speedway. Admission for spectators was $1. Here a driver receives a good-luck kiss before starting a race.

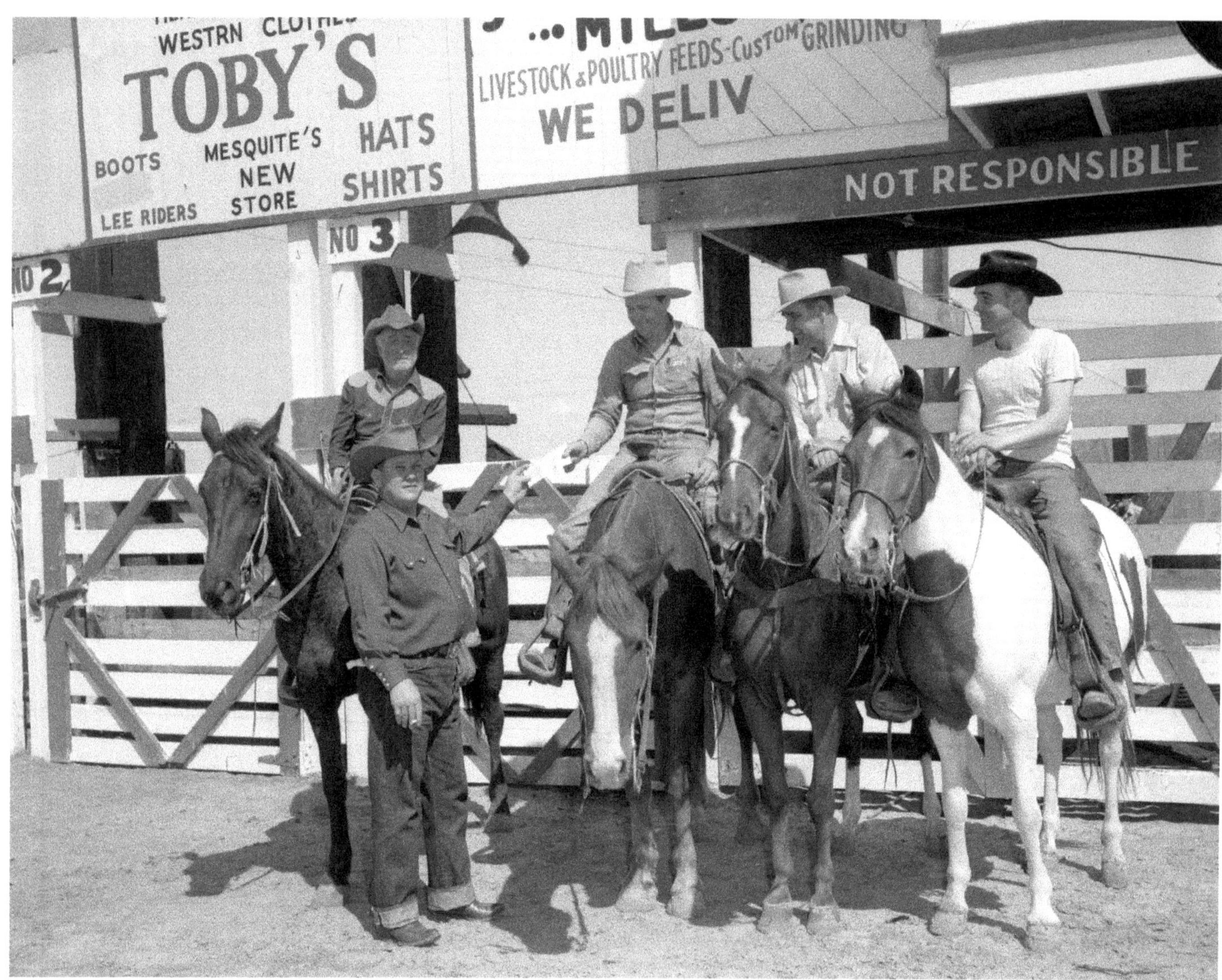

The small community of Mesquite in southeast Dallas County gained national attention with the Mesquite Championship Rodeo, founded in 1958. In 1993, the Texas legislature declared Mesquite the Rodeo Capital of Texas.

Elm Street remained Theater Row into the 1960s, until the proliferation of neighborhood movie houses showing first-run films killed off the downtown market.

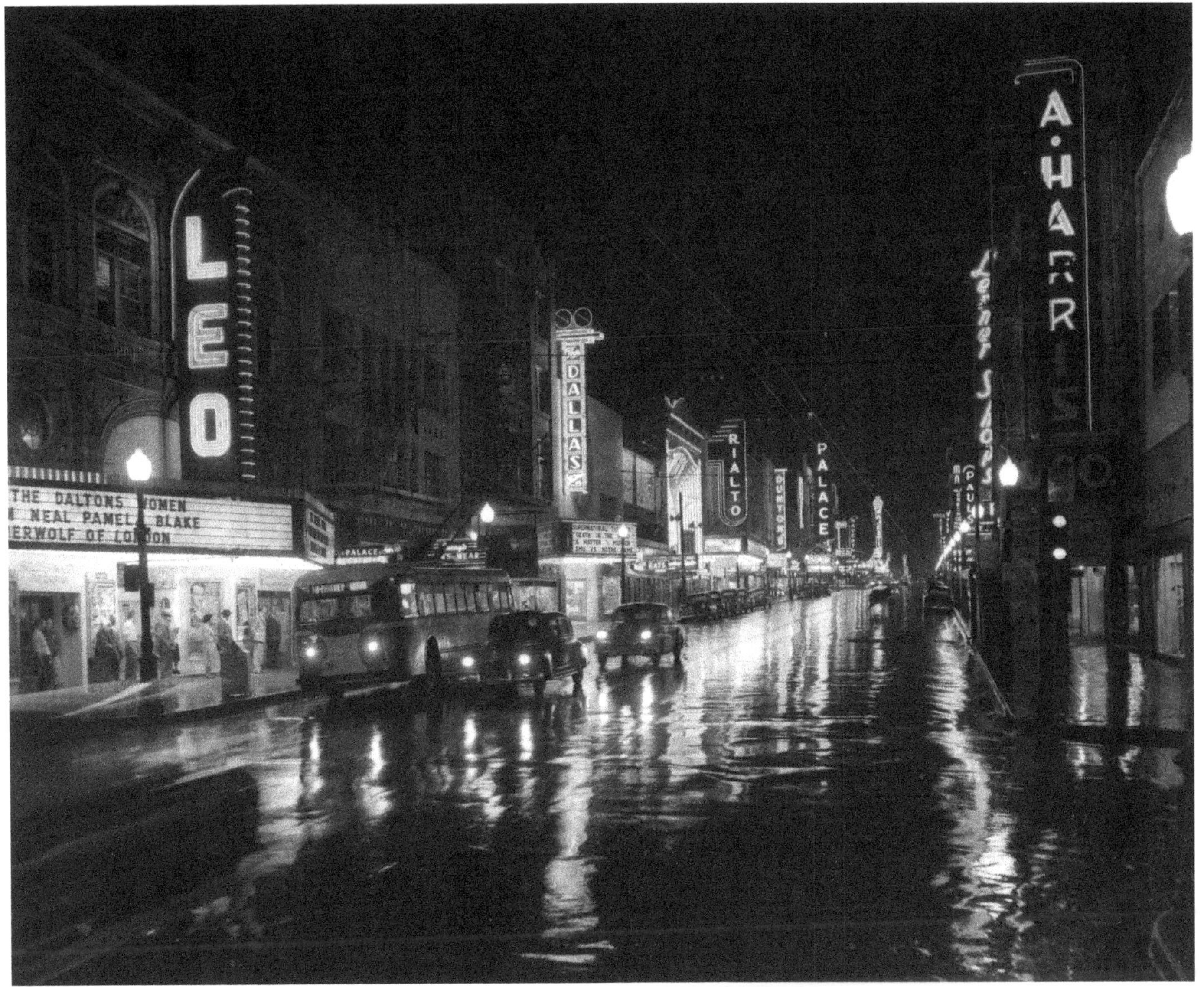

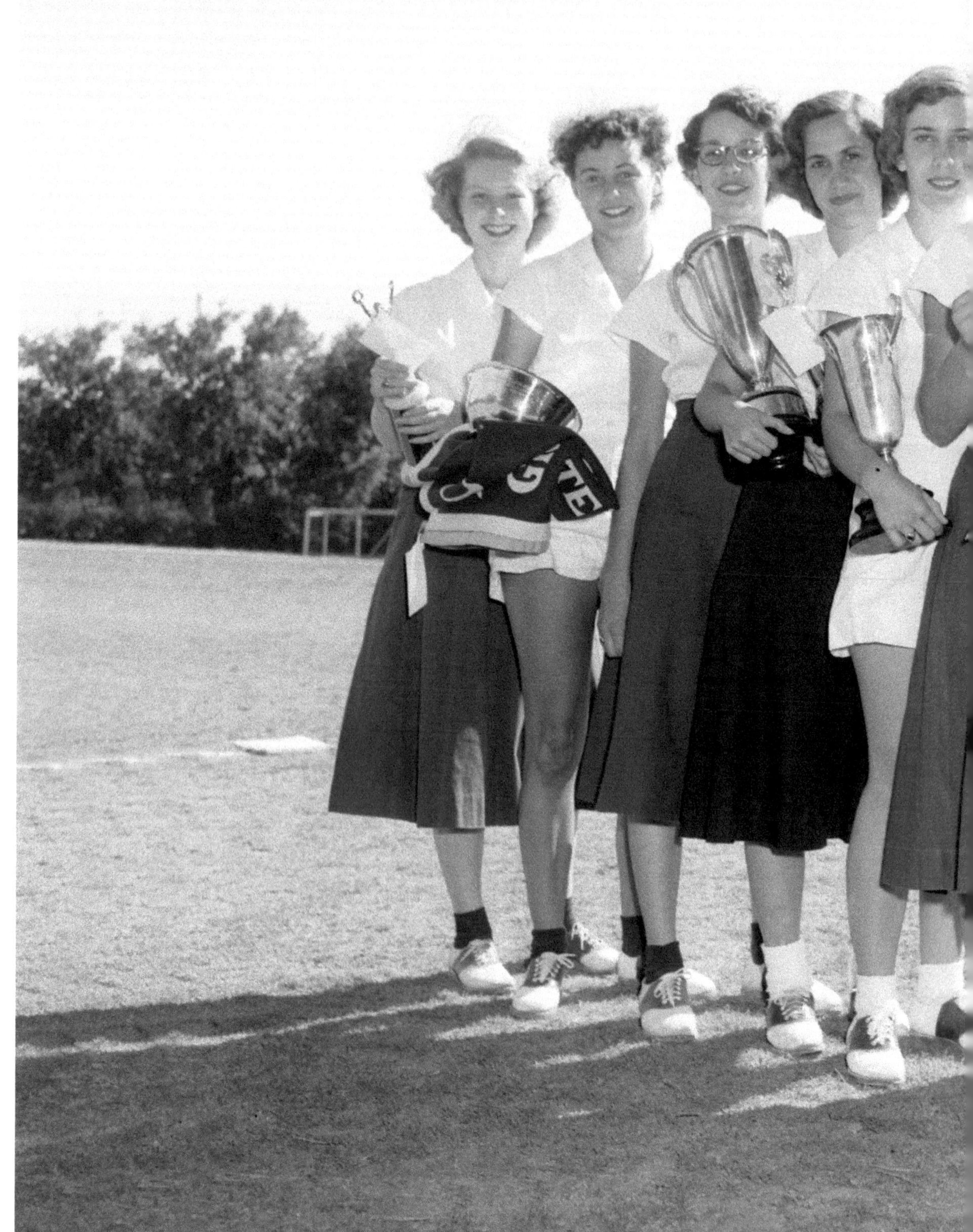

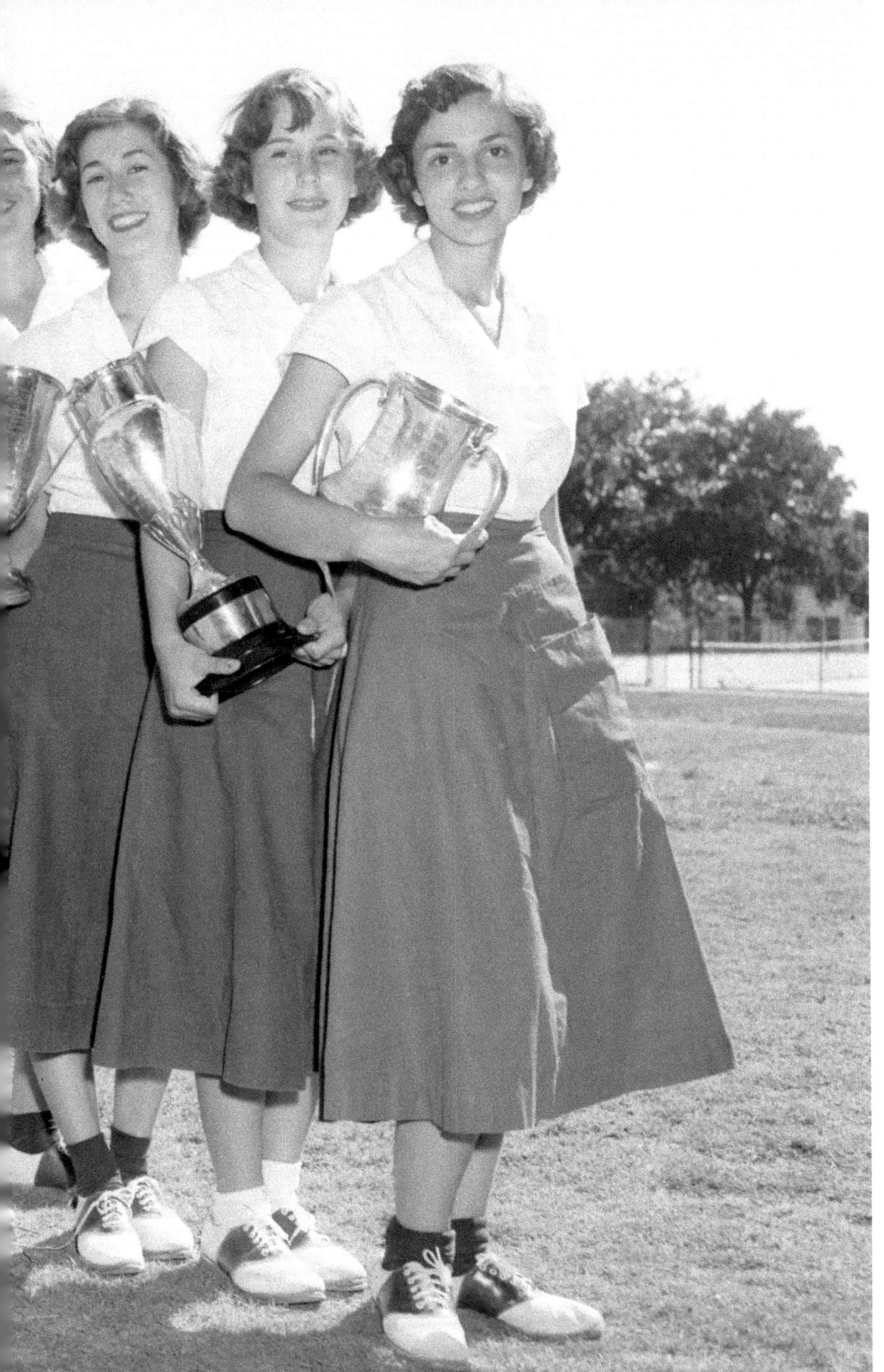

The Hockaday School was founded by Miss Ela Hockaday in 1913 and quickly gained a reputation for providing excellent education for young women. These students in the 1950s display school trophies.

Although Dallas was spared racial riots during the 1960s, it saw its share of peaceful protests. In 1965, some 3,000 people of all races marched through downtown expressing sympathy for recent struggles in Alabama.

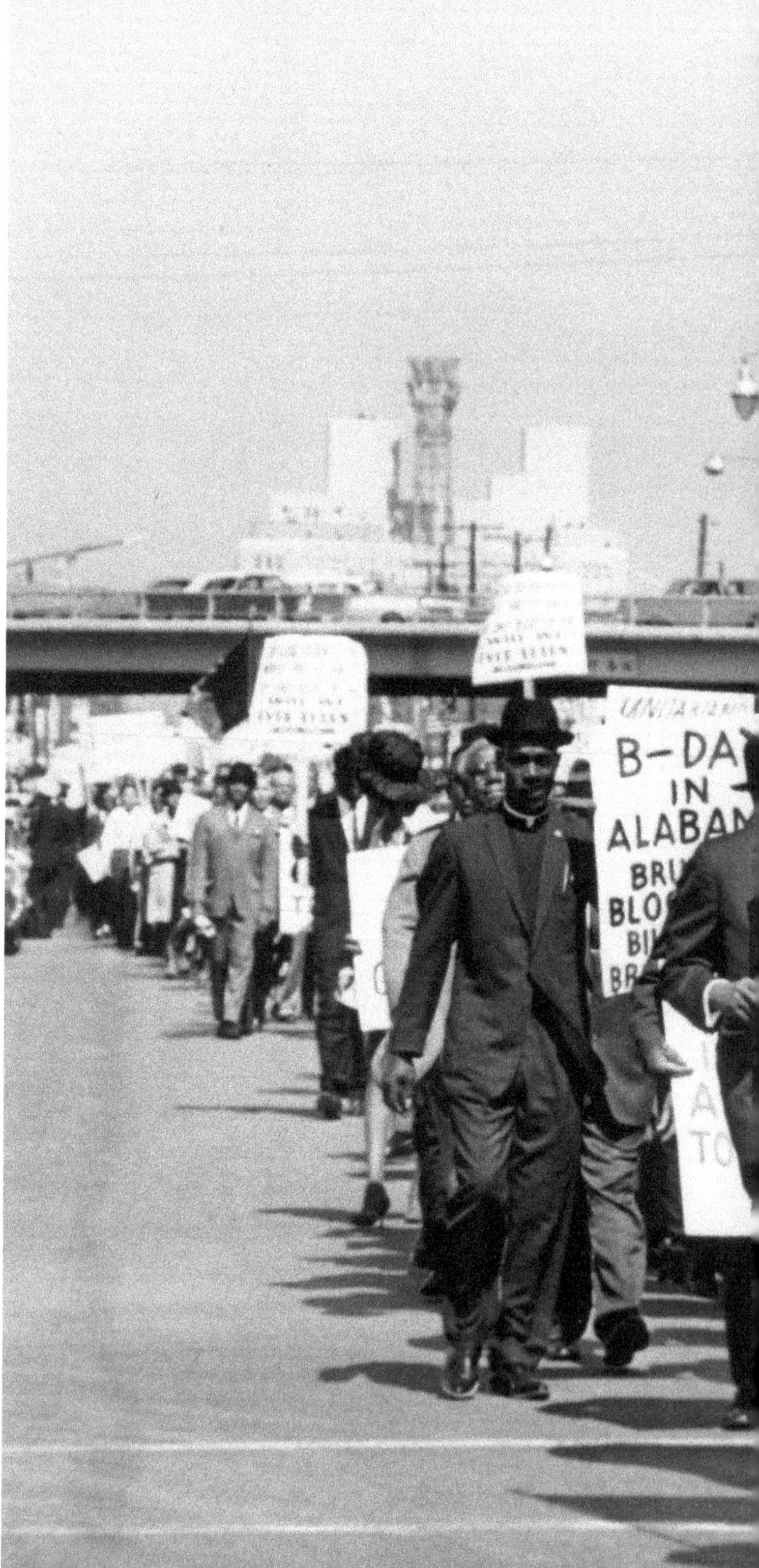

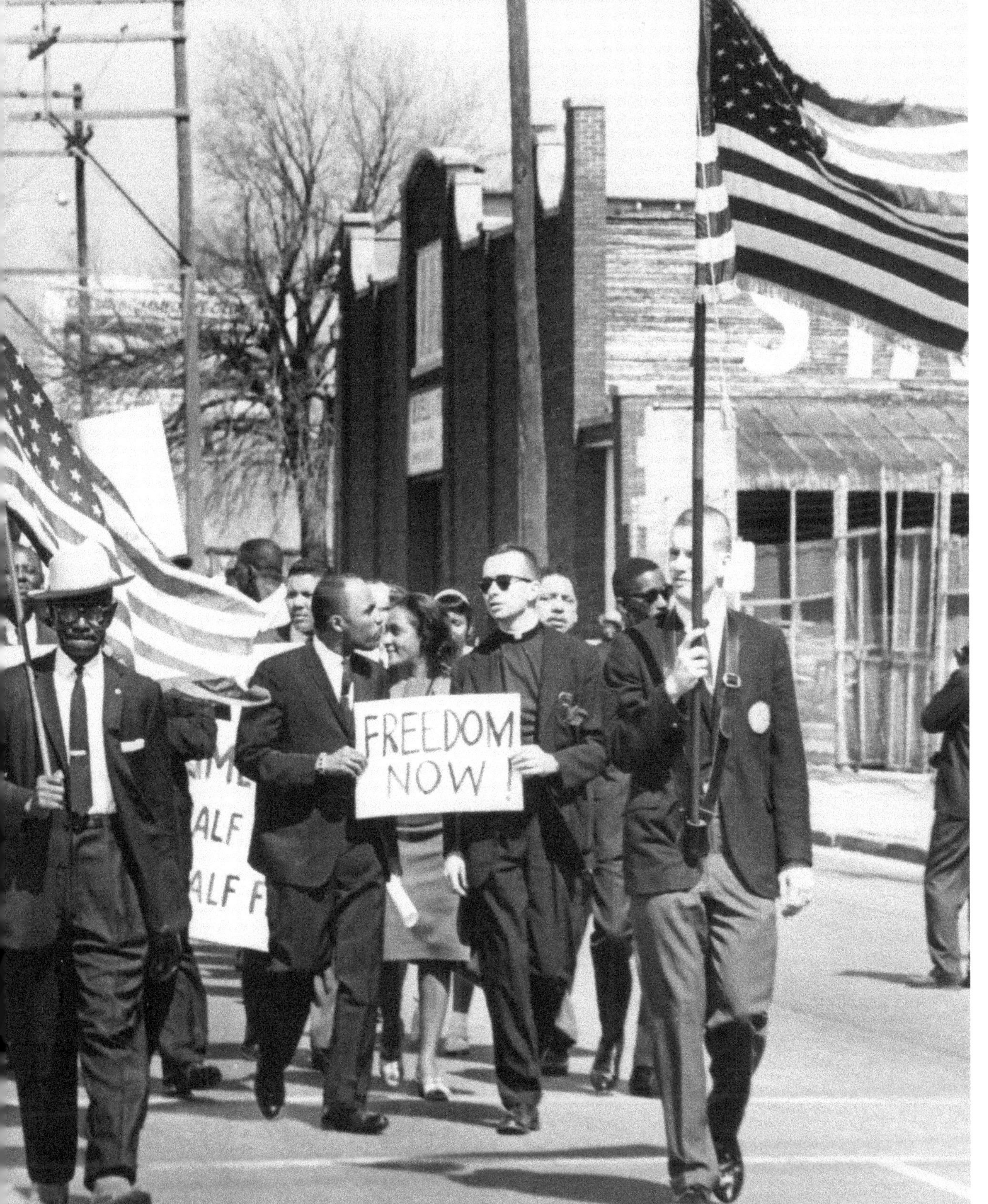
FREEDOM
NOW!

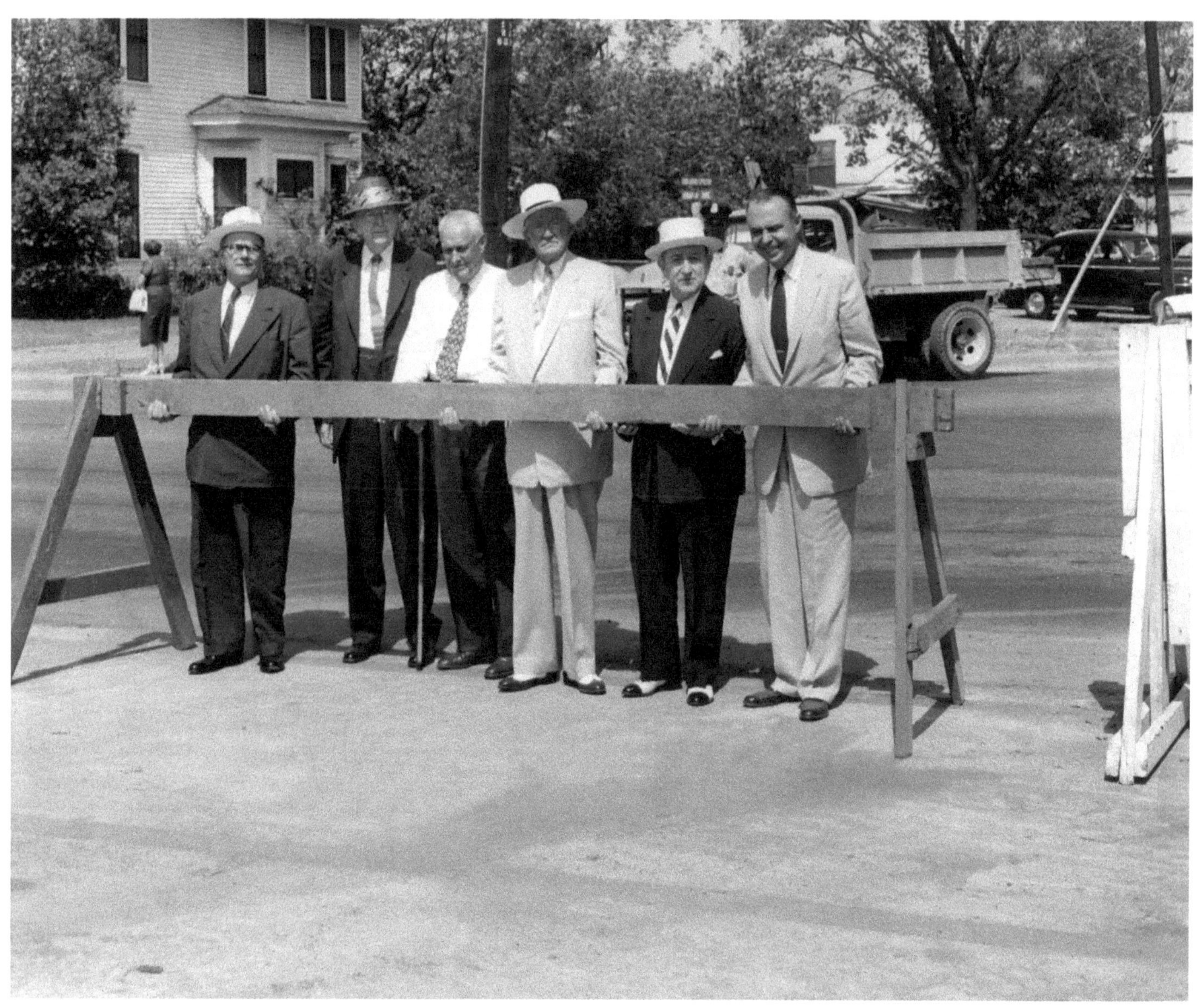

Six living Dallas mayors celebrated the "completion" of Central Expressway in 1958. In fact, the highway has continued to expand. Pictured left to right are George Sergeant (1935-37), George A. Sprague (1937-39), J. B. Adoue (1951-53), R. L. Thornton (1954-61), Woodall Rogers (1939-47), and Walter Savage (1949-51).

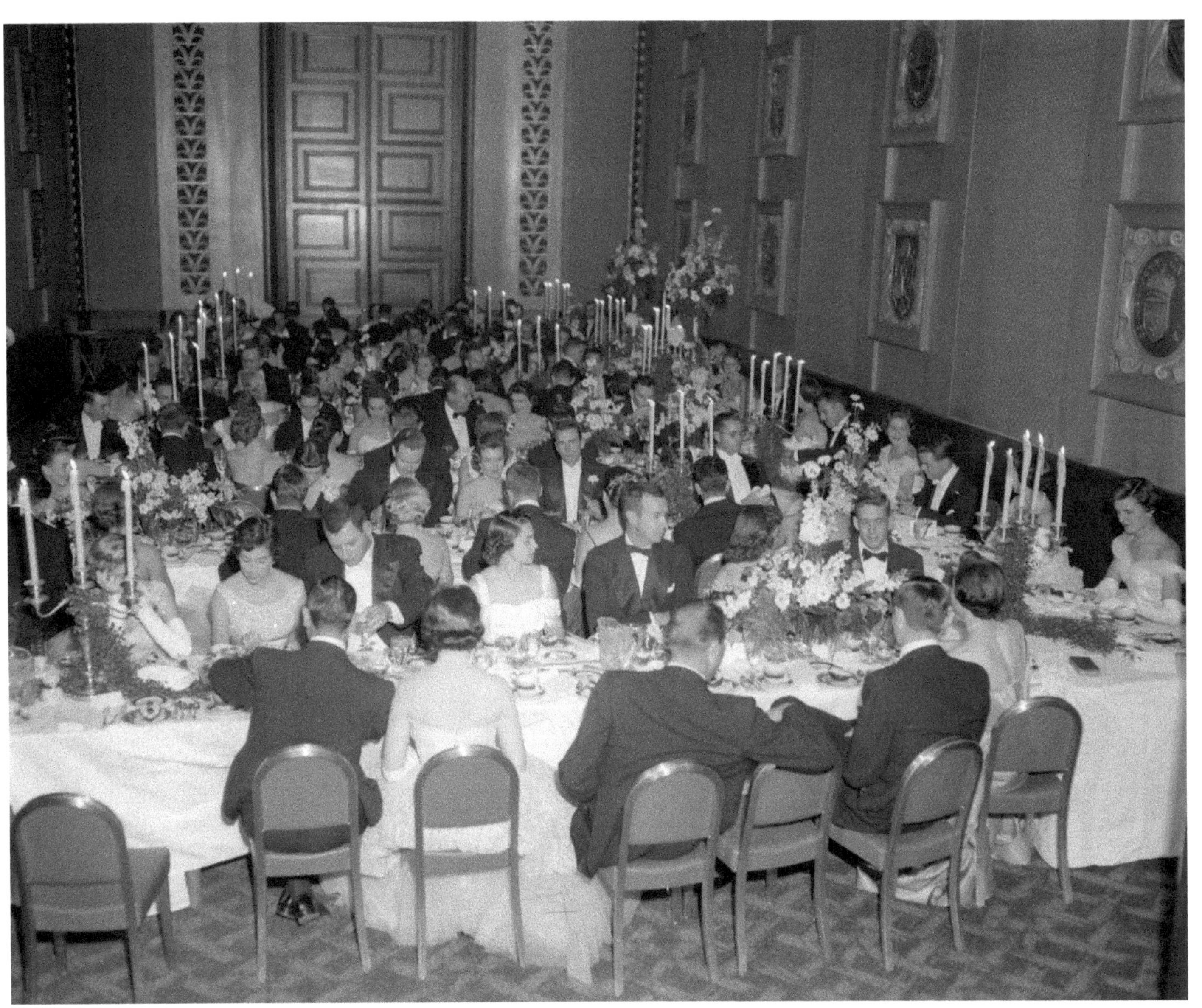

The introduction of new debutantes at the Idlewild Ball has opened the Dallas social season since the 1880s. The ball was held at the Baker Hotel every year from 1934 until 1960.

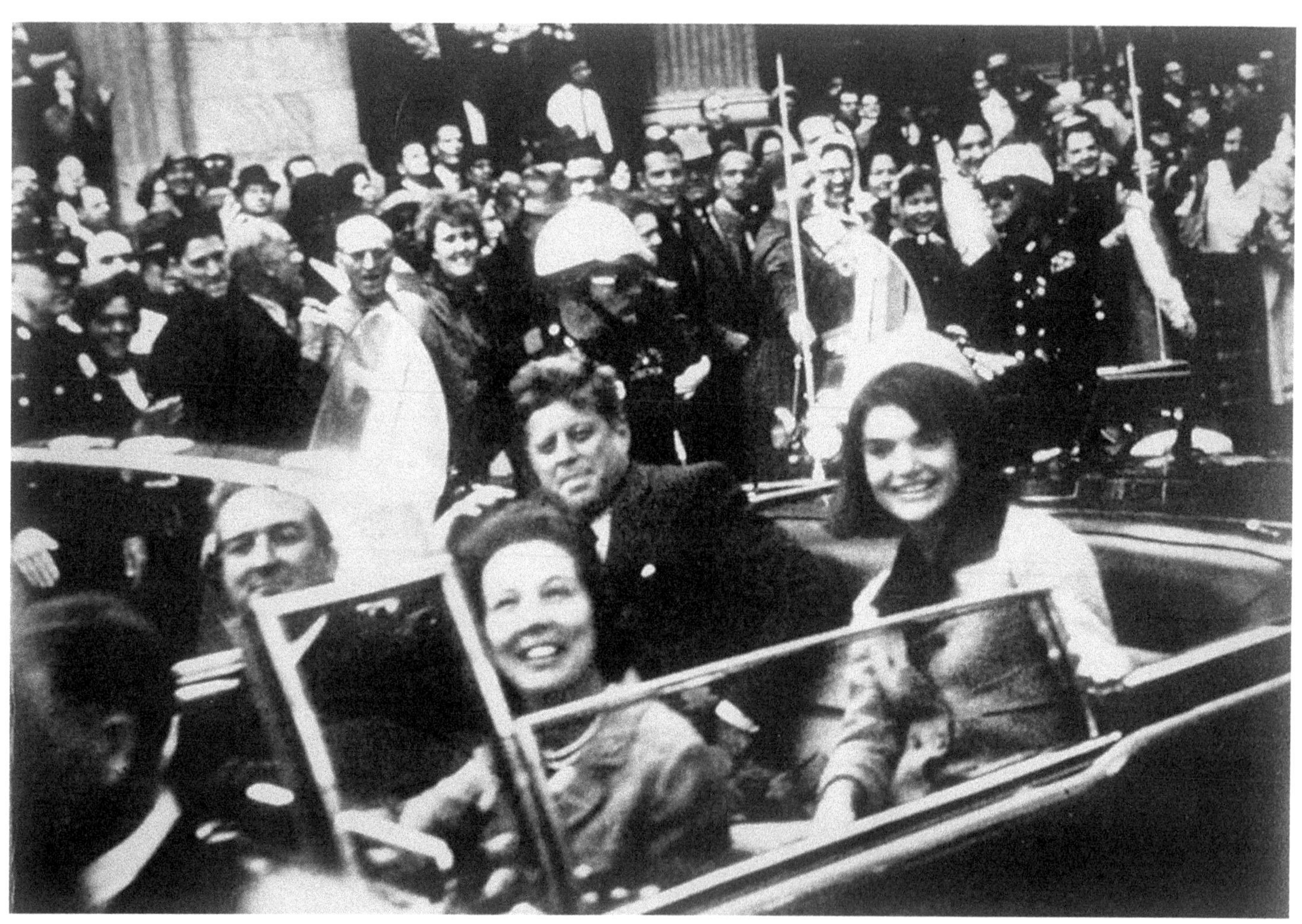

The sun shone and crowds cheered as President and Mrs. John F. Kennedy, and Texas Governor and Mrs. John Connally rode through downtown Dallas in a motorcade on the morning of November 22, 1963. Only minutes later, both men had been shot.

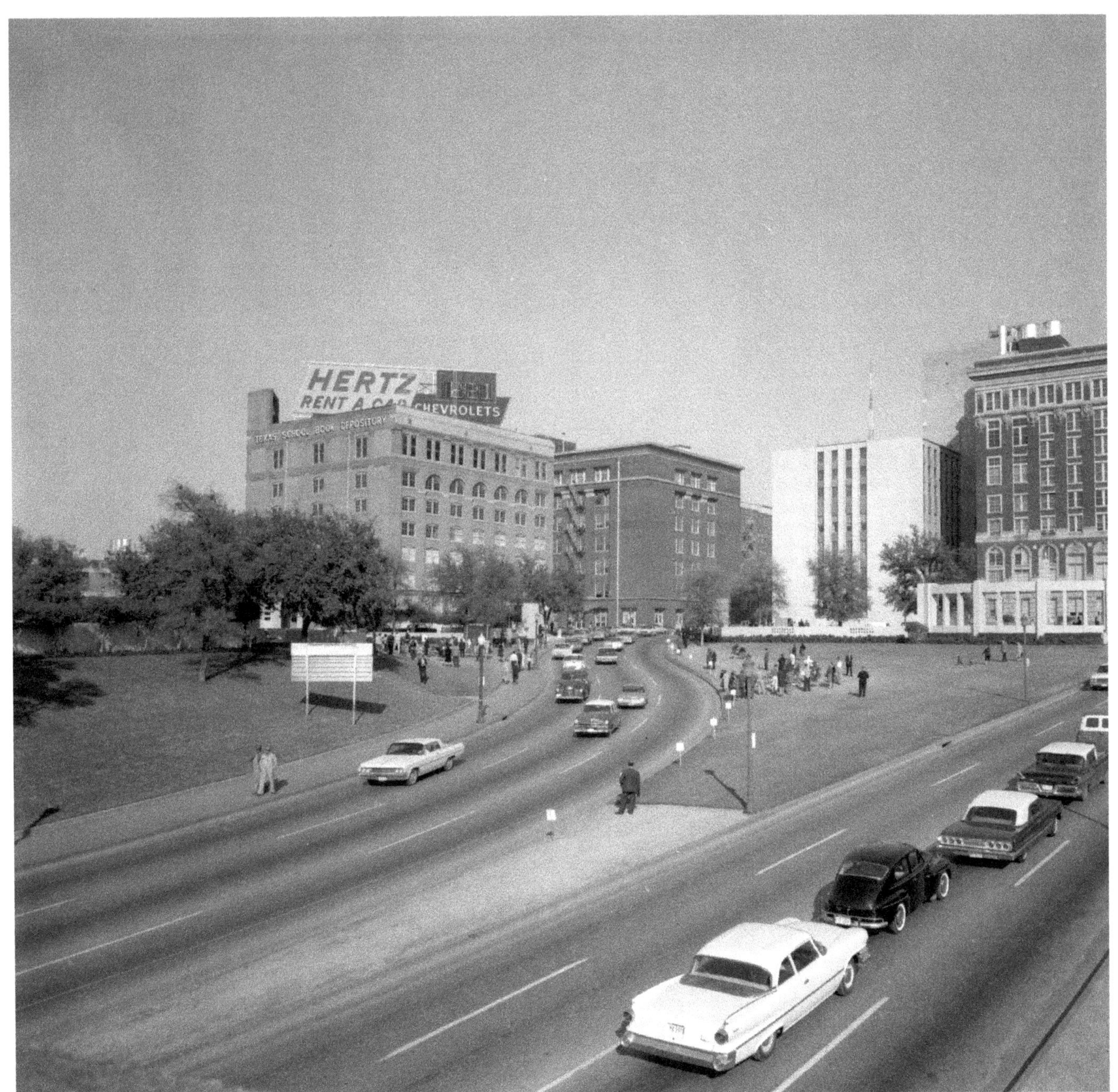

Lee Harvey Oswald, the alleged assassin of President Kennedy, worked in the Texas School Book Depository, the building to the left with the Hertz sign on the roof. The presidential motorcade had just turned down Elm Street, the curving street to the left, when the fatal shots were fired.

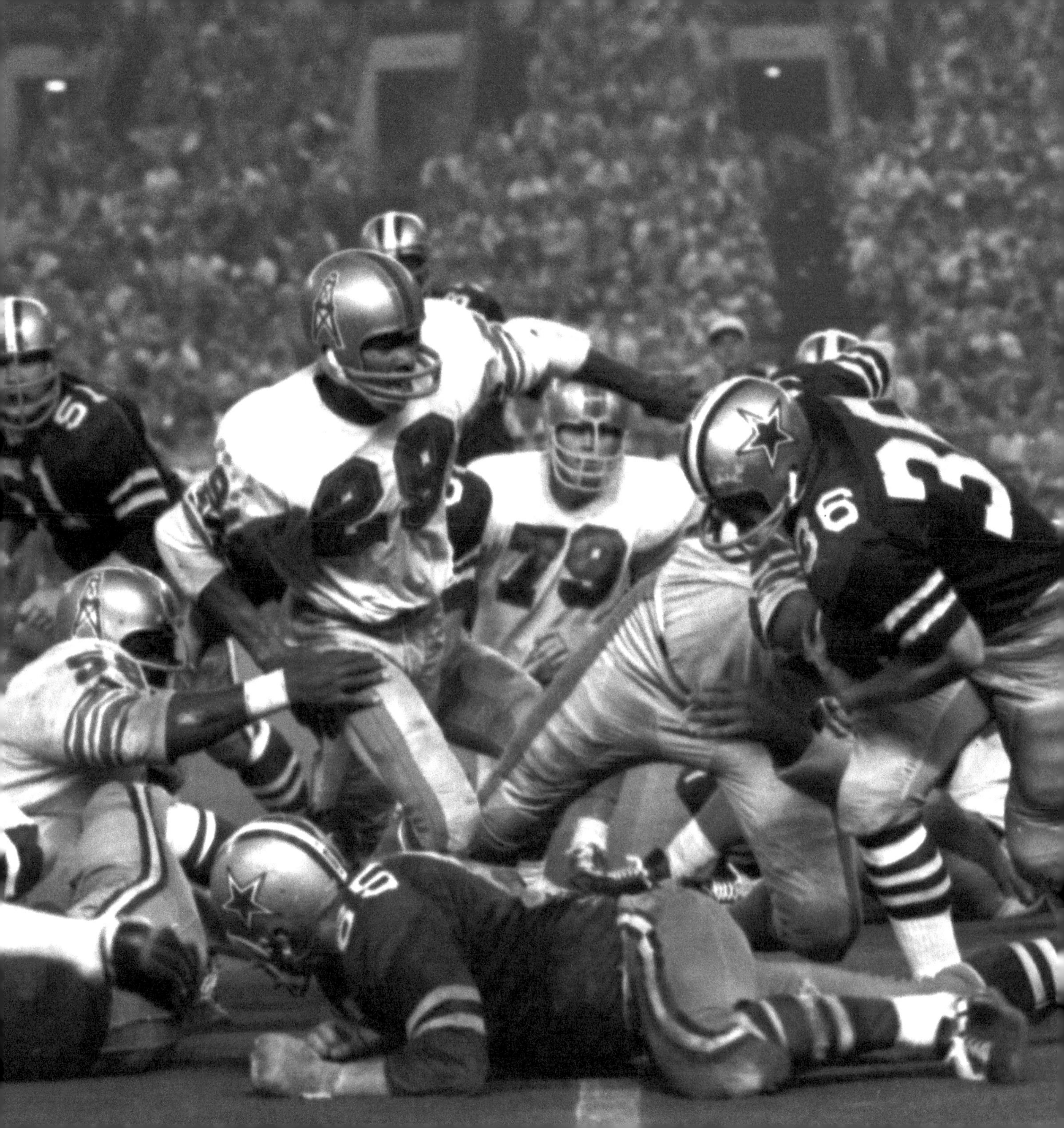

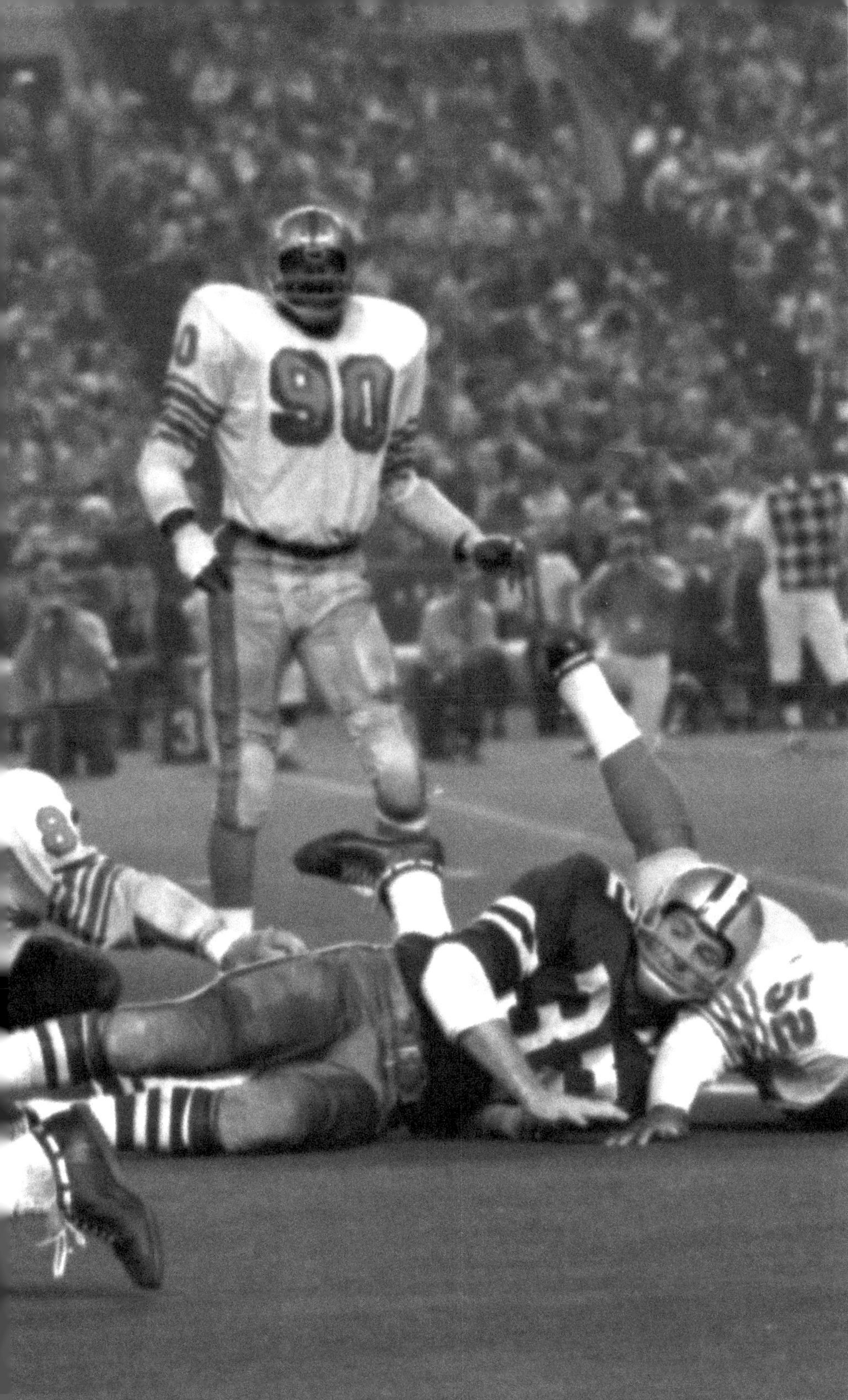

Organized in 1960, the Dallas Cowboys quickly gained a strong following in the region and eventually the nation, becoming known as "America's Team." This is a 1968 game at the Cotton Bowl.

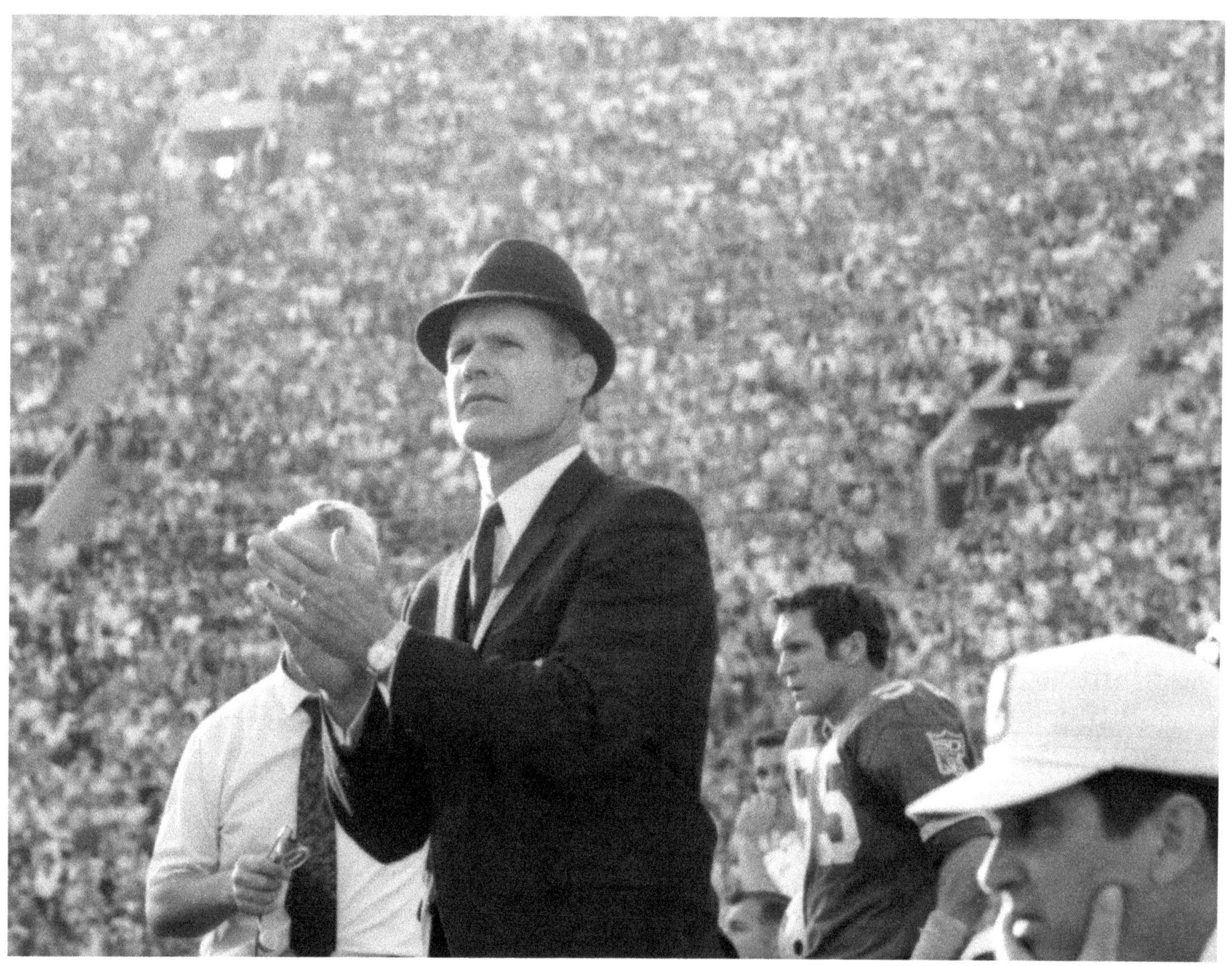

His fedora quickly became a trademark for Cowboys head coach Tom Landry as he paced the sidelines during games. Under his leadership, the Cowboys won the 1972 and 1978 Super Bowls.

Notes on the Photographs

These notes, listed by page number, attempt to include all aspects known of the photographs. Each of the photographs is identified by the page number, photograph's title or description, photographer and collection, archive, and call or box number when applicable. Although every attempt was made to collect all available data, in some cases complete data was unavailable due to the age and condition of some of the photographs and records.

II **Dallas Skyline, 1930s**
Dallas Historical Society
Centennial Collection

VI **Skyline with Reunion Tower**
Library of Congress
HAER TEX,57-DAL,8-

X **Arrival of the Harvey, 1893**
Dallas Historical Society
A.41.226

2 **1870s Street Scene**

3 **Mardi Gras Parade**
Dallas Historical Society
A10.21

4 **McCoy House**
Dallas Historical Society
A37.94.2

5 **Simpson House**
Dallas Historical Society
V84.132

6 **Wagon Yard by Courthouse**
Dallas Historical Society
F80.2.226

7 **Train**
Dallas Historical Society
A47.96.1

8 **Sanger Brothers Store**
Dallas Historical Society
A77.87.1042

9 **Mayer's Garden**
Dallas Public Library
Neg # 87-1/19-27-1

10 **Padgitt Brothers**
Dallas Historical Society
F80.7.6

12 **Streets in 1880s**
Dallas Historical Society
V91.2.20

13 **Dallas Opera House**
Dallas Historical Society
V48.65

14 **Gaston Building**
Dallas Historical Society
A48.65

15 **Courthouse, 1885**
Dallas Historical Society
V91.2.23

16 **U.S. Post Office**
Dallas Historical Society
A.6828.33

17 **Dallas City Hall**
Dallas Historical Society
V1998.6

18 **Intersection Commerce and Lamar**
Dallas Historical Society
V91.2.5

19 **Dallas Club**
Dallas Historical Society
V91.2.19

20 **Commercial Building on Akard**
Dallas Historical Society
V91.2.26

21 **Lawn Tennis Club**
Dallas Historical Society
V91.2.14

22 **Fishing Club**
Dallas Historical Society
V91.2.35

23 **Windsor Hotel**
Dallas Historical Society
F80.2.46

24 **Crowds Watching Arrival of Harvey from Bridge**
Dallas Historical Society
V91.2.51

25 **Harvey on Trinity**
Dallas Historical Society
V91.2.37

26 **Building Dam**
Dallas Historical Society
V91.2.40

27 **Dam**
Dallas Historical Society
V91.2.49

28 **Picnic Party Aboard Harvey**
Dallas Historical Society
V91.2

29 **Oriental Hotel, 1893**
Dallas Historical Society
F81.2.9

30 **Ivy Hall**
Dallas Historical Society
F81.2.7

31 **St. Paul's Sanitarium, 1898**
Dallas Historical Society
F81.2.5

32 **Temple Emanu-El**
Dallas Historical Society
F81.2.8

33 **St. Matthew's Cathedral**
Dallas Historical Society
F81.2.6

34 **Oak Cliff Baseball Team**
Dallas Historical Society
V.85.76

36 **Santa Fe Terminal**
Dallas Historical Society
F80.7.4

37 **Trolley Lines**
Dallas Historical Society
F81.2.3

38 **Streetcar Headed to Fair**
Dallas Historical Society
F80.2.35

40 **Dr. Pepper Wagon**
Dallas Historical Society
V.84.87

41 **Federal Building**
Dallas Historical Society
F81.2.4

42 **Newsboy**
Library of Congress
LOT 7480
v. 3, no.

45 **View from Courthouse Looking East, 1900**
Dallas Historical Society
A.45.68

46 **Scollard Building**
Dallas Historical Society
A.45.57

47 **H&TC Terminal**
Dallas Historical Society
A47.96.10

48 **African American Workers**
Dallas Historical Society
V80.2.78

49 **J. L. Patton's Elementary School Class**
Dallas Historical Society
V86.50.621

50 **Carnegie Library, Exterior**
Dallas Public Library
MA84-5/1

51 **Carnegie Library, Interior**
Dallas Public Library
MA84-5/6

52 **Crawford Art Gallery**
Dallas Historical Society
A 68.28.374

53 **Sarah Bernhardt by Tent**
Dallas Historical Society
F.79.12.67

54 **Racetrack at Fairgrounds**
Dallas Historical Society
V91.2.3

56 **Sanctuary, First Baptist Church**
Dallas Historical Society
A49.69

57 **Dallas Fire Fighters**
Dallas Historical Society
F80.2.37

58 Dallas Police, 1908
Dallas Historical Society
F80.2.13

60 Wilson Building
Dallas Historical Society
F.802.162

61 Huey & Philp Building
Dallas Historical Society
V81.5

62 Weaving Room
Dallas Historical Society
V.85.10.2

63 Dorsey Printing, Press Room
Dallas Historical Society
V.92.7.13

64 Underwood Typewriter Shop
Dallas Historical Society
A77.87.981

65 Men in Office
Dallas Historical Society
A77.87.132

66 Trinity River Flood
Dallas Historical Society
A36.17.3

68 Repairing Flood Damage
Dallas Historical Society
A36.17.5

69 Interurban Train
Dallas Historical Society
A68.28.405

70 Chalmers in Auto
Dallas Historical Society
F80.2.32

71 1907 State Fair Parade Auto
Dallas Historical Society
F80.2.36

72 Dallas Auto Device Co.
Dallas Historical Society
A80.48

73 Rudine Bicycle Repair Shop
Dallas Historical Society
V.91.8

74 Electric Crew, 1906
Dallas Historical Society
A42.196

75 Electric Crew, 1912
Dallas Historical Society
A42.196

76 Electric Crew in Motorized Vehicle
Dallas Historical Society
A42.196

77 Booker T. Washington High School's First Football Team
Dallas Historical Society
V86.50

78 Sheriff Ledbetter
Dallas Public Library
PA87-1/19-59-11

79 Baylor Graduates
Dallas Historical Society
A80.68

80 Early Dallas Golf & Country Club
Dallas Public Library
PA78-2/1234

82 Oak Lawn Lots for Sale
Dallas Historical Society
A4518

83 Tear-down of City Hall
Dallas Historical Society
F.802.221

84 Adolphus Hotel
Dallas Historical Society
F.802.222

85 Imperial Bar
Dallas Historical Society
F80.2.24

86 New City Hall
Dallas Public Library
PA76-1/37209

87 Neiman Marcus, Post-1913
Dallas Public Library
MA82-5/8

88 Huey & Philp Baseball Team
Dallas Historical Society
V81.5.16

89 Picnickers at State Fair
Dallas Historical Society
A77.87.1039

90 Fire Department Motorized Vehicle
Dallas Public Library
PA87-1/19-59-38

92 Assistant Fire Chief Car
Dallas Historical Society
A77.87.891

93 Cotton Belt Terminal
Dallas Public Library
PA87-1/19-59-135

94 New City Hall
Dallas Public Library
PA84-9/187

95 **Recruits on Houston Street**
Dallas Historical Society
A77.87.357

96 **World War I Thrift Association Parade**
Dallas Historical Society
A49.69

97 **Love Field**
Dallas Public Library
PA87-1/19-59-196

98 **Sheriff Dan Harston**
Dallas Public Library
PA87-1/19-59-14

99 **Budweiser Truck**
Dallas Historical Society
V84.99.11

100 **Sheriff's Deputies and Still**
Dallas Public Library
pa78-2/1311

101 **Weber's Root Beer Stand**
Dallas Historical Society
V.89.6.2

102 **Sanger Brothers Block**
Dallas Historical Society
F80.2

103 **Early Telephone Lines**
Dallas Historical Society
A68.28.391

104 **Telephone Operators**
Dallas Historical Society
F80.2.28

105 **Elm Street**
Dallas Historical Society
V.86.32

106 **Washington Theater**
Dallas Historical Society
A77.87.841

107 **Old Mill**
Dallas Historical Society
V1995.8.9

108 **Old Mill, Interior**
Dallas Historical Society
V84.99.8

109 **Hippodrome**
Dallas Historical Society
F80.2.103

110 **Plane at Love Field**
Dallas Public Library
pa78-2/1007

112 **St. Mary's Student Pageant**
Dallas Historical Society
A.44.58.24

113 **Girls on July 4**
Dallas Public Library
pa78-2/567

114 **Munger Place**
Dallas Historical Society
V.84.103

115 **Adolphus Hotel**
Dallas Historical Society
F.802.156

116 **Baker Hotel**
Dallas Historical Society
V1995.8.5

117 **Scott Hotel**
Dallas Public Library
pa87-1/19-59-122

118 **Harwood from Scottish Rite**
Dallas Historical Society
A.61.82

119 **East on Elm in 1927**
Dallas Historical Society
V1995.8.6

120 **West on Main**
Dallas Historical Society
V1995.8.2

121 **Cinco de Mayo Celebration**
Dallas Public Library
pa78-2/456

122 **Luna Tortilla Factory**
Dallas Historical Society

123 **Union Station**
Dallas Historical Society
A61.24

124 **Train Porter**
Dallas Public Library
PA78-2/92

125 **New Orleans at Love Field, 1924**
Dallas Historical Society
F.802.227

126 **Race Cars**
Dallas Historical Society
A77.87.308

127 **Dallas Baseball Team**
Dallas Historical Society
A77.87.974

128 **Deep Ellum**
Dallas Public Library
PA84-9/183

129 **Dr. Pepper Exhibit**
Dallas Historical Society
V.84.87

130 **Western Union Operators**
Dallas Historical Society
F.802.224

131 **G. B. Dealey in 1925**
Dallas Historical Society
V.89.17.11

132 Federal Reserve Bank
Dallas Historical Society
A61.24

134 Davis Building
Dallas Historical Society
A.59.46

135 Neiman Marcus
Dallas Historical Society
V.84.100.11

136 Savings Bank
Dallas Historical Society
V84.99.7

137 Elm Street in Late 1920s
Dallas Historical Society
A60.99

138 Harwood Street and Hilton Hotel
Dallas Historical Society
Centennial Collection––Dallas, Misc. Scenes

141 Elm Street in 1930s
Dallas Historical Society
V.87.9

142 Tower Petroleum Building
Dallas Historical Society
Centennial Collection––Dallas, Misc. Scenes

143 Highland Park Presbyterian Church
Dallas Historical Society
V.87.9.67

144 Dallas Hall, SMU
Dallas Historical Society
A61.24

146 Southwestern Bell Building
Dallas Historical Society
A.59.46

147 Lloyd Long's 1935 Skyline
Dallas Historical Society
M.40.4.1

148 Cotton
Dallas Historical Society
V.86.15.8

149 Discovery of Oil
Dallas Historical Society
V.83.139

150 Braniff Plane
Dallas Historical Society
V.84.9

151 Yates Laundry Co.
Dallas Historical Society
V.85.27

152 Hoisting Boat into Adolphus
Dallas Historical Society
V85.27 f7

153 Libecap Electric Co.
Dallas Historical Society
V.92.12.2

154 Hillcrest Drive-in Bank
Dallas Historical Society
A61.24

155 Bonnie and Clyde
Dallas Public Library
PA76-1/33022

156 Bullet-riddled Car
Dallas Public Library
Neg # 76-1/33022.1

157 Barrow-Harboring Trial
Dallas Public Library
PA76-1/37313

158 New Football Stadium
Dallas Historical Society
V.87.9

159 Old Coliseum Getting Facelift
Dallas Historical Society
State Fair of Texas Archives

160 Parry Avenue Entrance
Dallas Historical Society
A38.3

161 "Spirit of the Centennial"
Dallas Historical Society
Centennial Collection

162 FDR at Centennial
Dallas Historical Society
Centennial Collection

163 Cavalcade of Texas
Dallas Historical Society
A38.3.384

164 Armadillo Hunter and Collector
Dallas Historical Society
Centennial Collection

165 Crowd in Front of Federal Building
Dallas Historical Society
Centennial Collection

166 Street Scene
Dallas Historical Society
A77.47

167 Little Mexico
Dallas Historical Society
V.81.9.18

168 National Guardsmen
Dallas Historical Society
V83.154

169 People by Music Hall
Dallas Historical Society
A.46.178

170 **Ballots into Barrels**
Dallas Historical Society
A.46.178

171 **G. B. Dealey in Great Hall**
Dallas Historical Society
A.45.80

172 **Honor Guard for Nimitz**
Dallas Historical Society
A.46.201

173 **A&M Halftime Show**
Dallas Historical Society
V84.100.2

174 **Midway**
Dallas Historical Society
V1995.4.194

175 **Southland Corporation**
Dallas Historical Society
V84.94

176 **Main Street, 1947**
Dallas Historical Society
V84.99.3

177 **Ervay, 1948**
Dallas Historical Society
V84.99.33

178 **SMU Football Team**
Dallas Public Library
PA76-1/13335.4

180 **Big Tex**
Dallas Historical Society
State Fair of Texas Archives

181 **Mariachi Band and MKT Passengers**
Dallas Public Library
PA76-1/20385.5

182 **Interior, Dallas Cotton Exchange**
Dallas Historical Society

183 **Stokeley–Van Camp Plant**
Dallas Public Library
PA76-1/9142.6

184 **Clearing Land for Southland Center**
Dallas Historical Society
A80.55

185 **Dining Car in Texas Special**
Dallas Public Library
PA76-1/20384.4

186 **Mayor Thornton and Lyndon B. Johnson**
Dallas Public Library
PA76-1/11698

187 **Auto Racer and Girlfriend**
Dallas Historical Society
V.91.15

188 **Mesquite Rodeo**
Dallas Public Library
PA76-1/1074.1

189 **Elm Street**
Dallas Historical Society
V1995.4.477

190 **Hockaday School Students**
Dallas Public Library
PA76-1/2620

192 **Civil Rights March**
Dallas Public Library
PA83-42/1965-3-14.1

194 **Dallas Mayors at Central "Completion"**
Dallas Historical Society
V.90.6

195 **Idlewild Club Ball**
Dallas Public Library
PA76-1/19874.2

196 **President John F. Kennedy Motorcade**
Library of Congress
Unprocessed in PR 13 CN 2004:085

197 **Dealey Plaza**
Dallas Public Library
PA87-1/63110.7

198 **Dallas Cowboys Game**
Dallas Public Library
PA85-5/68-17-3.5

200 **Tom Landry**
Dallas Public Library
PA85-5/69-32-1-3

HISTORIC PHOTOS OF DALLAS

During the mid–nineteenth century, Dallas emerged as a vibrant, commercial American city. At the turn of the century, Dallas continued to prosper, overcoming adversity and becoming a leading center of commerce in the southwestern United States.

Historic Photos of Dallas captures this journey through still photography selected from the finest archives. From the Civil War and the Great Depression, to the building of a modern metropolis, *Historic Photos of Dallas* follows life, government, education, and events throughout the city's history.

This volume captures unique and rare scenes as depicted in nearly 200 historic photographs. Published in striking black and white, these images communicate historic events and everyday life of two centuries of people building a unique and prosperous city.

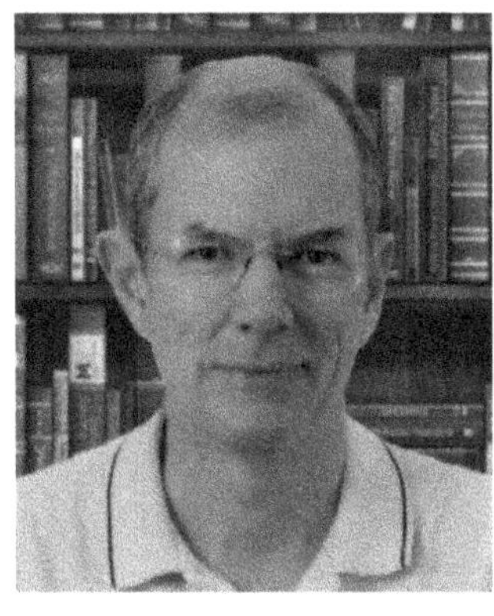

Michael V. Hazel is a native Dallasite. He earned his B.A. in history from Southern Methodist University and his M.A. and Ph.D. degrees from the University of Chicago. Since 1989, he has edited *Legacies*, a regional history journal jointly published by four local historical organizations. He has also edited and written several books, including *Dallas Reconsidered* (1995, revised 2000), *Dallas: A History of Big D* (1997), *Dallas: A Dynamic Century* (1998), *Stanley Marcus from A to Z* (2000), and *The Dallas Public Library: Celebrating a Century of Service* (2001). He served as photo editor for *Dynamic Dallas* (2003). Dr. Hazel has also taught Dallas history at S.M.U. and museum studies at the University of North Texas. For the past ten years, he has coordinated a Dallas History Conference co-sponsored by twelve local history groups.

WWW.TURNERPUBLISHING.COM